A TOR/SEVEN SEAS BOOK

AFRO SAMURAI®

VOLUME 2

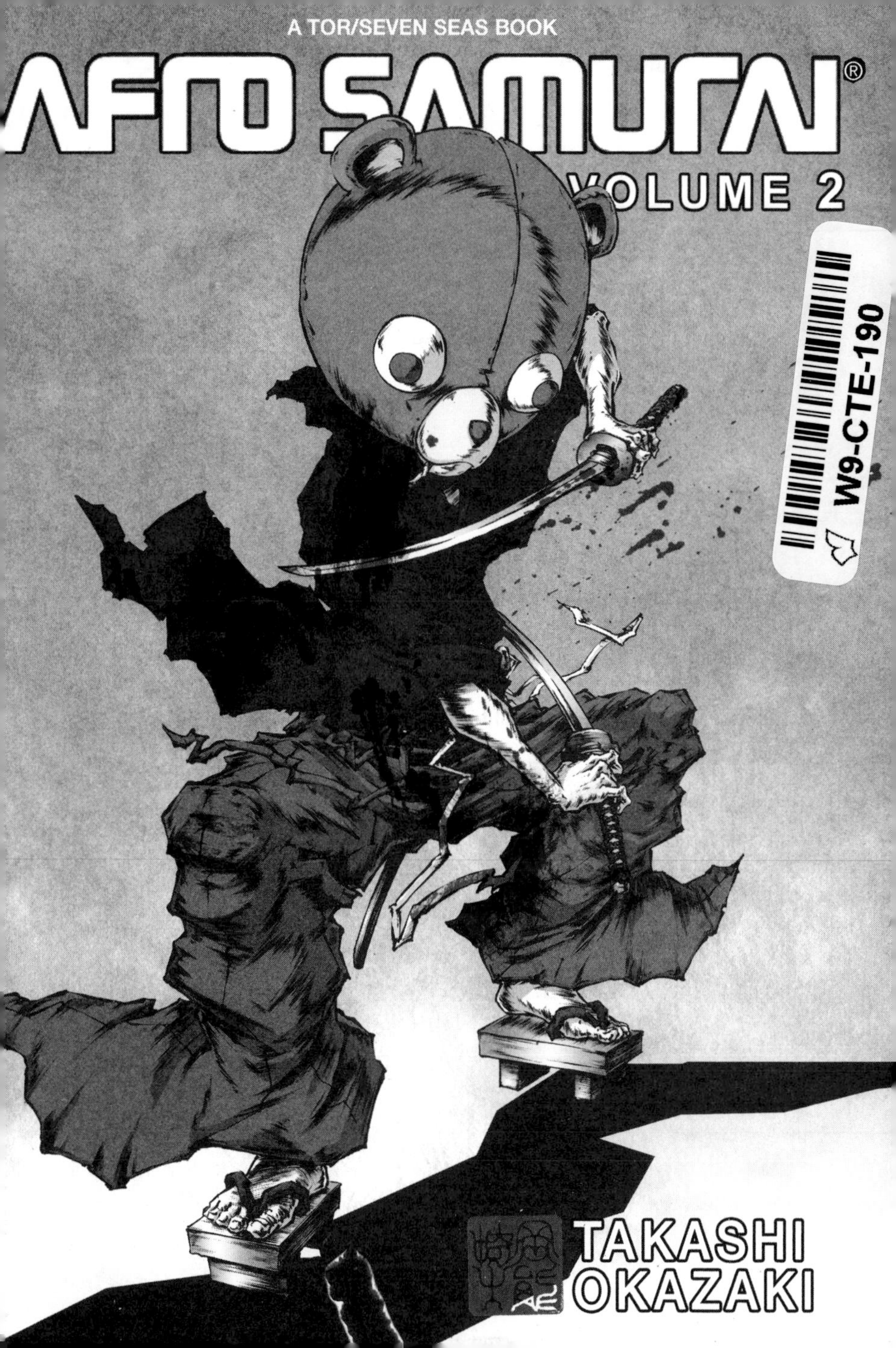

TAKASHI OKAZAKI

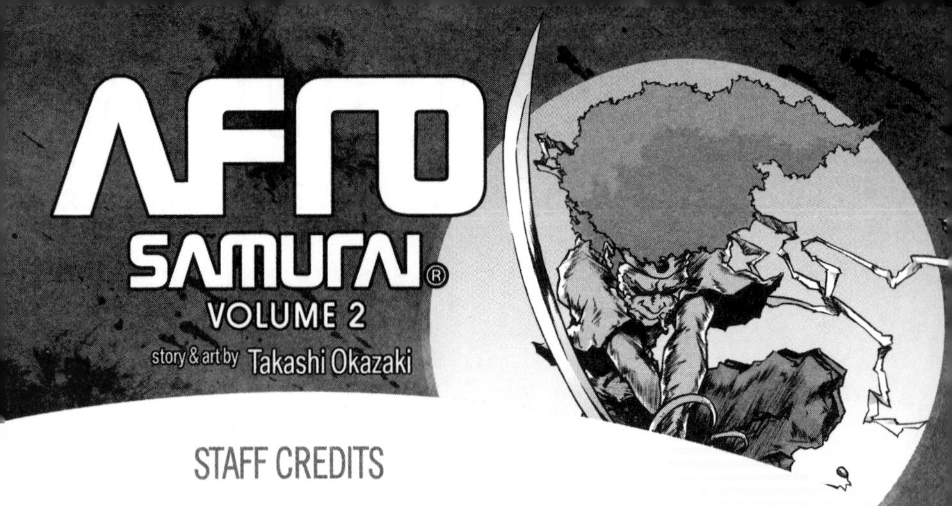

ΛFꞄ SΛMUꞄΛI ®

VOLUME 2

story & art by Takashi Okazaki

STAFF CREDITS

translation	**Greg Moore**
adaptation	**Joshua Fialkov**
cover design	**Pablo Defendini**
lettering & design	**Roland Amago**
layout	**Bambi Eloriaga-Amago**
editor	**Adam Arnold**

A Tor/Seven Seas Publication

AFRO SAMURAI VOL. 2
Copyright © 2008 TAKASHI OKAZAKI, GONZO

Visit us online at www.gomanga.com and www.tor-forge.com.

ISBN-13: 978-0-7653-2239-5
ISBN-10: 0-7653-2239-0

Printed in the USA

First printing: February 2009

10 9 8 7 6 5 4 3 2 1

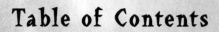

Table of Contents

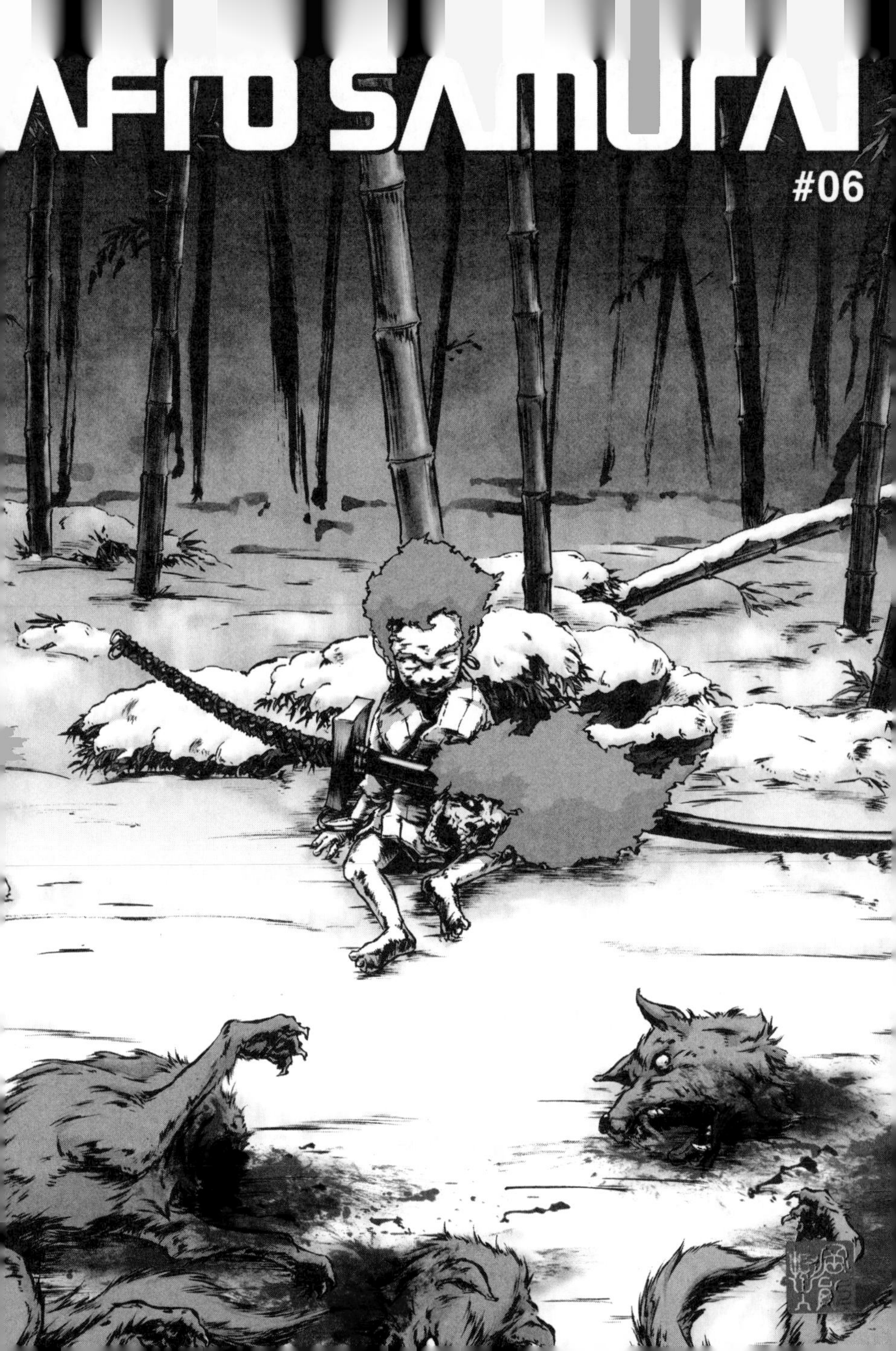
AFRO SAMURAI
#06

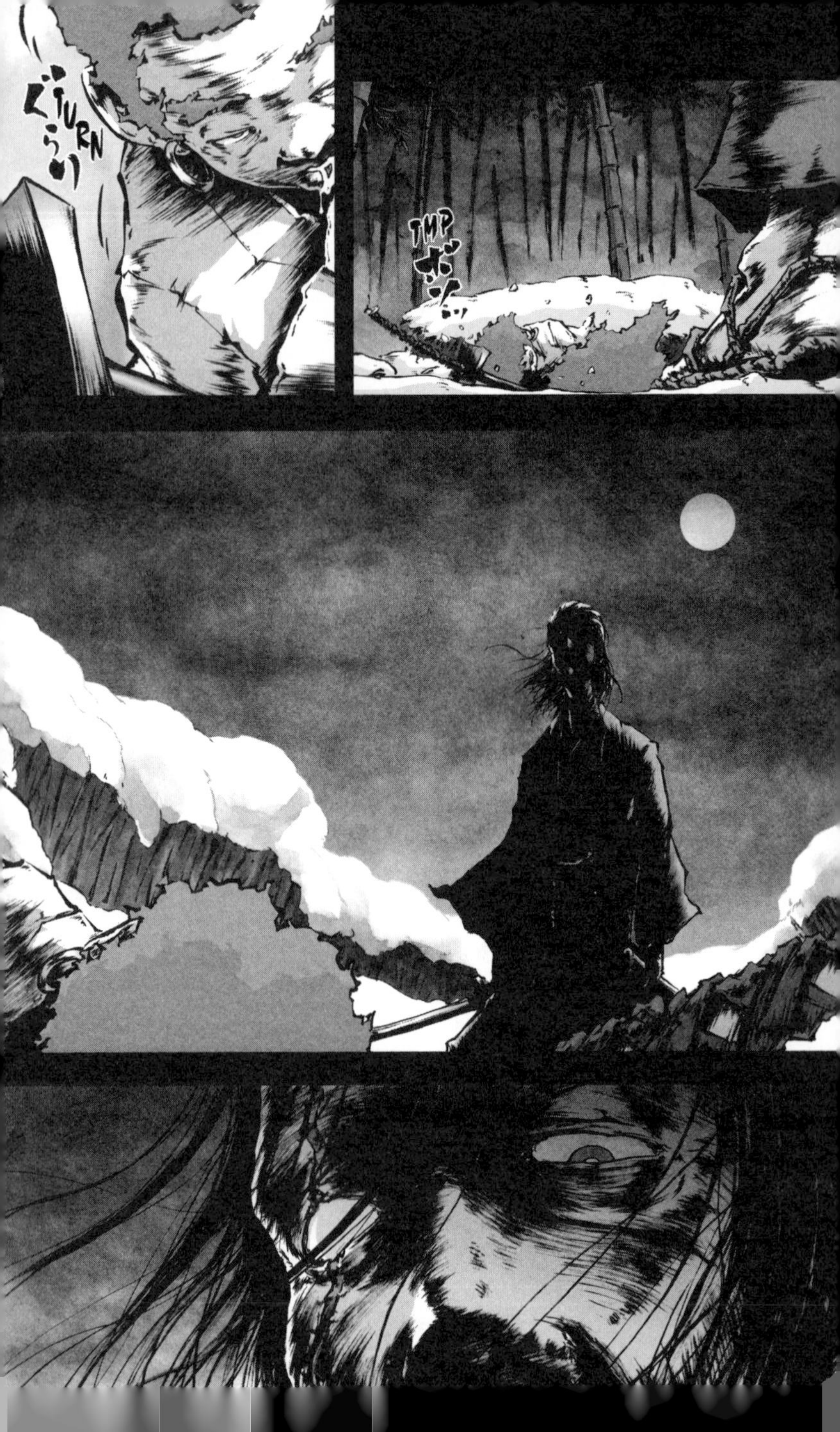
ぐらり
TURN
TMP
ボソ…

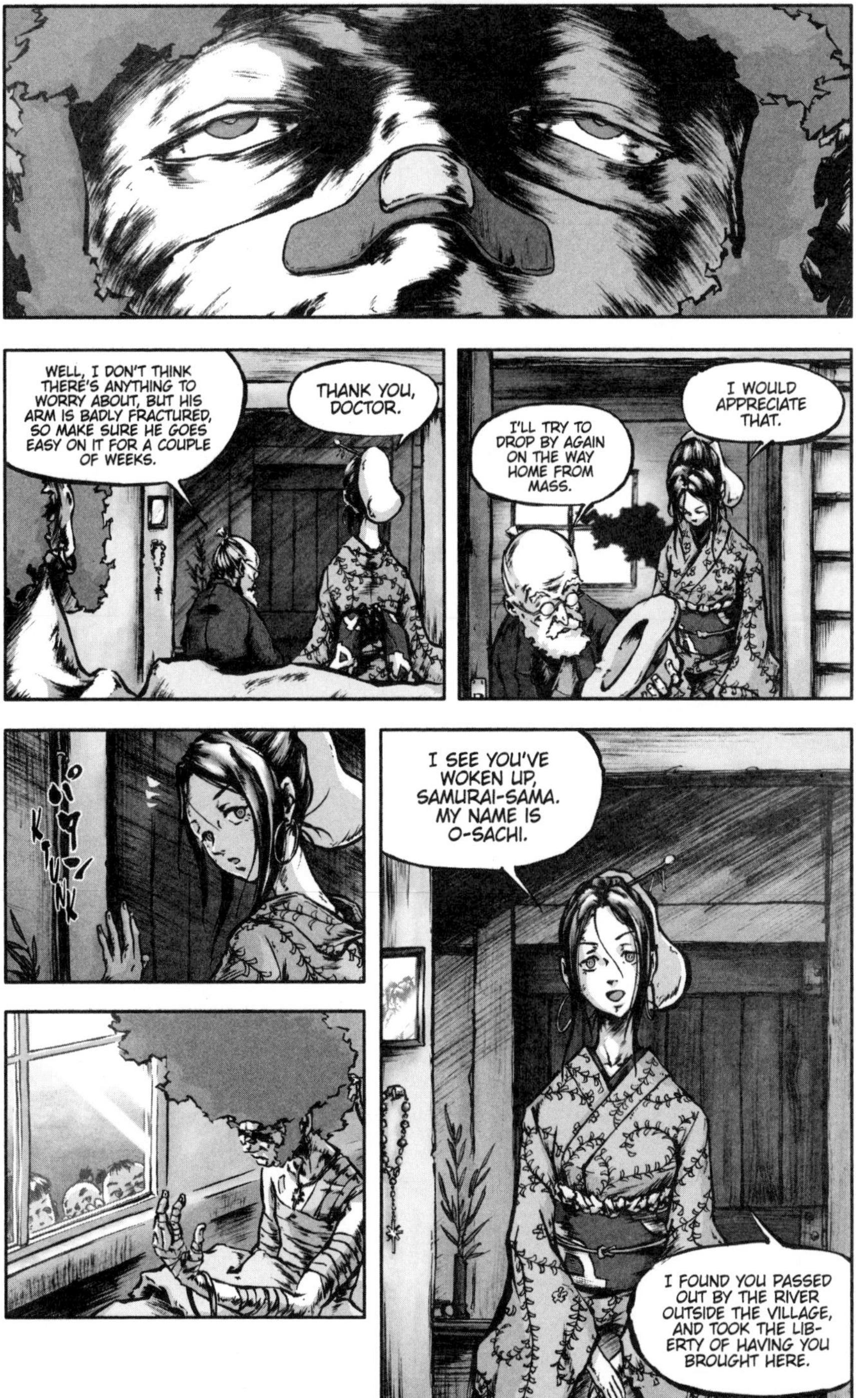
WELL, I DON'T THINK THERE'S ANYTHING TO WORRY ABOUT, BUT HIS ARM IS BADLY FRACTURED, SO MAKE SURE HE GOES EASY ON IT FOR A COUPLE OF WEEKS.
THANK YOU, DOCTOR.
I'LL TRY TO DROP BY AGAIN ON THE WAY HOME FROM MASS.
I WOULD APPRECIATE THAT.
KATUNK
I SEE YOU'VE WOKEN UP, SAMURAI-SAMA. MY NAME IS O-SACHI.
I FOUND YOU PASSED OUT BY THE RIVER OUTSIDE THE VILLAGE, AND TOOK THE LIB-ERTY OF HAVING YOU BROUGHT HERE.

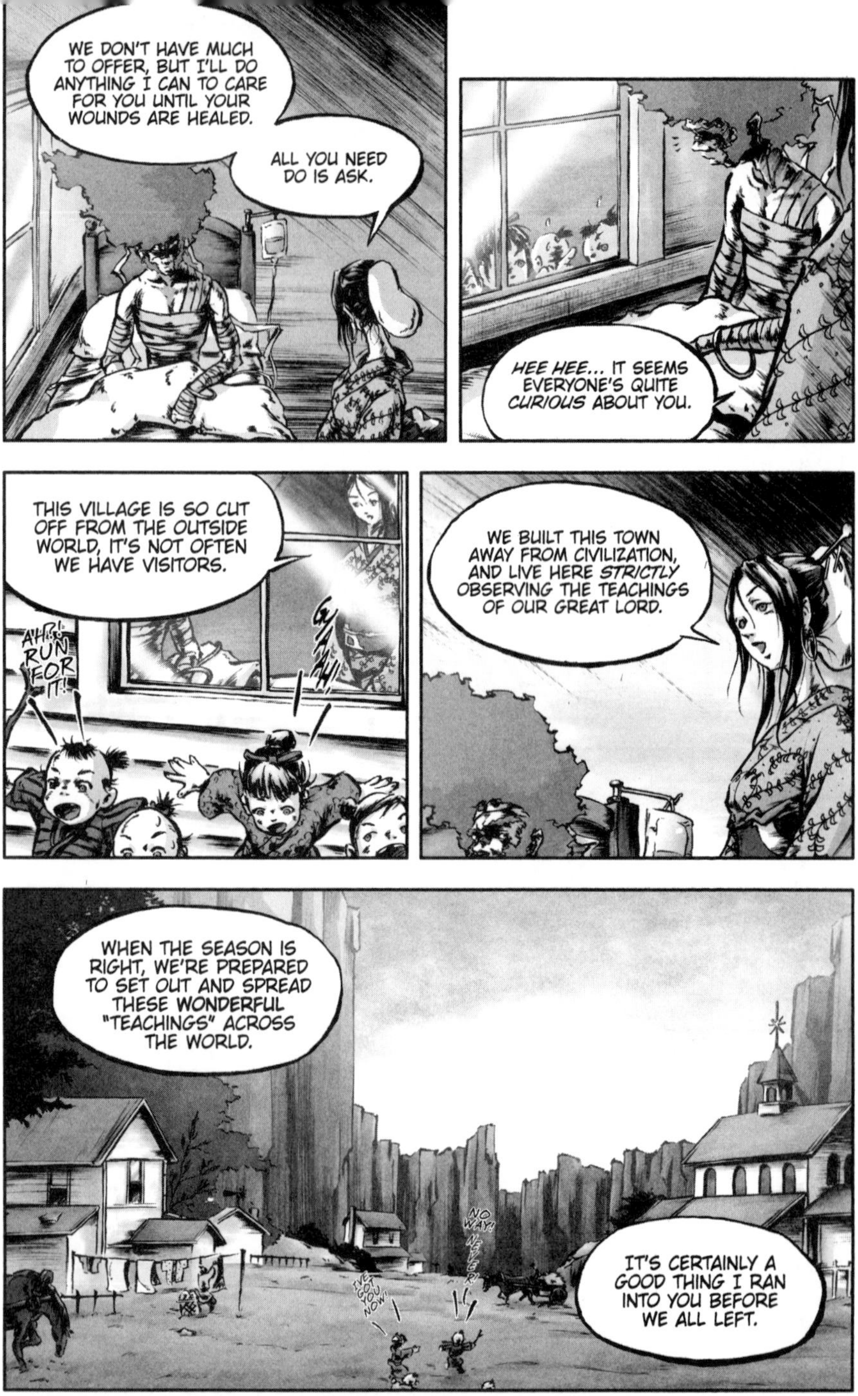
WE DON'T HAVE MUCH TO OFFER, BUT I'LL DO ANYTHING I CAN TO CARE FOR YOU UNTIL YOUR WOUNDS ARE HEALED.
ALL YOU NEED DO IS ASK.
HEE HEE... IT SEEMS EVERYONE'S QUITE *CURIOUS* ABOUT YOU.
THIS VILLAGE IS SO CUT OFF FROM THE OUTSIDE WORLD, IT'S NOT OFTEN WE HAVE VISITORS.
AH?! RUN FOR IT!
WE BUILT THIS TOWN AWAY FROM CIVILIZATION, AND LIVE HERE *STRICTLY* OBSERVING THE TEACHINGS OF OUR GREAT LORD.
WHEN THE SEASON IS RIGHT, WE'RE PREPARED TO SET OUT AND SPREAD THESE **WONDERFUL** "TEACHINGS" ACROSS THE WORLD.
I'VE GOT YOU NOW!
NO WAY! NEVER!
IT'S CERTAINLY A GOOD THING I RAN INTO YOU BEFORE WE ALL LEFT.

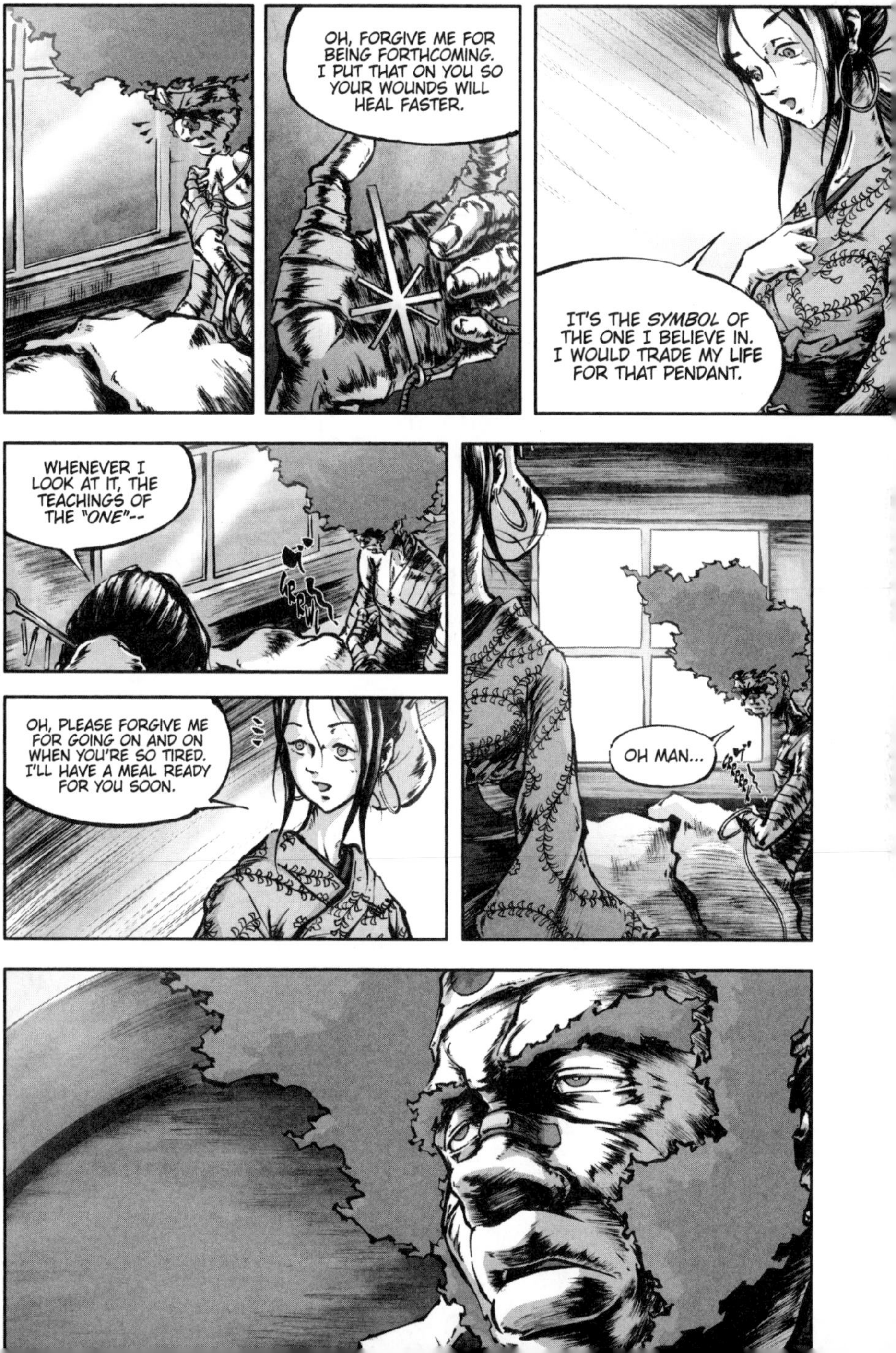
OH, FORGIVE ME FOR BEING FORTHCOMING. I PUT THAT ON YOU SO YOUR WOUNDS WILL HEAL FASTER.
IT'S THE *SYMBOL* OF THE ONE I BELIEVE IN. I WOULD TRADE MY LIFE FOR THAT PENDANT.
WHENEVER I LOOK AT IT, THE TEACHINGS OF THE "*ONE*"--
OH, PLEASE FORGIVE ME FOR GOING ON AND ON WHEN YOU'RE SO TIRED. I'LL HAVE A MEAL READY FOR YOU SOON.
OH MAN...

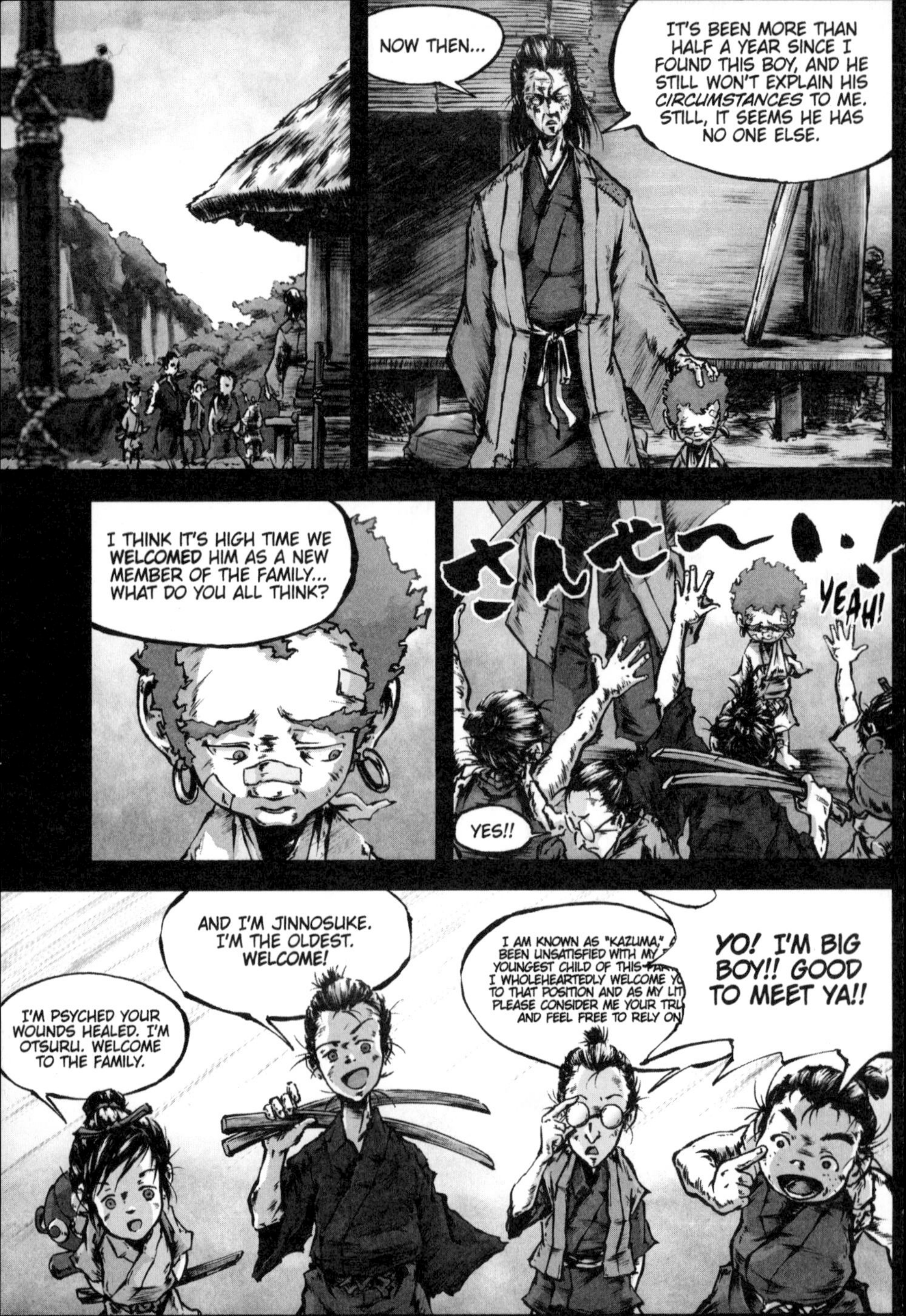
NOW THEN...
IT'S BEEN MORE THAN HALF A YEAR SINCE I FOUND THIS BOY, AND HE STILL WON'T EXPLAIN HIS *CIRCUMSTANCES* TO ME. STILL, IT SEEMS HE HAS NO ONE ELSE.
I THINK IT'S HIGH TIME WE WELCOMED HIM AS A NEW MEMBER OF THE FAMILY... WHAT DO YOU ALL THINK?
さんせ〜!!
YEAH!
YES!!
I'M PSYCHED YOUR WOUNDS HEALED. I'M OTSURU. WELCOME TO THE FAMILY.
AND I'M JINNOSUKE. I'M THE OLDEST. WELCOME!
I AM KNOWN AS "KAZUMA," BEEN UNSATISFIED WITH MY YOUNGEST CHILD OF THIS I WHOLEHEARTEDLY WELCOME TO THAT POSITION AND AS MY PLEASE CONSIDER ME YOUR AND FEEL FREE TO RELY
YO! I'M BIG BOY!! GOOD TO MEET YA!!

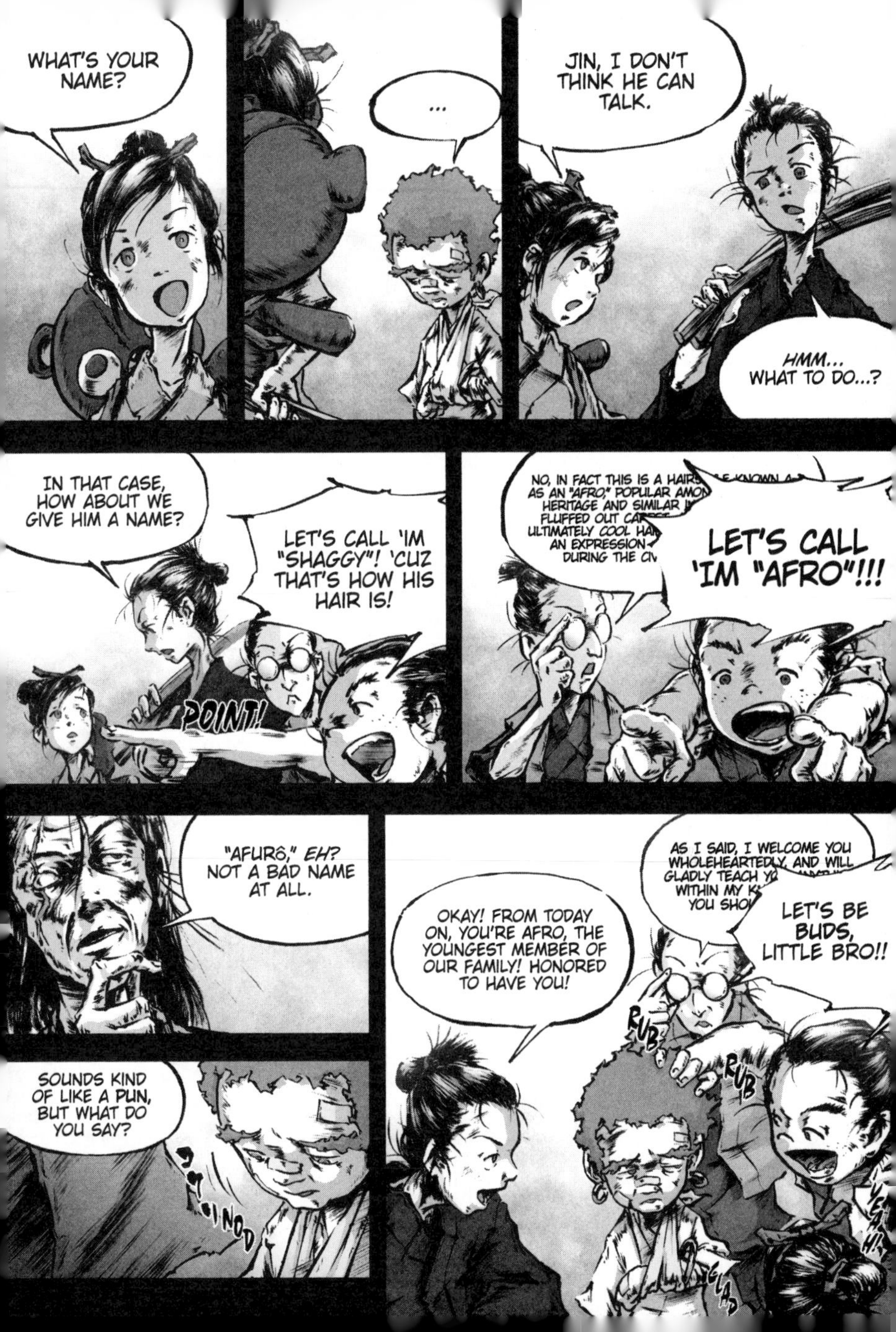

WHAT'S YOUR NAME?
...
JIN, I DON'T THINK HE CAN TALK.
HMM... WHAT TO DO...?
IN THAT CASE, HOW ABOUT WE GIVE HIM A NAME?
LET'S CALL 'IM "SHAGGY"! 'CUZ THAT'S HOW HIS HAIR IS!
POINT!
NO, IN FACT THIS IS A AS AN "AFRO," POPULAR HERITAGE AND SIMILAR FLUFFED OUT ULTIMATELY COOL AN EXPRESSION DURING THE
LET'S CALL 'IM "AFRO"!!!
"AFURÔ," EH? NOT A BAD NAME AT ALL.
SOUNDS KIND OF LIKE A PUN, BUT WHAT DO YOU SAY?
NOD
OKAY! FROM TODAY ON, YOU'RE AFRO, THE YOUNGEST MEMBER OF OUR FAMILY! HONORED TO HAVE YOU!
AS I SAID, I WELCOME YOU WHOLEHEARTEDLY, AND WILL GLADLY TEACH WITHIN MY YOU
LET'S BE BUDS, LITTLE BRO!!
RUB
RUB

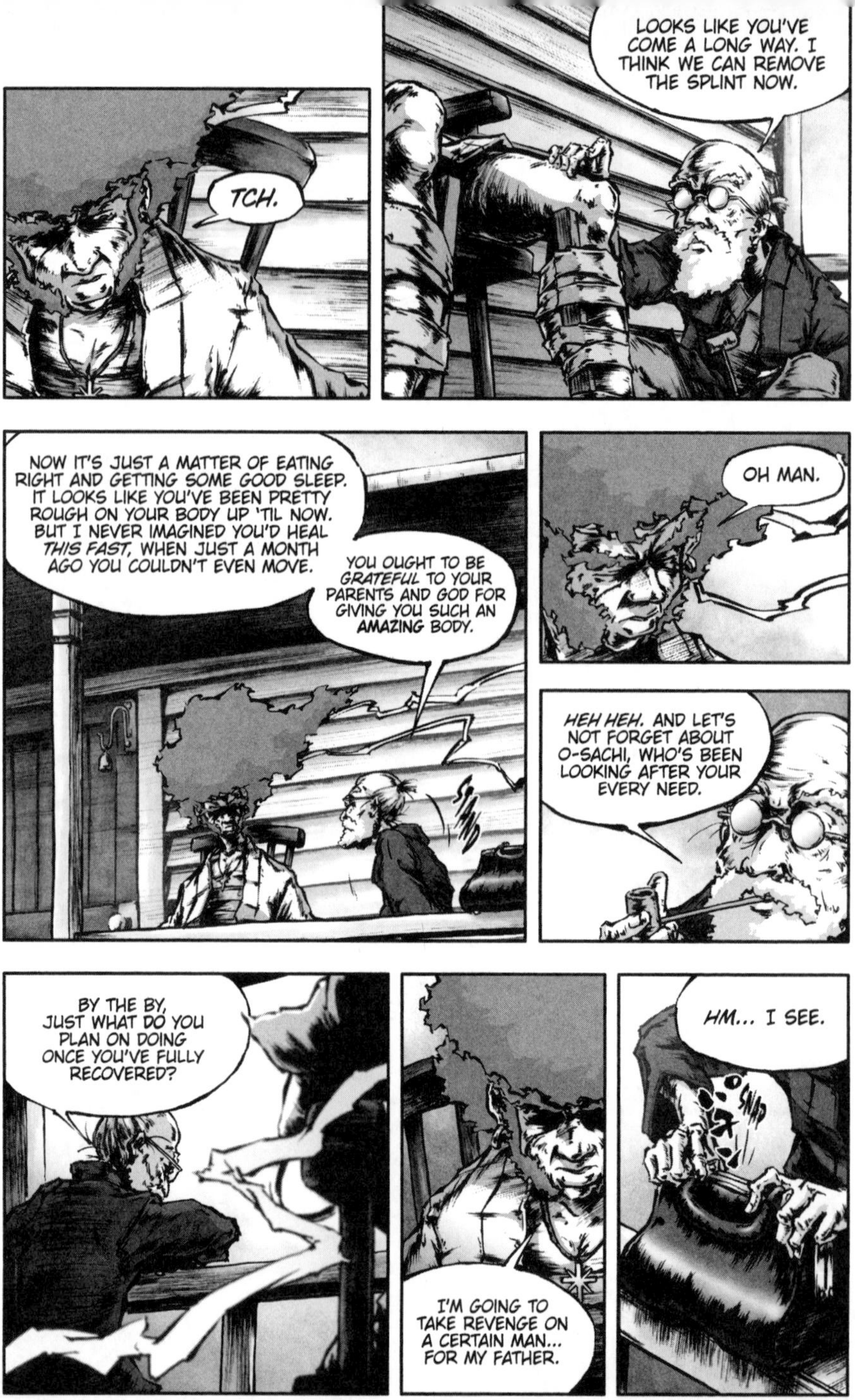
TCH.
LOOKS LIKE YOU'VE COME A LONG WAY. I THINK WE CAN REMOVE THE SPLINT NOW.
NOW IT'S JUST A MATTER OF EATING RIGHT AND GETTING SOME GOOD SLEEP. IT LOOKS LIKE YOU'VE BEEN PRETTY ROUGH ON YOUR BODY UP 'TIL NOW. BUT I NEVER IMAGINED YOU'D HEAL *THIS FAST*, WHEN JUST A MONTH AGO YOU COULDN'T EVEN MOVE.
YOU OUGHT TO BE *GRATEFUL* TO YOUR PARENTS AND GOD FOR GIVING YOU SUCH AN **AMAZING** BODY.
OH MAN.
HEH HEH. AND LET'S NOT FORGET ABOUT O-SACHI, WHO'S BEEN LOOKING AFTER YOUR EVERY NEED.
BY THE BY, JUST WHAT DO YOU PLAN ON DOING ONCE YOU'VE FULLY RECOVERED?
I'M GOING TO TAKE REVENGE ON A CERTAIN MAN... FOR MY FATHER.
HM... I SEE.
SNAP

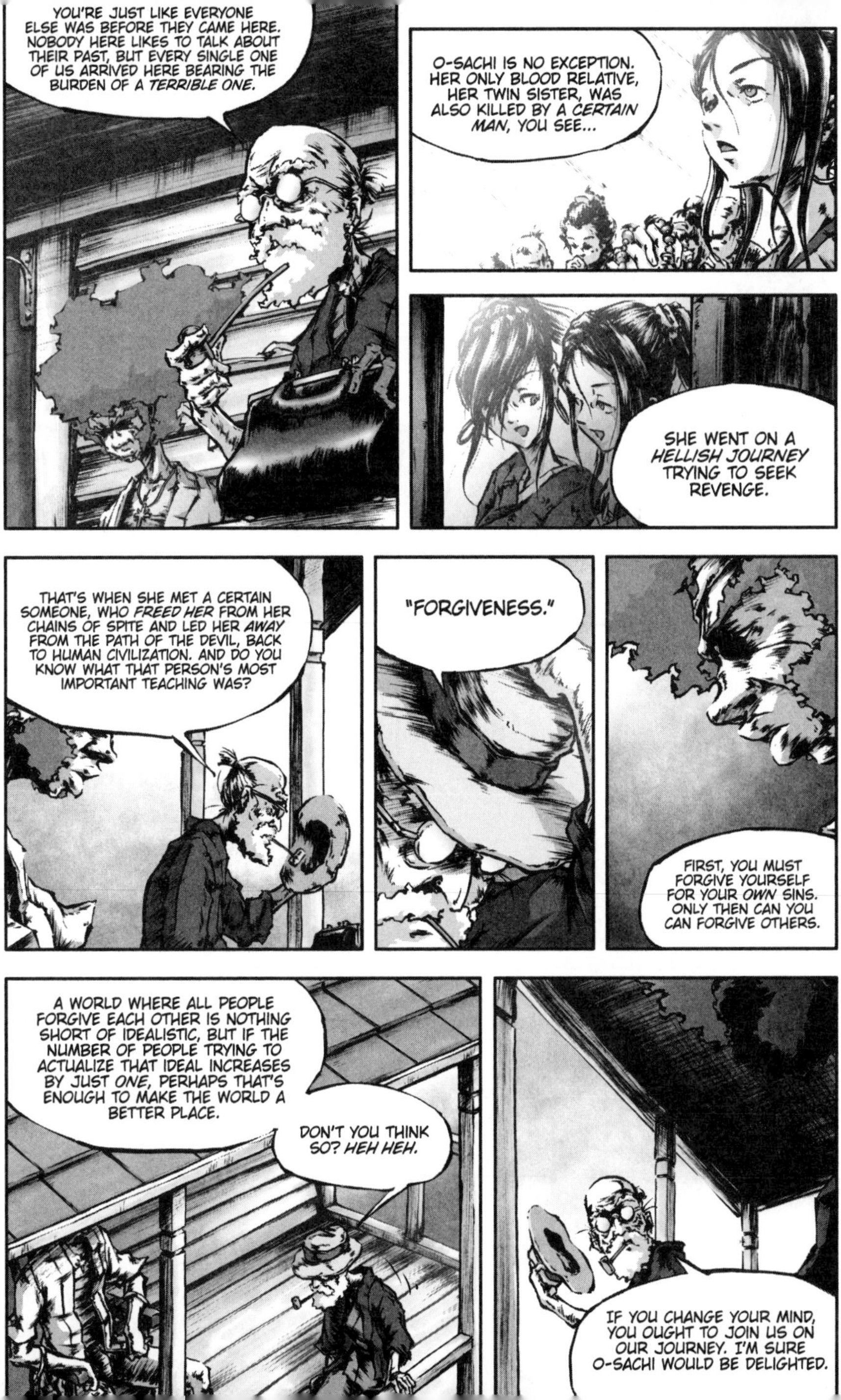
YOU'RE JUST LIKE EVERYONE ELSE WAS BEFORE THEY CAME HERE. NOBODY HERE LIKES TO TALK ABOUT THEIR PAST, BUT EVERY SINGLE ONE OF US ARRIVED HERE BEARING THE BURDEN OF A *TERRIBLE ONE*.
O-SACHI IS NO EXCEPTION. HER ONLY BLOOD RELATIVE, HER TWIN SISTER, WAS ALSO KILLED BY A *CERTAIN MAN*, YOU SEE...
SHE WENT ON A *HELLISH JOURNEY* TRYING TO SEEK REVENGE.
THAT'S WHEN SHE MET A CERTAIN SOMEONE, WHO *FREED HER* FROM HER CHAINS OF SPITE AND LED HER *AWAY* FROM THE PATH OF THE DEVIL, BACK TO HUMAN CIVILIZATION. AND DO YOU KNOW WHAT THAT PERSON'S MOST IMPORTANT TEACHING WAS?
"FORGIVENESS."
FIRST, YOU MUST FORGIVE YOURSELF FOR YOUR *OWN* SINS. ONLY THEN CAN YOU CAN FORGIVE OTHERS.
A WORLD WHERE ALL PEOPLE FORGIVE EACH OTHER IS NOTHING SHORT OF IDEALISTIC, BUT IF THE NUMBER OF PEOPLE TRYING TO ACTUALIZE THAT IDEAL INCREASES BY JUST *ONE*, PERHAPS THAT'S ENOUGH TO MAKE THE WORLD A BETTER PLACE.
DON'T YOU THINK SO? *HEH HEH*.
IF YOU CHANGE YOUR MIND, YOU OUGHT TO JOIN US ON OUR JOURNEY. I'M SURE O-SACHI WOULD BE DELIGHTED.

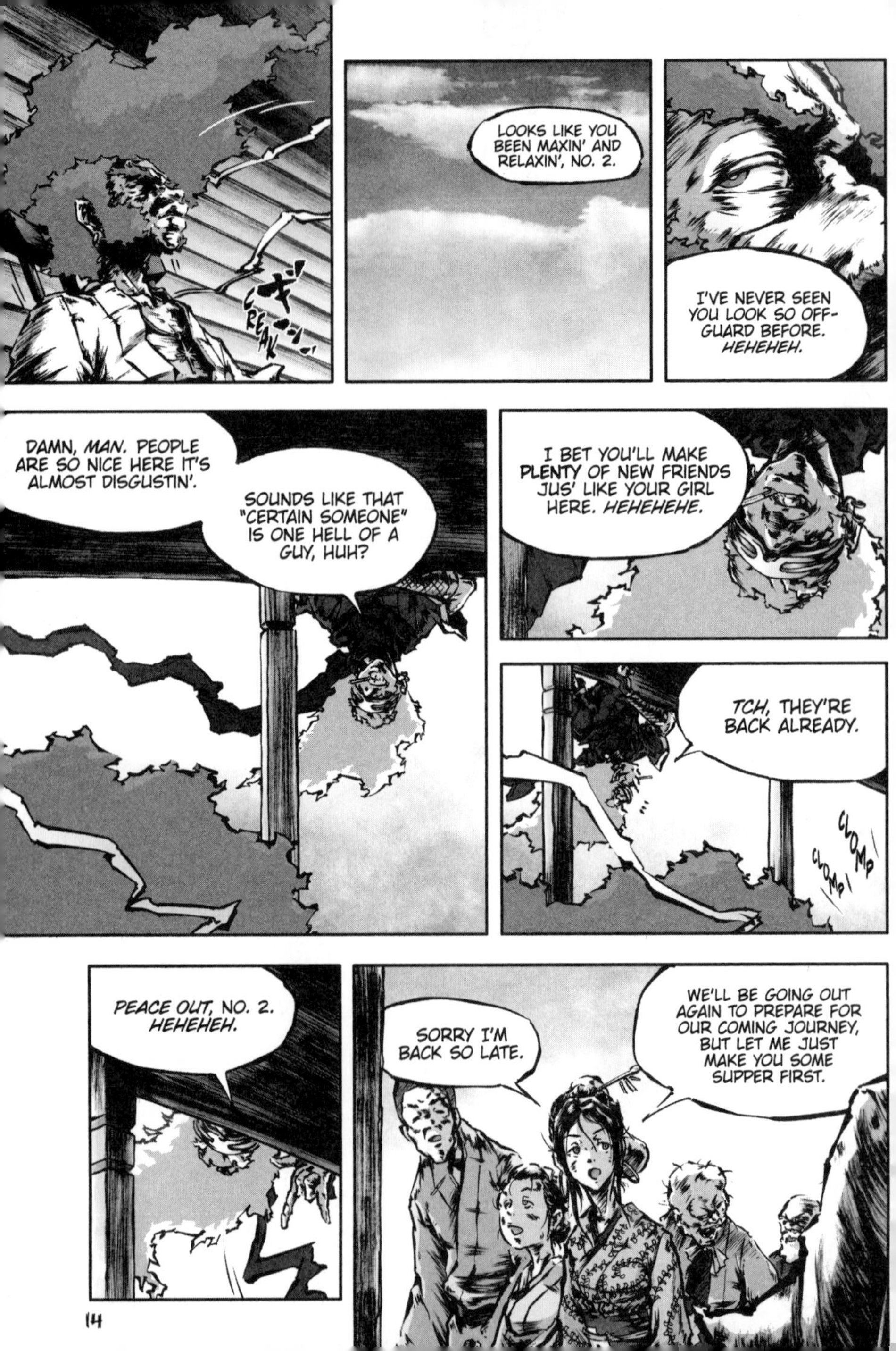
CREAK
LOOKS LIKE YOU BEEN MAXIN' AND RELAXIN', NO. 2.
I'VE NEVER SEEN YOU LOOK SO OFF-GUARD BEFORE. *HEHEHEH.*
DAMN, *MAN.* PEOPLE ARE SO NICE HERE IT'S ALMOST DISGUSTIN'.
SOUNDS LIKE THAT "CERTAIN SOMEONE" IS ONE HELL OF A GUY, HUH?
I BET YOU'LL MAKE **PLENTY** OF NEW FRIENDS JUS' LIKE YOUR GIRL HERE. *HEHEHEHE.*
TCH, THEY'RE BACK ALREADY.
CLOMP CLOMP
PEACE OUT, NO. 2. *HEHEHEH.*
SORRY I'M BACK SO LATE.
WE'LL BE GOING OUT AGAIN TO PREPARE FOR OUR COMING JOURNEY, BUT LET ME JUST MAKE YOU SOME SUPPER FIRST.

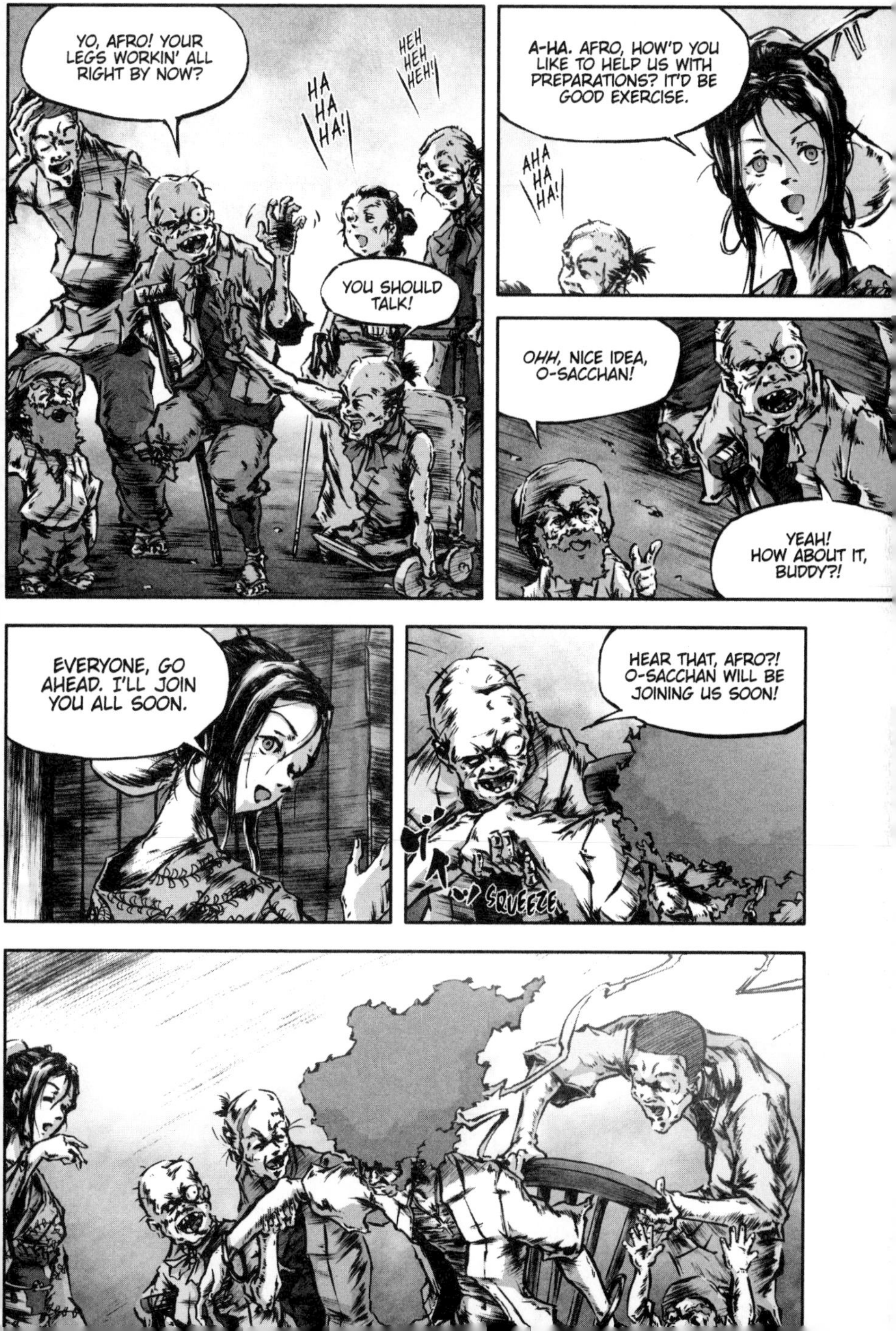
YO, AFRO! YOUR LEGS WORKIN' ALL RIGHT BY NOW?
HA HA HA!
HEH HEH HEH!
YOU SHOULD TALK!
A-HA. AFRO, HOW'D YOU LIKE TO HELP US WITH PREPARATIONS? IT'D BE GOOD EXERCISE.
AHA HA HA!
OHH, NICE IDEA, O-SACCHAN!
YEAH! HOW ABOUT IT, BUDDY?!
EVERYONE, GO AHEAD. I'LL JOIN YOU ALL SOON.
HEAR THAT, AFRO?! O-SACCHAN WILL BE JOINING US SOON!
SQUEEZE

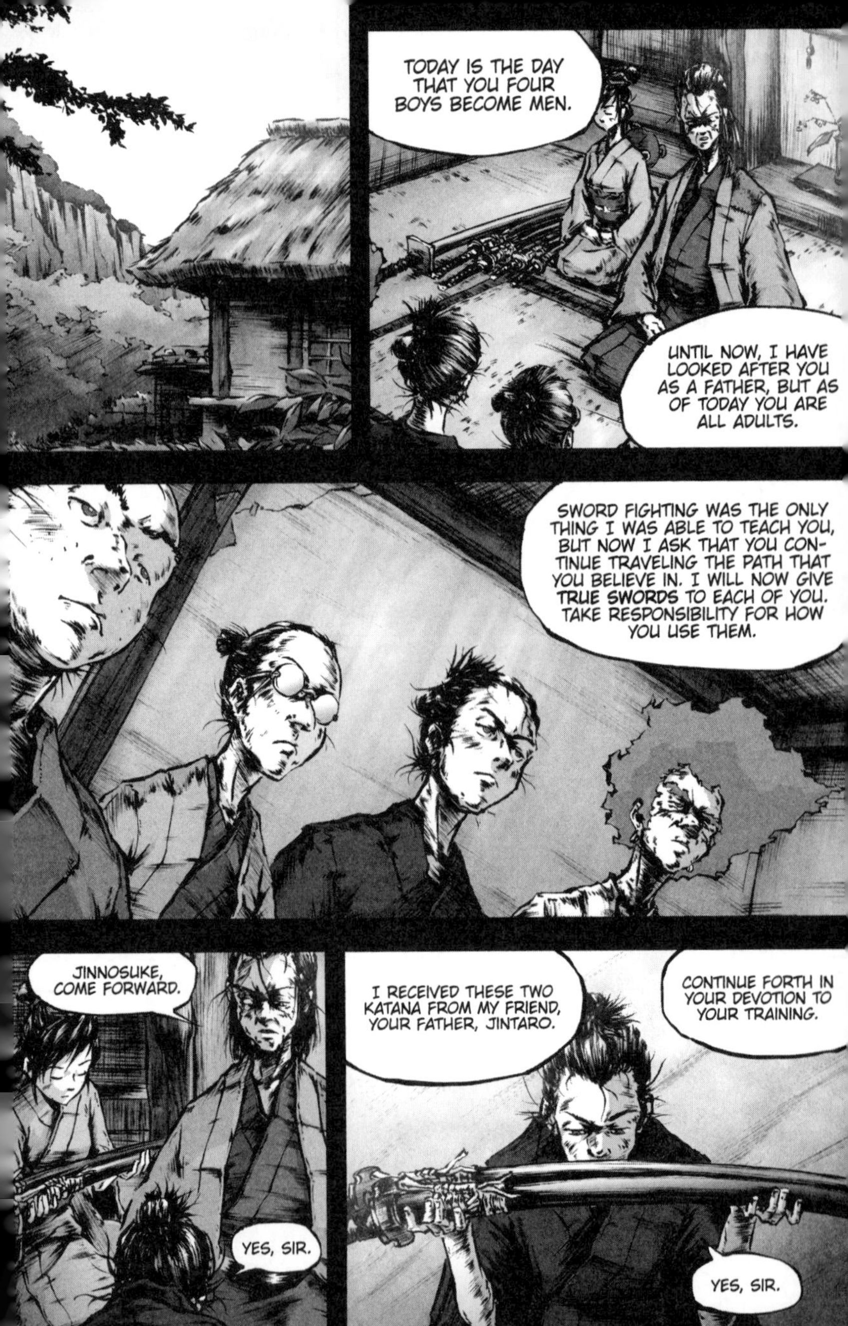
TODAY IS THE DAY THAT YOU FOUR BOYS BECOME MEN.
UNTIL NOW, I HAVE LOOKED AFTER YOU AS A FATHER, BUT AS OF TODAY YOU ARE ALL ADULTS.
SWORD FIGHTING WAS THE ONLY THING I WAS ABLE TO TEACH YOU, BUT NOW I ASK THAT YOU CONTINUE TRAVELING THE PATH THAT YOU BELIEVE IN. I WILL NOW GIVE **TRUE SWORDS** TO EACH OF YOU. TAKE RESPONSIBILITY FOR HOW YOU USE THEM.
JINNOSUKE, COME FORWARD.
YES, SIR.
I RECEIVED THESE TWO KATANA FROM MY FRIEND, YOUR FATHER, JINTARO.
CONTINUE FORTH IN YOUR DEVOTION TO YOUR TRAINING.
YES, SIR.

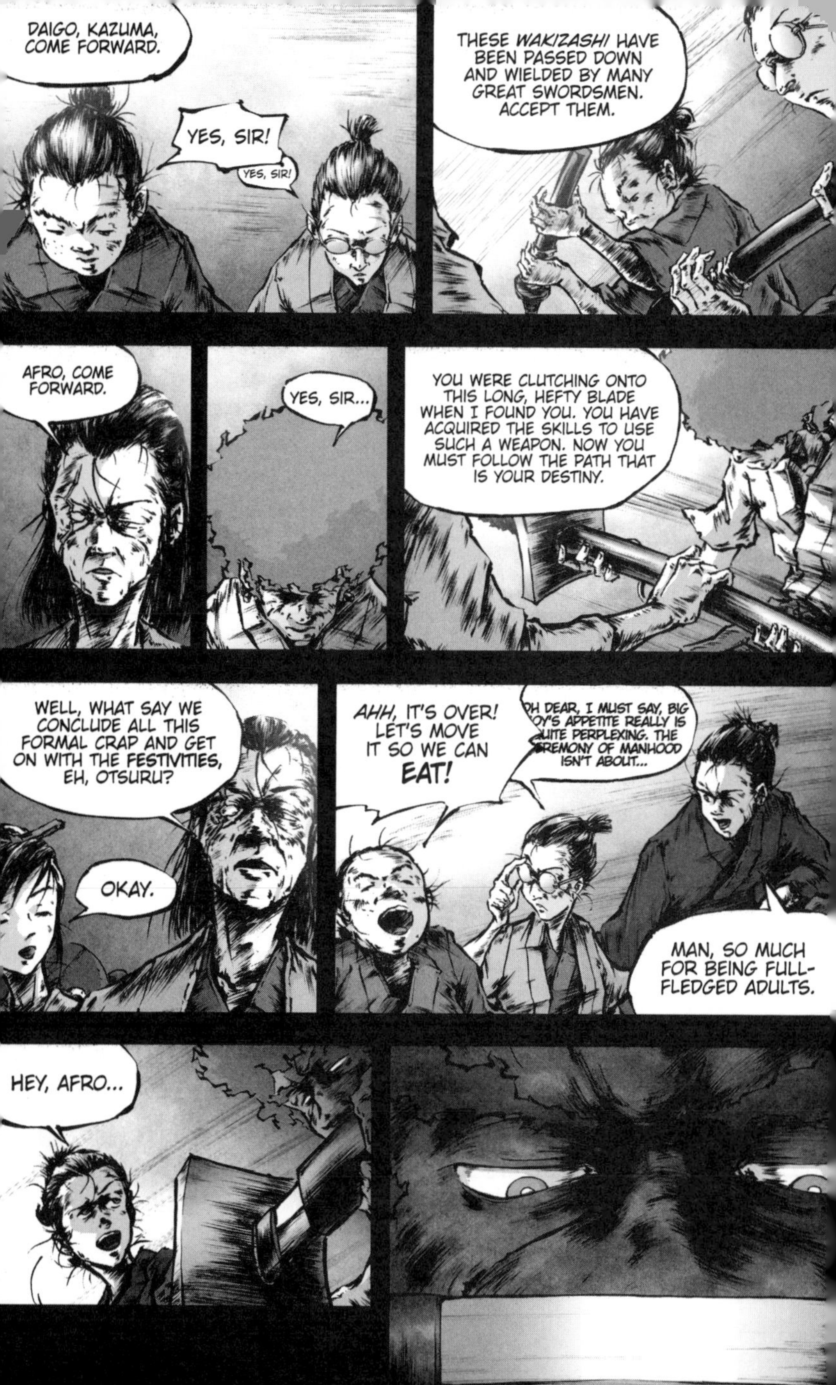
DAIGO, KAZUMA, COME FORWARD.
YES, SIR!
YES, SIR!
THESE *WAKIZASHI* HAVE BEEN PASSED DOWN AND WIELDED BY MANY GREAT SWORDSMEN. ACCEPT THEM.
AFRO, COME FORWARD.
YES, SIR...
YOU WERE CLUTCHING ONTO THIS LONG, HEFTY BLADE WHEN I FOUND YOU. YOU HAVE ACQUIRED THE SKILLS TO USE SUCH A WEAPON. NOW YOU MUST FOLLOW THE PATH THAT IS YOUR DESTINY.
WELL, WHAT SAY WE CONCLUDE ALL THIS FORMAL CRAP AND GET ON WITH THE FESTIVITIES, EH, OTSURU?
OKAY.
AHH, IT'S OVER! LET'S MOVE IT SO WE CAN **EAT!**
H DEAR, I MUST SAY, BIG OY'S APPETITE REALLY IS UITE PERPLEXING. THE REMONY OF MANHOOD ISN'T ABOUT...
MAN, SO MUCH FOR BEING FULL-FLEDGED ADULTS.
HEY, AFRO...

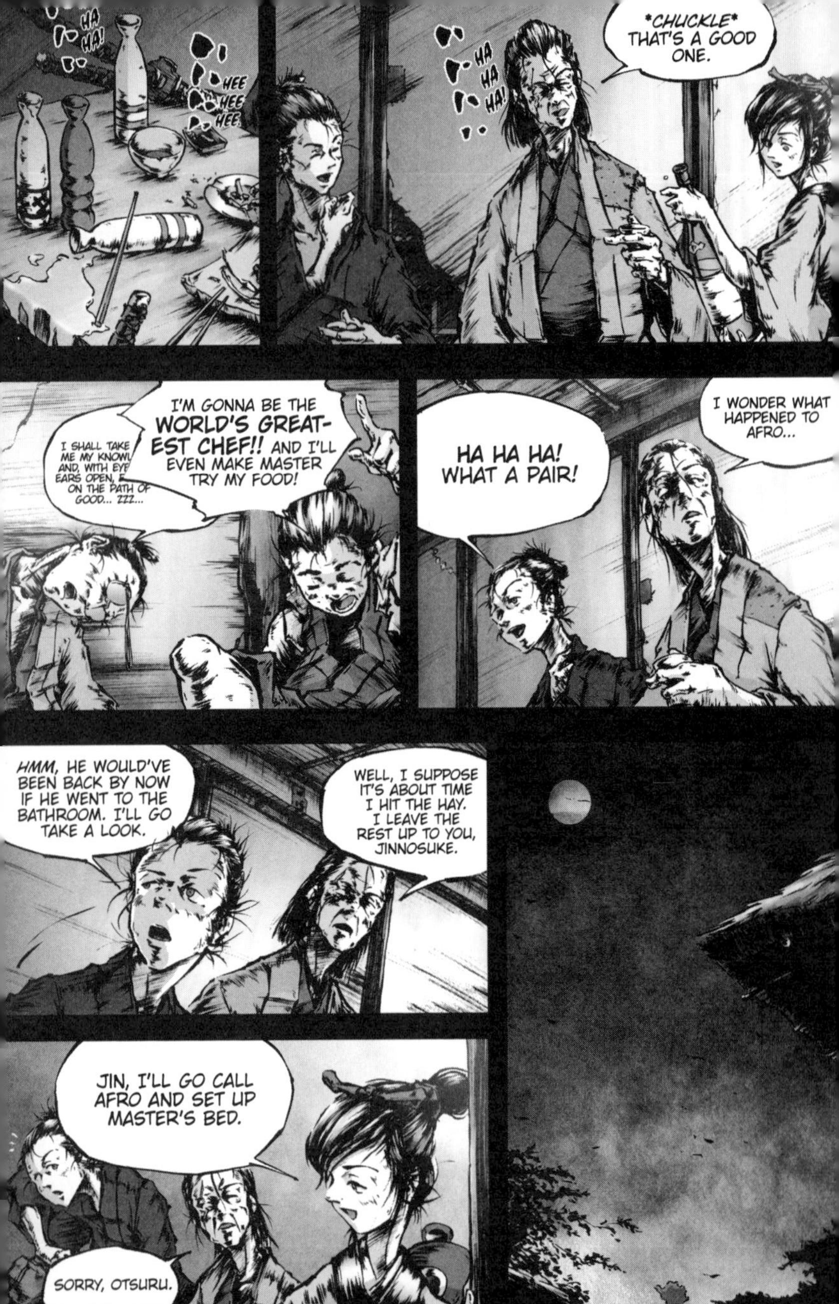
HA HA!
HEE HEE HEE
HA HA HA!
CHUCKLE THAT'S A GOOD ONE.
I SHALL TAKE ME MY KNOWL AND, WITH EYE EARS OPEN, ON THE PATH OF GOOD... ZZZ...
I'M GONNA BE THE **WORLD'S GREATEST CHEF!!** AND I'LL EVEN MAKE MASTER TRY MY FOOD!
HA HA HA! WHAT A PAIR!
I WONDER WHAT HAPPENED TO AFRO...
HMM, HE WOULD'VE BEEN BACK BY NOW IF HE WENT TO THE BATHROOM. I'LL GO TAKE A LOOK.
WELL, I SUPPOSE IT'S ABOUT TIME I HIT THE HAY. I LEAVE THE REST UP TO YOU, JINNOSUKE.
JIN, I'LL GO CALL AFRO AND SET UP MASTER'S BED.
SORRY, OTSURU.

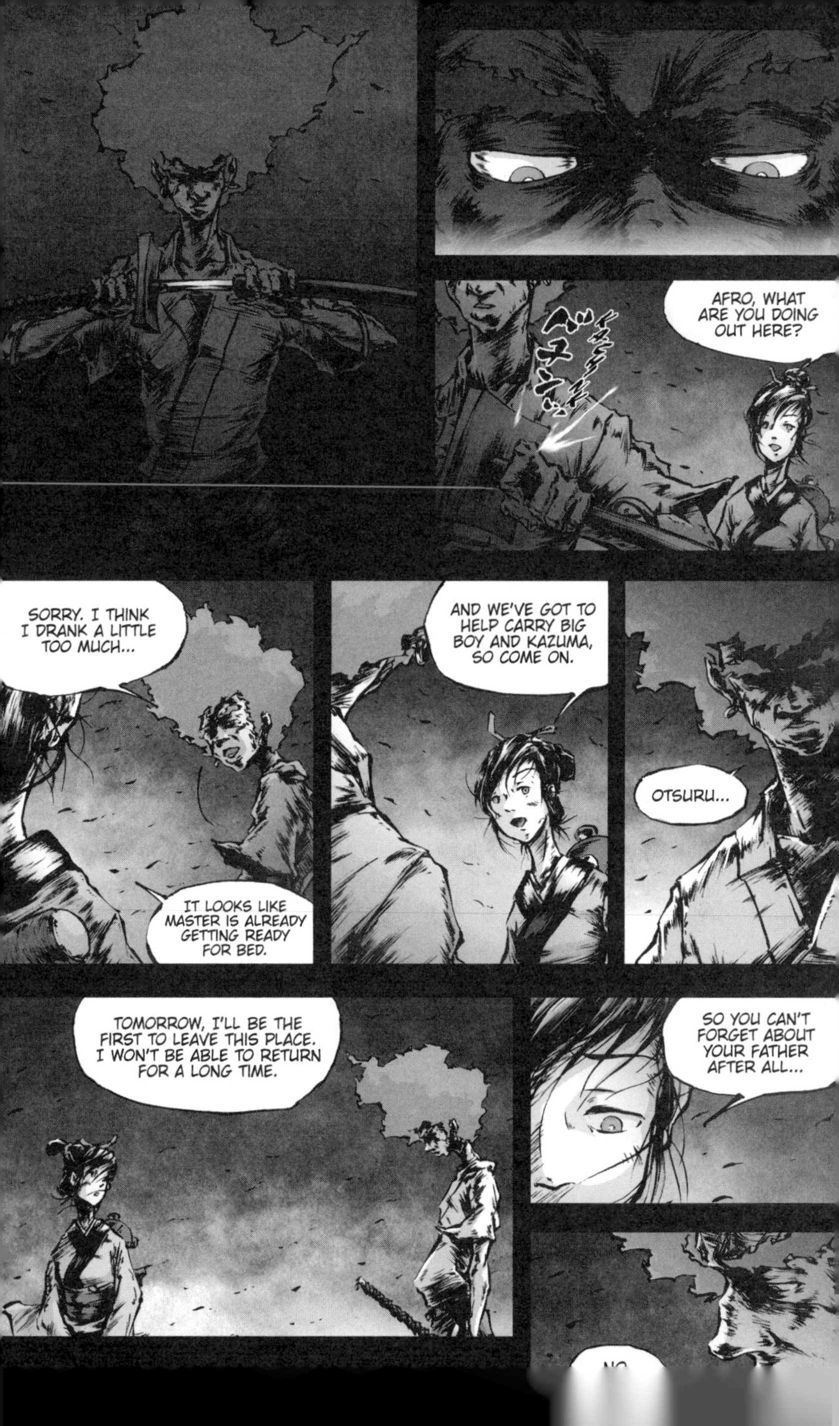
AFRO, WHAT ARE YOU DOING OUT HERE?
SORRY. I THINK I DRANK A LITTLE TOO MUCH...
IT LOOKS LIKE MASTER IS ALREADY GETTING READY FOR BED.
AND WE'VE GOT TO HELP CARRY BIG BOY AND KAZUMA, SO COME ON.
OTSURU...
TOMORROW, I'LL BE THE FIRST TO LEAVE THIS PLACE. I WON'T BE ABLE TO RETURN FOR A LONG TIME.
SO YOU CAN'T FORGET ABOUT YOUR FATHER AFTER ALL...
NO

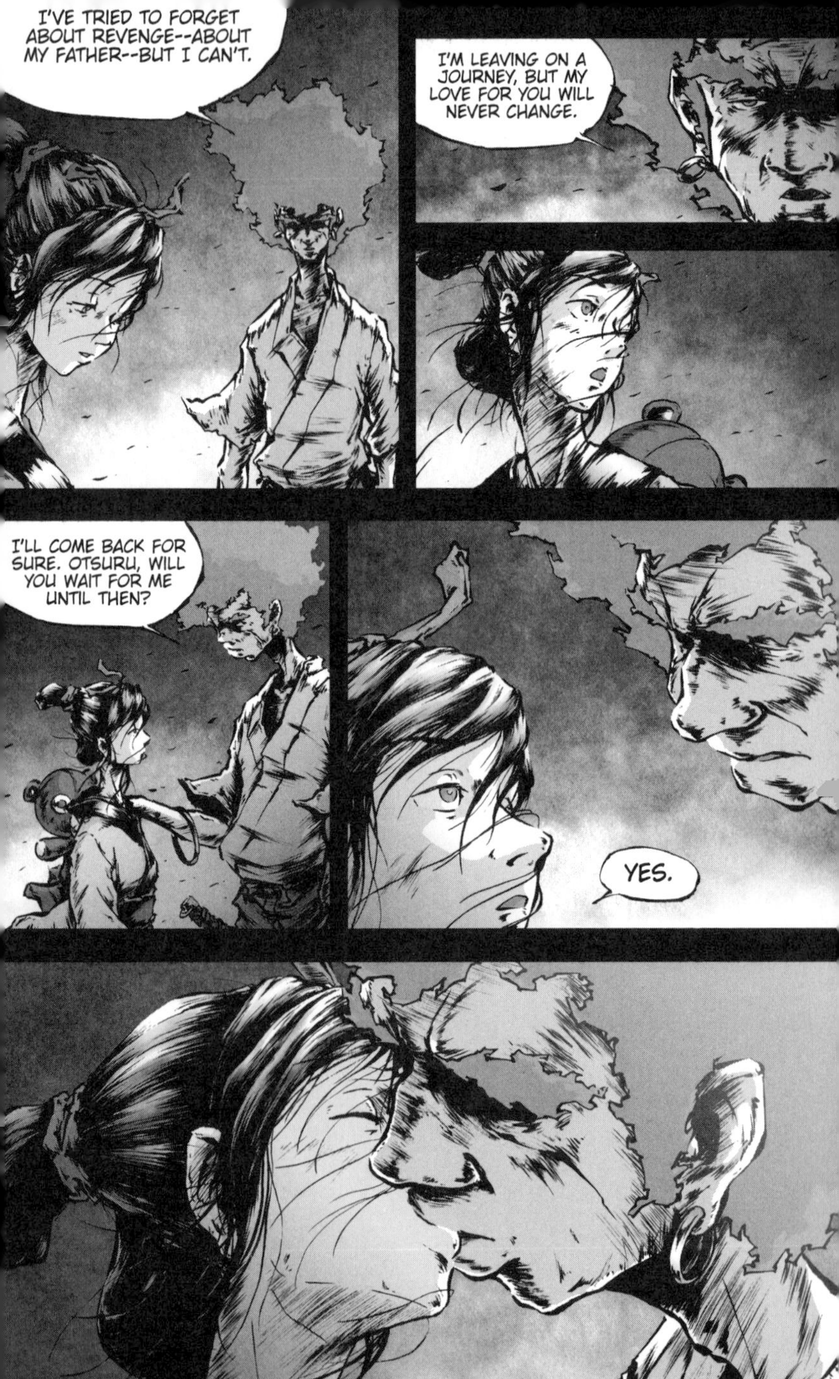
I'VE TRIED TO FORGET ABOUT REVENGE--ABOUT MY FATHER--BUT I CAN'T.
I'M LEAVING ON A JOURNEY, BUT MY LOVE FOR YOU WILL NEVER CHANGE.
I'LL COME BACK FOR SURE. OTSURU, WILL YOU WAIT FOR ME UNTIL THEN?
YES.

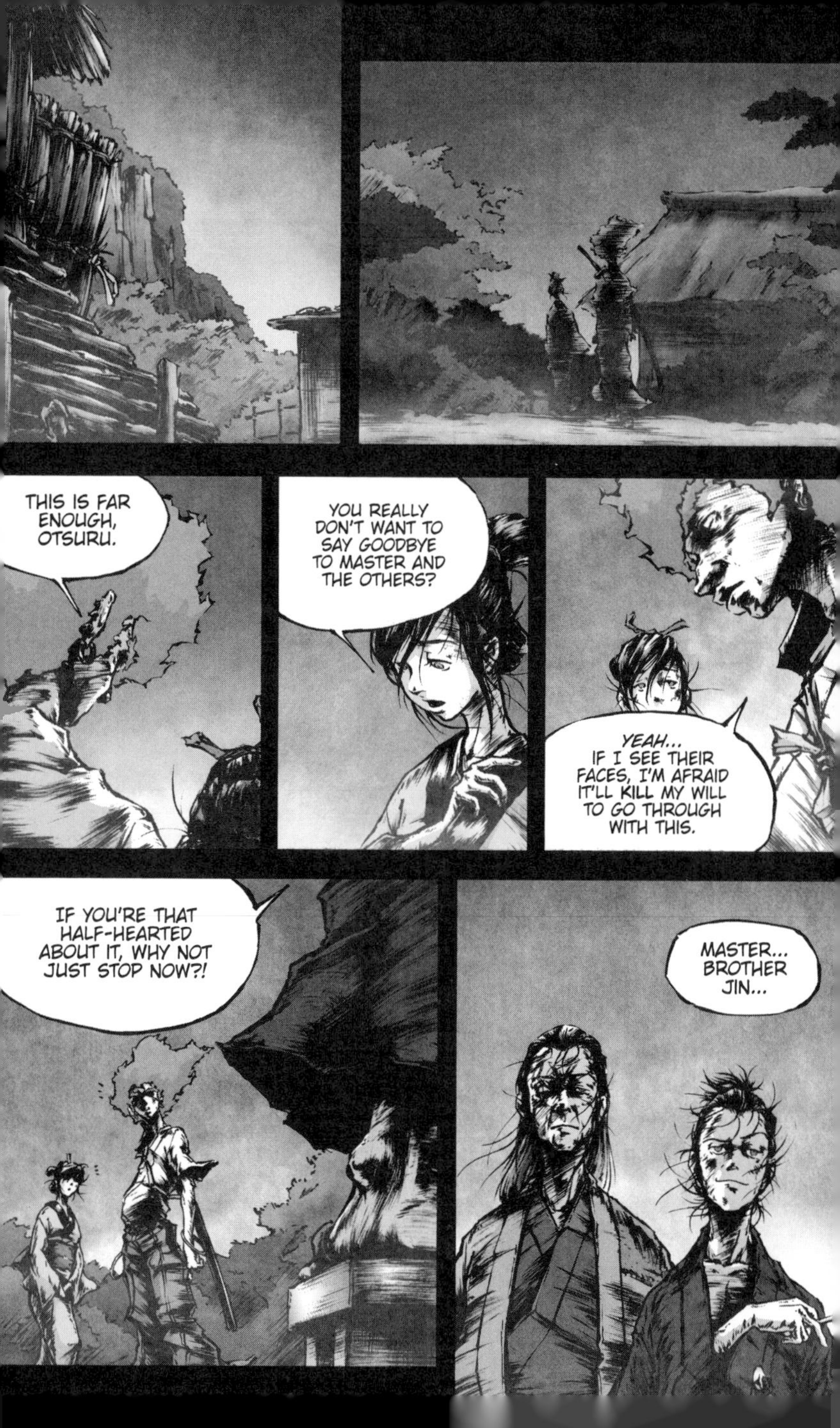
THIS IS FAR ENOUGH, OTSURU.
YOU REALLY DON'T WANT TO SAY GOODBYE TO MASTER AND THE OTHERS?
YEAH... IF I SEE THEIR FACES, I'M AFRAID IT'LL **KILL** MY WILL TO GO THROUGH WITH THIS.
IF YOU'RE THAT HALF-HEARTED ABOUT IT, WHY NOT JUST STOP NOW?!
MASTER... BROTHER JIN...

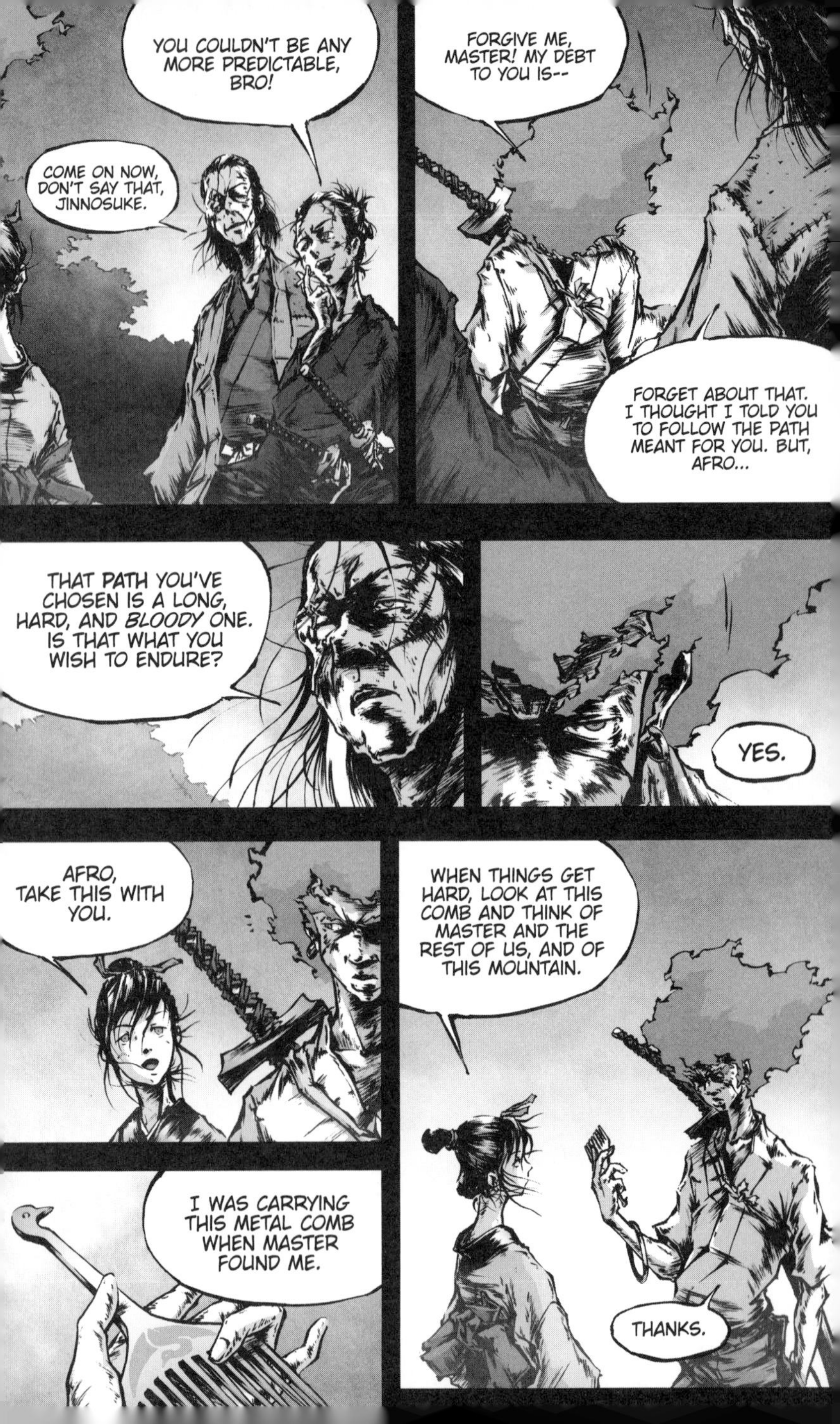
YOU COULDN'T BE ANY MORE PREDICTABLE, BRO!
COME ON NOW, DON'T SAY THAT, JINNOSUKE.
FORGIVE ME, MASTER! MY DEBT TO YOU IS--
FORGET ABOUT THAT. I THOUGHT I TOLD YOU TO FOLLOW THE PATH MEANT FOR YOU. BUT, AFRO...
THAT PATH YOU'VE CHOSEN IS A LONG, HARD, AND *BLOODY* ONE. IS THAT WHAT YOU WISH TO ENDURE?
YES.
AFRO, TAKE THIS WITH YOU.
I WAS CARRYING THIS METAL COMB WHEN MASTER FOUND ME.
WHEN THINGS GET HARD, LOOK AT THIS COMB AND THINK OF MASTER AND THE REST OF US, AND OF THIS MOUNTAIN.
THANKS.

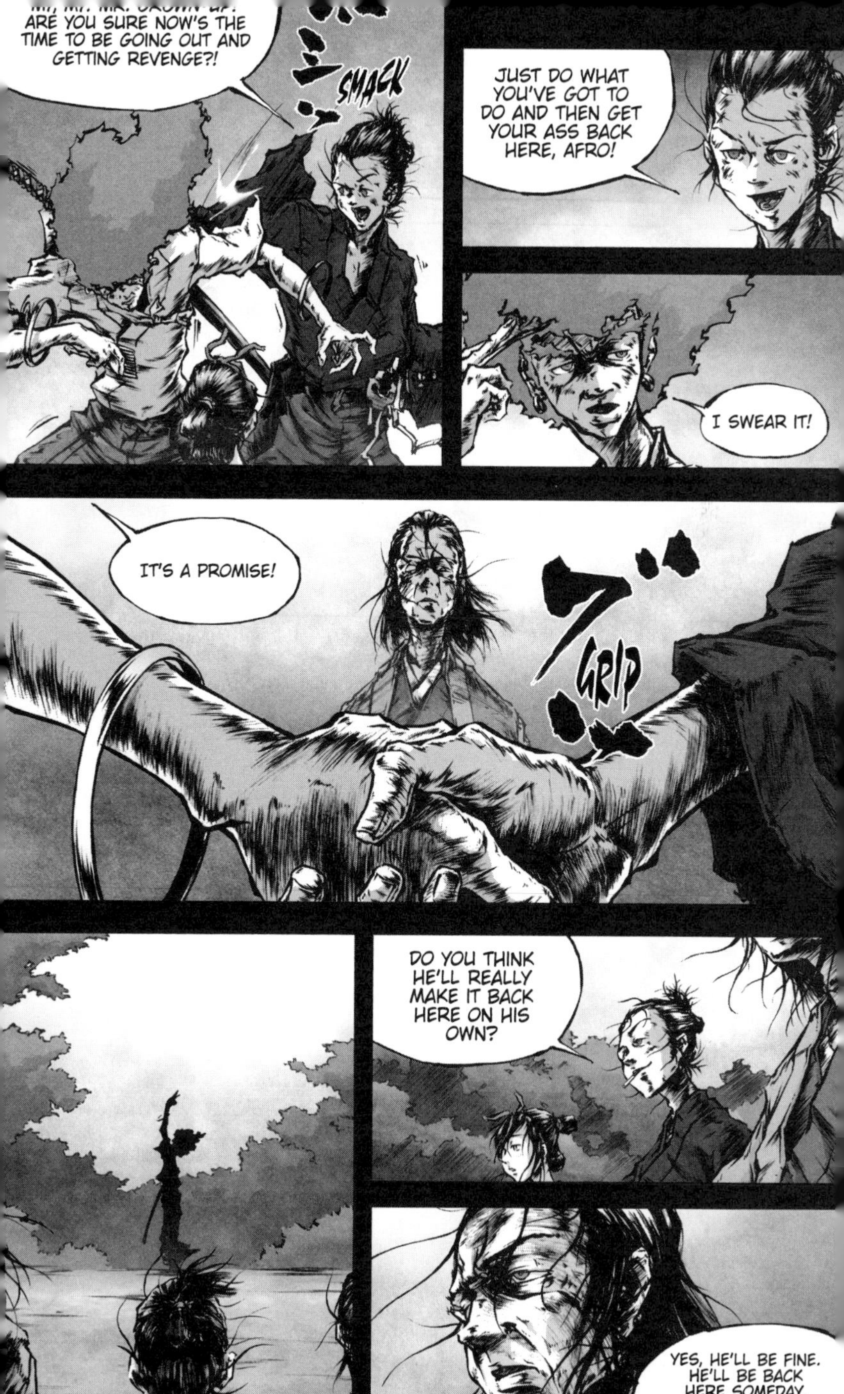
ARE YOU SURE NOW'S THE TIME TO BE GOING OUT AND GETTING REVENGE?!
SMACK
JUST DO WHAT YOU'VE GOT TO DO AND THEN GET YOUR ASS BACK HERE, AFRO!
I SWEAR IT!
IT'S A PROMISE!
GRIP
DO YOU THINK HE'LL REALLY MAKE IT BACK HERE ON HIS OWN?
YES, HE'LL BE FINE. HE'LL BE BACK HERE SOMEDAY.

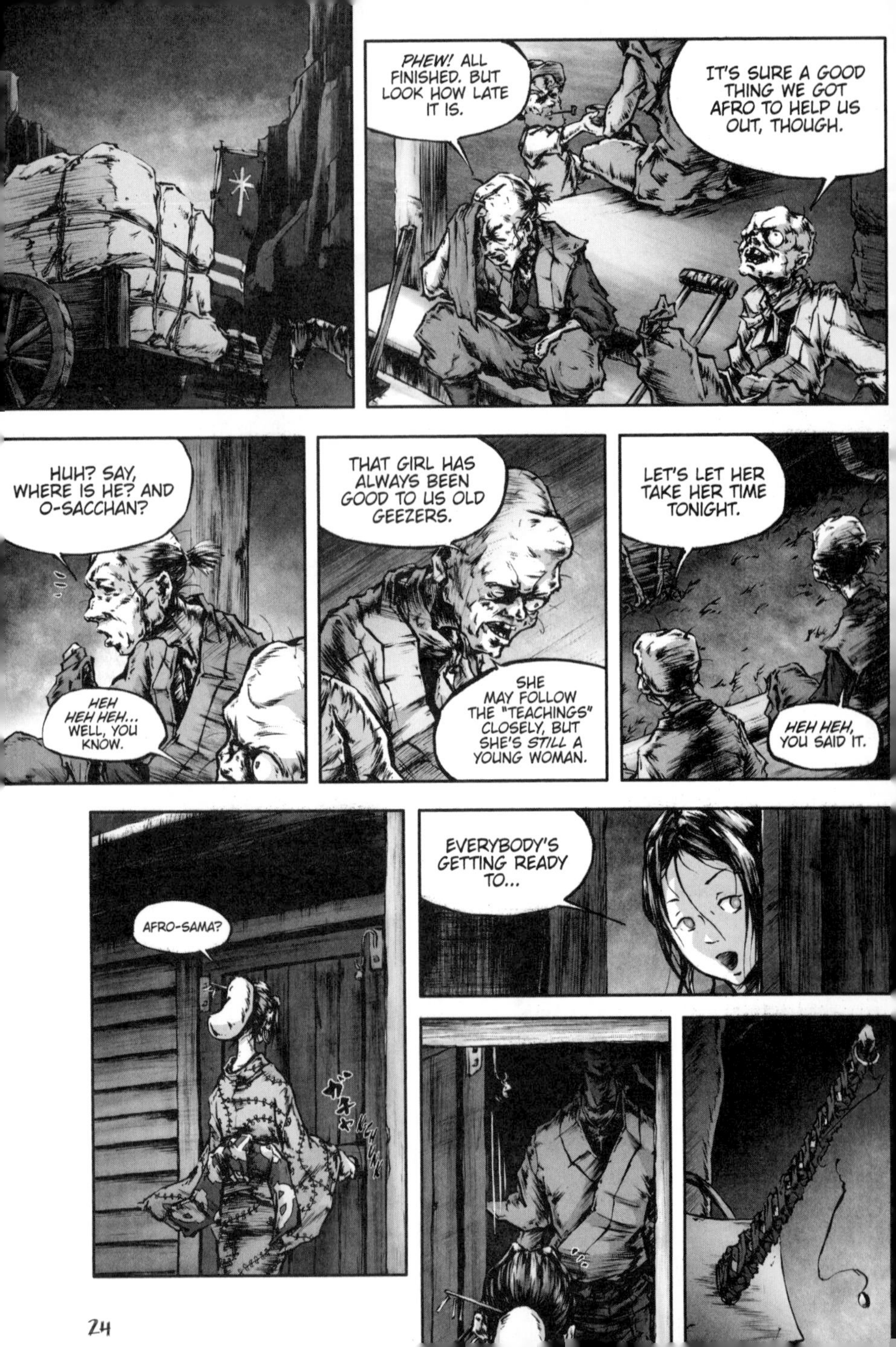
PHEW! ALL FINISHED. BUT LOOK HOW LATE IT IS.
IT'S SURE A GOOD THING WE GOT AFRO TO HELP US OUT, THOUGH.
HUH? SAY, WHERE IS HE? AND O-SACCHAN?
HEH HEH HEH... WELL, YOU KNOW.
THAT GIRL HAS ALWAYS BEEN GOOD TO US OLD GEEZERS.
SHE MAY FOLLOW THE "TEACHINGS" CLOSELY, BUT SHE'S STILL A YOUNG WOMAN.
LET'S LET HER TAKE HER TIME TONIGHT.
HEH HEH, YOU SAID IT.
AFRO-SAMA?
ガチャ
KCHUNK
EVERYBODY'S GETTING READY TO...

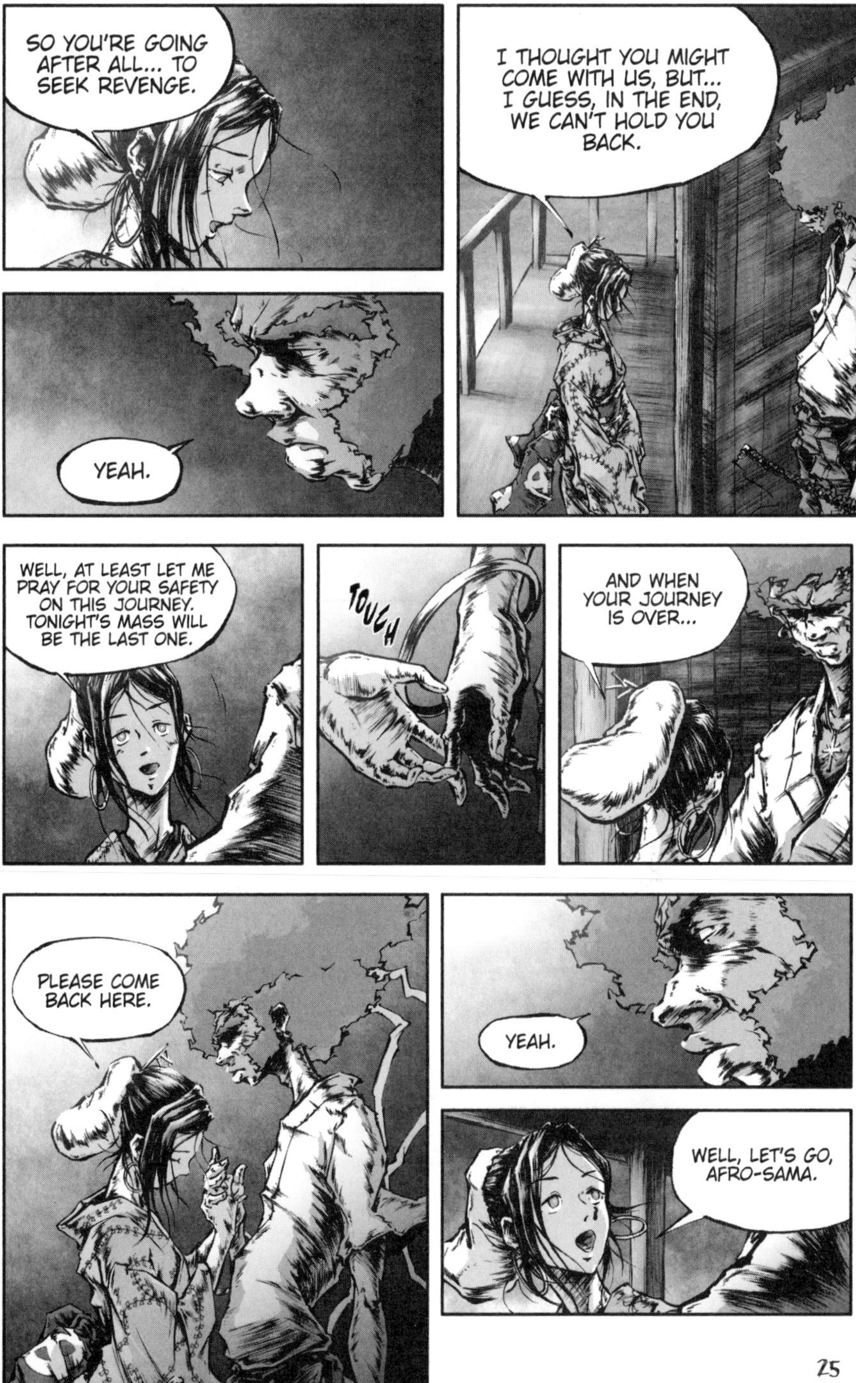
SO YOU'RE GOING AFTER ALL... TO SEEK REVENGE.
YEAH.
I THOUGHT YOU MIGHT COME WITH US, BUT... I GUESS, IN THE END, WE CAN'T HOLD YOU BACK.
WELL, AT LEAST LET ME PRAY FOR YOUR SAFETY ON THIS JOURNEY. TONIGHT'S MASS WILL BE THE LAST ONE.
TOUCH
AND WHEN YOUR JOURNEY IS OVER...
PLEASE COME BACK HERE.
YEAH.
WELL, LET'S GO, AFRO-SAMA.

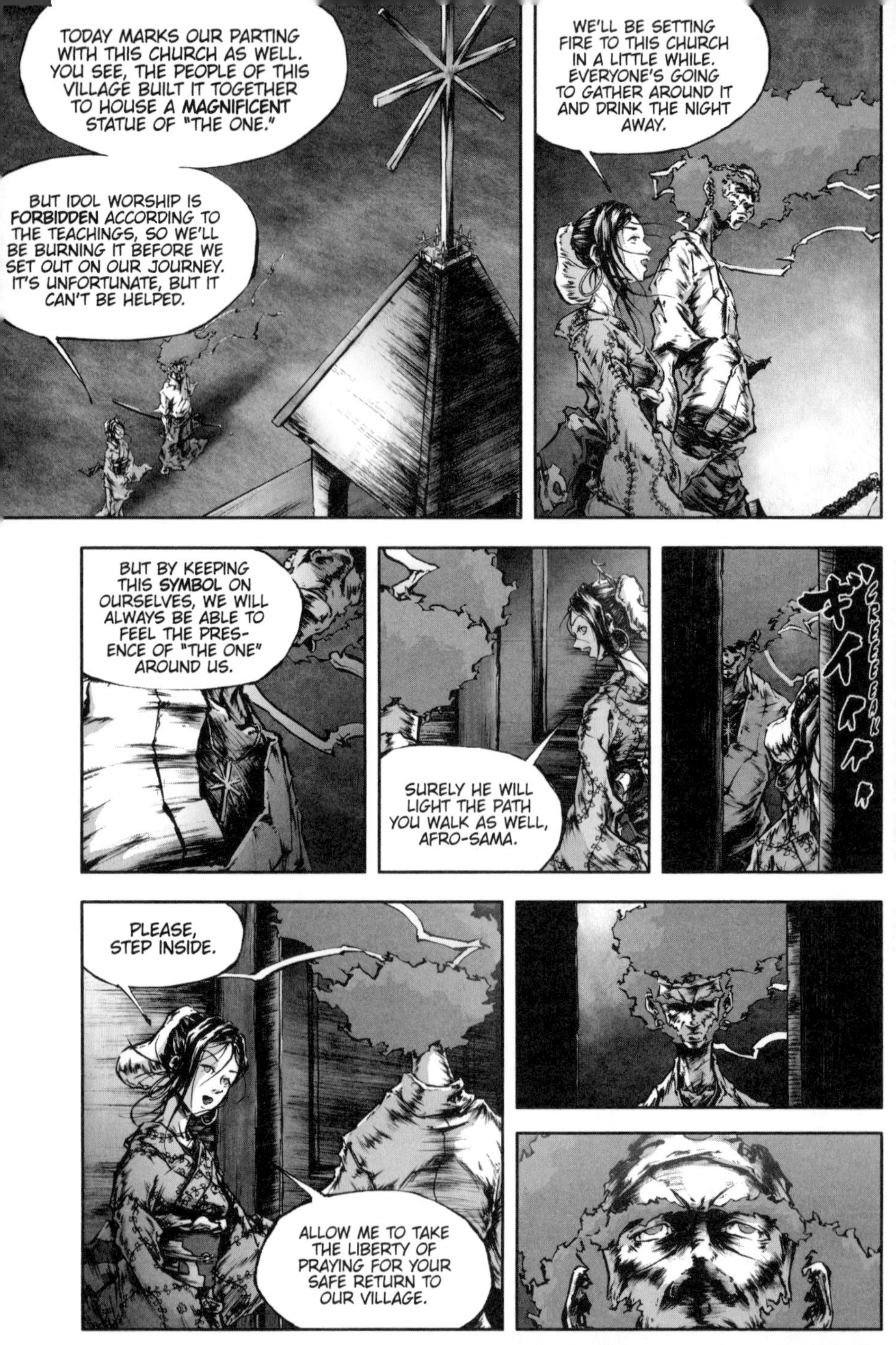
TODAY MARKS OUR PARTING WITH THIS CHURCH AS WELL. YOU SEE, THE PEOPLE OF THIS VILLAGE BUILT IT TOGETHER TO HOUSE A **MAGNIFICENT** STATUE OF "THE ONE."
BUT IDOL WORSHIP IS **FORBIDDEN** ACCORDING TO THE TEACHINGS, SO WE'LL BE BURNING IT BEFORE WE SET OUT ON OUR JOURNEY. IT'S UNFORTUNATE, BUT IT CAN'T BE HELPED.
WE'LL BE SETTING FIRE TO THIS CHURCH IN A LITTLE WHILE. EVERYONE'S GOING TO GATHER AROUND IT AND DRINK THE NIGHT AWAY.
BUT BY KEEPING THIS **SYMBOL** ON OURSELVES, WE WILL ALWAYS BE ABLE TO FEEL THE PRES-ENCE OF "THE ONE" AROUND US.
SURELY HE WILL LIGHT THE PATH YOU WALK AS WELL, AFRO-SAMA.
ギイイイィ
CREEEEEAK
PLEASE, STEP INSIDE.
ALLOW ME TO TAKE THE LIBERTY OF PRAYING FOR YOUR SAFE RETURN TO OUR VILLAGE.

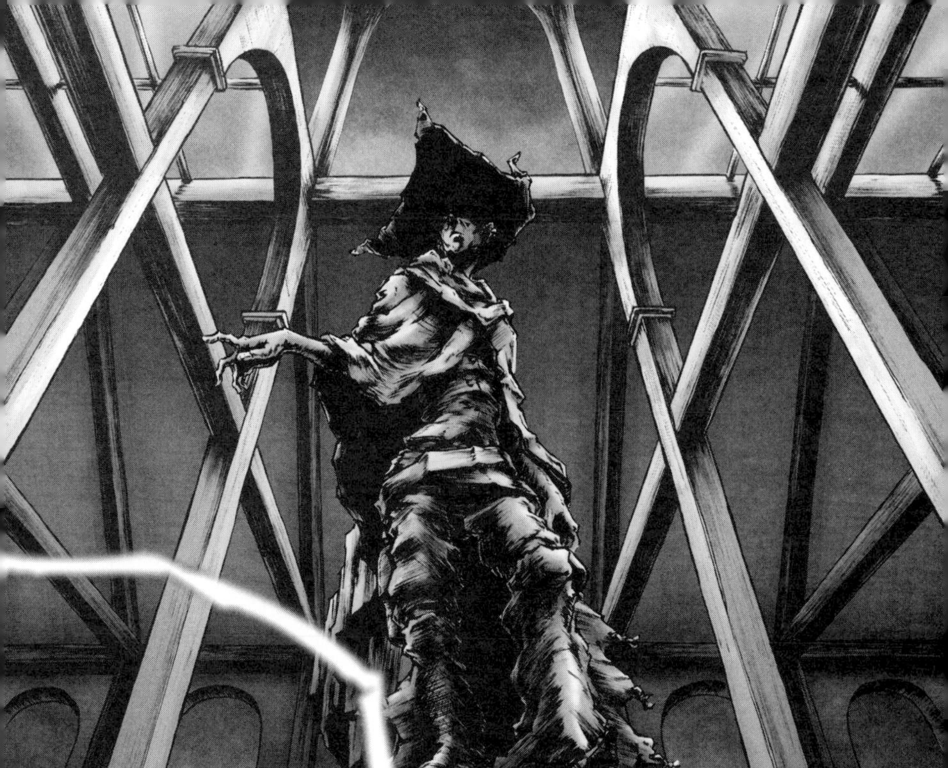

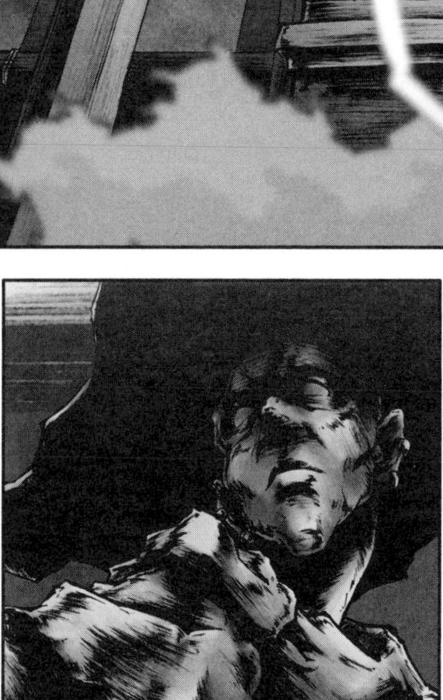

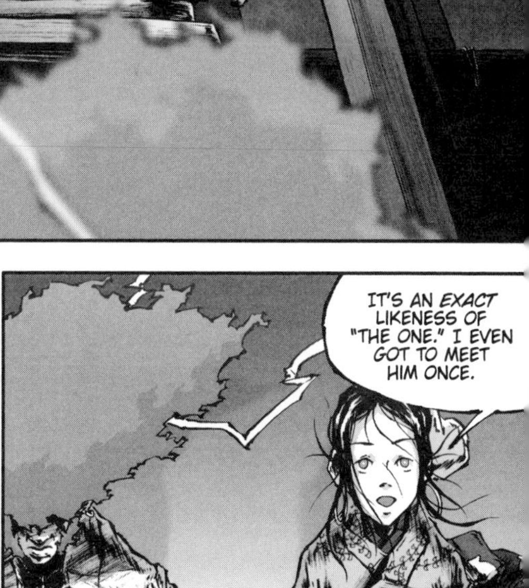
IT'S AN *EXACT* LIKENESS OF "THE ONE." I EVEN GOT TO MEET HIM ONCE.

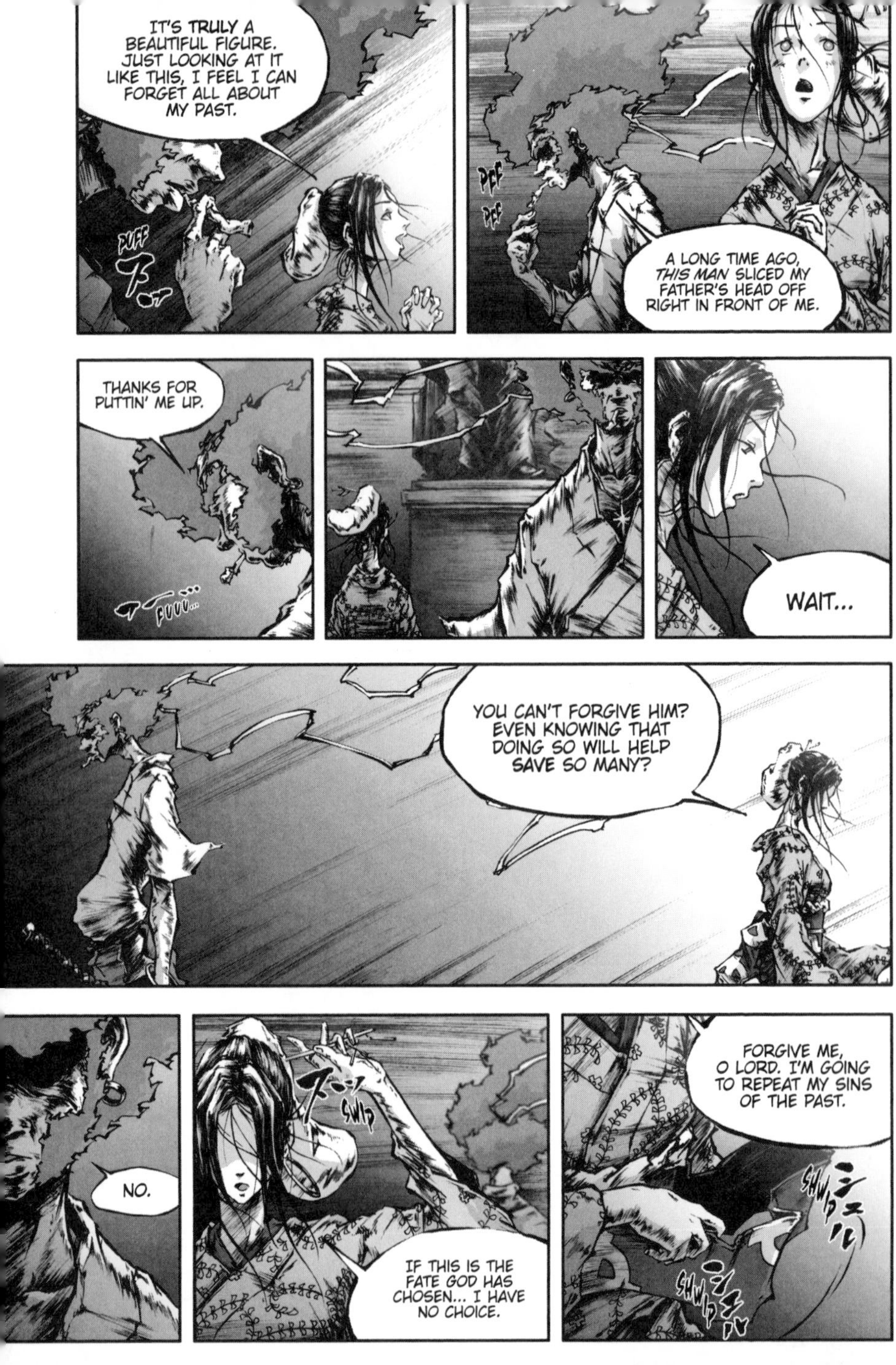
IT'S TRULY A BEAUTIFUL FIGURE. JUST LOOKING AT IT LIKE THIS, I FEEL I CAN FORGET ALL ABOUT MY PAST.
PUFF
PFF
PFF
A LONG TIME AGO, *THIS MAN* SLICED MY FATHER'S HEAD OFF RIGHT IN FRONT OF ME.
THANKS FOR PUTTIN' ME UP.
FUUU...
WAIT...
YOU CAN'T FORGIVE HIM? EVEN KNOWING THAT DOING SO WILL HELP SAVE SO MANY?
NO.
SWIP
IF THIS IS THE FATE GOD HAS CHOSEN... I HAVE NO CHOICE.
FORGIVE ME, O LORD. I'M GOING TO REPEAT MY SINS OF THE PAST.
SHWIP
SHWIP

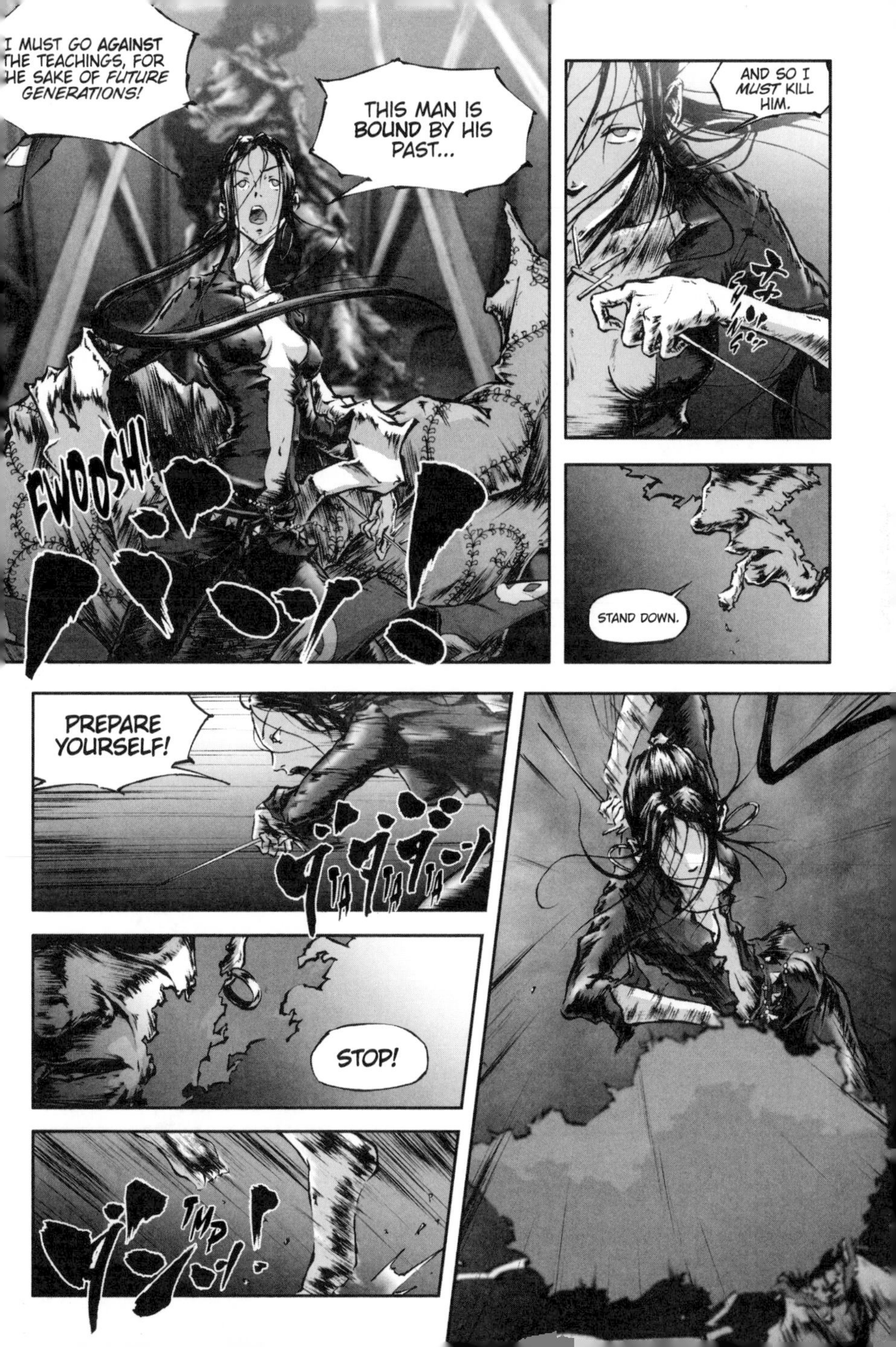
I MUST GO AGAINST THE TEACHINGS, FOR HE SAKE OF FUTURE GENERATIONS!
THIS MAN IS BOUND BY HIS PAST...
FWOOSH!
AND SO I MUST KILL HIM.
STAND DOWN.
PREPARE YOURSELF!
TA TA TA
STOP!
TMP

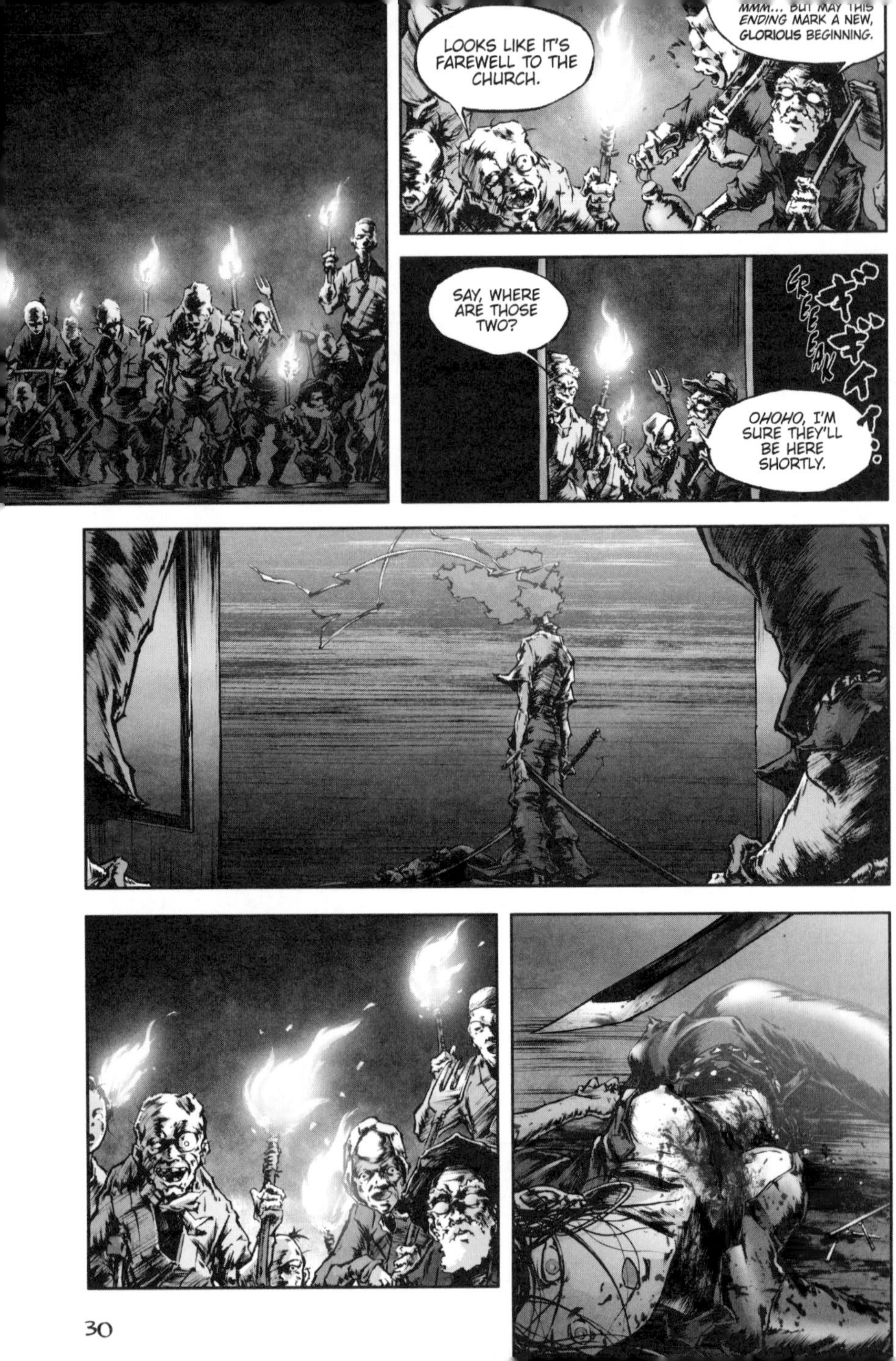
LOOKS LIKE IT'S FAREWELL TO THE CHURCH.
MMM... BUT MAY THIS ENDING MARK A NEW, GLORIOUS BEGINNING.
SAY, WHERE ARE THOSE TWO?
CREEEAK
OHOHO, I'M SURE THEY'LL BE HERE SHORTLY.

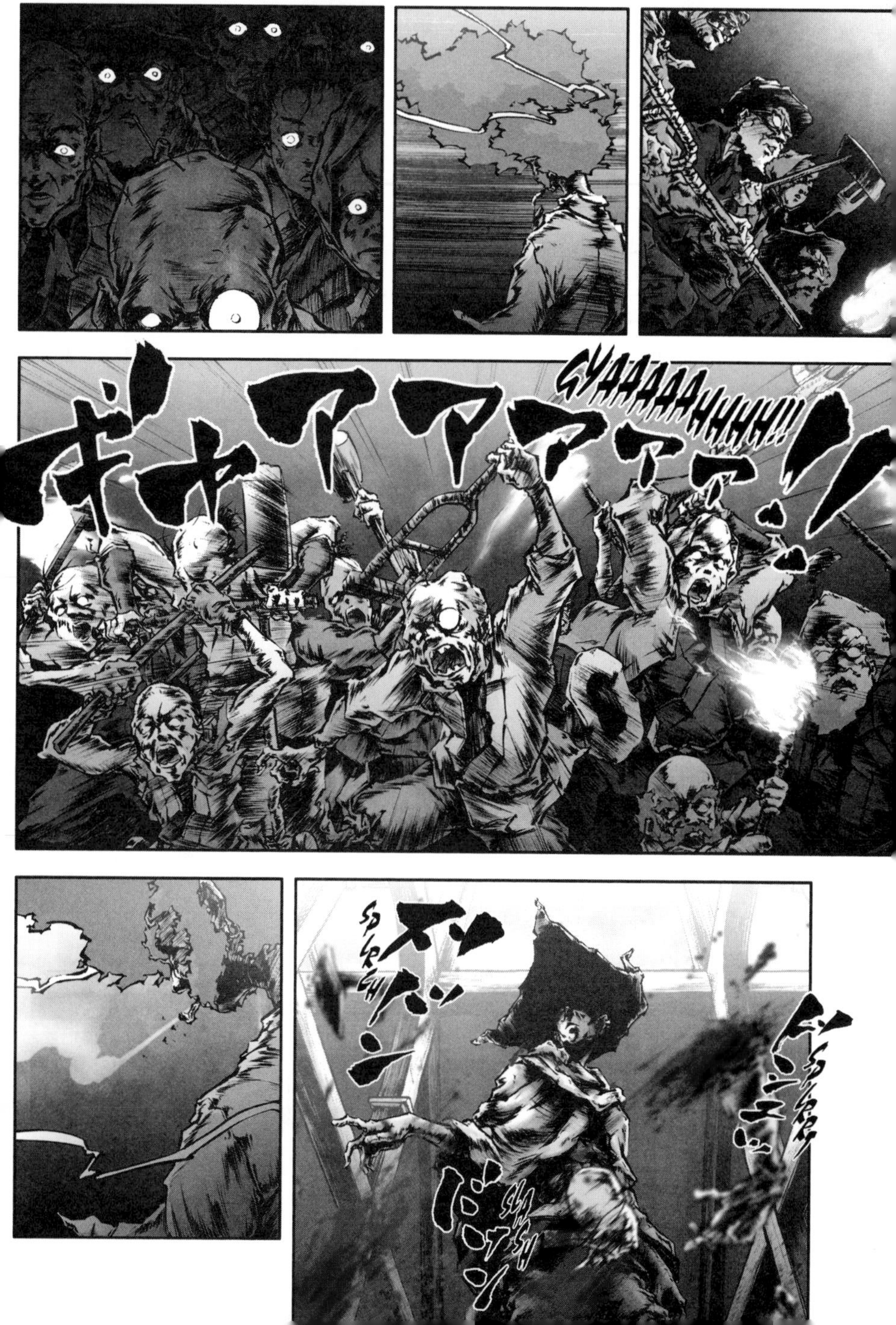
ギャアアアァ!!
GYAAAAAAHHHH!!
ズバン
SPLRCH
SPLORK
SLASH

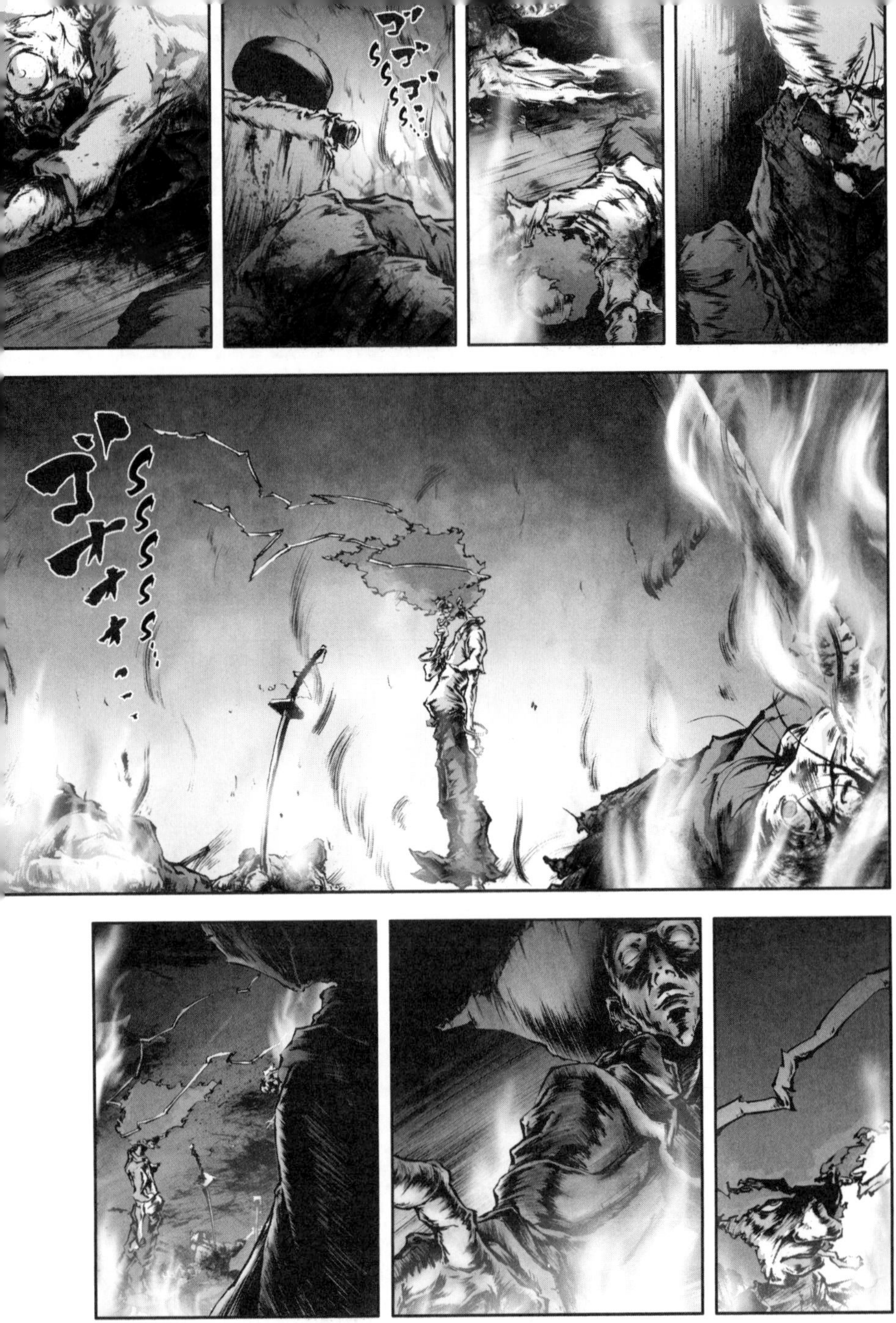
ゴゴゴ…
ゴオォォ…

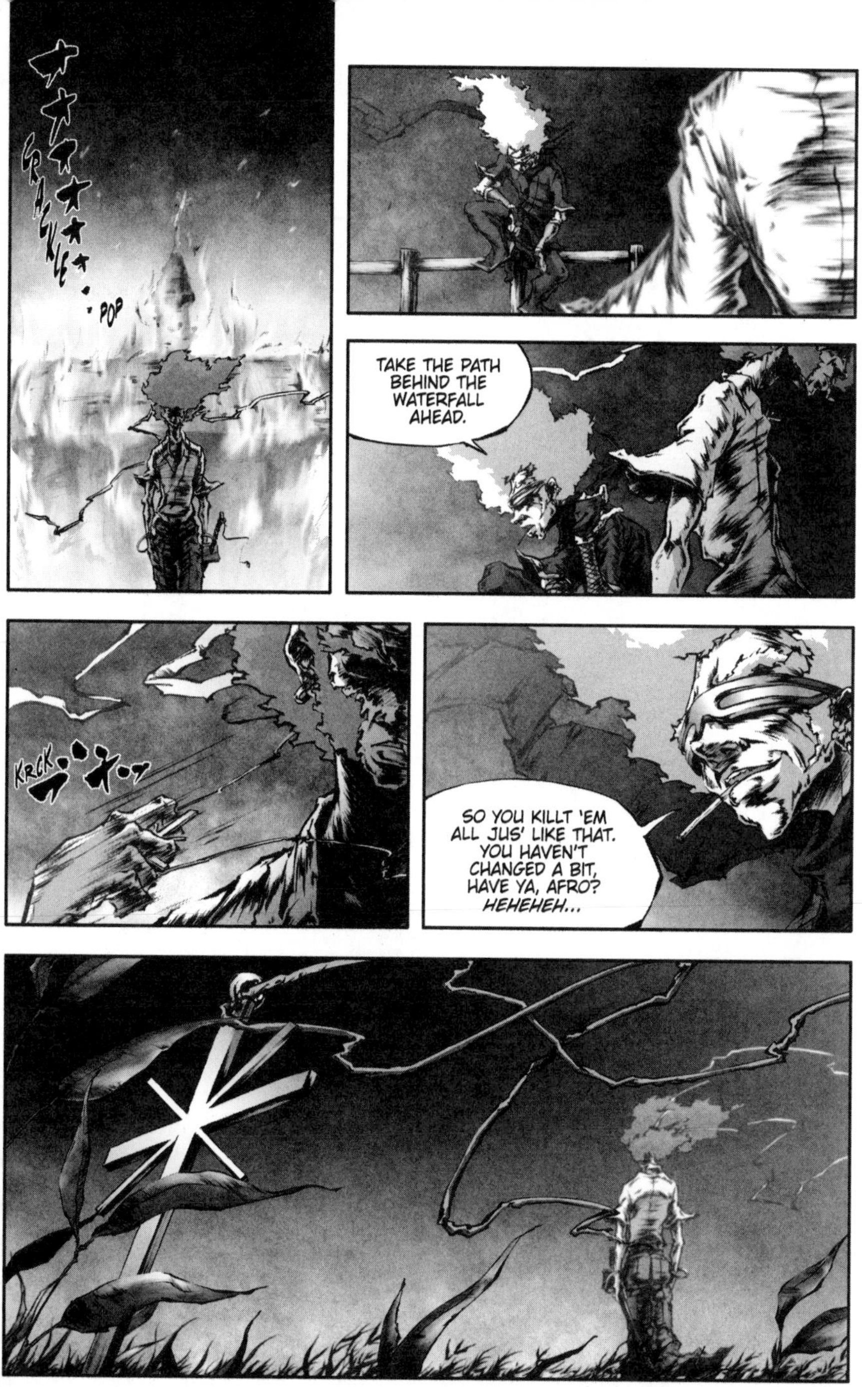
CRACKLE... POP
TAKE THE PATH BEHIND THE WATERFALL AHEAD.
KRCK
SO YOU KILLT 'EM ALL JUS' LIKE THAT. YOU HAVEN'T CHANGED A BIT, HAVE YA, AFRO? *HEHEHEH...*

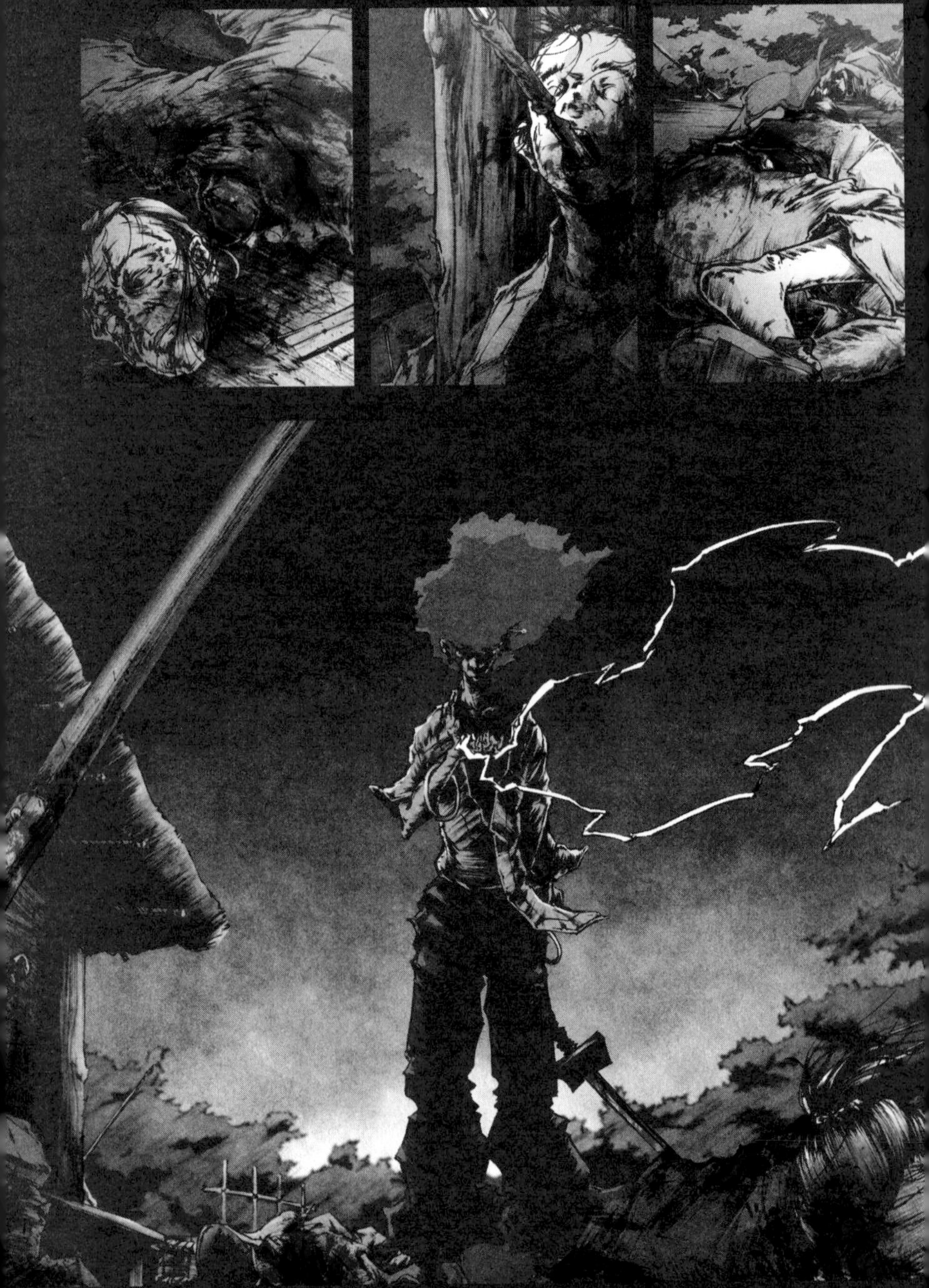

END OF #06

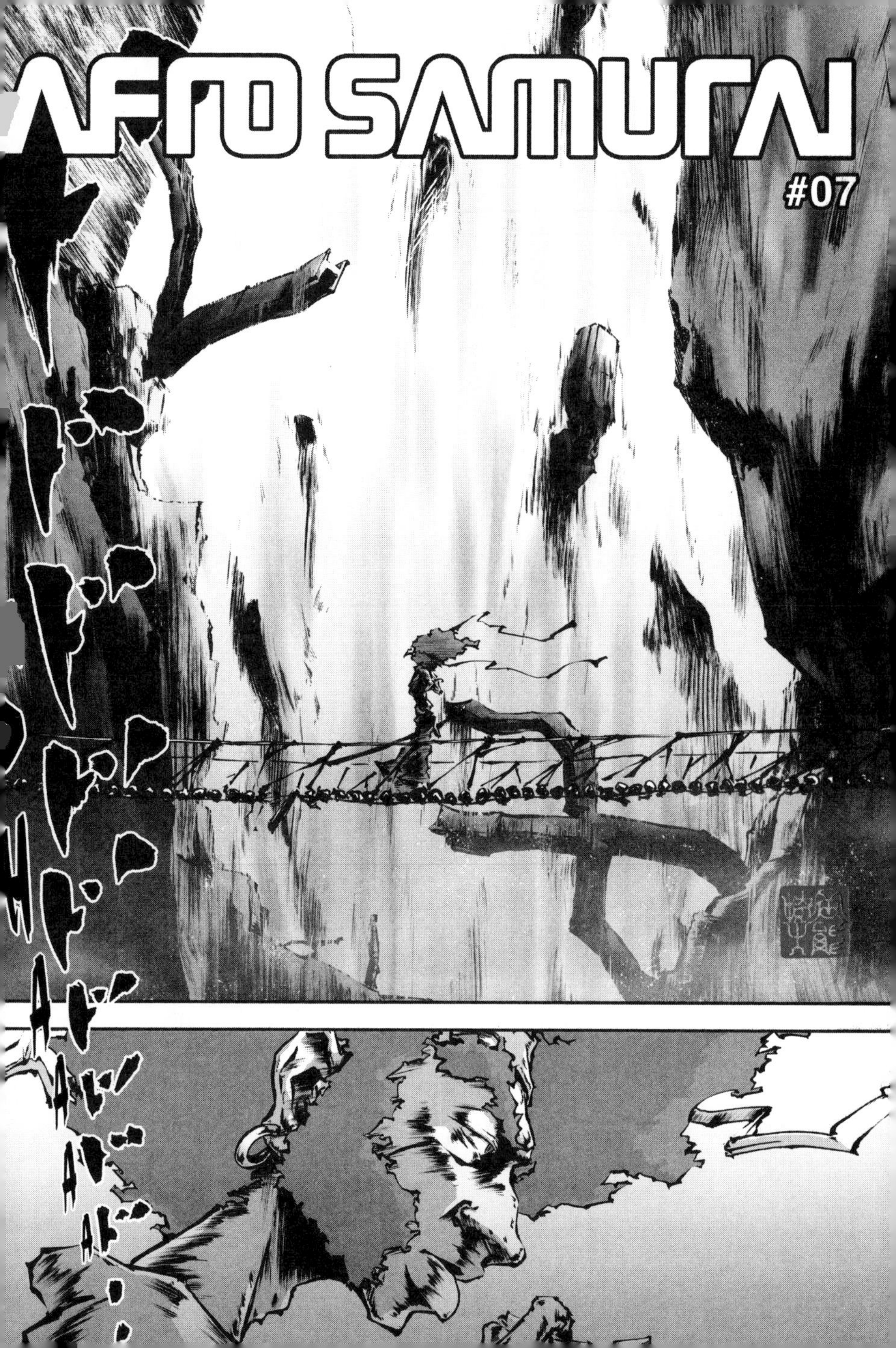
AFRO SAMURAI
#07

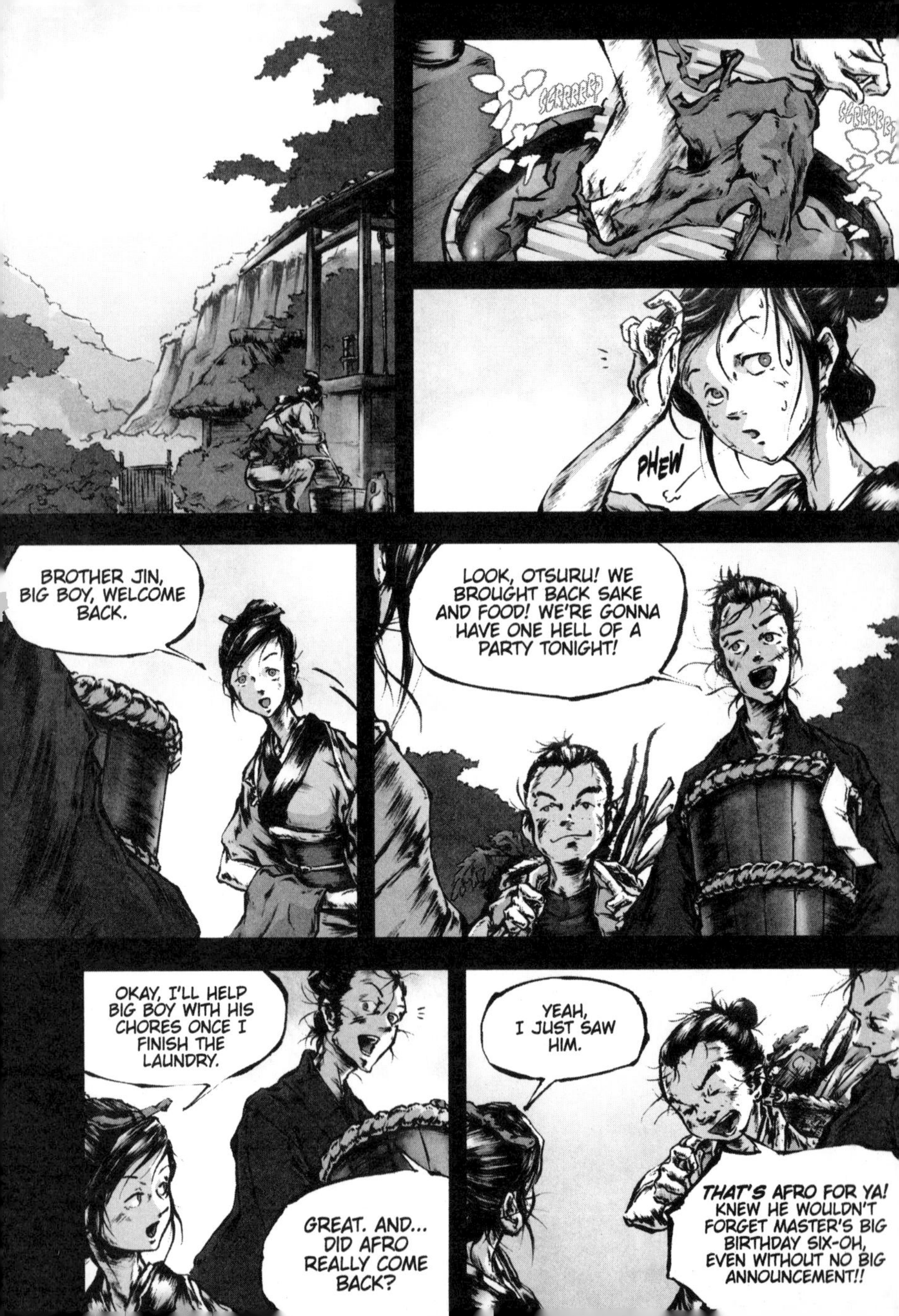
PHEW
BROTHER JIN, BIG BOY, WELCOME BACK.
LOOK, OTSURU! WE BROUGHT BACK SAKE AND FOOD! WE'RE GONNA HAVE ONE HELL OF A PARTY TONIGHT!
OKAY, I'LL HELP BIG BOY WITH HIS CHORES ONCE I FINISH THE LAUNDRY.
GREAT. AND... DID AFRO REALLY COME BACK?
YEAH, I JUST SAW HIM.
THAT'S AFRO FOR YA! KNEW HE WOULDN'T FORGET MASTER'S BIG BIRTHDAY SIX-OH, EVEN WITHOUT NO BIG ANNOUNCEMENT!!

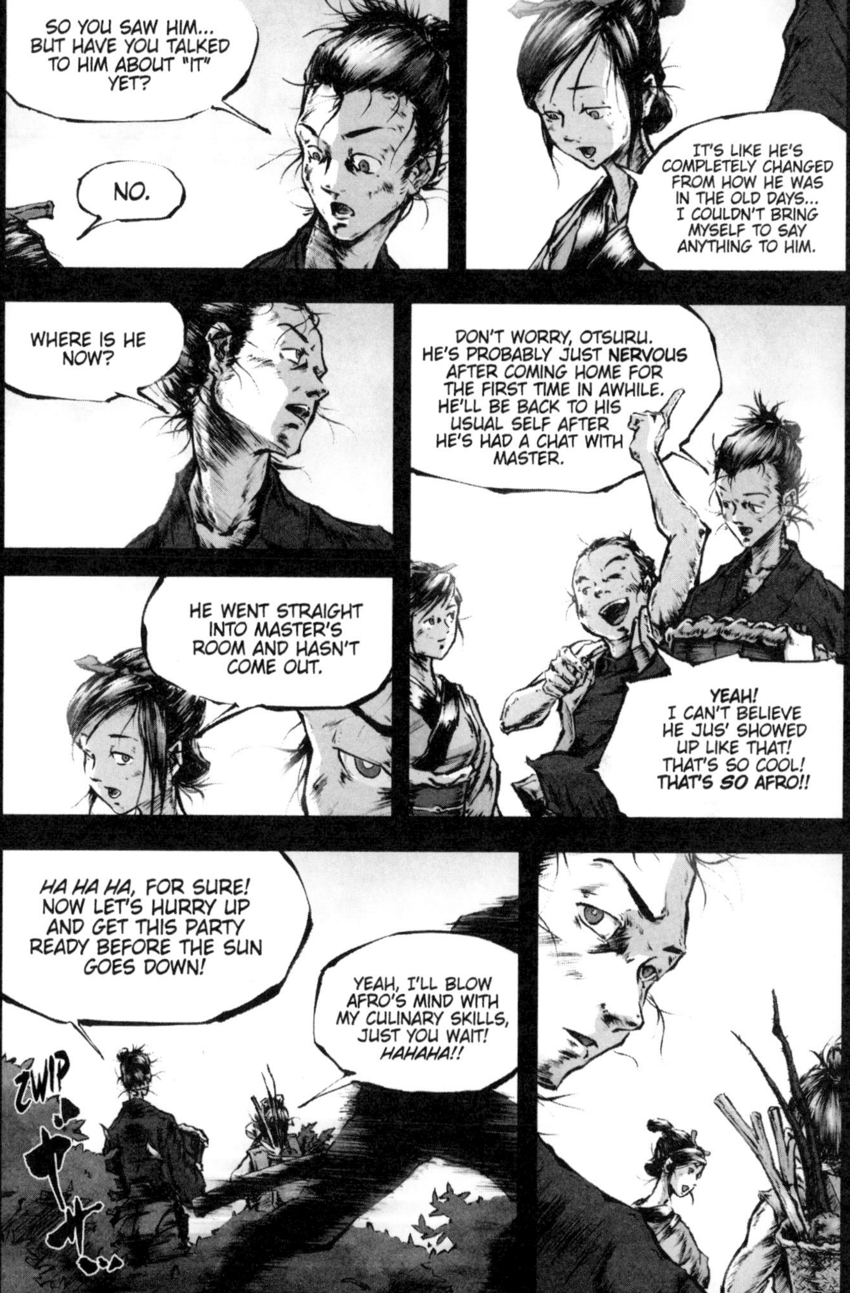
SO YOU SAW HIM... BUT HAVE YOU TALKED TO HIM ABOUT "IT" YET?
NO.
IT'S LIKE HE'S COMPLETELY CHANGED FROM HOW HE WAS IN THE OLD DAYS... I COULDN'T BRING MYSELF TO SAY ANYTHING TO HIM.
WHERE IS HE NOW?
HE WENT STRAIGHT INTO MASTER'S ROOM AND HASN'T COME OUT.
DON'T WORRY, OTSURU. HE'S PROBABLY JUST NERVOUS AFTER COMING HOME FOR THE FIRST TIME IN AWHILE. HE'LL BE BACK TO HIS USUAL SELF AFTER HE'S HAD A CHAT WITH MASTER.
YEAH! I CAN'T BELIEVE HE JUS' SHOWED UP LIKE THAT! THAT'S SO COOL! THAT'S SO AFRO!!
HA HA HA, FOR SURE! NOW LET'S HURRY UP AND GET THIS PARTY READY BEFORE THE SUN GOES DOWN!
YEAH, I'LL BLOW AFRO'S MIND WITH MY CULINARY SKILLS, JUST YOU WAIT! HAHAHA!!
ZWIP

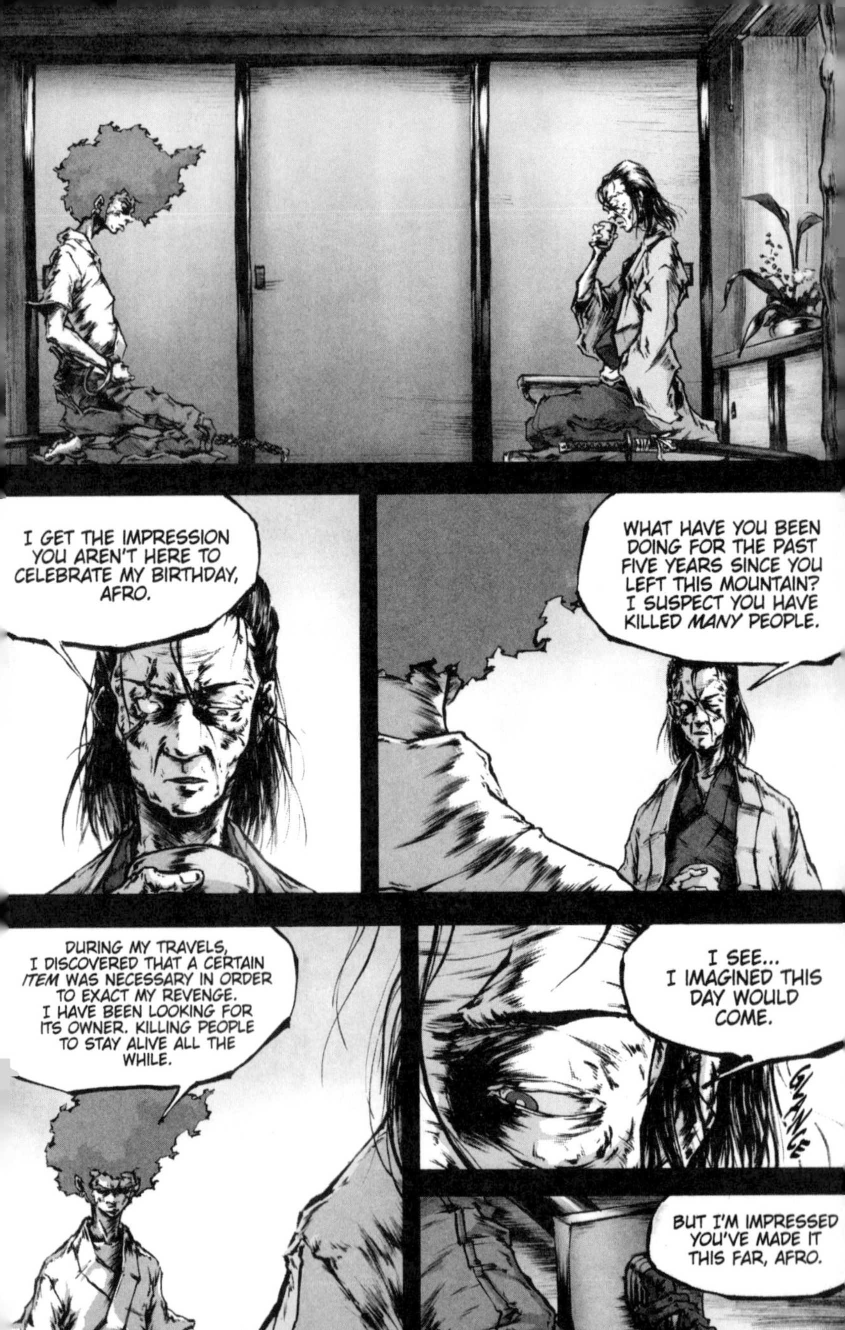
I GET THE IMPRESSION YOU AREN'T HERE TO CELEBRATE MY BIRTHDAY, AFRO.
WHAT HAVE YOU BEEN DOING FOR THE PAST FIVE YEARS SINCE YOU LEFT THIS MOUNTAIN? I SUSPECT YOU HAVE KILLED *MANY* PEOPLE.
DURING MY TRAVELS, I DISCOVERED THAT A CERTAIN *ITEM* WAS NECESSARY IN ORDER TO EXACT MY REVENGE. I HAVE BEEN LOOKING FOR ITS OWNER. KILLING PEOPLE TO STAY ALIVE ALL THE WHILE.
I SEE... I IMAGINED THIS DAY WOULD COME.
GLANCE
BUT I'M IMPRESSED YOU'VE MADE IT THIS FAR, AFRO.

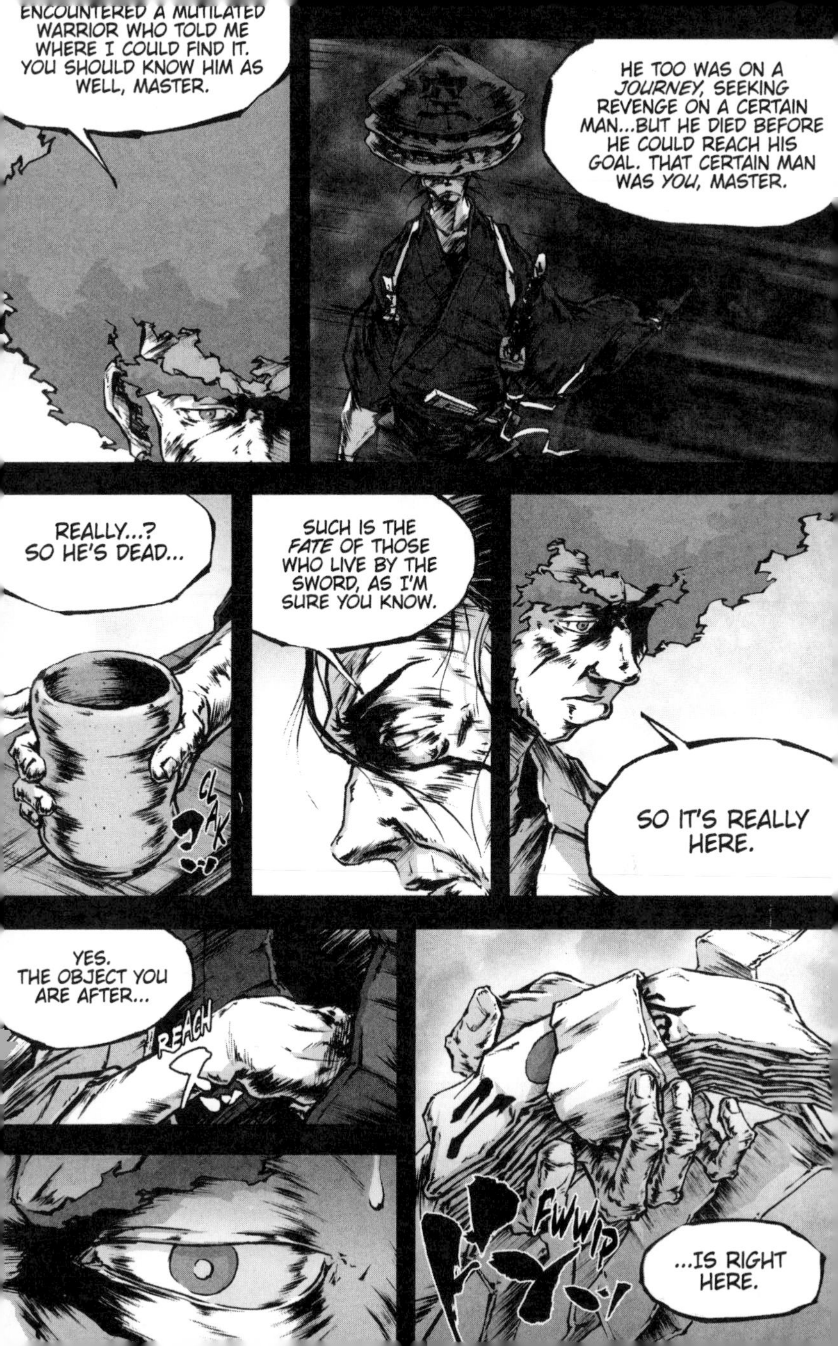
ENCOUNTERED A MUTILATED WARRIOR WHO TOLD ME WHERE I COULD FIND IT. YOU SHOULD KNOW HIM AS WELL, MASTER.
HE TOO WAS ON A *JOURNEY*, SEEKING REVENGE ON A CERTAIN MAN...BUT HE DIED BEFORE HE COULD REACH HIS GOAL. THAT CERTAIN MAN WAS *YOU*, MASTER.
REALLY...? SO HE'S DEAD...
CLAK
SUCH IS THE *FATE* OF THOSE WHO LIVE BY THE SWORD, AS I'M SURE YOU KNOW.
SO IT'S REALLY HERE.
YES. THE OBJECT YOU ARE AFTER...
REACH
FWWIP
...IS RIGHT HERE.

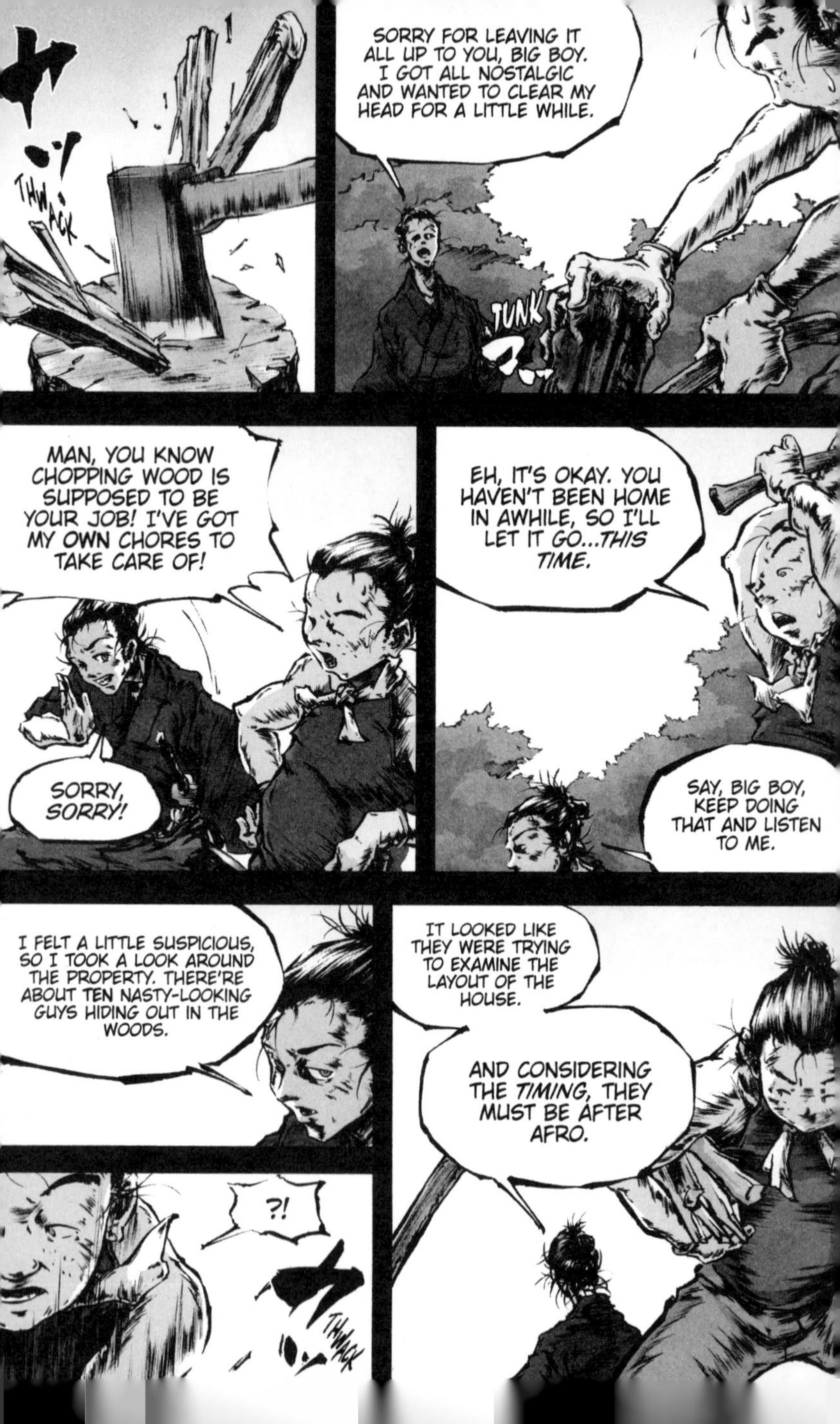
THWACK
SORRY FOR LEAVING IT ALL UP TO YOU, BIG BOY. I GOT ALL NOSTALGIC AND WANTED TO CLEAR MY HEAD FOR A LITTLE WHILE.
TUNK
MAN, YOU KNOW CHOPPING WOOD IS SUPPOSED TO BE YOUR JOB! I'VE GOT MY OWN CHORES TO TAKE CARE OF!
SORRY, SORRY!
EH, IT'S OKAY. YOU HAVEN'T BEEN HOME IN AWHILE, SO I'LL LET IT GO...THIS TIME.
SAY, BIG BOY, KEEP DOING THAT AND LISTEN TO ME.
I FELT A LITTLE SUSPICIOUS, SO I TOOK A LOOK AROUND THE PROPERTY. THERE'RE ABOUT TEN NASTY-LOOKING GUYS HIDING OUT IN THE WOODS.
?!
THWACK
IT LOOKED LIKE THEY WERE TRYING TO EXAMINE THE LAYOUT OF THE HOUSE.
AND CONSIDERING THE TIMING, THEY MUST BE AFTER AFRO.

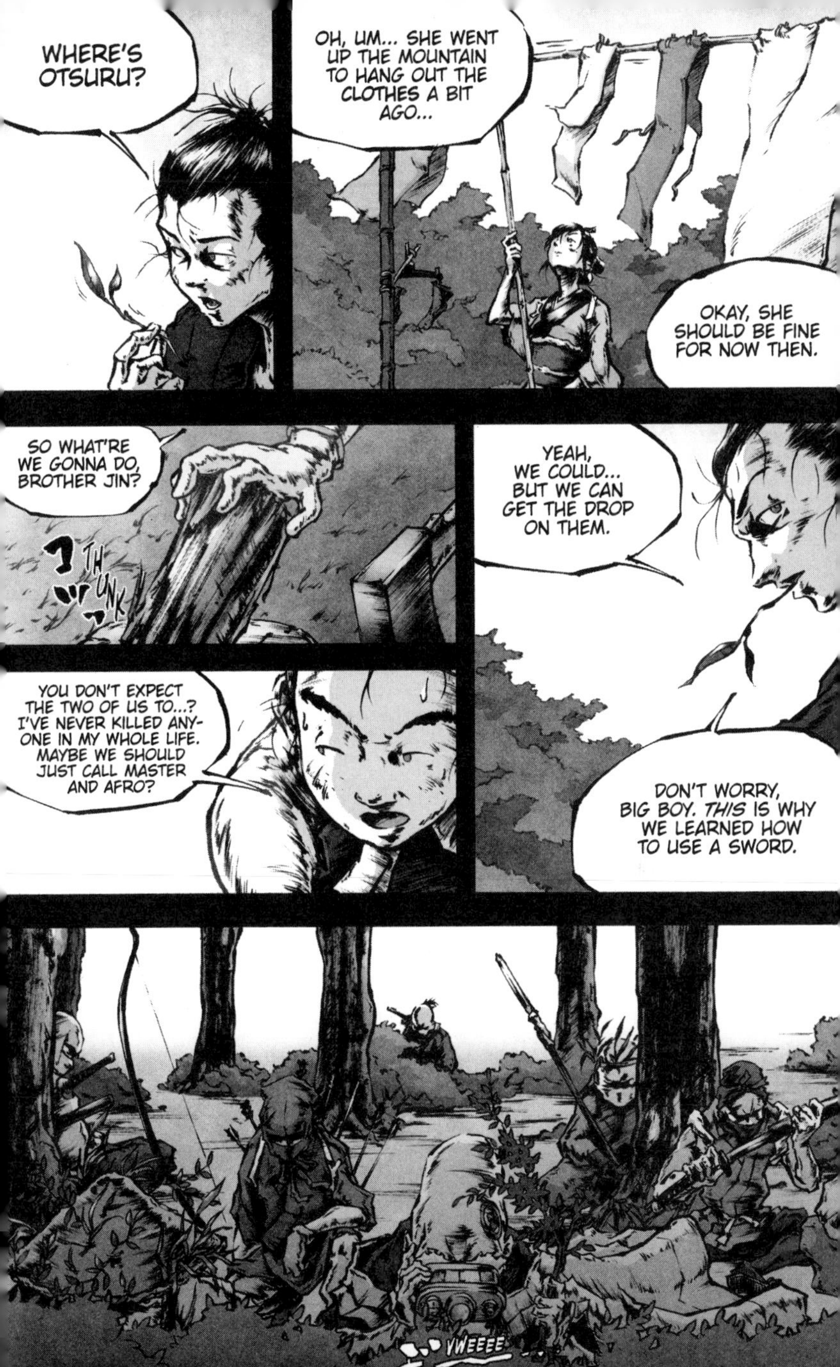

WHERE'S OTSURU?
OH, UM... SHE WENT UP THE MOUNTAIN TO HANG OUT THE CLOTHES A BIT AGO...
OKAY, SHE SHOULD BE FINE FOR NOW THEN.
SO WHAT'RE WE GONNA DO, BROTHER JIN?
THUNK
YEAH, WE COULD... BUT WE CAN GET THE DROP ON THEM.
YOU DON'T EXPECT THE TWO OF US TO...? I'VE NEVER KILLED ANY-ONE IN MY WHOLE LIFE. MAYBE WE SHOULD JUST CALL MASTER AND AFRO?
DON'T WORRY, BIG BOY. *THIS* IS WHY WE LEARNED HOW TO USE A SWORD.
VWEEEE

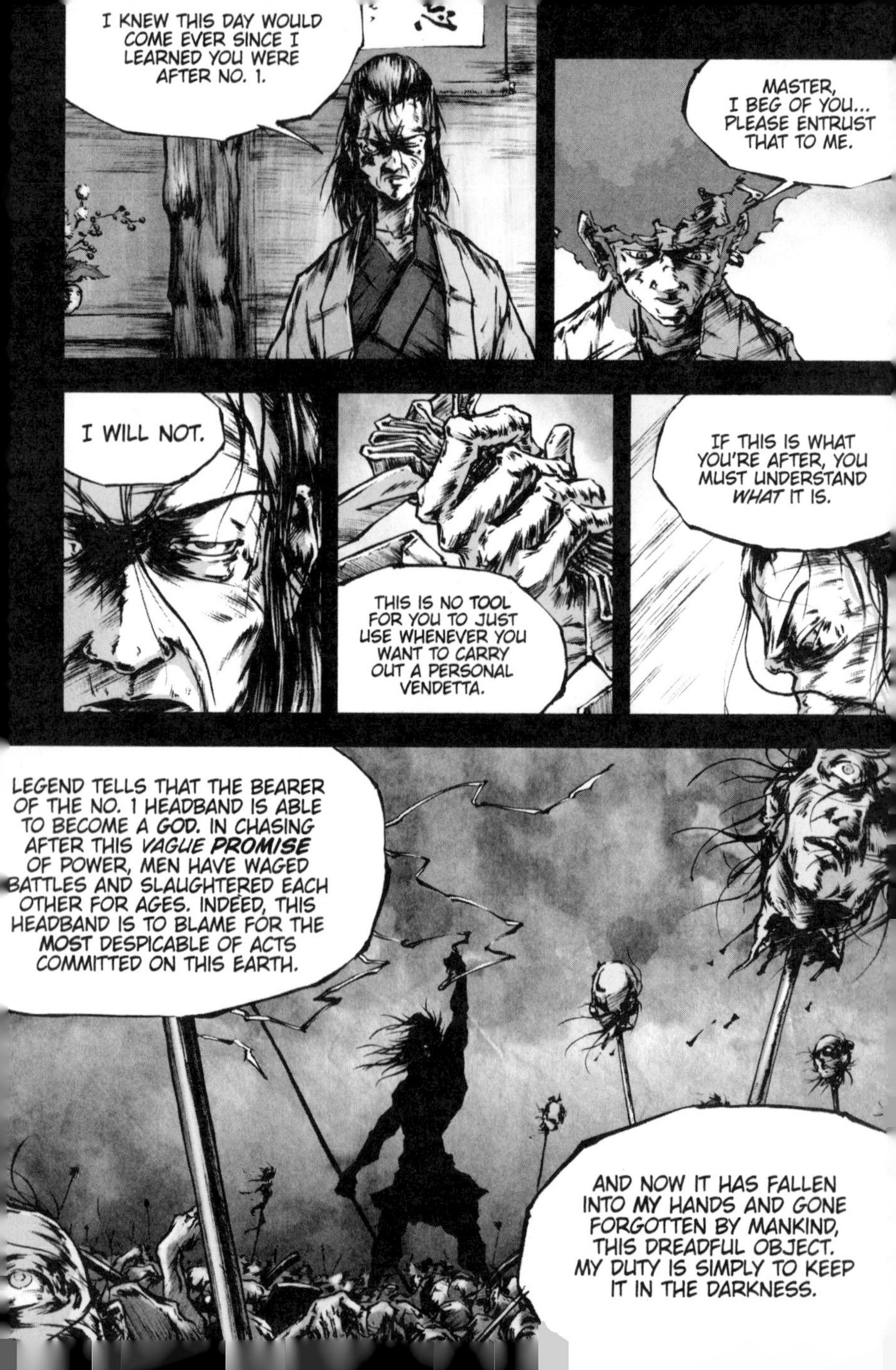
I KNEW THIS DAY WOULD COME EVER SINCE I LEARNED YOU WERE AFTER NO. 1.
MASTER, I BEG OF YOU... PLEASE ENTRUST THAT TO ME.
I WILL NOT.
THIS IS NO TOOL FOR YOU TO JUST USE WHENEVER YOU WANT TO CARRY OUT A PERSONAL VENDETTA.
IF THIS IS WHAT YOU'RE AFTER, YOU MUST UNDERSTAND *WHAT* IT IS.
LEGEND TELLS THAT THE BEARER OF THE NO. 1 HEADBAND IS ABLE TO BECOME A **GOD.** IN CHASING AFTER THIS *VAGUE* ***PROMISE*** OF POWER, MEN HAVE WAGED BATTLES AND SLAUGHTERED EACH OTHER FOR AGES. INDEED, THIS HEADBAND IS TO BLAME FOR THE **MOST DESPICABLE** OF ACTS COMMITTED ON THIS EARTH.
AND NOW IT HAS FALLEN INTO **MY** HANDS AND GONE FORGOTTEN BY MANKIND, THIS DREADFUL OBJECT. MY DUTY IS SIMPLY TO KEEP IT IN THE DARKNESS.

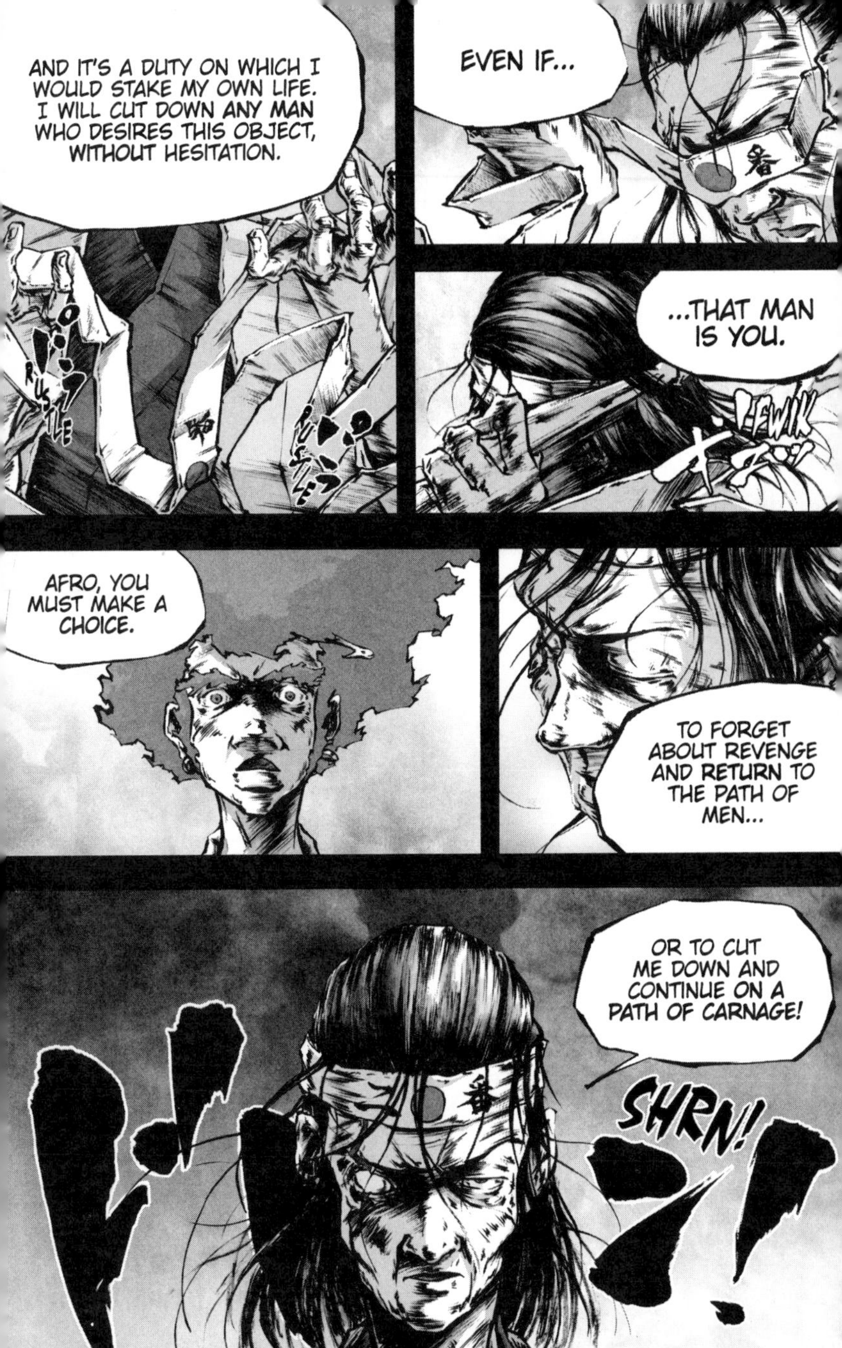
AND IT'S A DUTY ON WHICH I WOULD STAKE MY OWN LIFE. I WILL CUT DOWN ANY MAN WHO DESIRES THIS OBJECT, WITHOUT HESITATION.
RUSTLE
EVEN IF...
...THAT MAN IS YOU.
FWIK
AFRO, YOU MUST MAKE A CHOICE.
TO FORGET ABOUT REVENGE AND RETURN TO THE PATH OF MEN...
OR TO CUT ME DOWN AND CONTINUE ON A PATH OF CARNAGE!
SHRN!

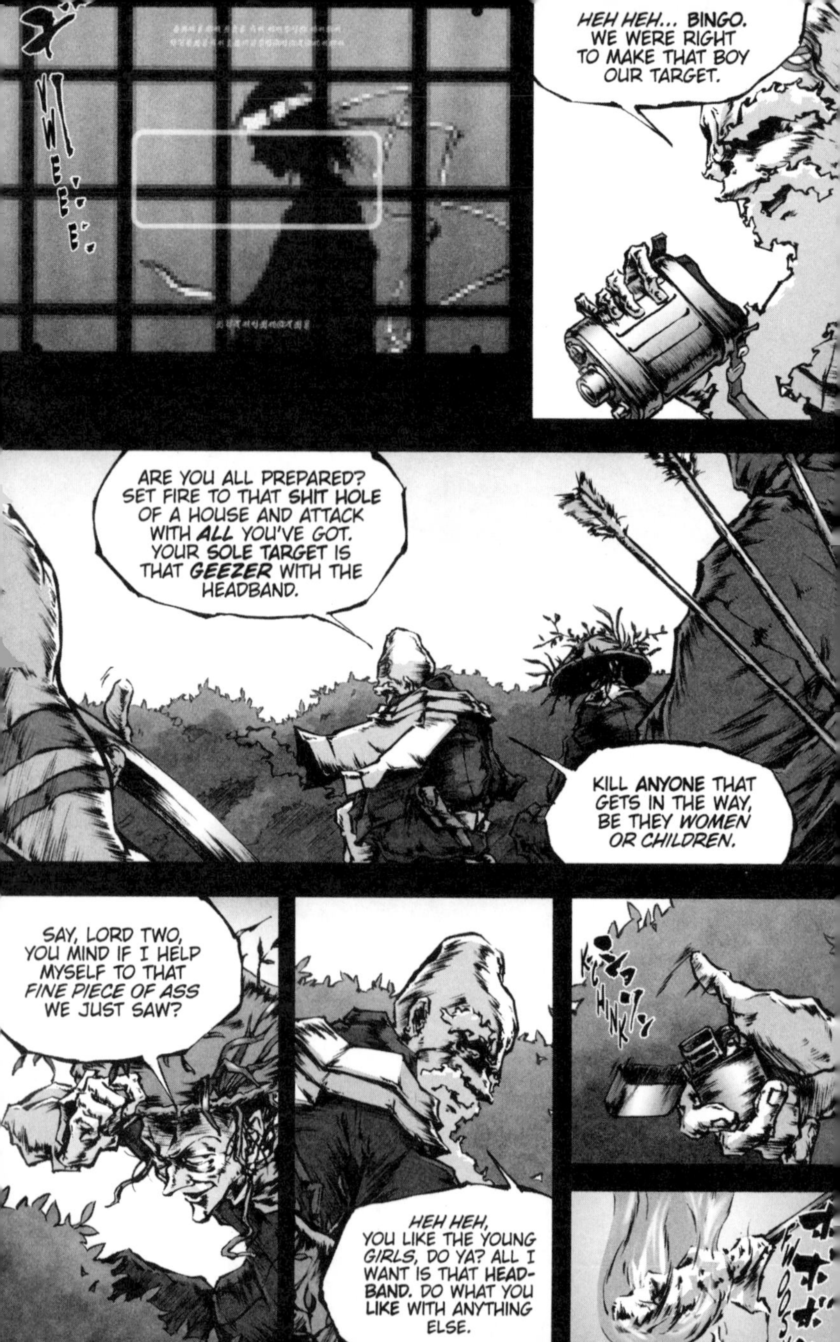
VWEEE...
HEH HEH... BINGO. WE WERE RIGHT TO MAKE THAT BOY OUR TARGET.
ARE YOU ALL PREPARED? SET FIRE TO THAT SHIT HOLE OF A HOUSE AND ATTACK WITH ALL YOU'VE GOT. YOUR SOLE TARGET IS THAT GEEZER WITH THE HEADBAND.
KILL ANYONE THAT GETS IN THE WAY, BE THEY WOMEN OR CHILDREN.
SAY, LORD TWO, YOU MIND IF I HELP MYSELF TO THAT FINE PIECE OF ASS WE JUST SAW?
HEH HEH, YOU LIKE THE YOUNG GIRLS, DO YA? ALL I WANT IS THAT HEAD-BAND. DO WHAT YOU LIKE WITH ANYTHING ELSE.
KCHINK
FWOOSH

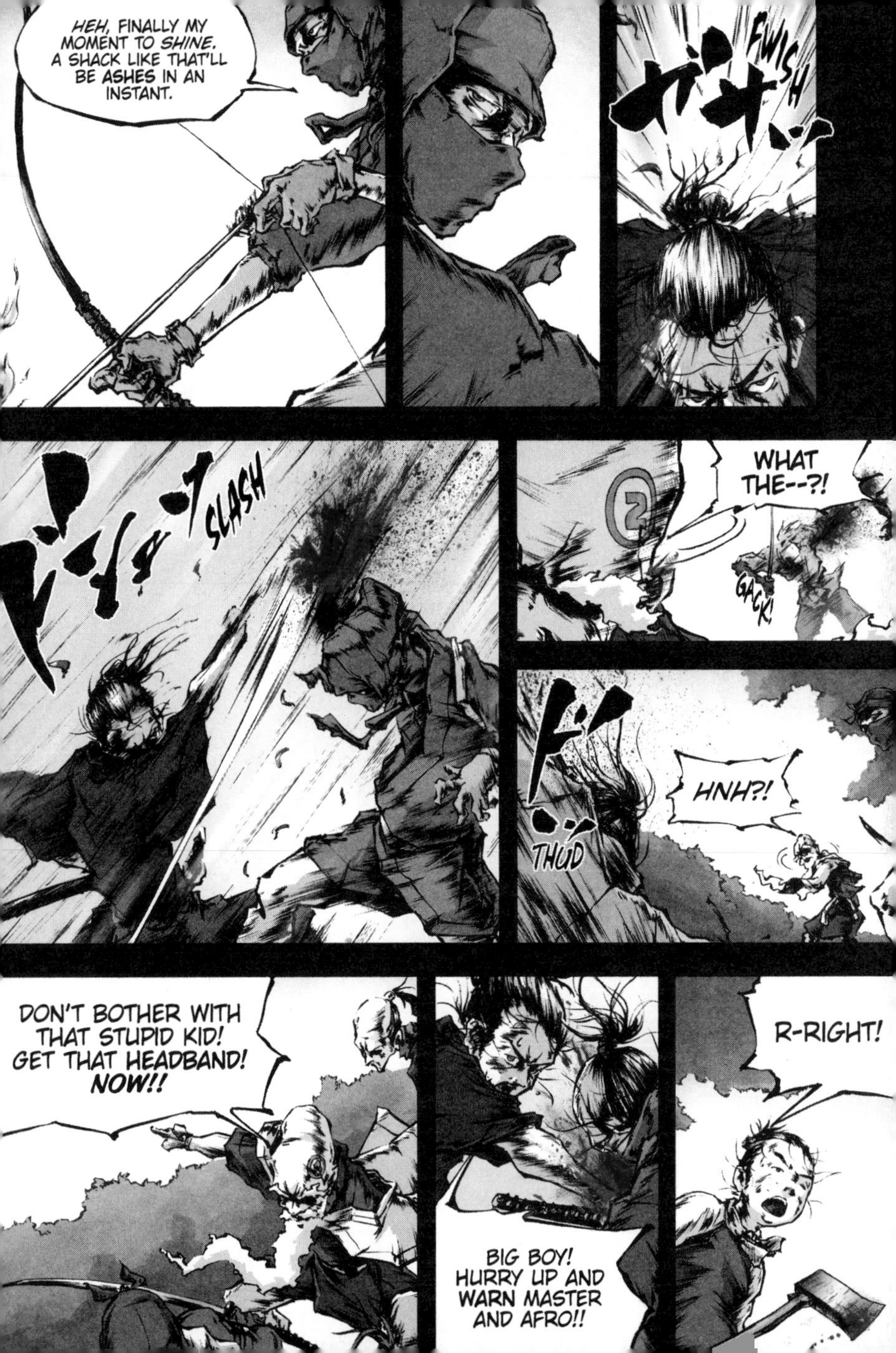
HEH, FINALLY MY MOMENT TO SHINE. A SHACK LIKE THAT'LL BE ASHES IN AN INSTANT.
FWISH
SLASH
WHAT THE--?!
GACK!
HNH?!
THUD
DON'T BOTHER WITH THAT STUPID KID! GET THAT HEADBAND! NOW!!
BIG BOY! HURRY UP AND WARN MASTER AND AFRO!!
R-RIGHT!

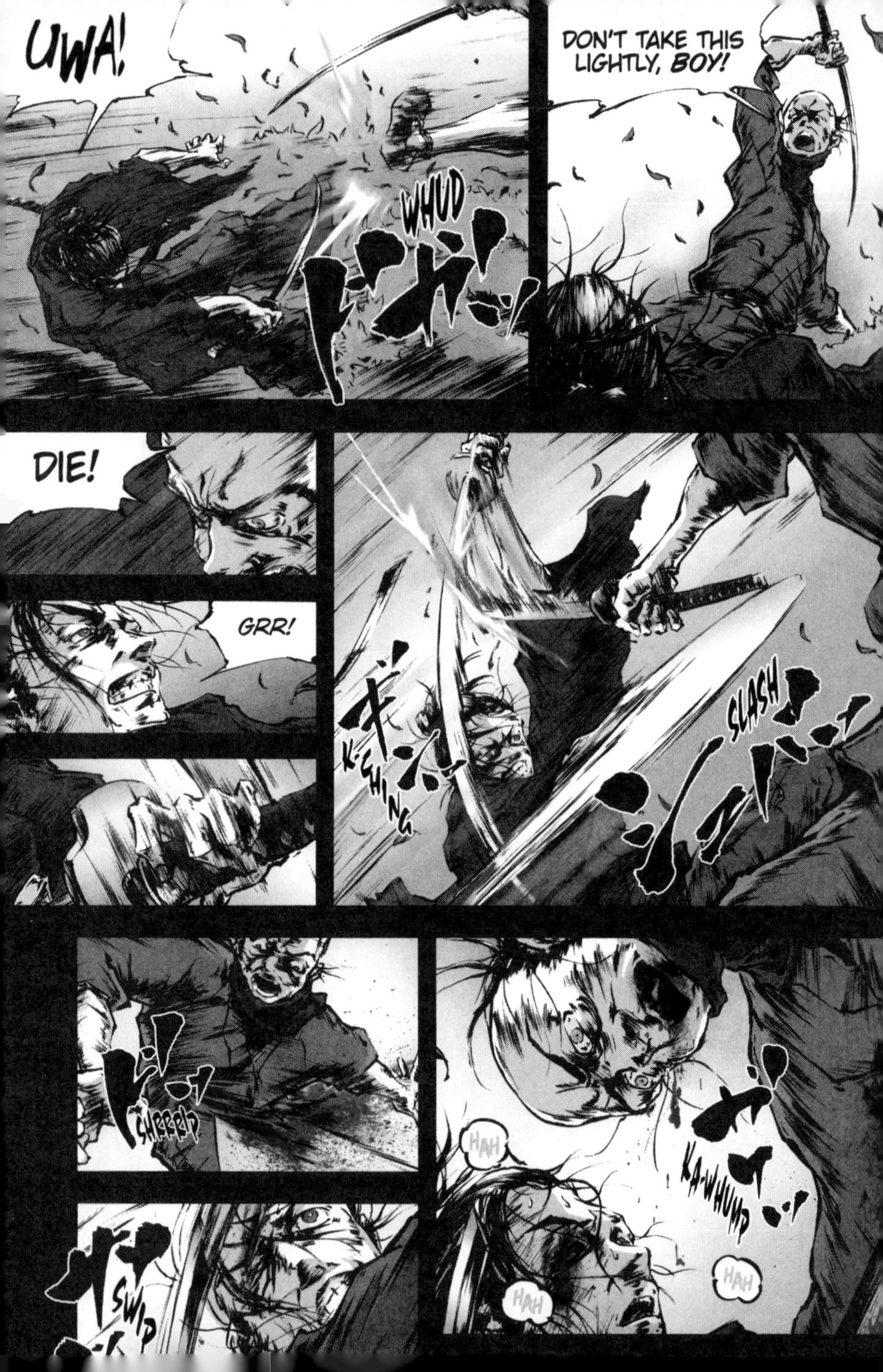
UWA!
WHUD
DON'T TAKE THIS LIGHTLY, BOY!
DIE!
GRR!
K-CHING
SLASH
SHRRRIP
SWIP
HAH
KA-WHUMP
HAH
HAH

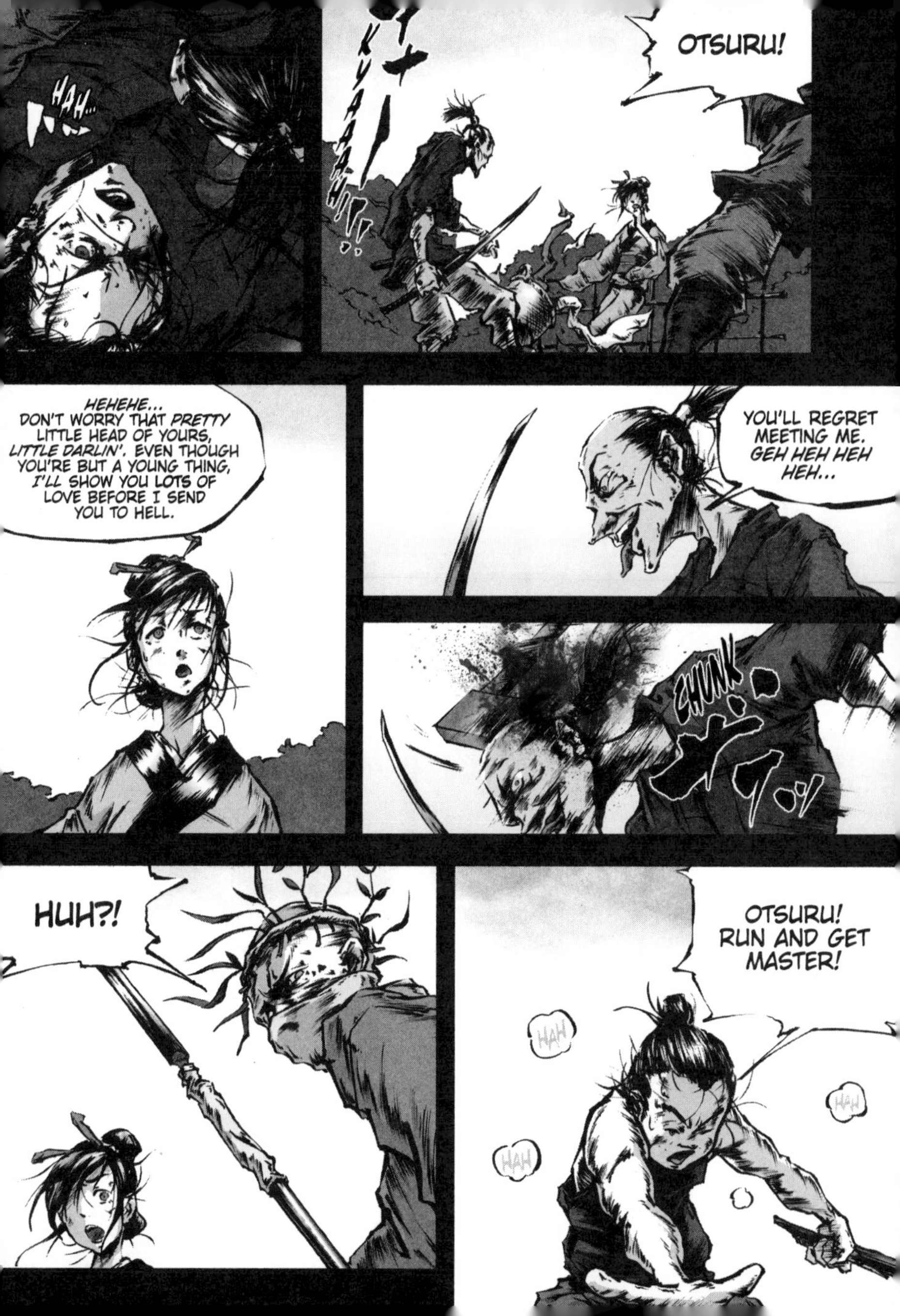
HAH...
KYAAAAAH!!
OTSURU!
HEHEHE... DON'T WORRY THAT PRETTY LITTLE HEAD OF YOURS, LITTLE DARLIN'. EVEN THOUGH YOU'RE BUT A YOUNG THING, I'LL SHOW YOU LOTS OF LOVE BEFORE I SEND YOU TO HELL.
YOU'LL REGRET MEETING ME. GEH HEH HEH HEH...
CHUNK
HUH?!
OTSURU! RUN AND GET MASTER!
HAH
HAH
HAH

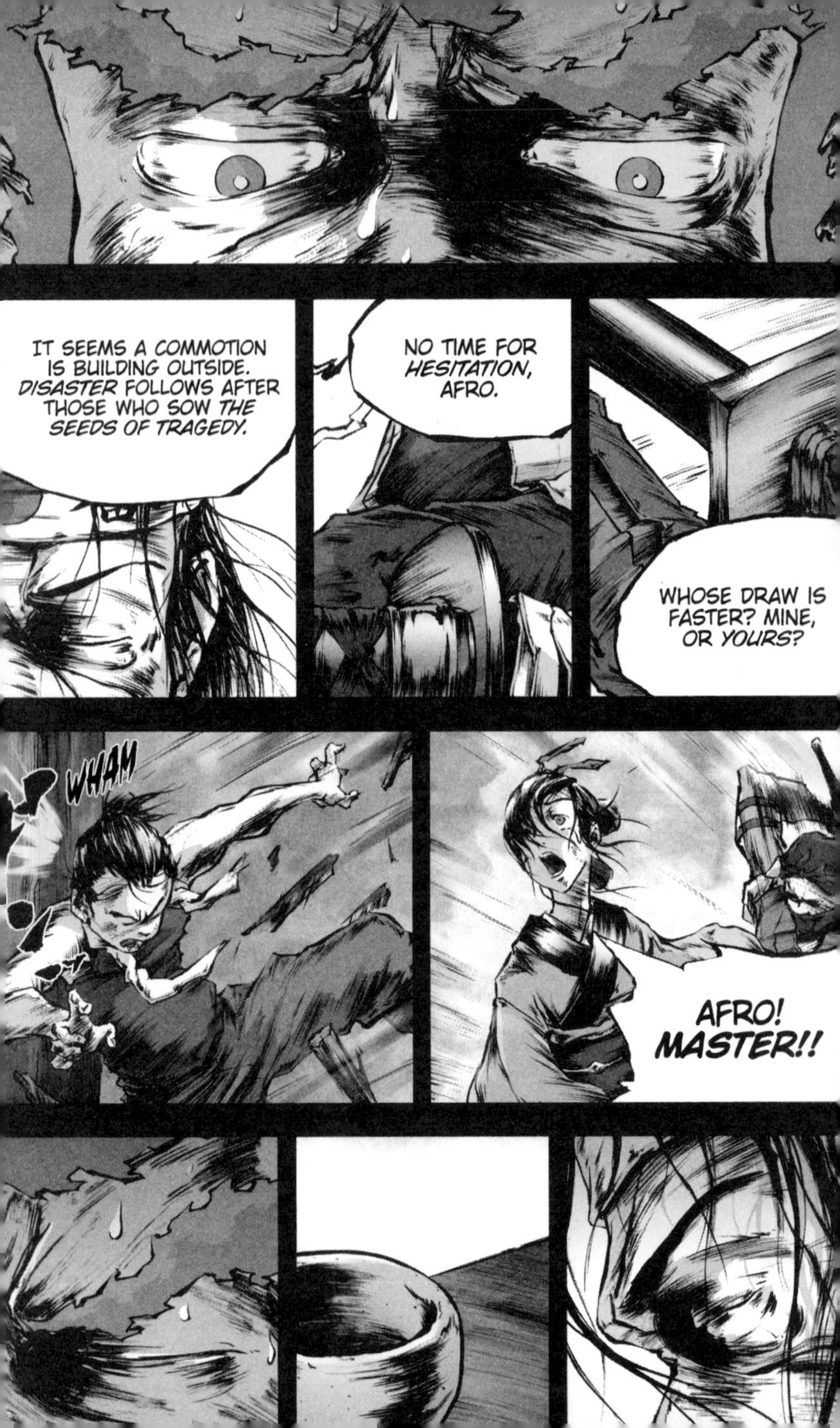
IT SEEMS A COMMOTION IS BUILDING OUTSIDE. *DISASTER* FOLLOWS AFTER THOSE WHO SOW *THE SEEDS OF TRAGEDY.*
NO TIME FOR *HESITATION,* AFRO.
WHOSE DRAW IS FASTER? MINE, OR *YOURS?*
WHAM
AFRO! **MASTER!!**

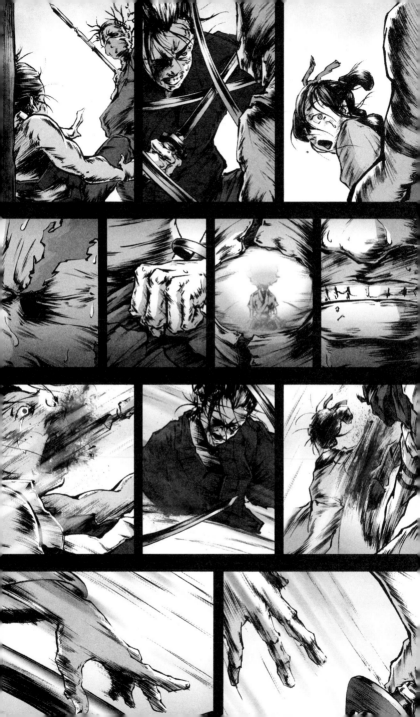

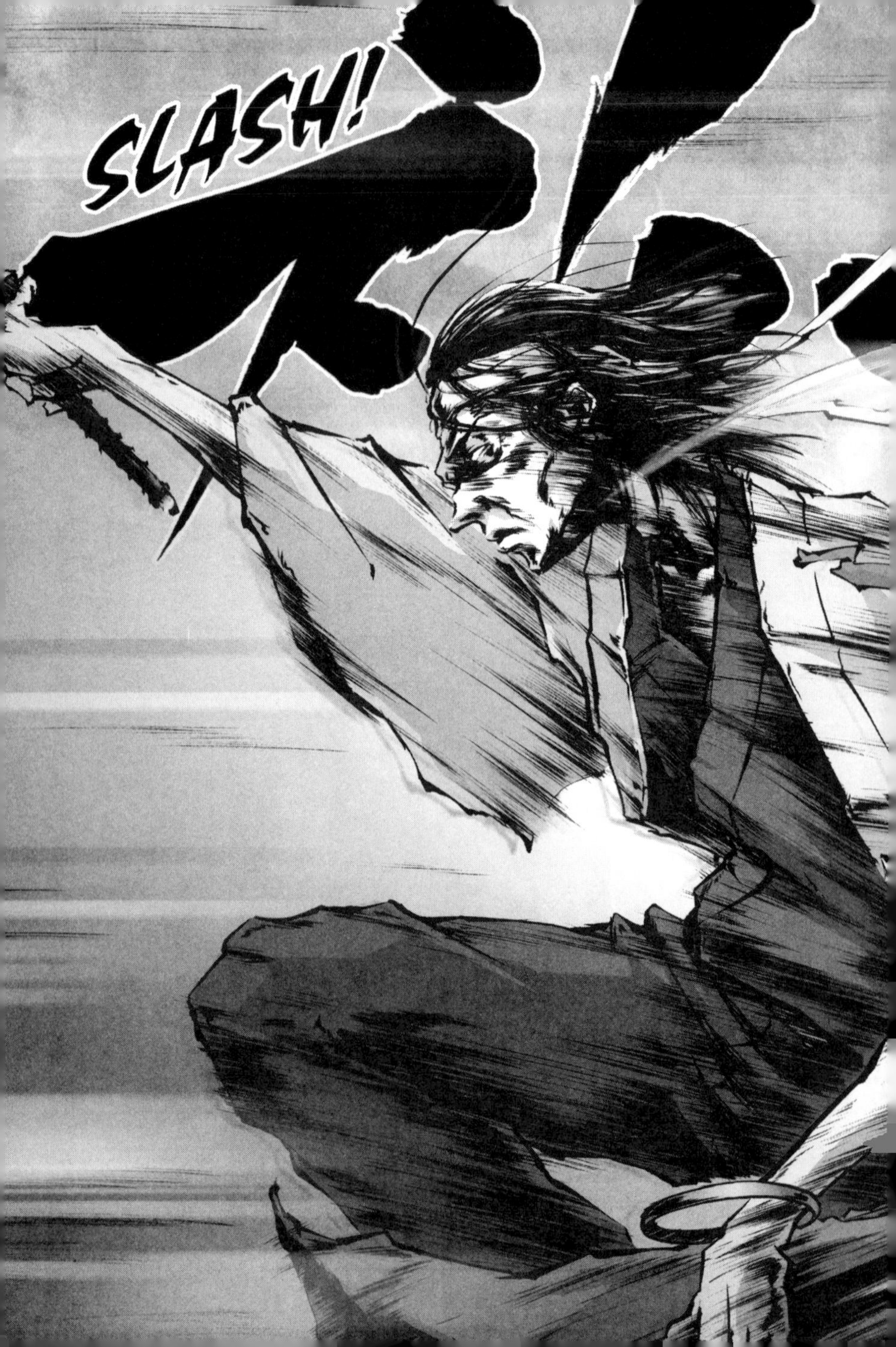
SLASH!

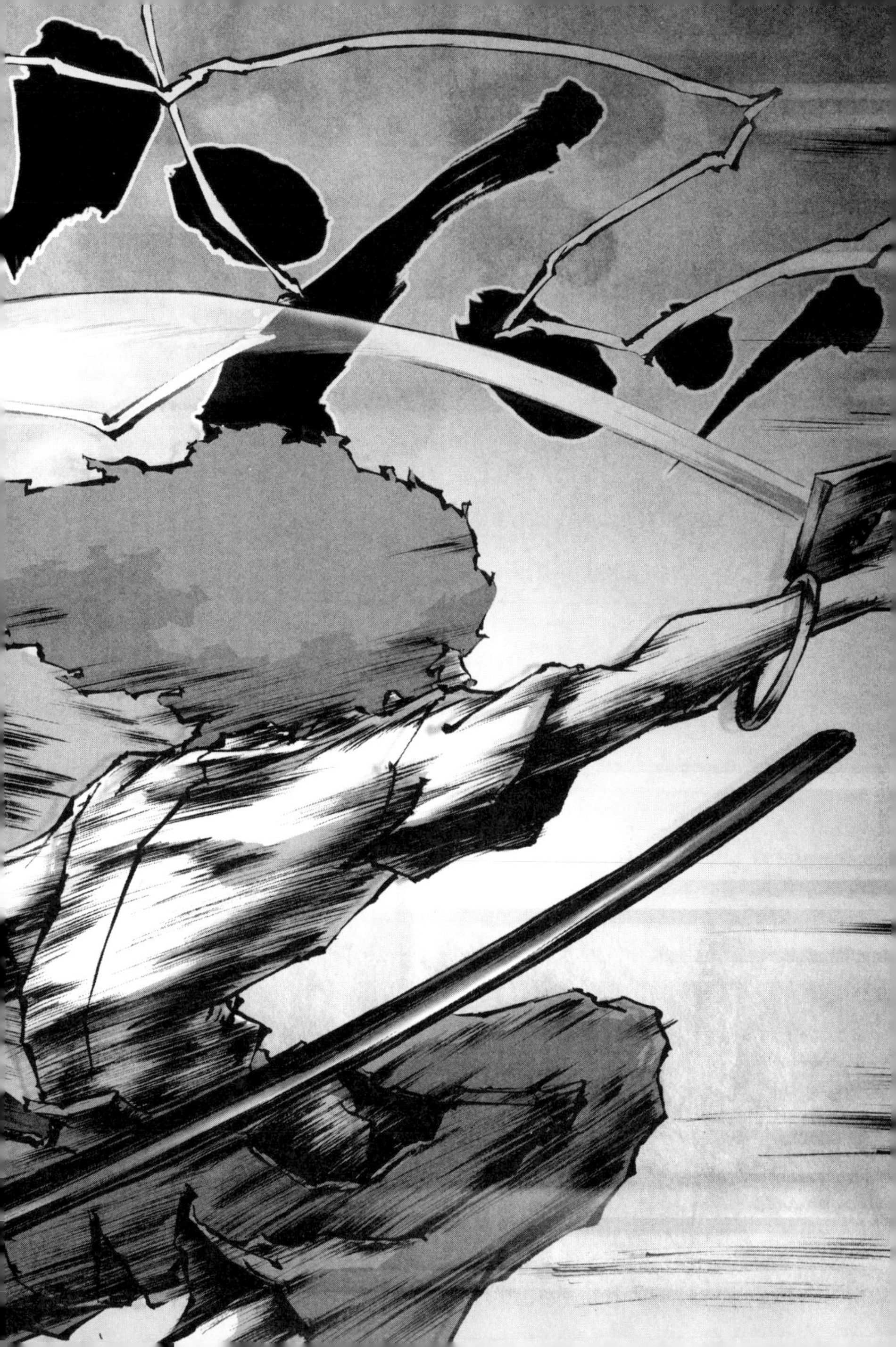

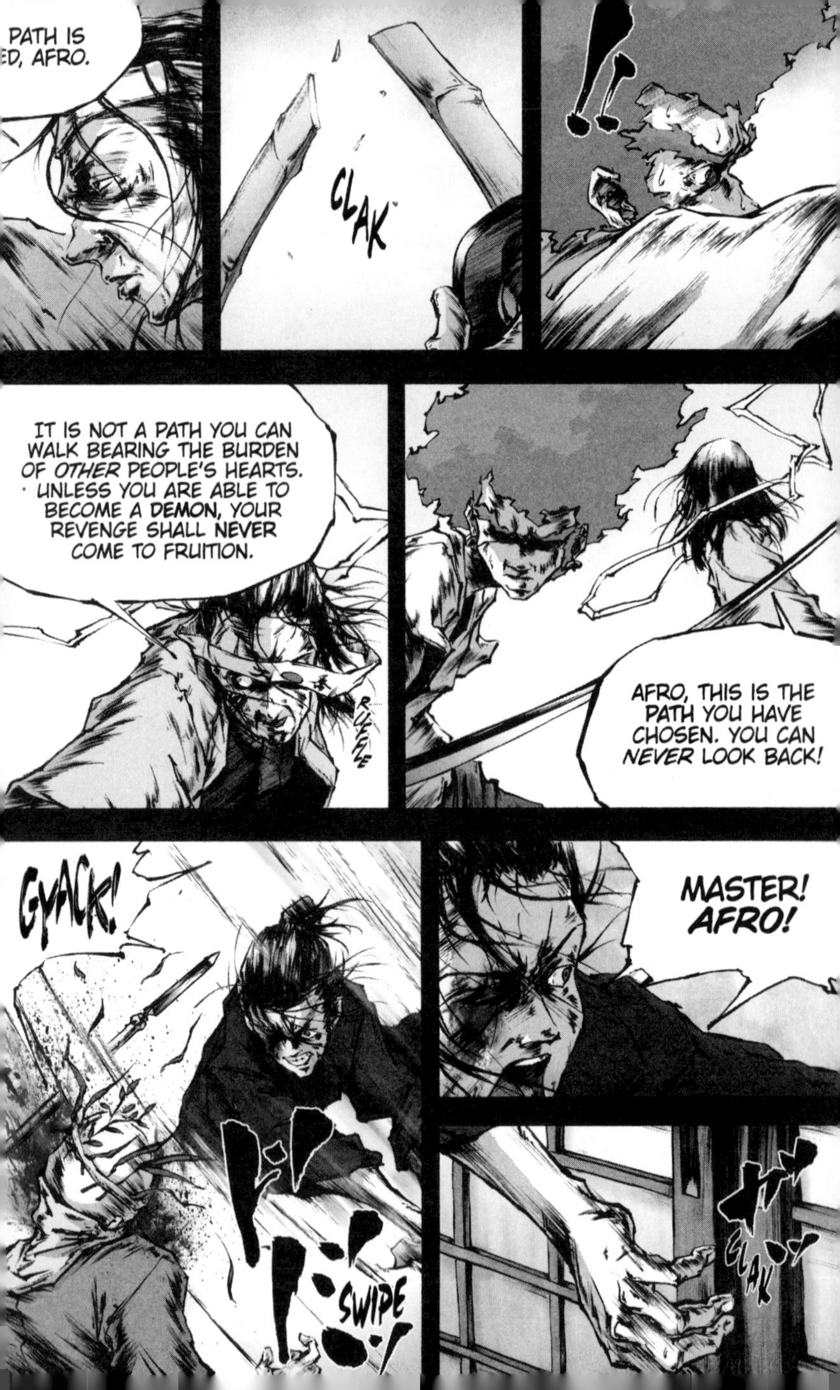
PATH IS
ED, AFRO.
CLAK
IT IS NOT A PATH YOU CAN WALK BEARING THE BURDEN OF *OTHER* PEOPLE'S HEARTS. UNLESS YOU ARE ABLE TO BECOME A **DEMON**, YOUR REVENGE SHALL **NEVER** COME TO FRUITION.
AFRO, THIS IS THE PATH YOU HAVE CHOSEN. YOU CAN *NEVER* LOOK BACK!
GYACK!
SWIPE
MASTER! AFRO!
CLAK

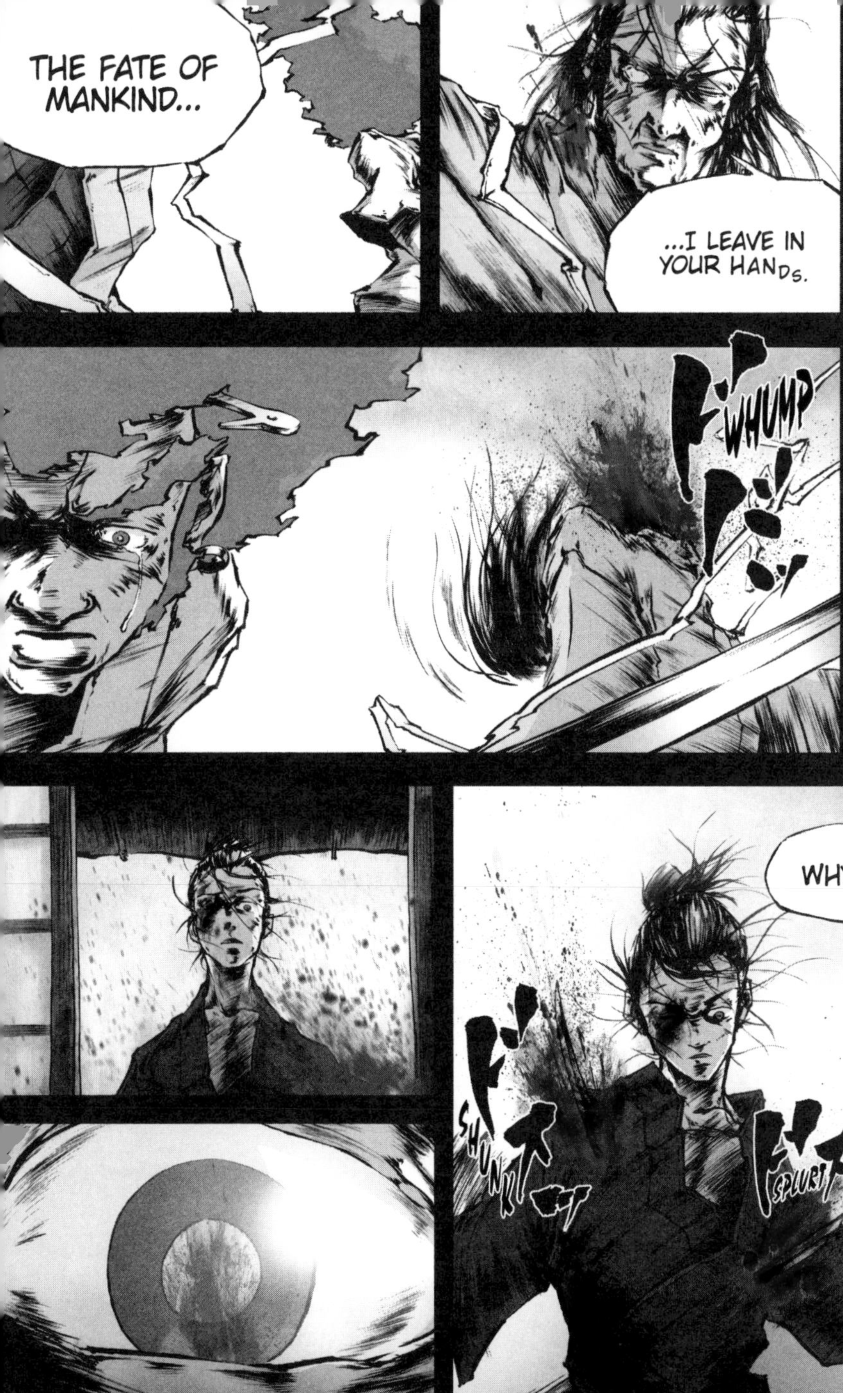
THE FATE OF MANKIND...
...I LEAVE IN YOUR HANDs.
WHUMP
WHY...?
SHUNK
SPLURT

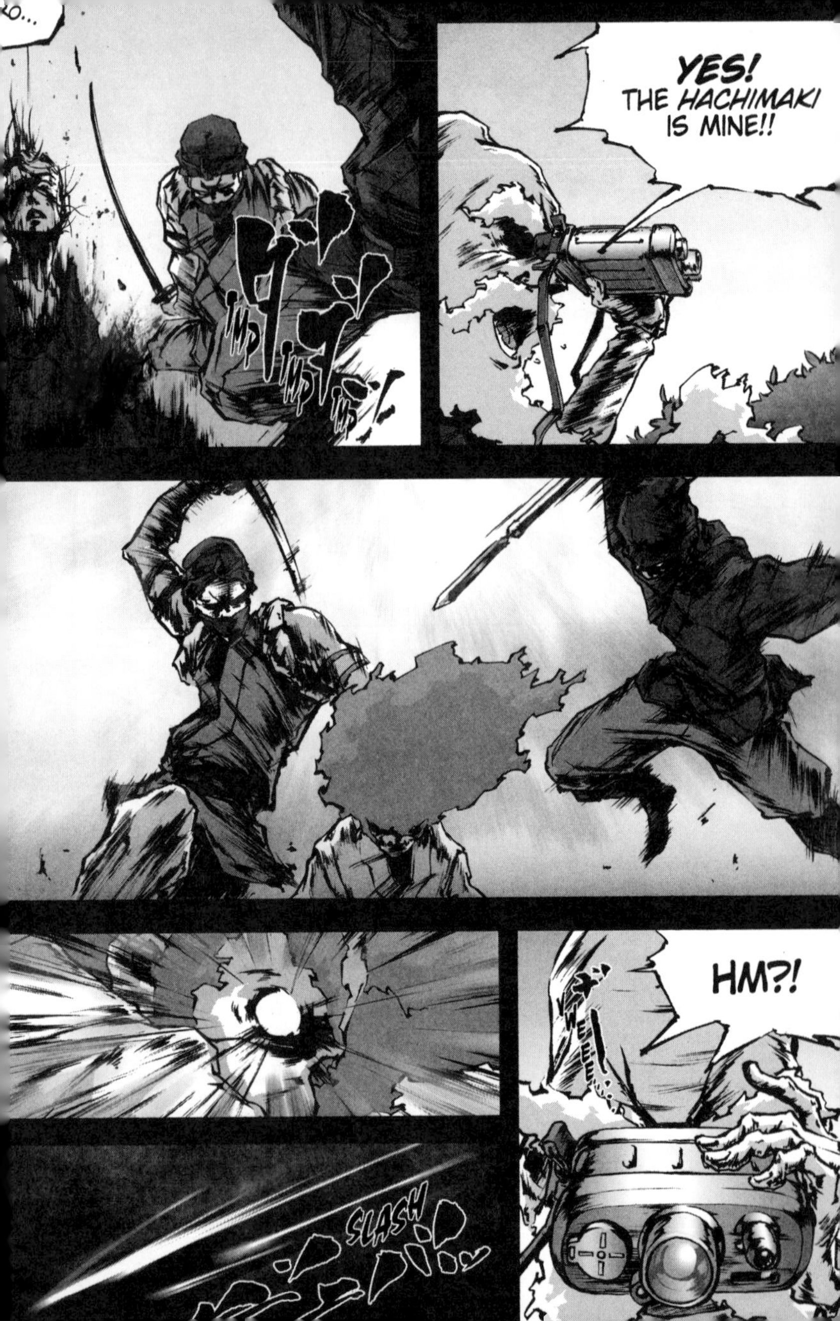
LO...
TMP TMP TMP TMP
YES! THE HACHIMAKI IS MINE!!
SLASH
HM?!
VWEEEE...

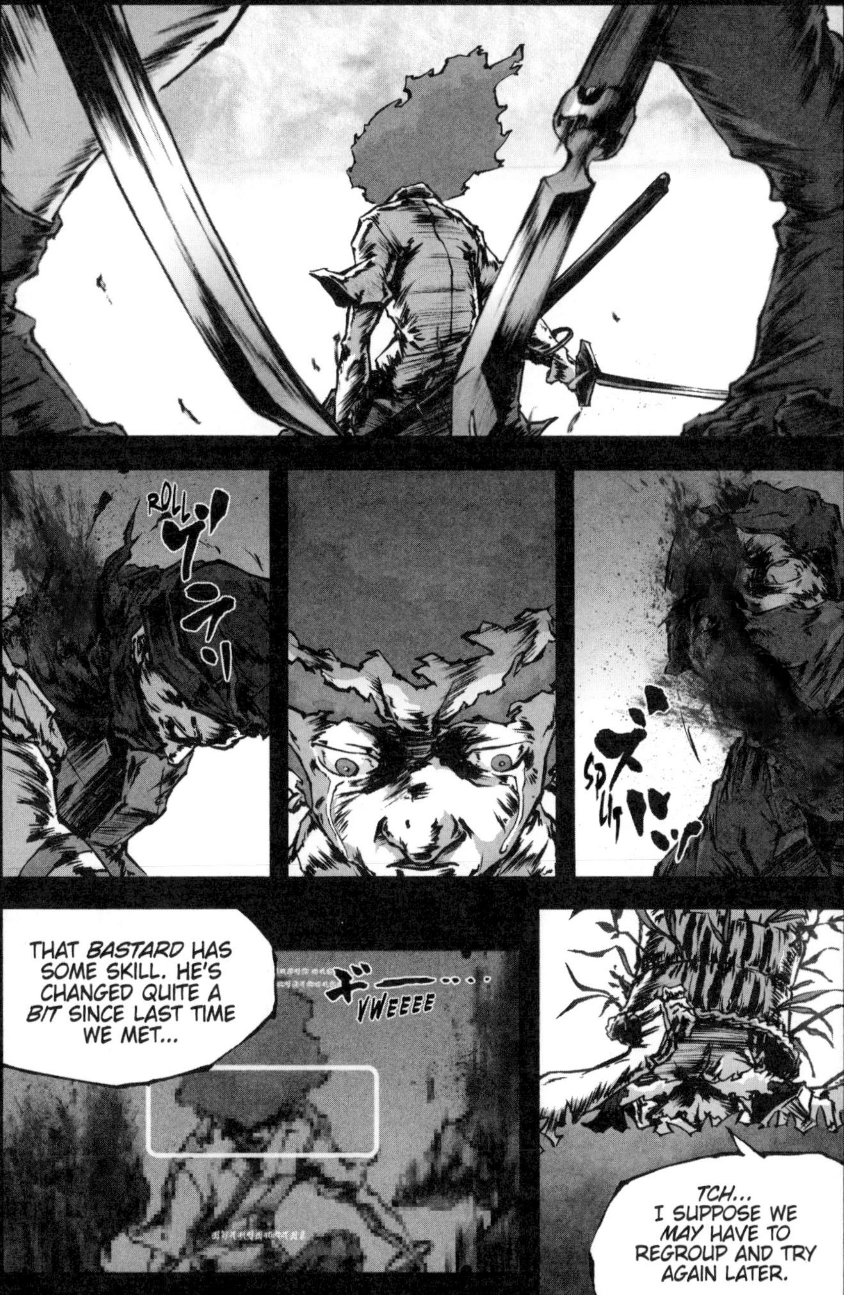
ROLL
SPLIT
THAT BASTARD HAS SOME SKILL. HE'S CHANGED QUITE A BIT SINCE LAST TIME WE MET...
VWEEEE
TCH... I SUPPOSE WE MAY HAVE TO REGROUP AND TRY AGAIN LATER.

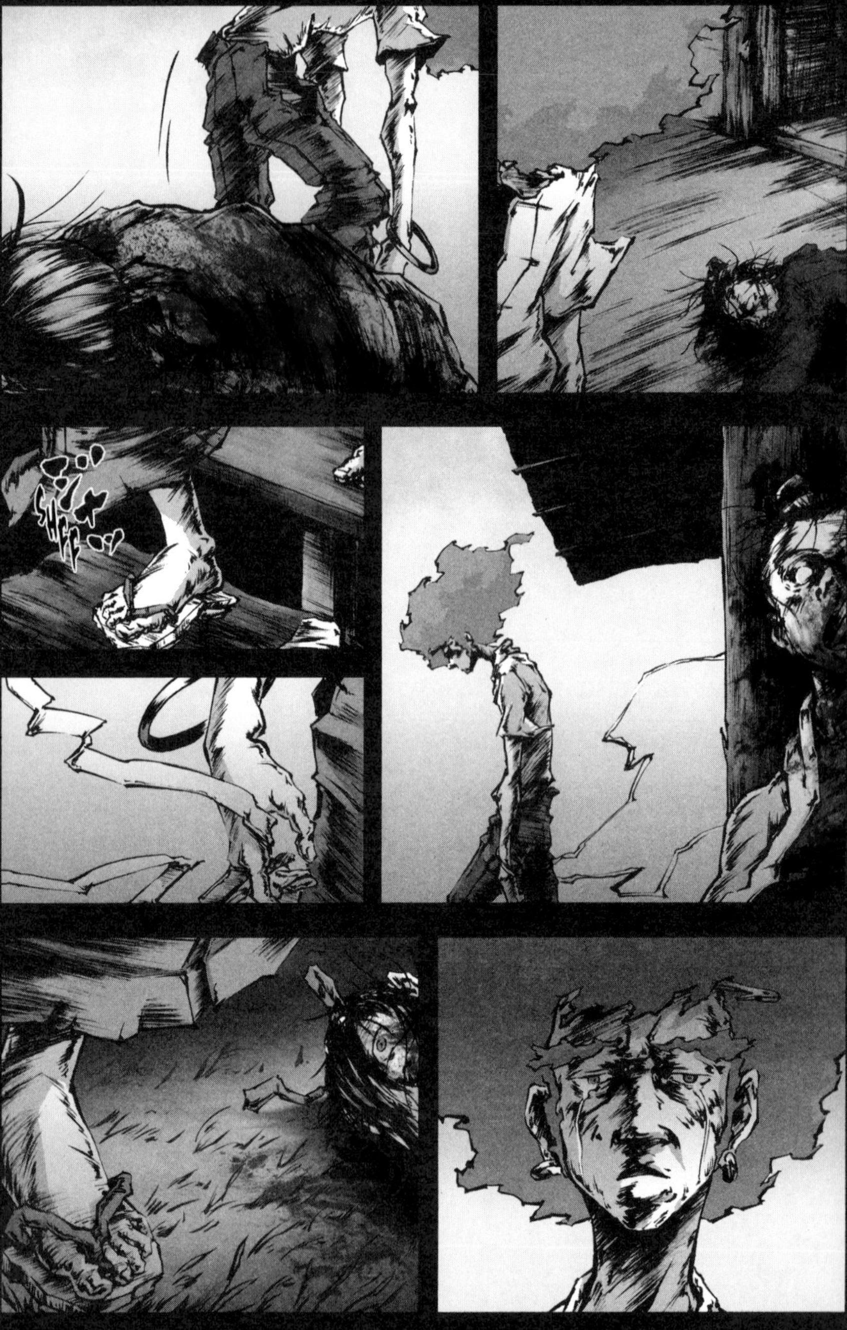
SHFF

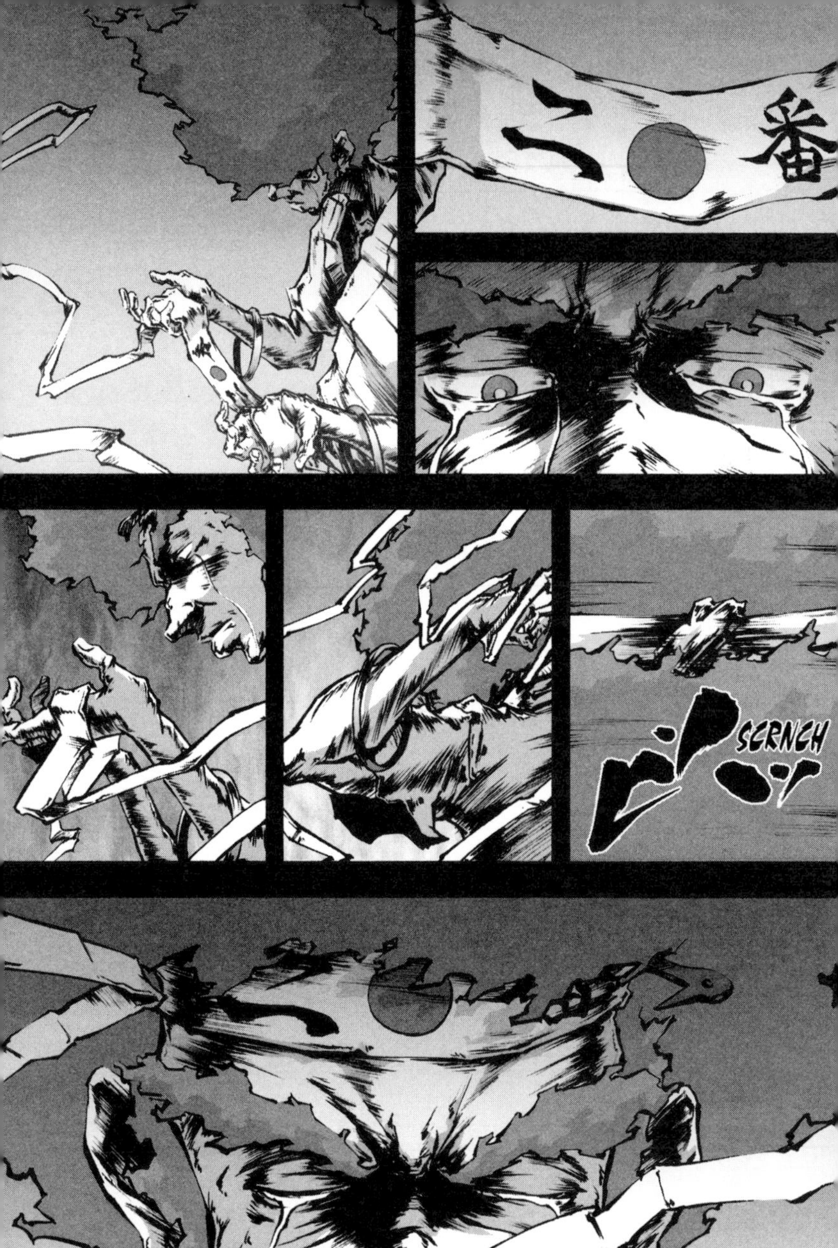
SCRNCH

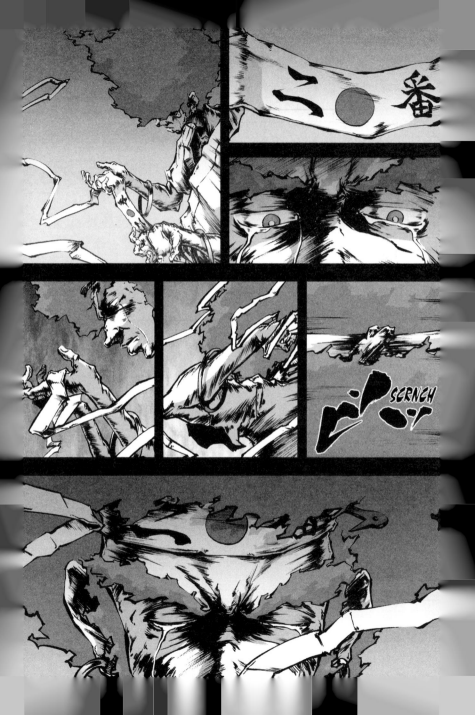

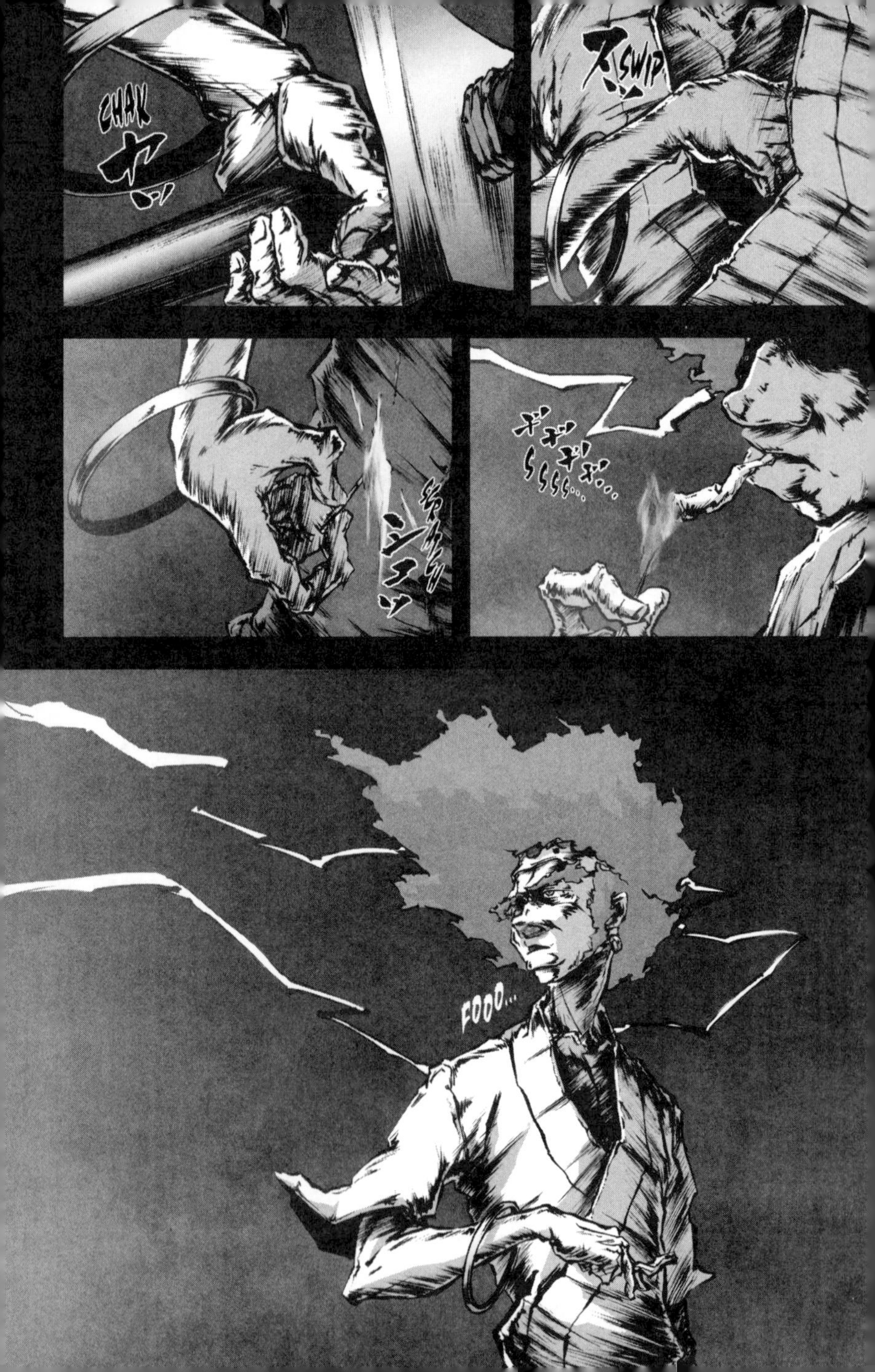
CHAK
ヤッ
スッ
SWIP
シュッ
ジジジジ...
SSSS...
FOOO...

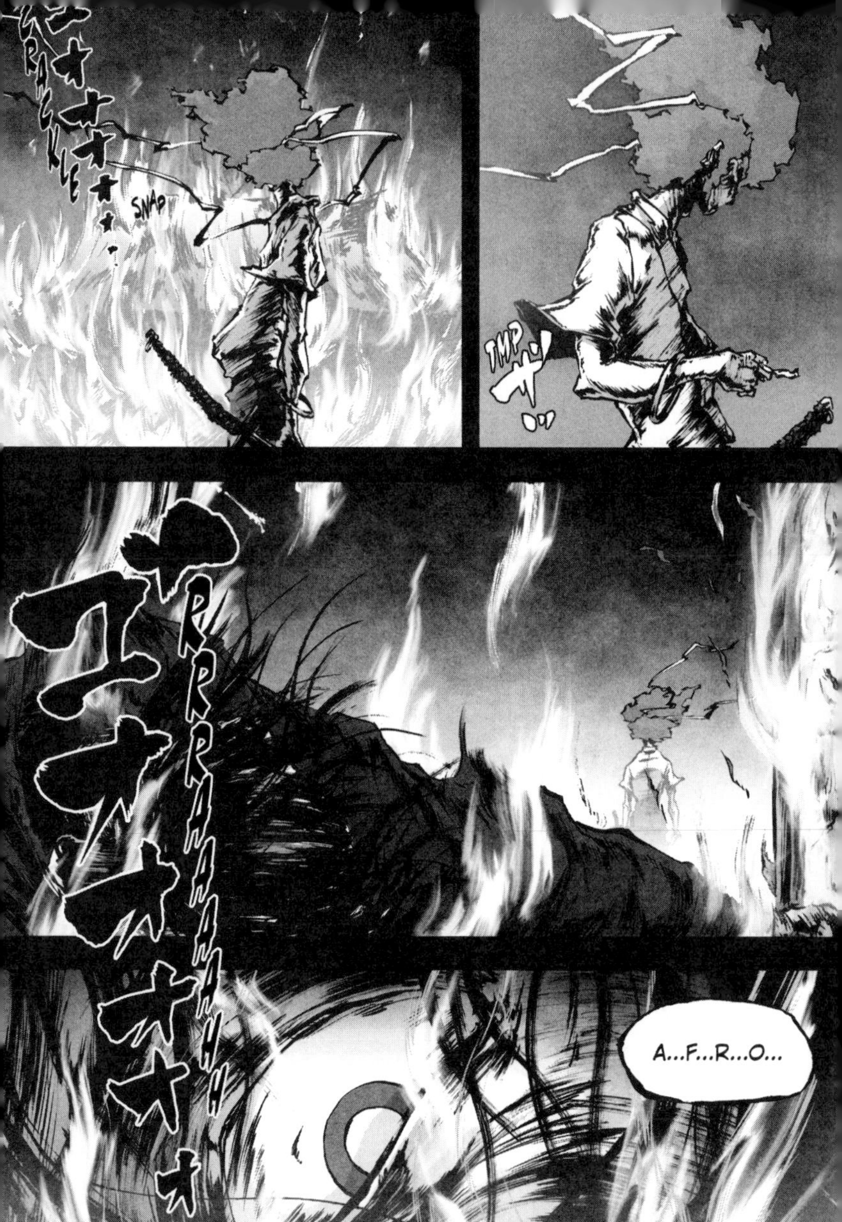
RACKLE
SNAP
TMP
RRRAAAAHH
A...F...R...O...

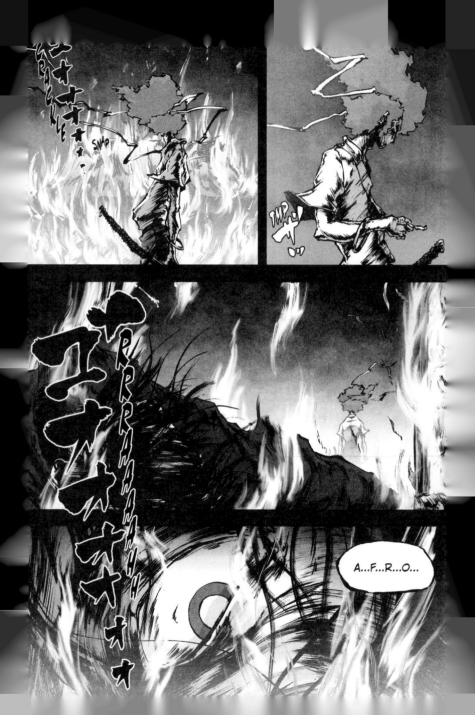

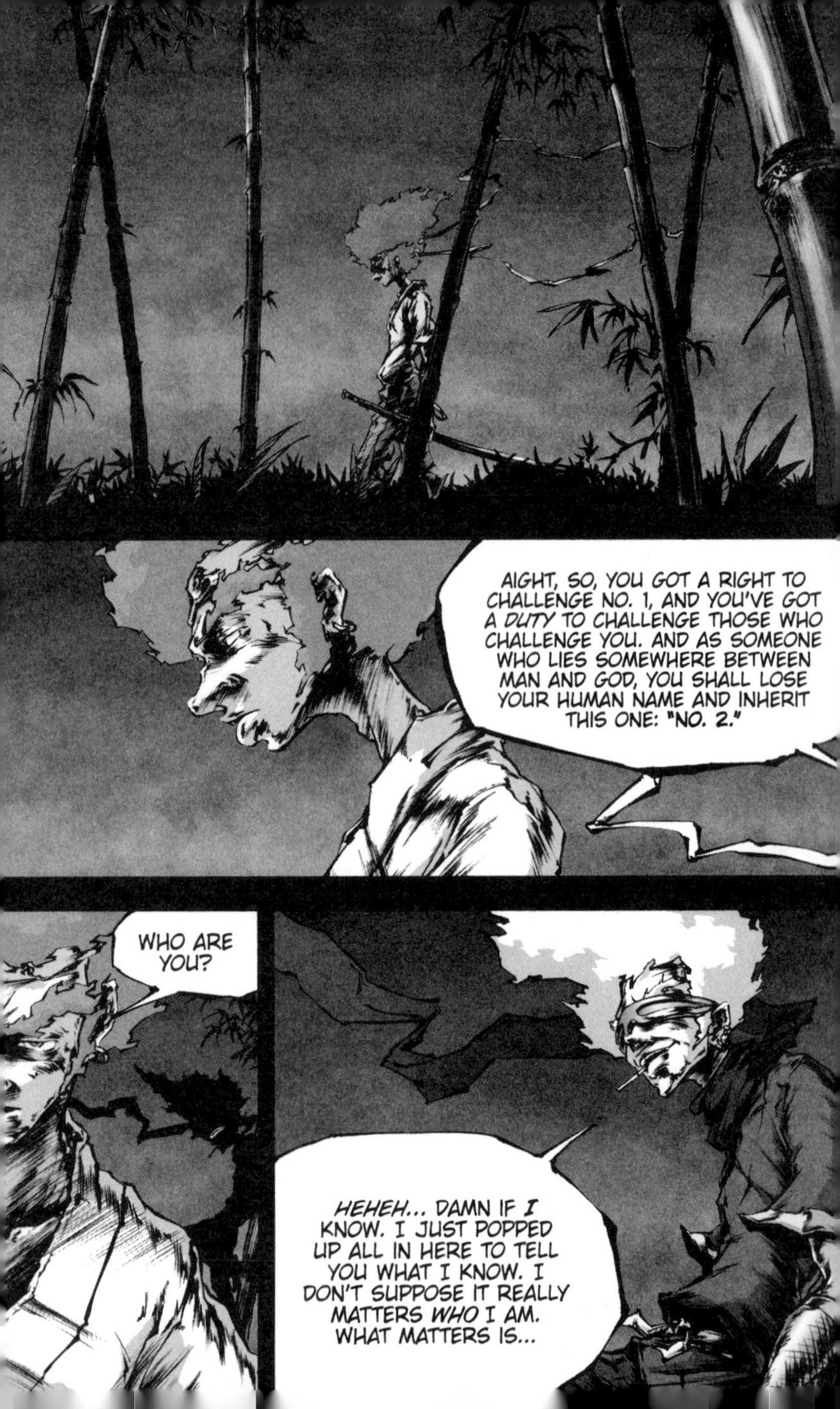
AIGHT, SO, YOU GOT A RIGHT TO CHALLENGE NO. 1, AND YOU'VE GOT A *DUTY* TO CHALLENGE THOSE WHO CHALLENGE YOU. AND AS SOMEONE WHO LIES SOMEWHERE BETWEEN MAN AND GOD, YOU SHALL LOSE YOUR HUMAN NAME AND INHERIT THIS ONE: "NO. 2."
WHO ARE YOU?
HEHEH... DAMN IF *I* KNOW. I JUST POPPED UP ALL IN HERE TO TELL YOU WHAT I KNOW. I DON'T SUPPOSE IT REALLY MATTERS *WHO* I AM. WHAT MATTERS IS...

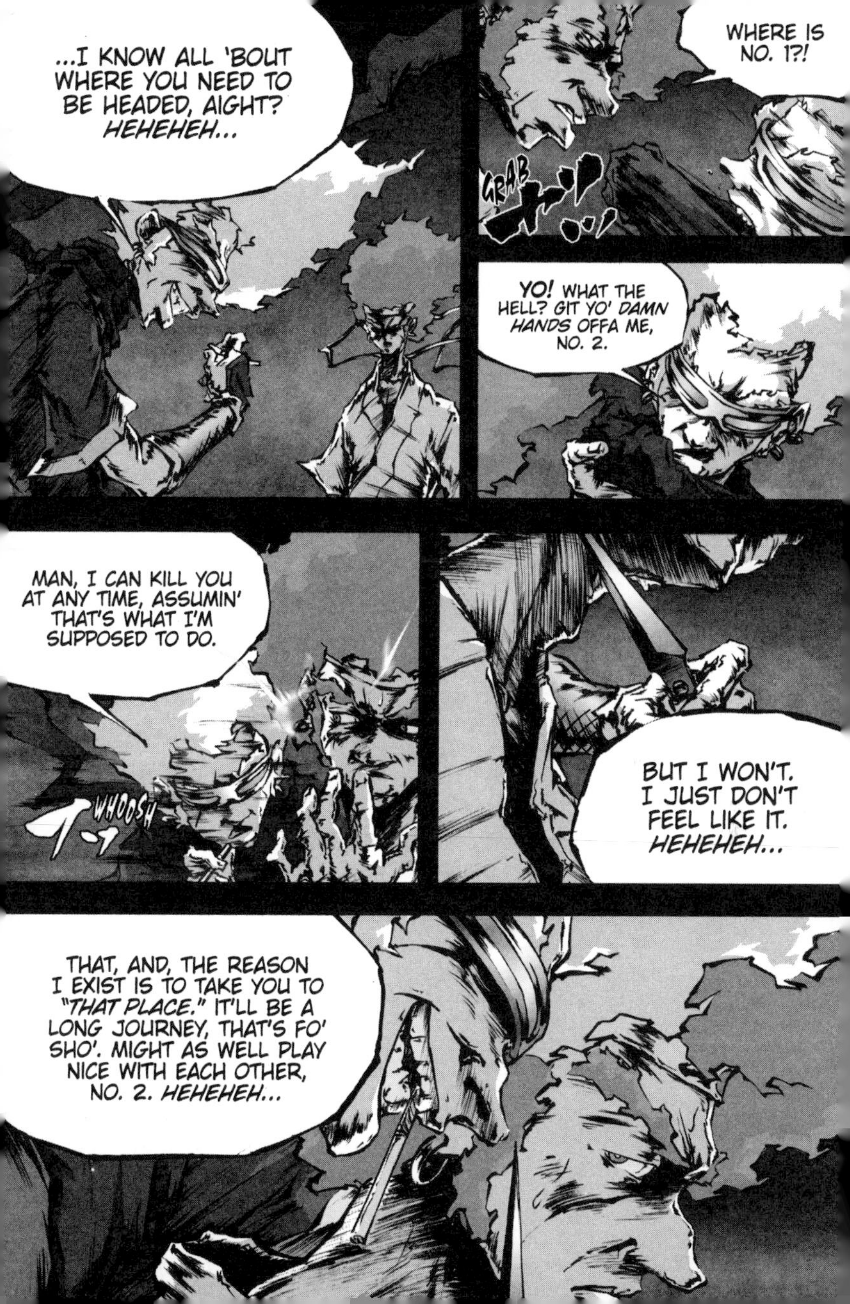
...I KNOW ALL 'BOUT WHERE YOU NEED TO BE HEADED, AIGHT? *HEHEHEH...*
WHERE IS NO. 1?!
GRAB
YO! WHAT THE HELL? GIT YO' *DAMN HANDS* OFFA ME, NO. 2.
MAN, I CAN KILL YOU AT ANY TIME, ASSUMIN' THAT'S WHAT I'M SUPPOSED TO DO.
WHOOSH
BUT I WON'T. I JUST DON'T FEEL LIKE IT. *HEHEHEH...*
THAT, AND, THE REASON I EXIST IS TO TAKE YOU TO "*THAT PLACE.*" IT'LL BE A LONG JOURNEY, THAT'S FO' SHO'. MIGHT AS WELL PLAY NICE WITH EACH OTHER, NO. 2. *HEHEHEH...*

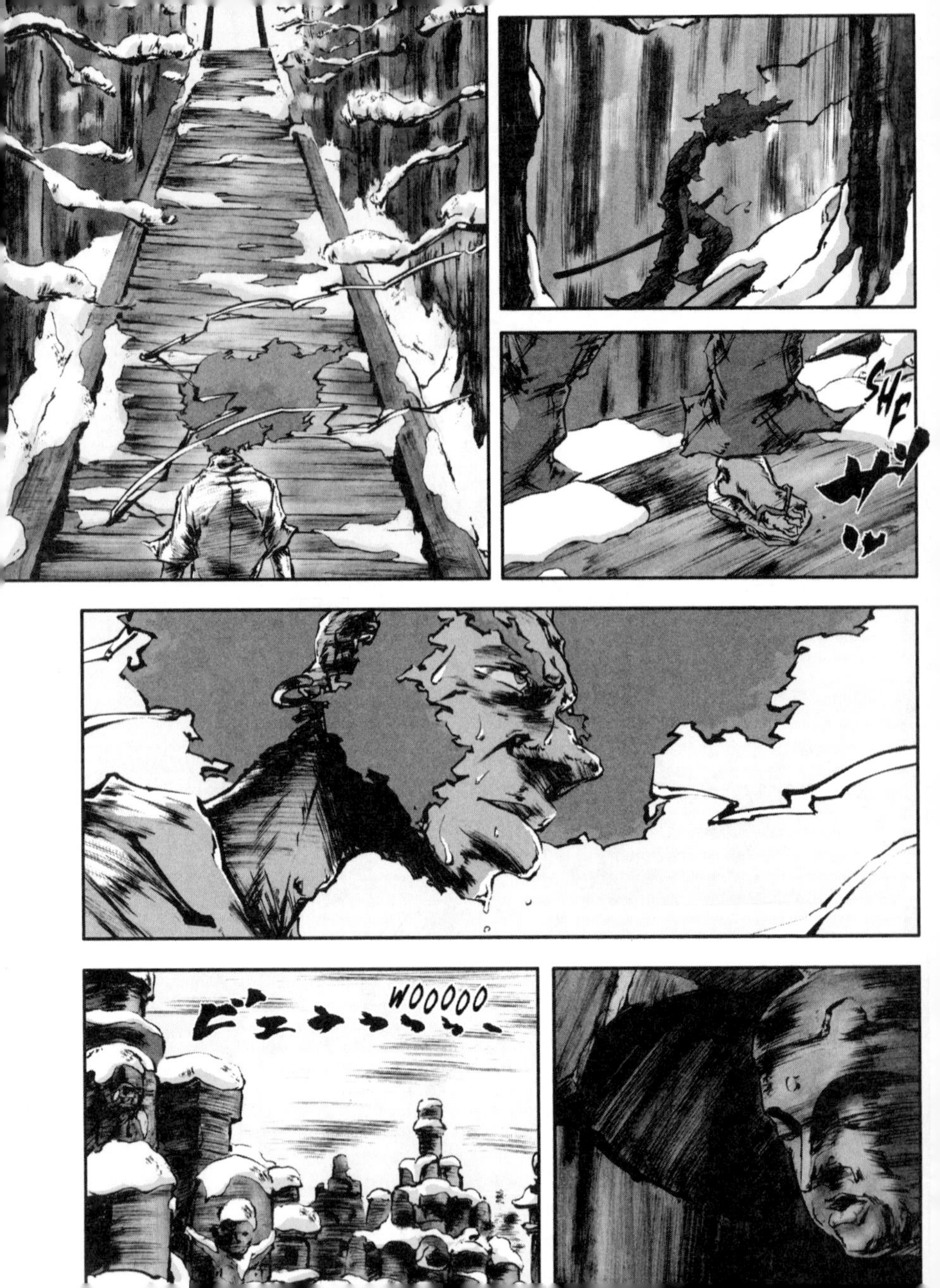
SHF
WOOOOO

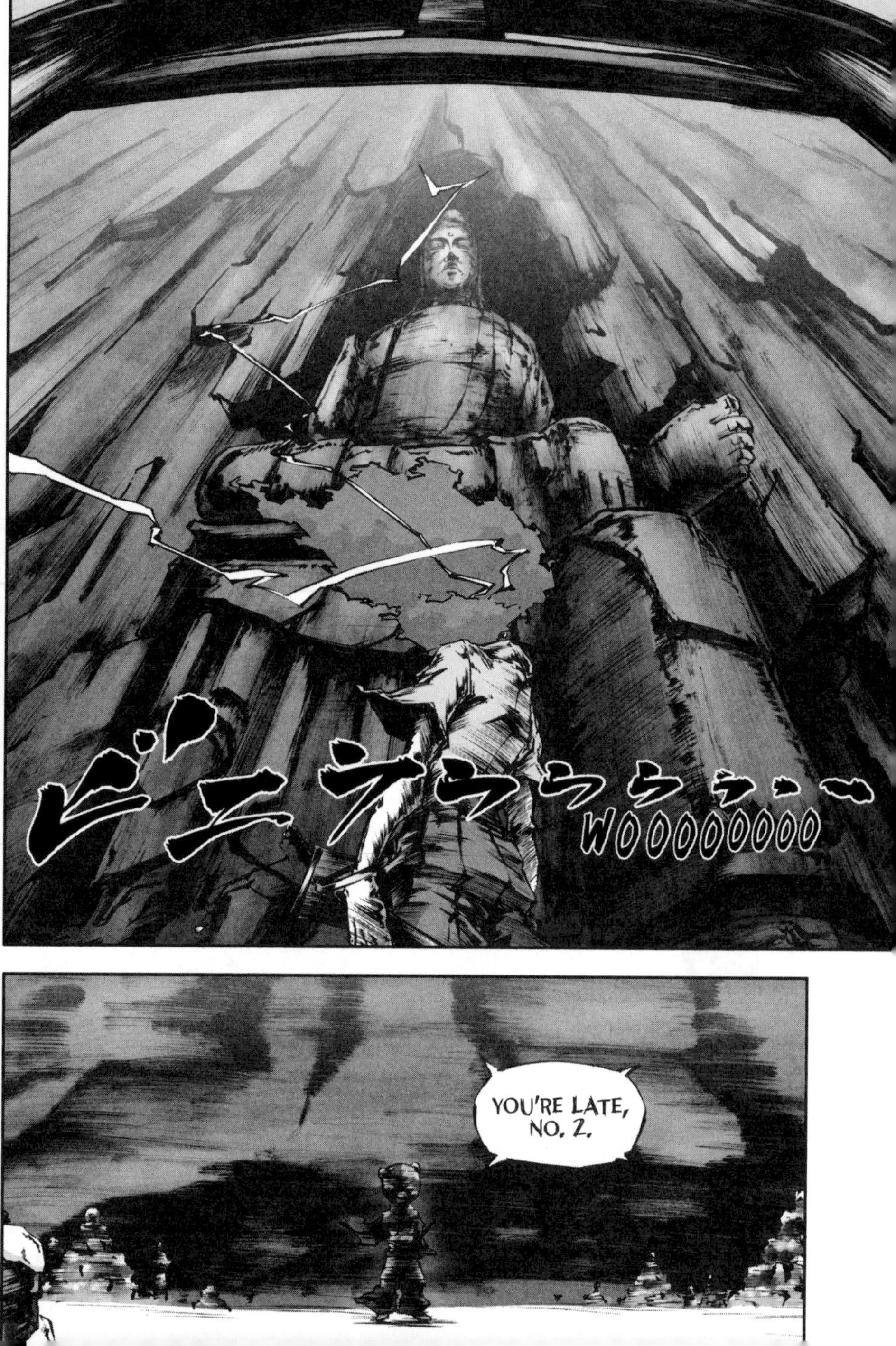
WOOOOOOOO
YOU'RE LATE, NO. 2.

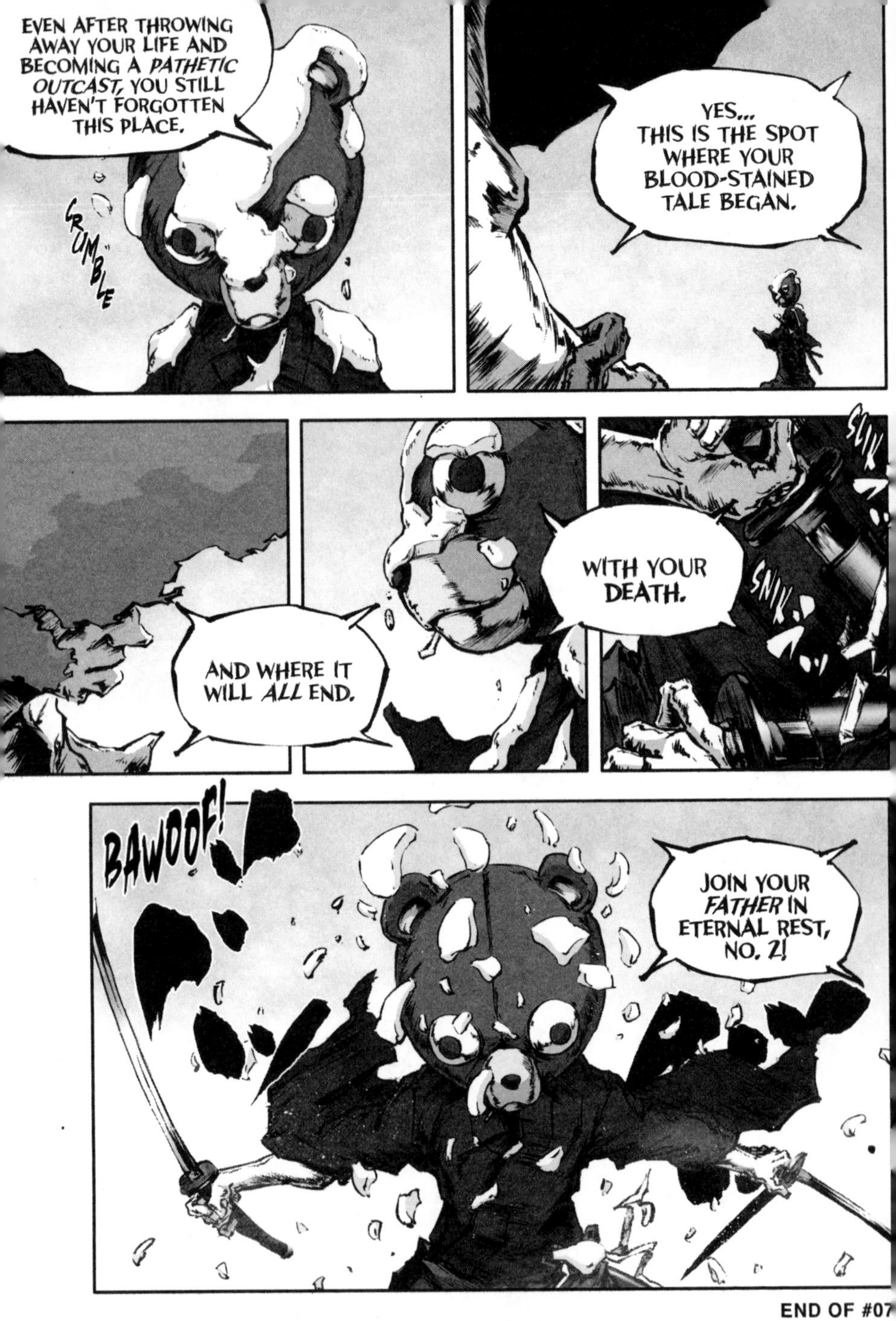
EVEN AFTER THROWING AWAY YOUR LIFE AND BECOMING A *PATHETIC OUTCAST,* YOU STILL HAVEN'T FORGOTTEN THIS PLACE.
CRUMBLE
YES... THIS IS THE SPOT WHERE YOUR BLOOD-STAINED TALE BEGAN.
AND WHERE IT WILL *ALL* END.
WITH YOUR **DEATH.**
SLIK
SNIK
BAWOOF!
JOIN YOUR *FATHER* IN ETERNAL REST, NO. 2!

END OF #07

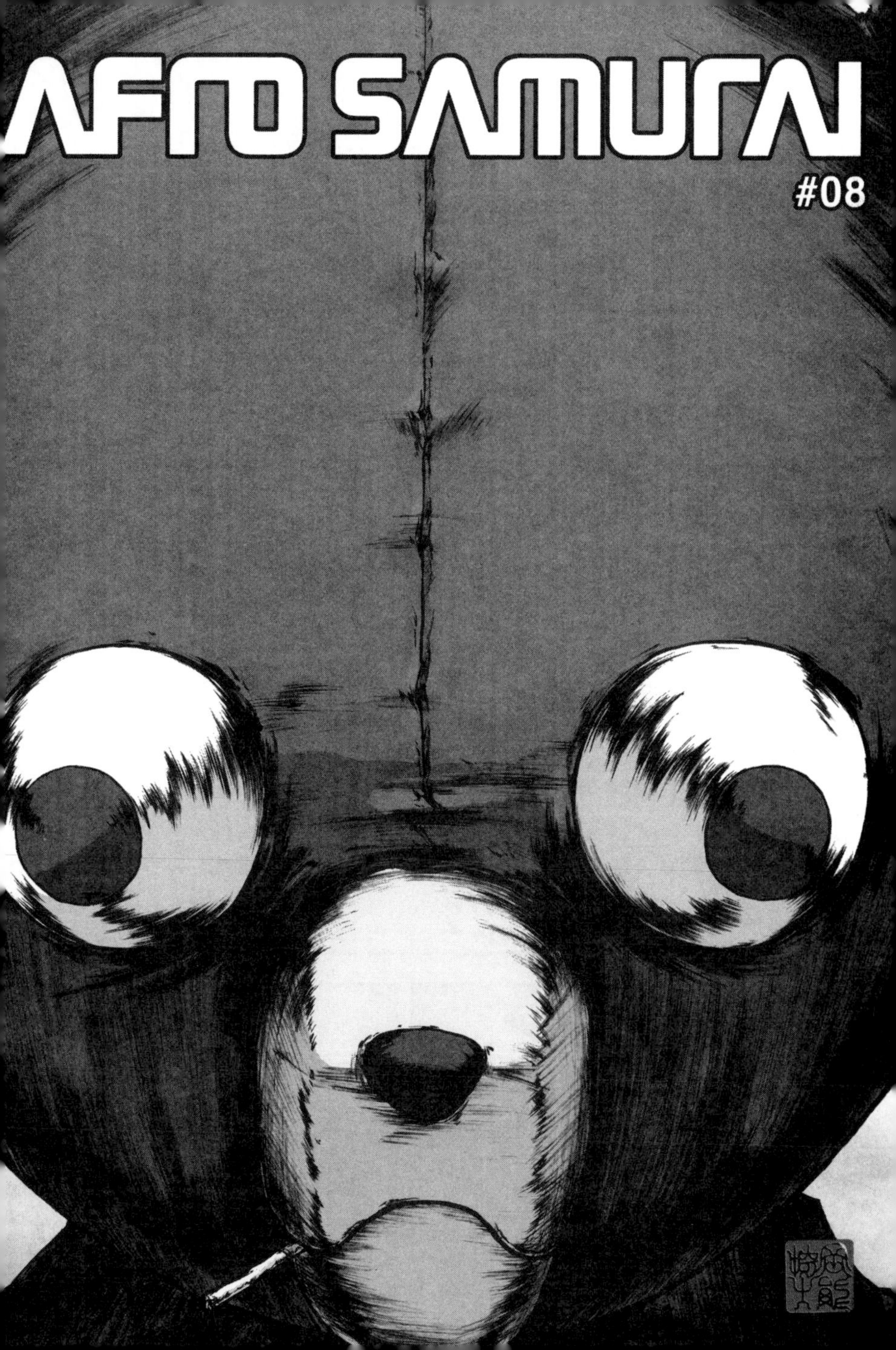
AFRO SAMURAI
#08

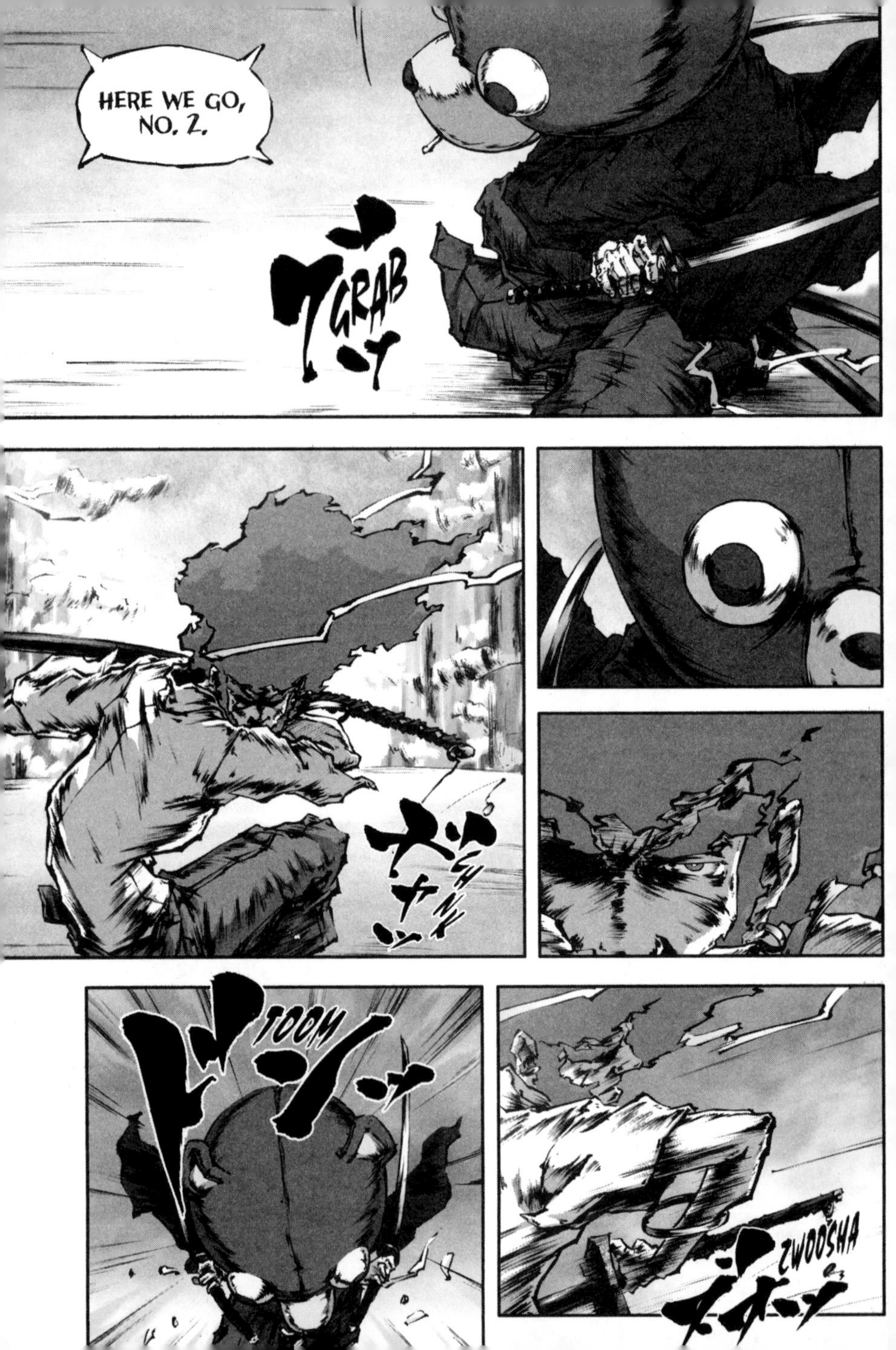
HERE WE GO, NO. 2.
GRAB
CHINK
TOOM
ZWOOSHA

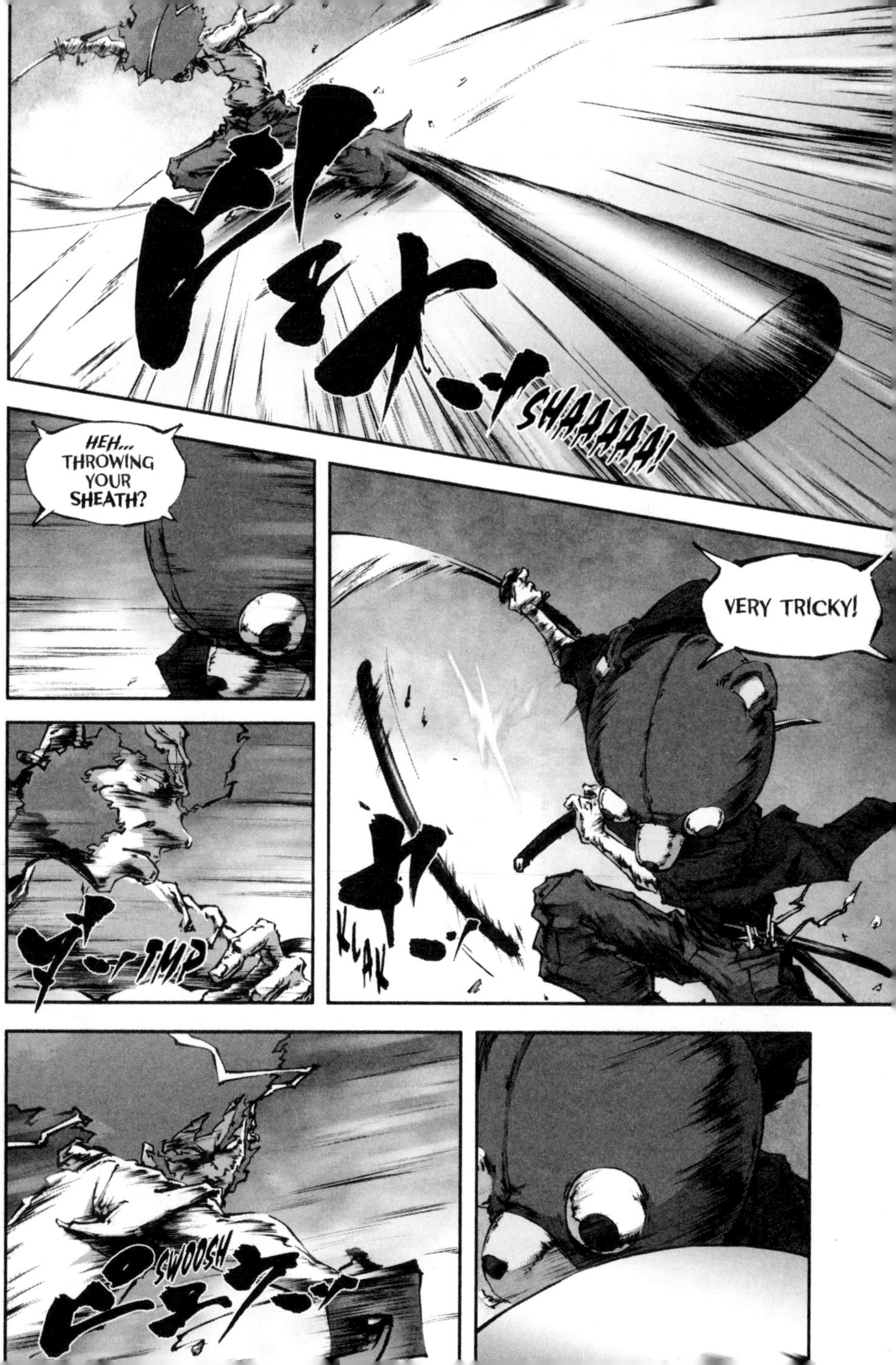

SHAAAAAA!
HEH... THROWING YOUR SHEATH?
TMP
VERY TRICKY!
KLAK
SWOOSH

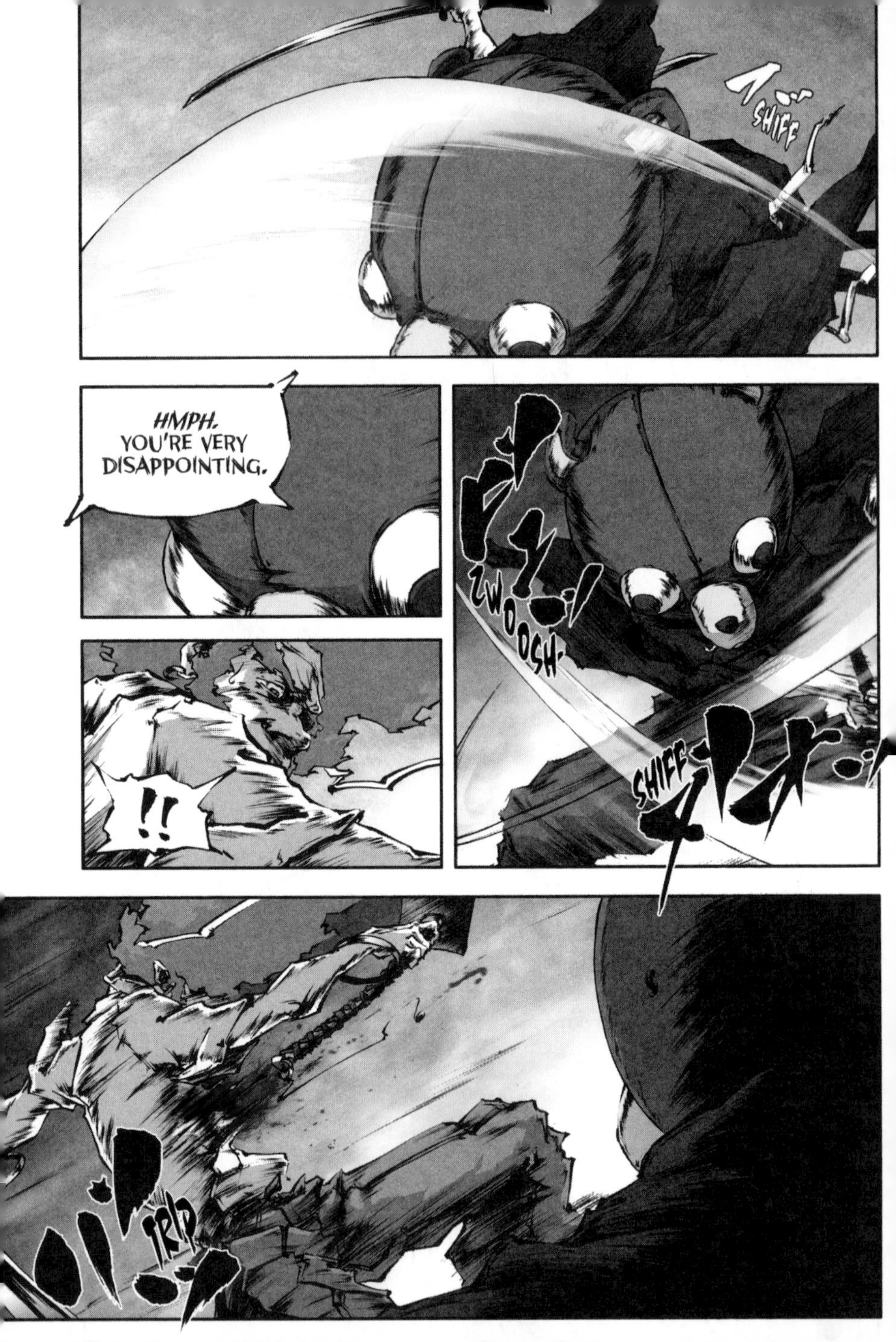
SHIFF
HMPH. YOU'RE VERY DISAPPOINTING.
!!
ZWOOSH
SHIFF
RIP

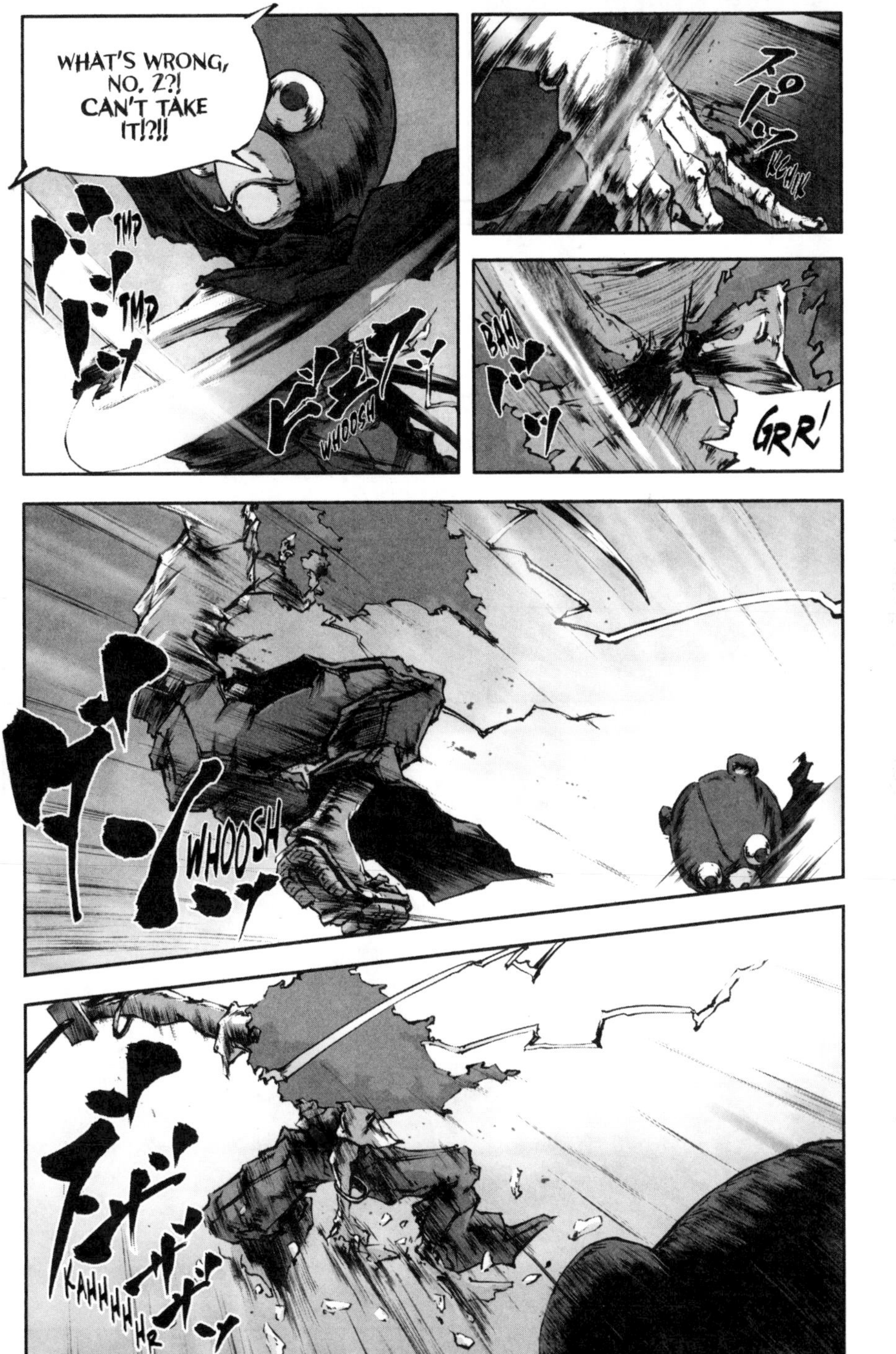
WHAT'S WRONG, NO. 2?! CAN'T TAKE IT!?!!
TMP
TMP
WHOOSH
KCHIK
BAM
GRR!
WHOOSH
KAHHHHHR

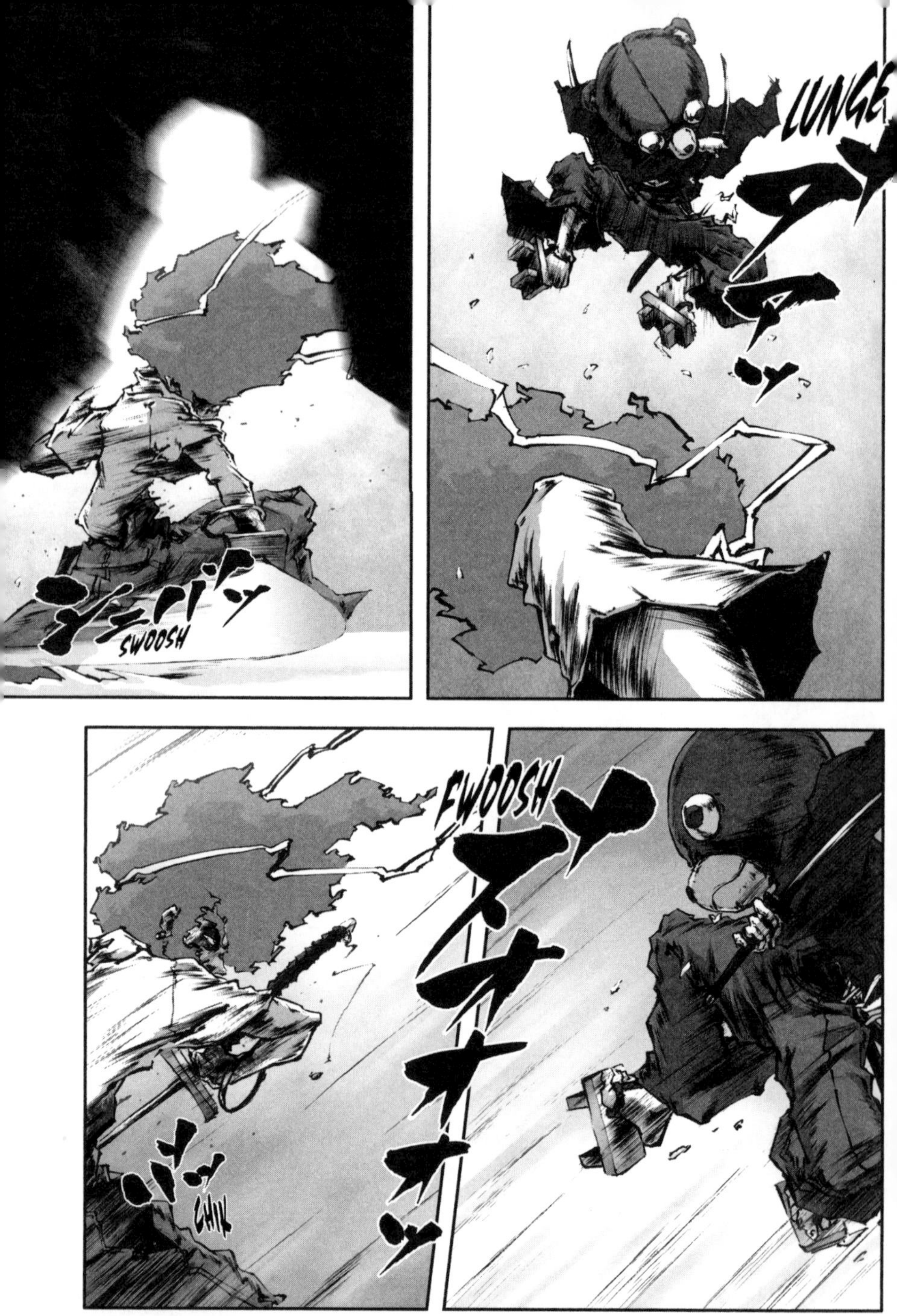
SWOOSH
LUNGE
CHIK
FWOOSH

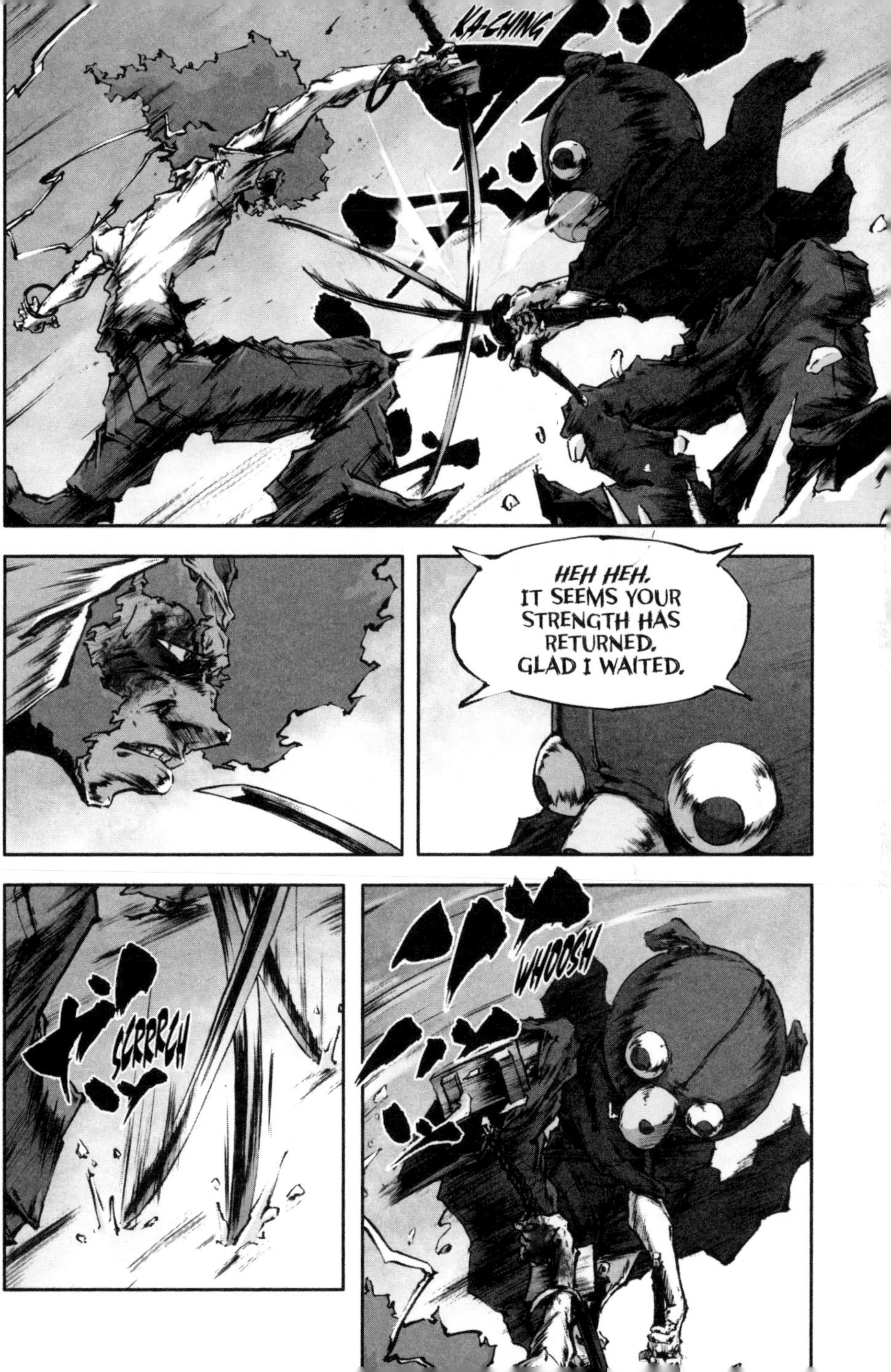
KA-CHING
HEH HEH.
IT SEEMS YOUR
STRENGTH HAS
RETURNED.
GLAD I WAITED.
SCRRRCH
WHOOSH

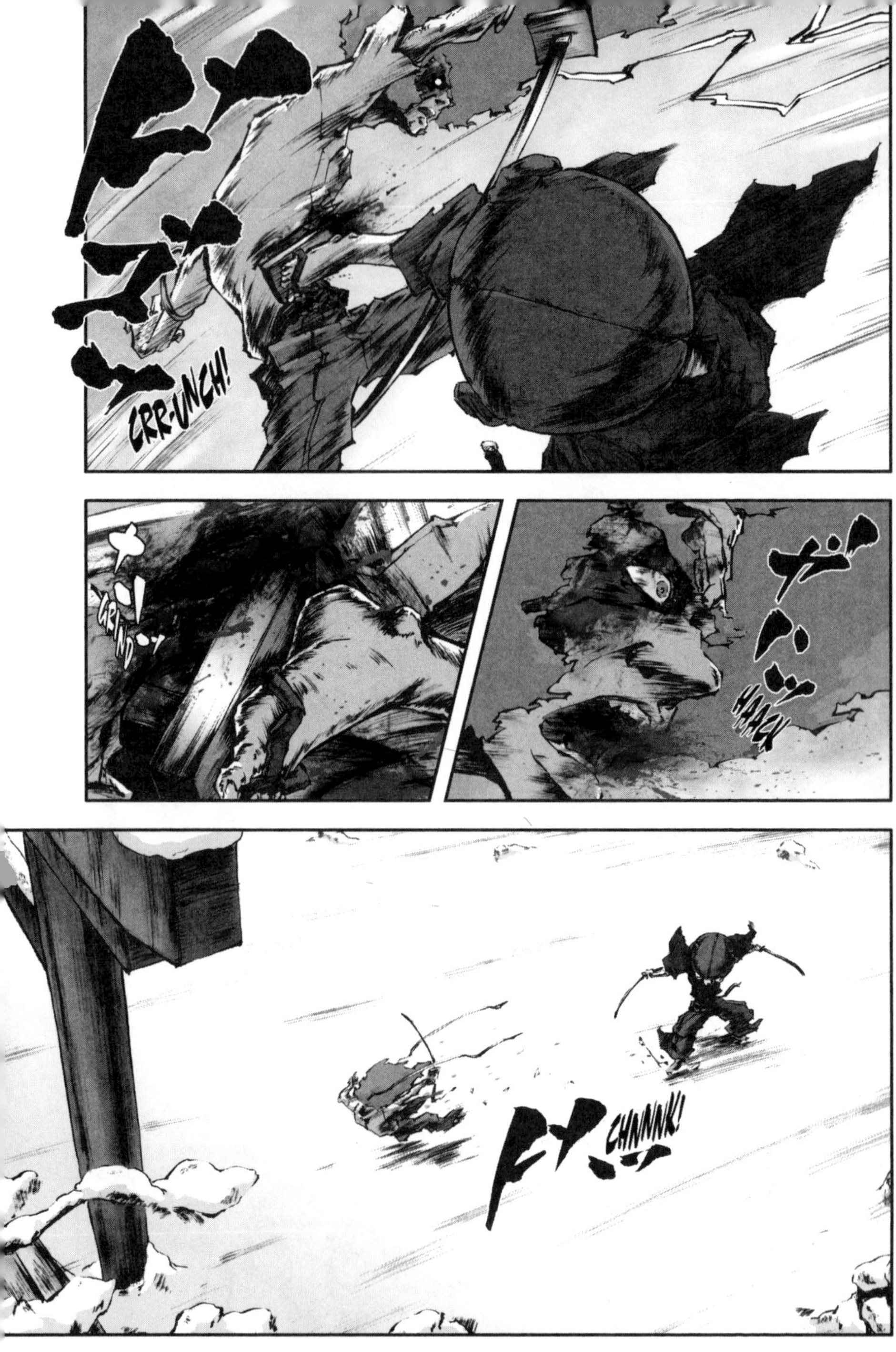
CRR-UNCH!
GRIND
HAACK
CHNNNK!

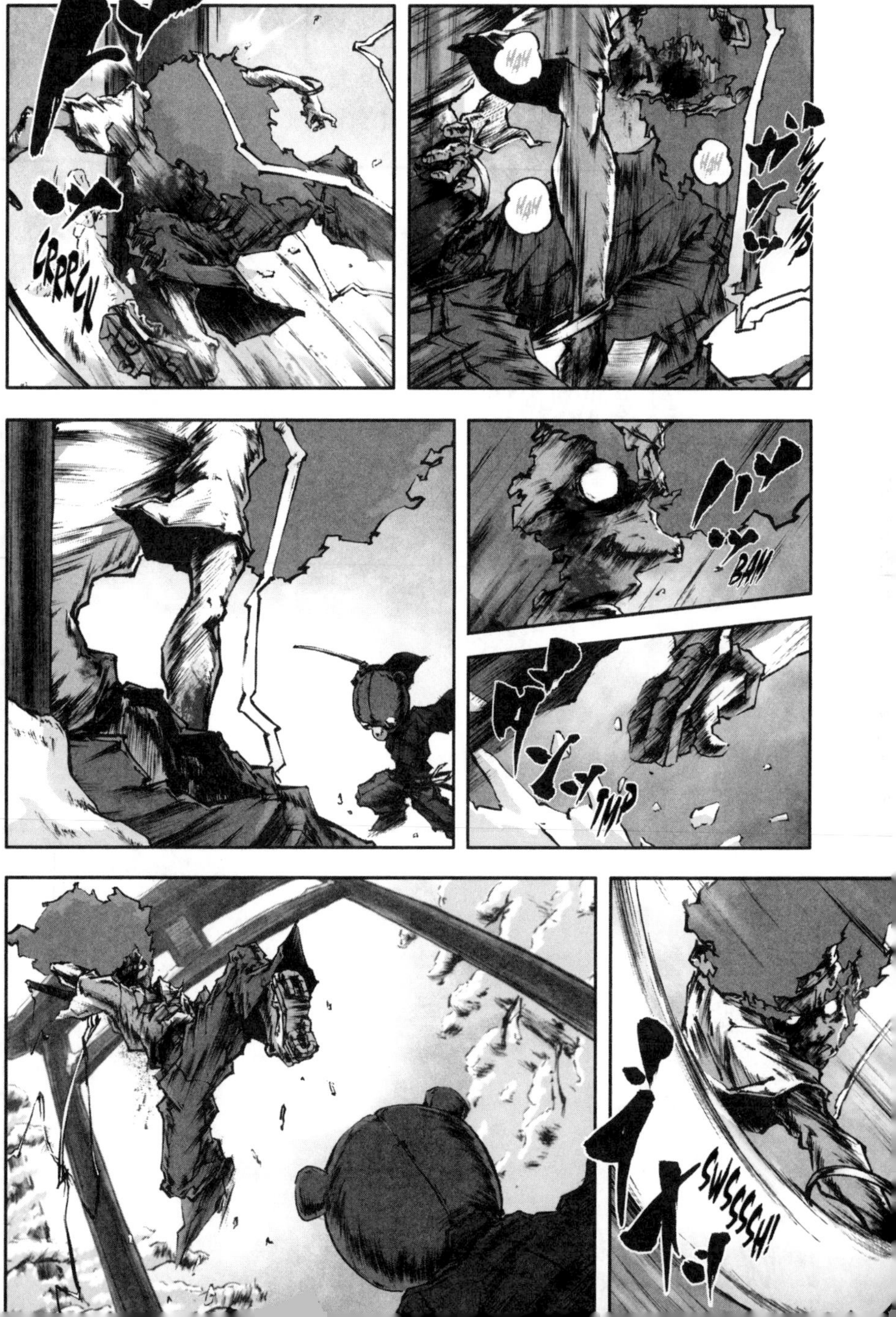

HAH
HAH
HAH
BAM
TMP
SWSSSH!

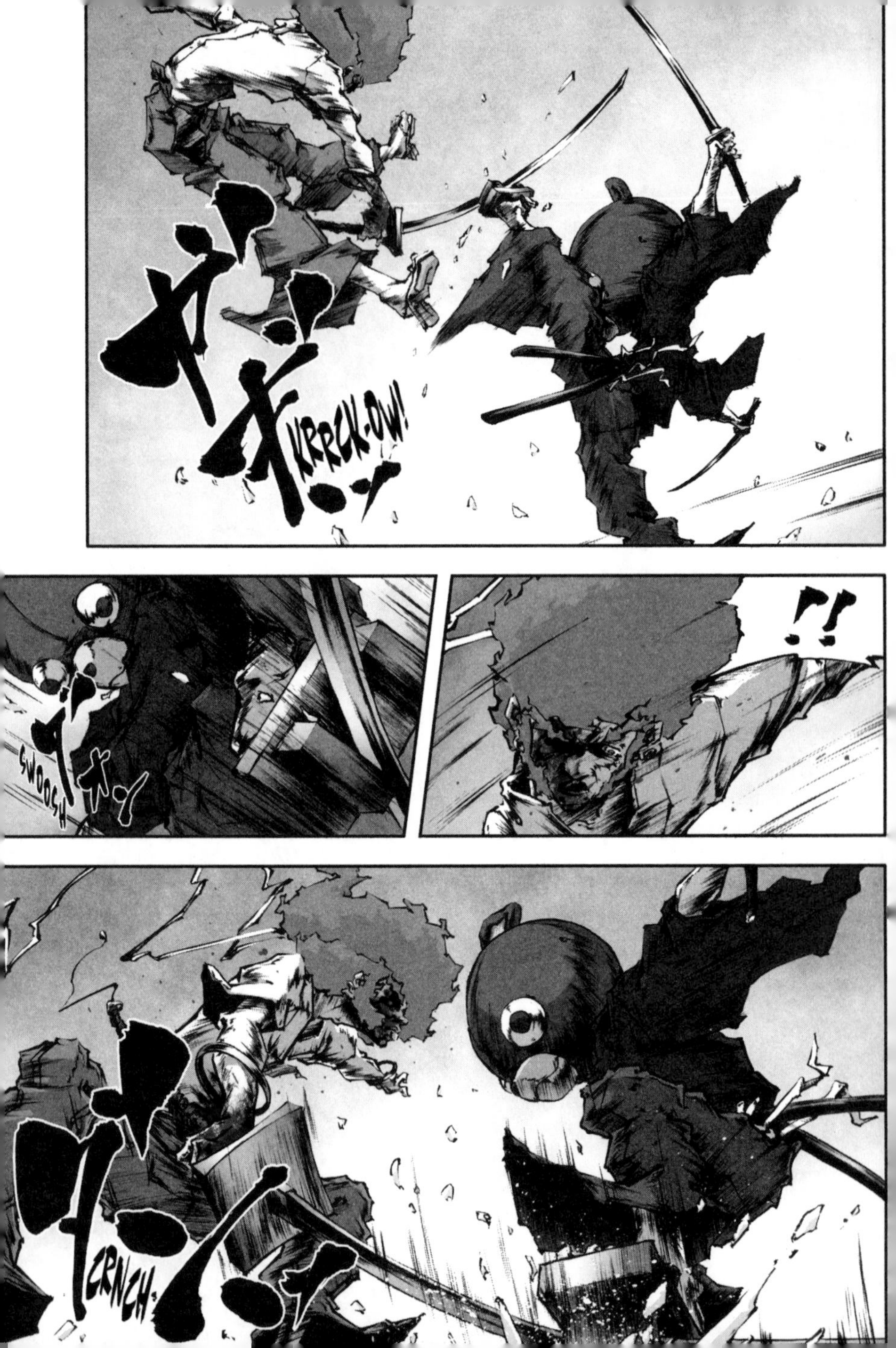
KRRCK-OW!
SWOOSH
!?!
CRNCH

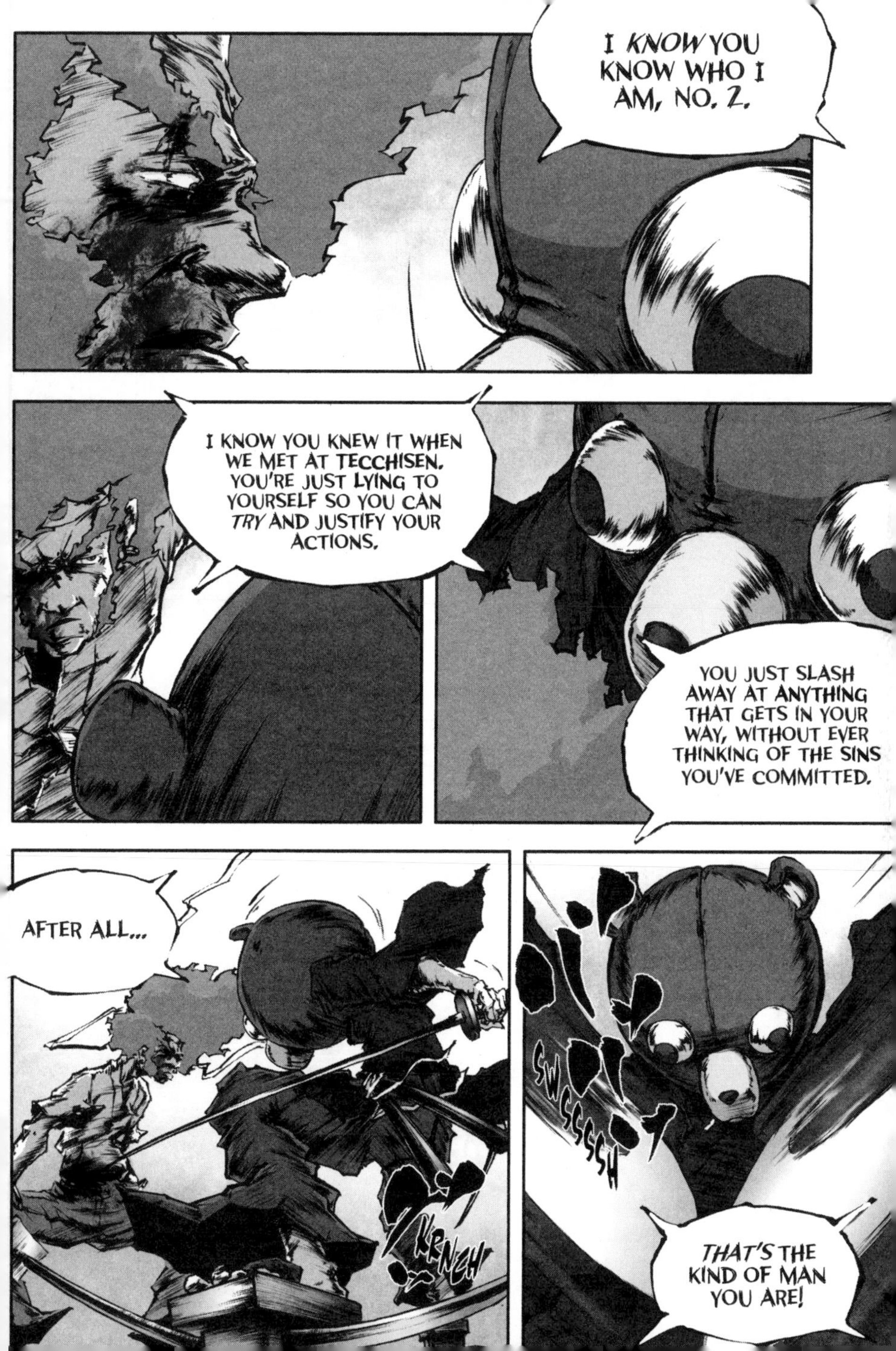
I *KNOW* YOU KNOW WHO I AM, NO. 2.
I KNOW YOU KNEW IT WHEN WE MET AT TECCHISEN. YOU'RE JUST LYING TO YOURSELF SO YOU CAN *TRY* AND JUSTIFY YOUR ACTIONS.
YOU JUST SLASH AWAY AT ANYTHING THAT GETS IN YOUR WAY, WITHOUT EVER THINKING OF THE SINS YOU'VE COMMITTED.
AFTER ALL...
KRNCH
SWSSSSSH
THAT'S THE KIND OF MAN YOU ARE!

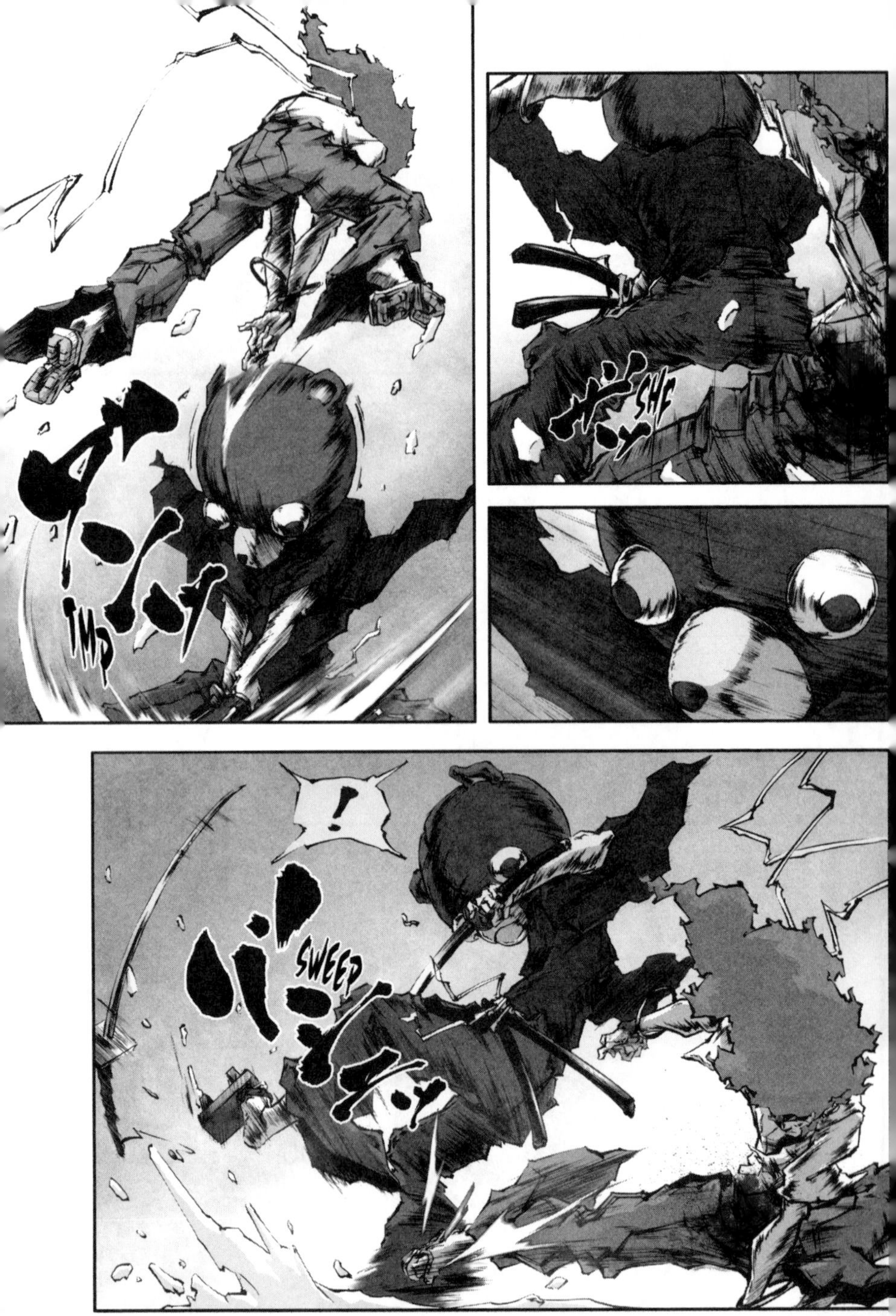

TMP
SHF
!
SWEEP

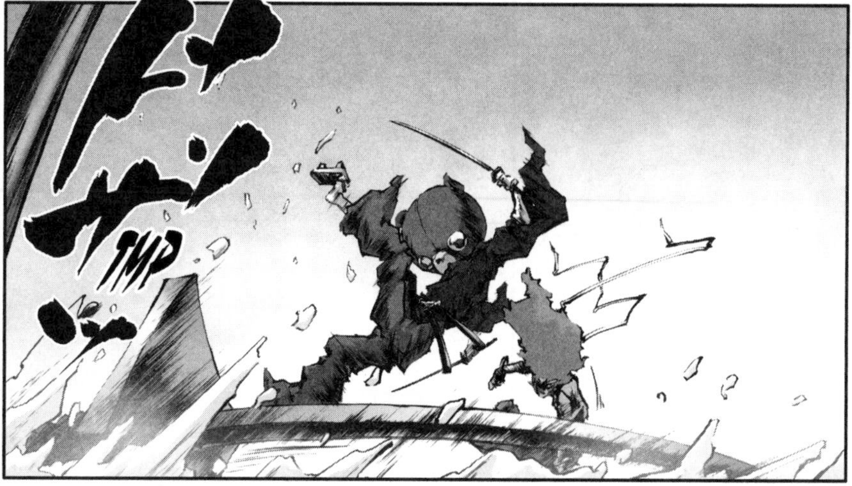
TMP
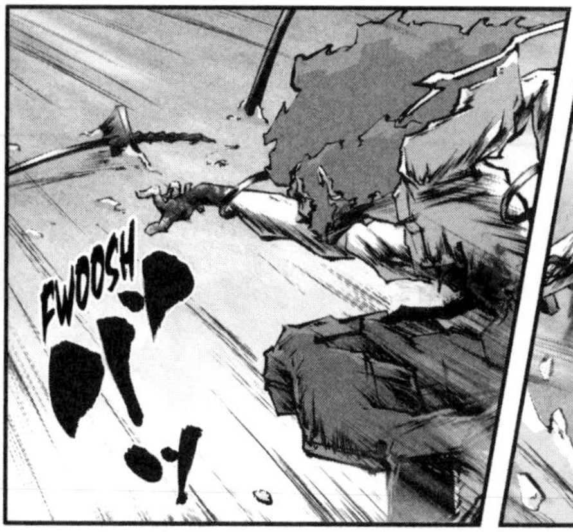
FWOOSH
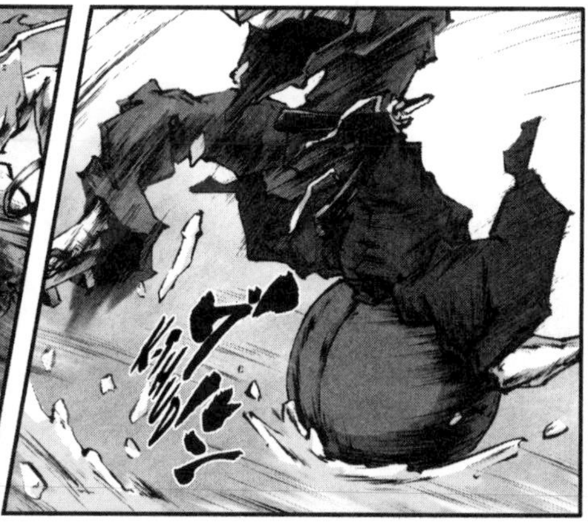
KTHUD
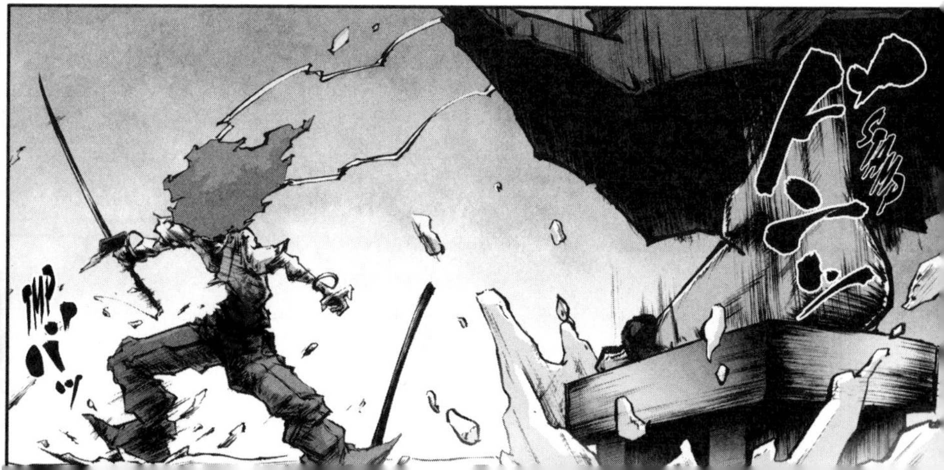
STAMP
TMP

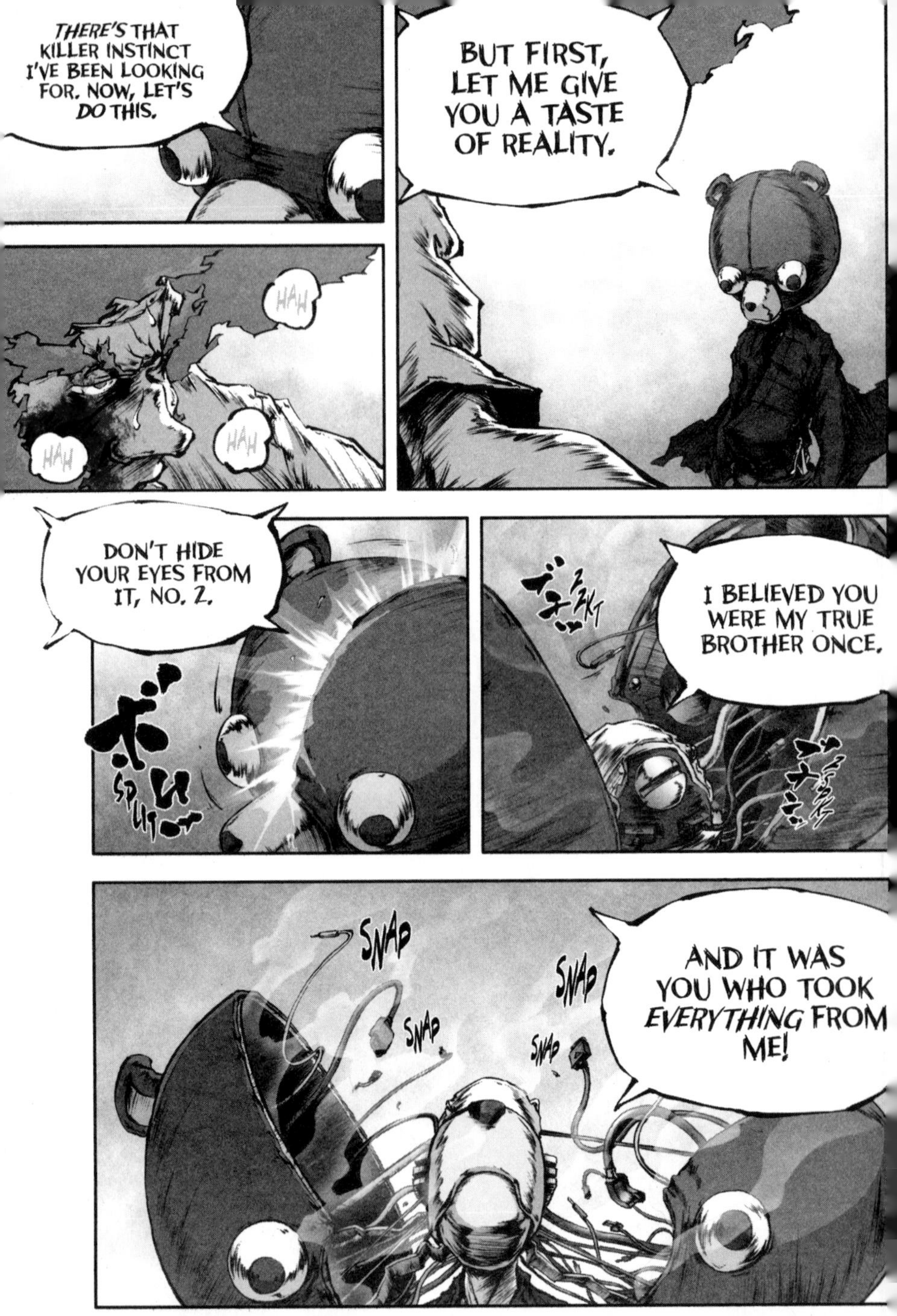

THERE'S THAT KILLER INSTINCT I'VE BEEN LOOKING FOR. NOW, LET'S *DO* THIS.
BUT FIRST, LET ME GIVE YOU A TASTE OF REALITY.
HAH
HAH
HAH
DON'T HIDE YOUR EYES FROM IT, NO. 2.
SPLIT
I BELIEVED YOU WERE MY TRUE BROTHER ONCE.
SNAP
SNAP
SNAP
SNAP
AND IT WAS YOU WHO TOOK *EVERYTHING* FROM ME!

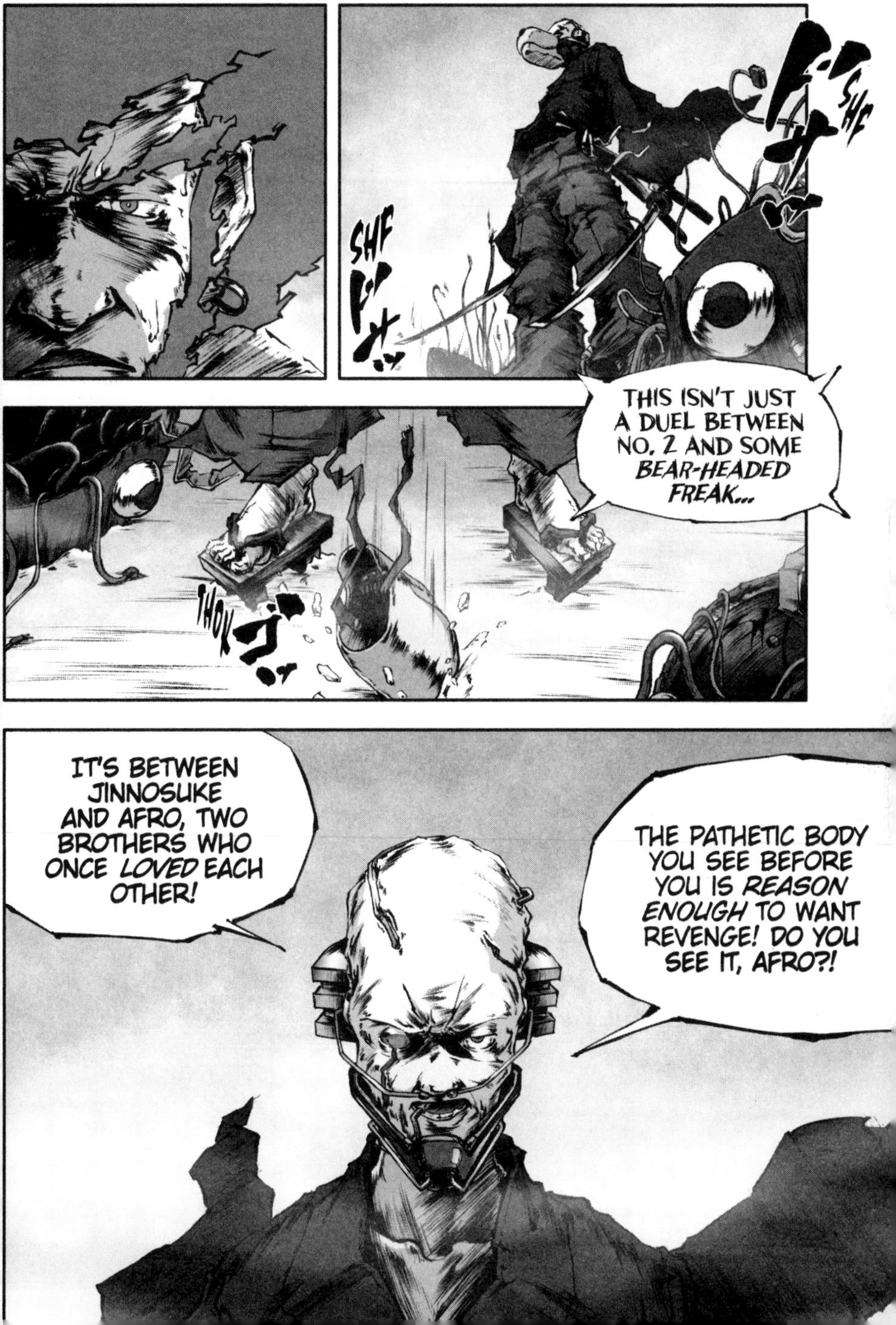
SHF
SHF
THIS ISN'T JUST A DUEL BETWEEN NO. 2 AND SOME *BEAR-HEADED* FREAK...
THOK
IT'S BETWEEN JINNOSUKE AND AFRO, TWO BROTHERS WHO ONCE *LOVED* EACH OTHER!
THE PATHETIC BODY YOU SEE BEFORE YOU IS *REASON ENOUGH* TO WANT REVENGE! DO YOU SEE IT, AFRO?!

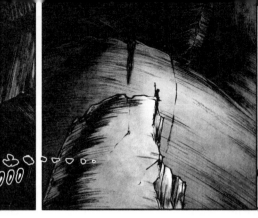

WOOOOOOOO

GETTING RATHER RILED UP, EH, JINNOSUKE? HE'S LEARNED TO SUPPRESS HIS EMOTIONS, BUT I *DOUBT* THAT WILL BE ENOUGH WITH A SKILLED MURDERER LIKE THIS ONE. *HEH HEH.*

AFTER ALL, THE END OF THIS CHALLENGE IS ALREADY CLEAR. IT IS *HIGHLY UNLIKELY* THAT THE AFRO SAMURAI WILL LOSE. HE *IS* THE MAN WITH THE POWER TO HELP US PROTECT NO. 1.

BUT... HE IS CONTROLLED SOLELY BY NEGATIVE EMOTIONS. DESPITE HIS SKILL, HE WILL BRING ABOUT HIS *OWN* DESTRUCTION. *HEHEHEH.*

YET... THERE'S THIS STRANGE *FEELING* HE EXUDES? SOMEHOW IT FEELS LIKE I'VE SENSED THIS BEFORE, LONG AGO... WHAT A FOUL MEMORY...

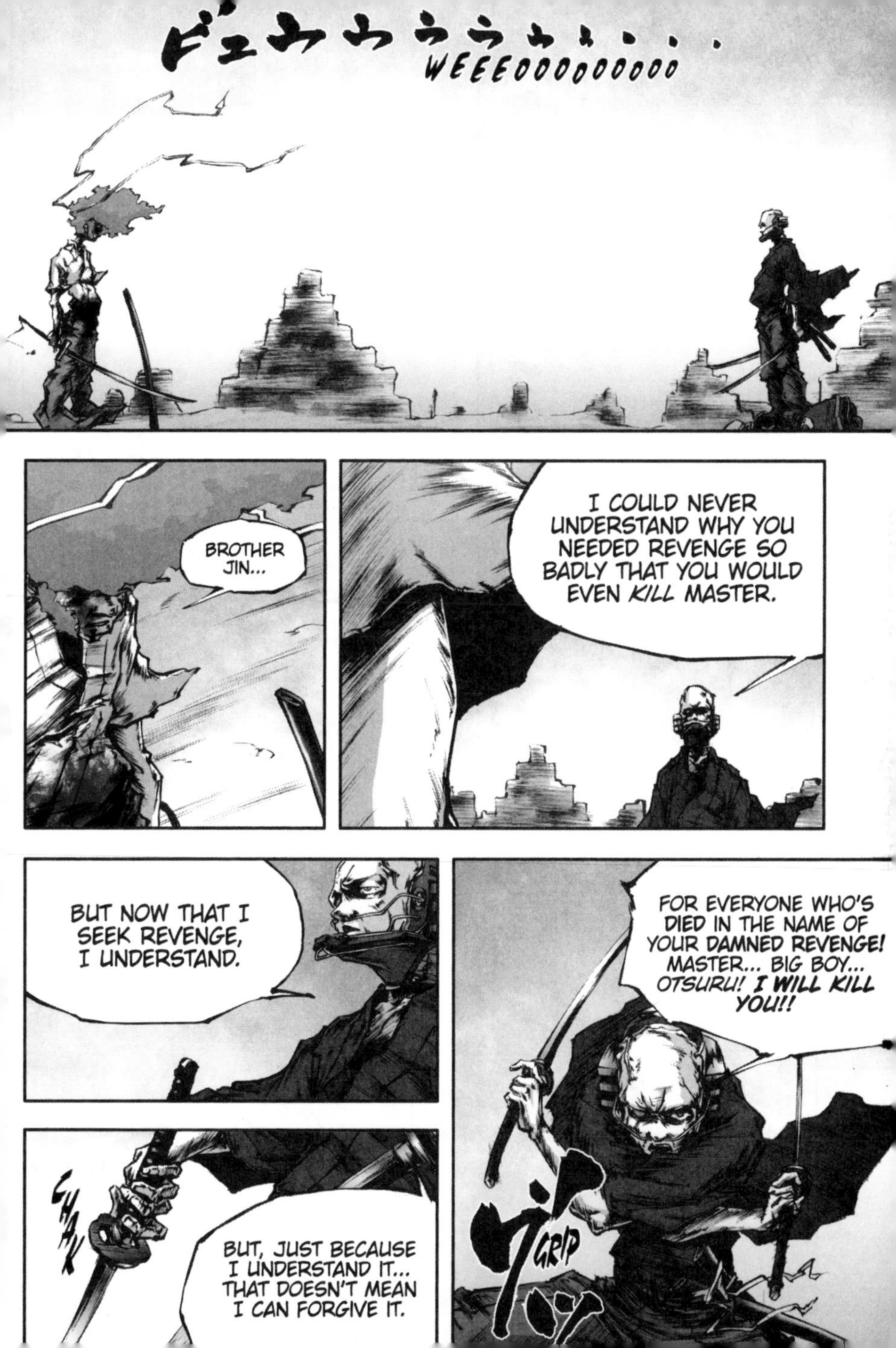
WEEEOOOOOOOOO
BROTHER JIN...
I COULD NEVER UNDERSTAND WHY YOU NEEDED REVENGE SO BADLY THAT YOU WOULD EVEN *KILL* MASTER.
BUT NOW THAT I SEEK REVENGE, I UNDERSTAND.
CHAK
BUT, JUST BECAUSE I UNDERSTAND IT... THAT DOESN'T MEAN I CAN FORGIVE IT.
FOR EVERYONE WHO'S DIED IN THE NAME OF YOUR DAMNED REVENGE! MASTER... BIG BOY... OTSURU! ***I WILL KILL YOU!!***
GRIP

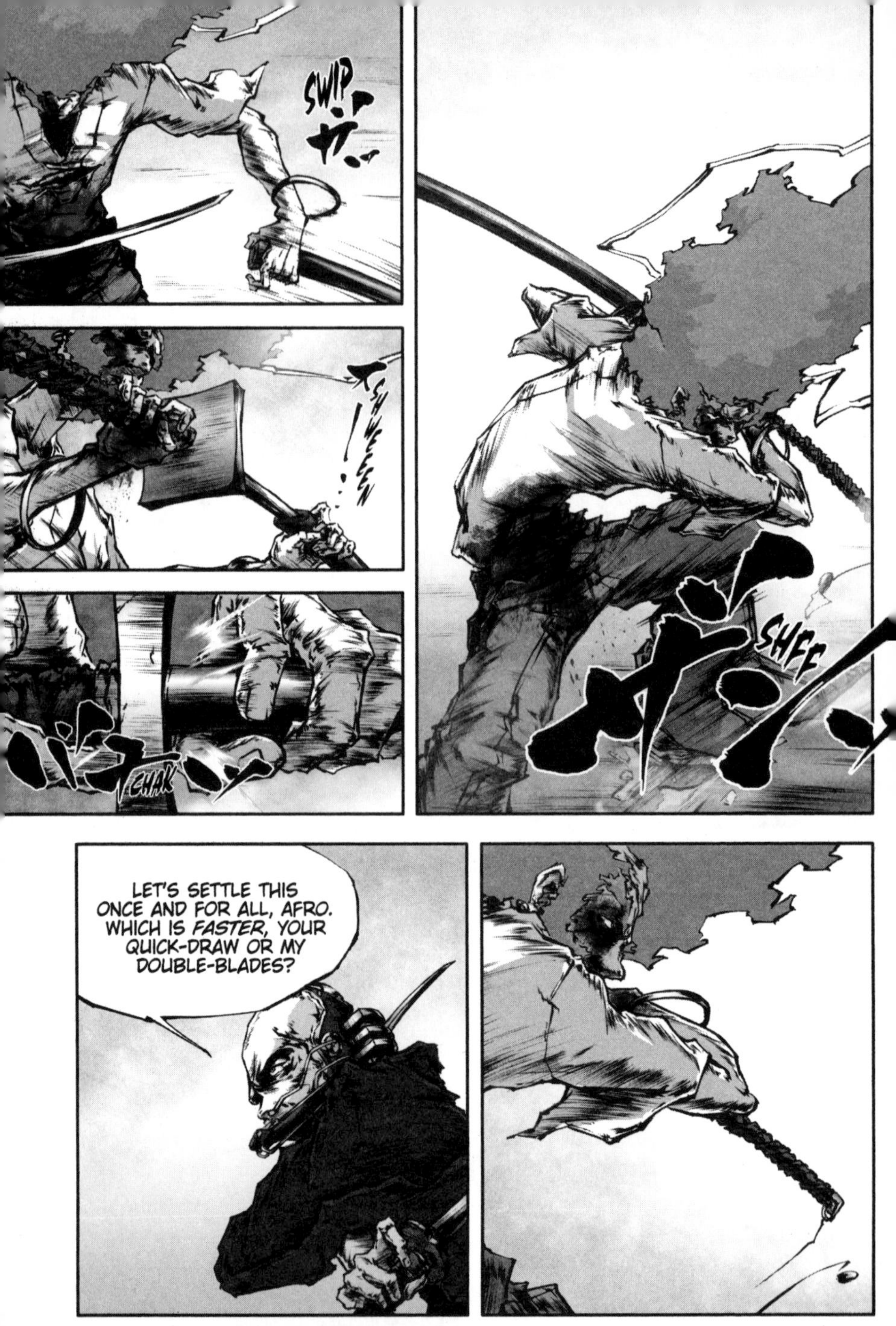
SWIP
TSHWEEEN
CHAK
SHFF
LET'S SETTLE THIS ONCE AND FOR ALL, AFRO. WHICH IS *FASTER*, YOUR QUICK-DRAW OR MY DOUBLE-BLADES?

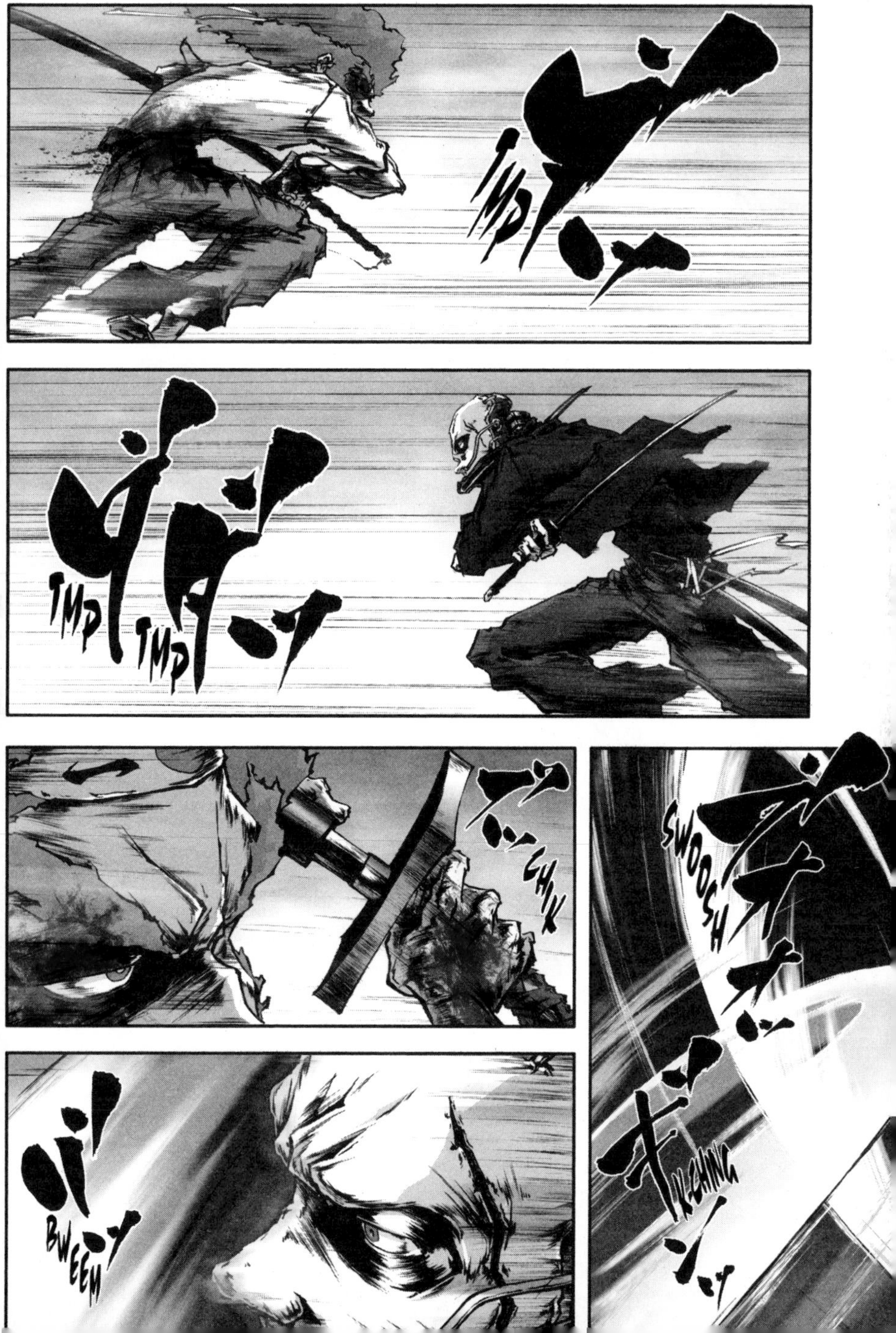
TMP
TMP
TMP
CHIK
BWEEM
SWOOSH
CHING

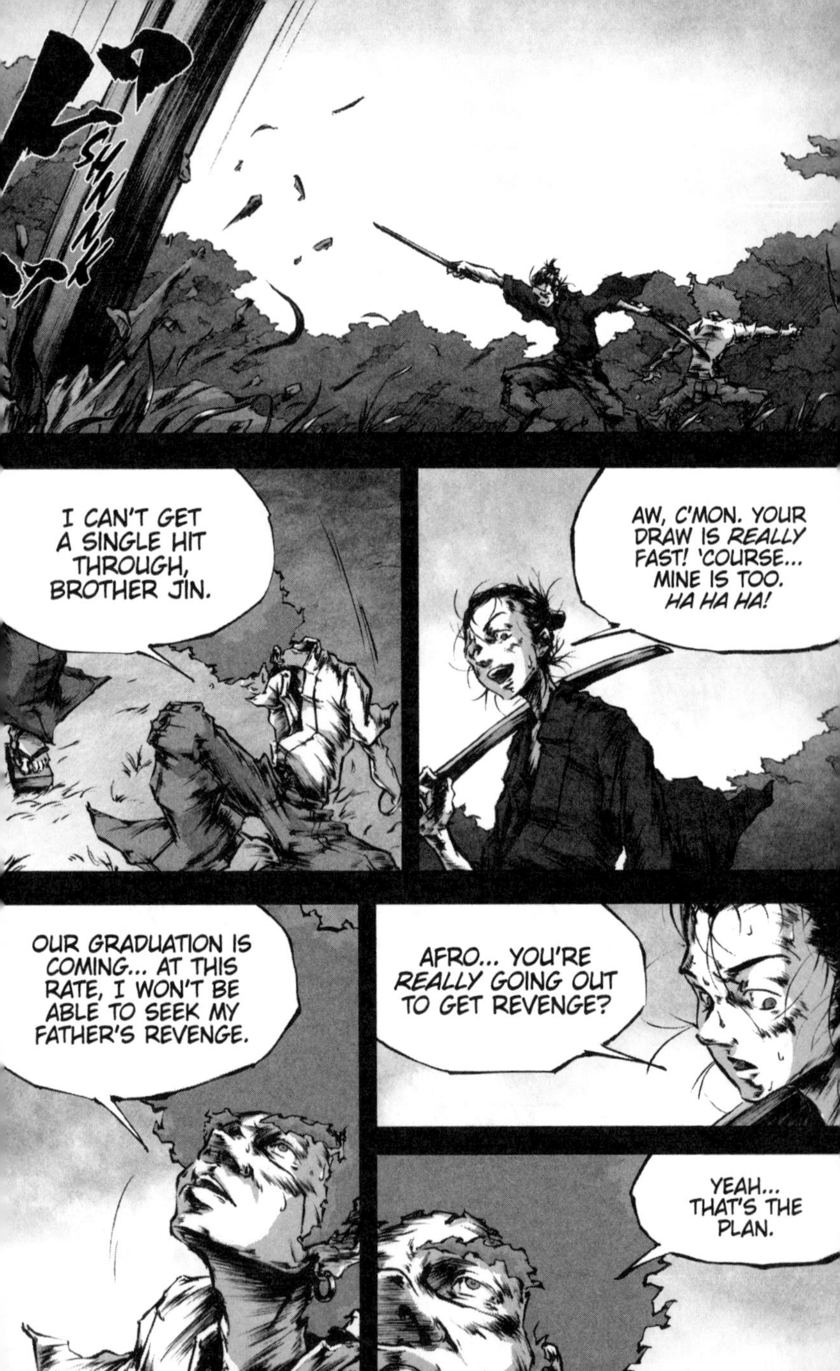
SHWANK
I CAN'T GET A SINGLE HIT THROUGH, BROTHER JIN.
AW, C'MON. YOUR DRAW IS *REALLY* FAST! 'COURSE... MINE IS TOO. *HA HA HA!*
OUR GRADUATION IS COMING... AT THIS RATE, I WON'T BE ABLE TO SEEK MY FATHER'S REVENGE.
AFRO... YOU'RE *REALLY* GOING OUT TO GET REVENGE?
YEAH... THAT'S THE PLAN.

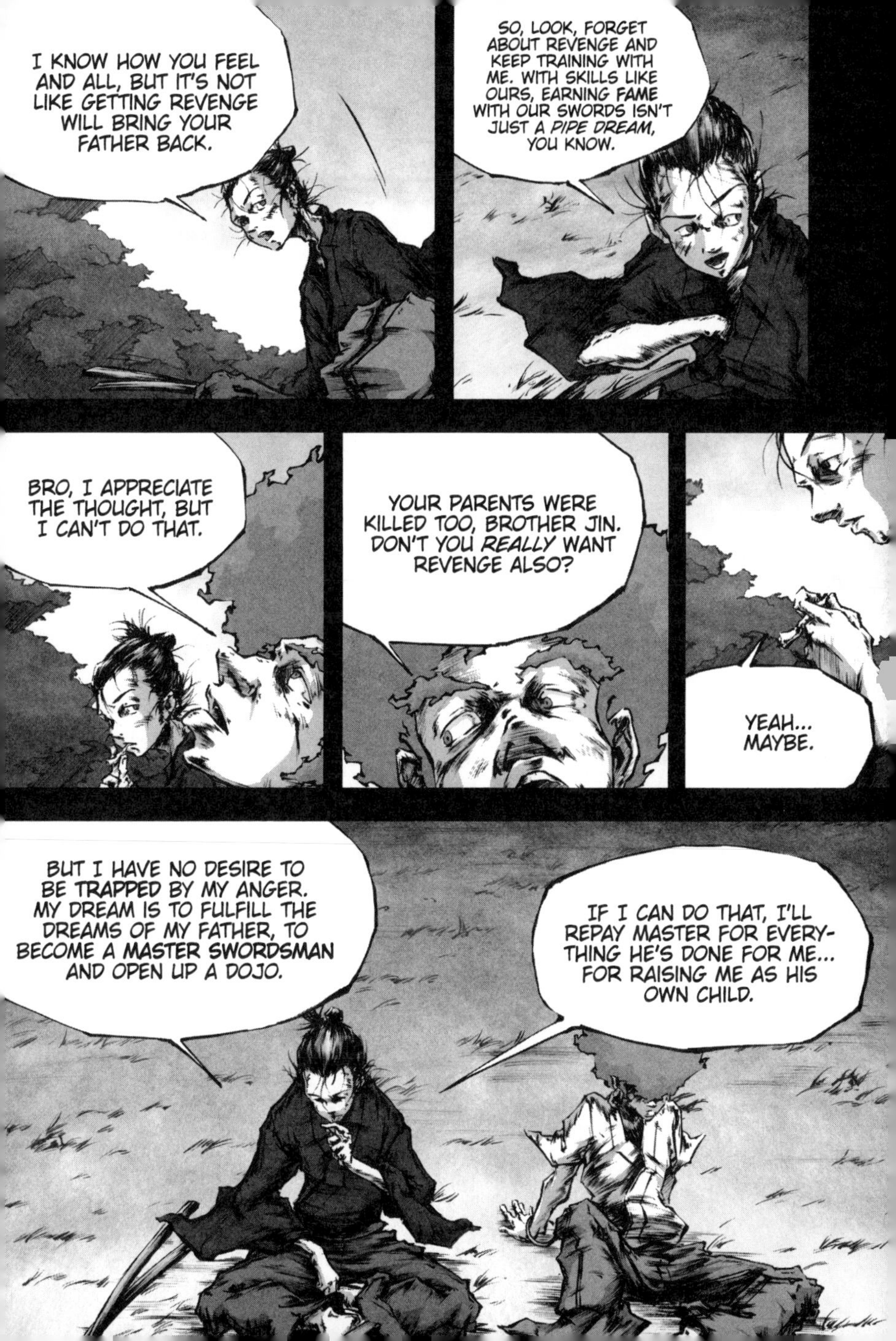
I KNOW HOW YOU FEEL AND ALL, BUT IT'S NOT LIKE GETTING REVENGE WILL BRING YOUR FATHER BACK.
SO, LOOK, FORGET ABOUT REVENGE AND KEEP TRAINING WITH ME. WITH SKILLS LIKE OURS, EARNING FAME WITH OUR SWORDS ISN'T JUST A *PIPE DREAM*, YOU KNOW.
BRO, I APPRECIATE THE THOUGHT, BUT I CAN'T DO THAT.
YOUR PARENTS WERE KILLED TOO, BROTHER JIN. DON'T YOU *REALLY* WANT REVENGE ALSO?
YEAH... MAYBE.
BUT I HAVE NO DESIRE TO BE **TRAPPED** BY MY ANGER. MY DREAM IS TO FULFILL THE DREAMS OF MY FATHER, TO BECOME A **MASTER SWORDSMAN** AND OPEN UP A DOJO.
IF I CAN DO THAT, I'LL REPAY MASTER FOR EVERYTHING HE'S DONE FOR ME... FOR RAISING ME AS HIS OWN CHILD.

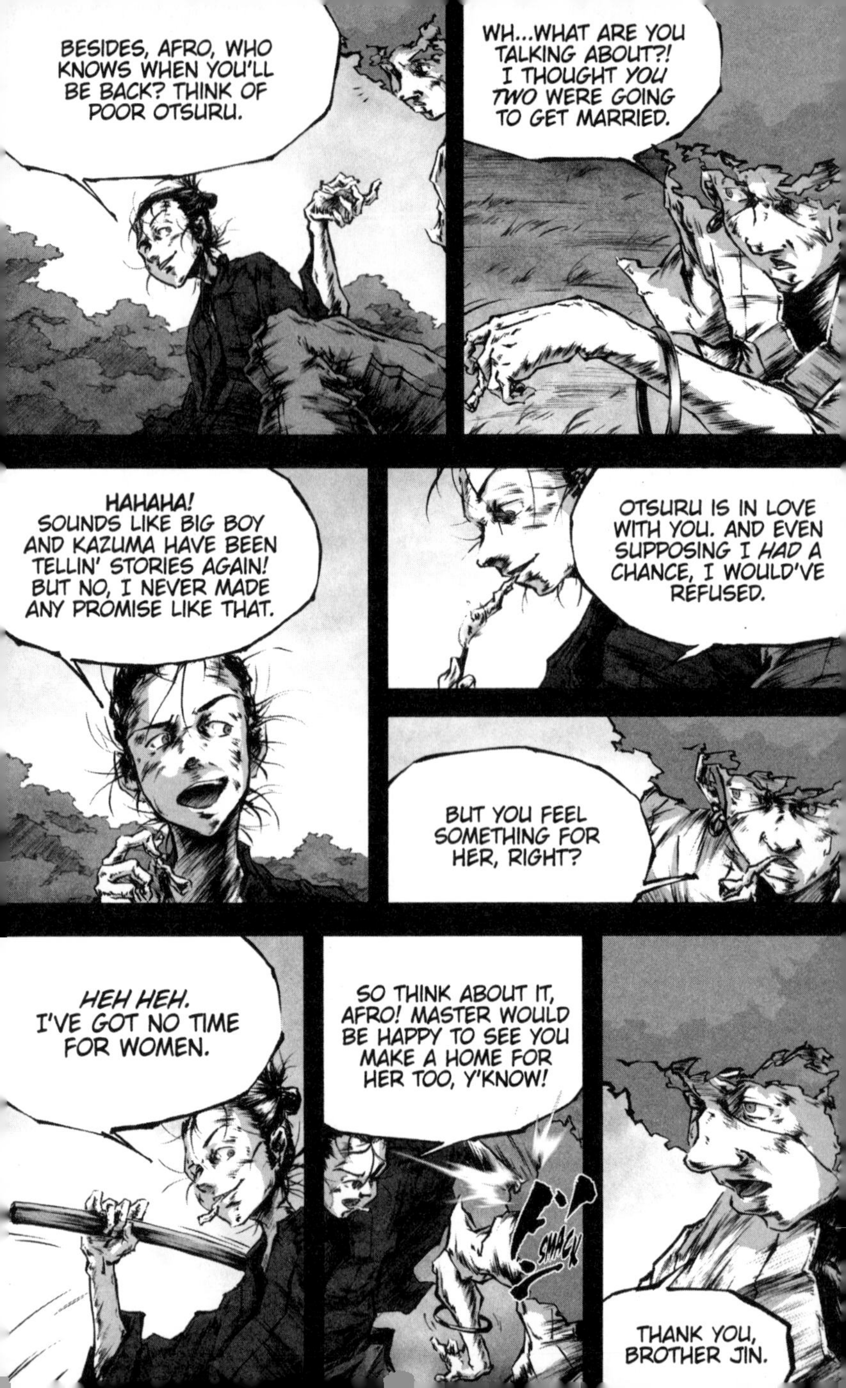
BESIDES, AFRO, WHO KNOWS WHEN YOU'LL BE BACK? THINK OF POOR OTSURU.
WH...WHAT ARE YOU TALKING ABOUT?! I THOUGHT *YOU TWO* WERE GOING TO GET MARRIED.
HAHAHA! SOUNDS LIKE BIG BOY AND KAZUMA HAVE BEEN TELLIN' STORIES AGAIN! BUT NO, I NEVER MADE ANY PROMISE LIKE THAT.
OTSURU IS IN LOVE WITH YOU. AND EVEN SUPPOSING I *HAD* A CHANCE, I WOULD'VE REFUSED.
BUT YOU FEEL SOMETHING FOR HER, RIGHT?
HEH HEH. I'VE GOT NO TIME FOR WOMEN.
SO THINK ABOUT IT, AFRO! MASTER WOULD BE HAPPY TO SEE YOU MAKE A HOME FOR HER TOO, Y'KNOW!
SMACK
THANK YOU, BROTHER JIN.

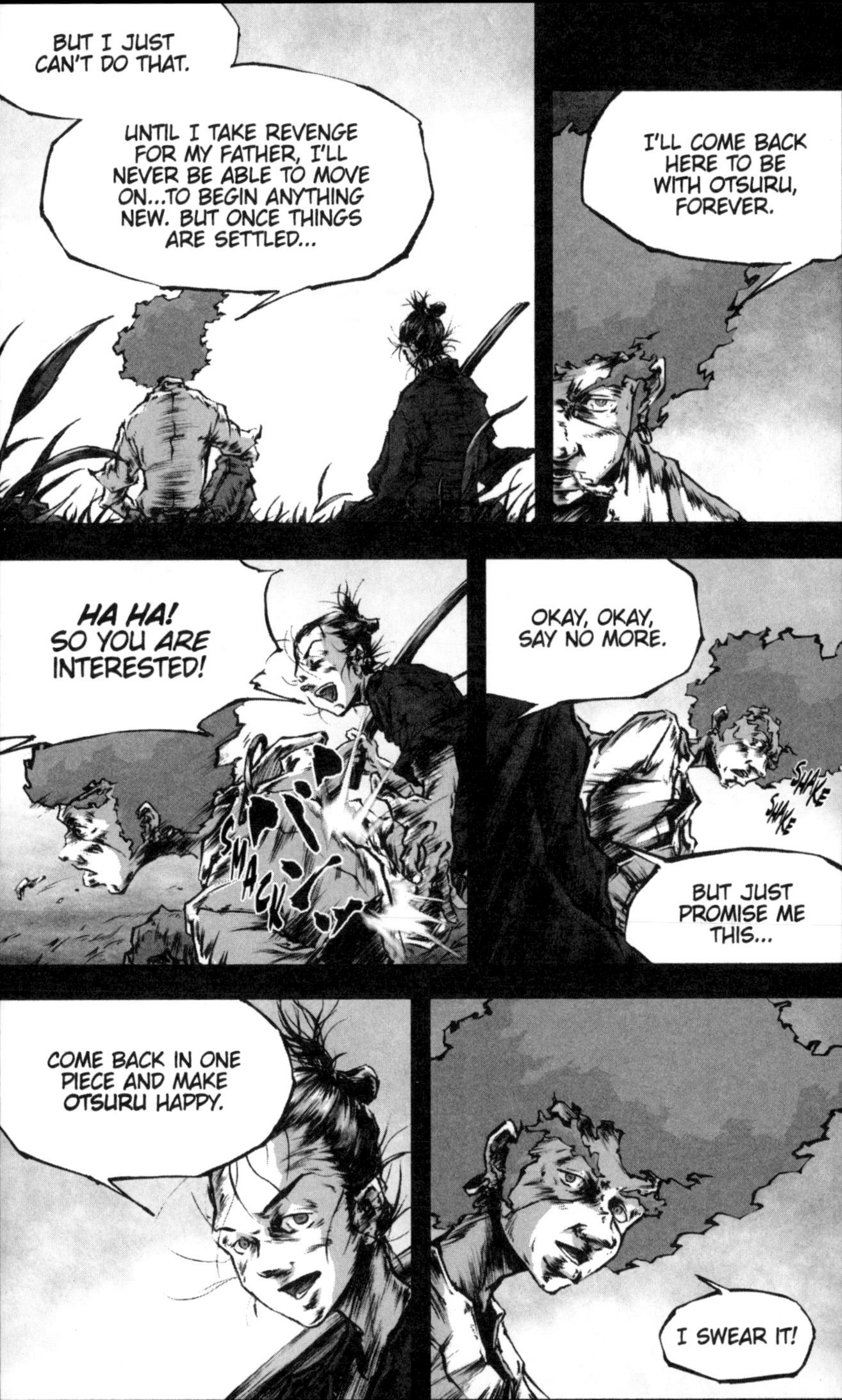
BUT I JUST CAN'T DO THAT.
UNTIL I TAKE REVENGE FOR MY FATHER, I'LL NEVER BE ABLE TO MOVE ON...TO BEGIN ANYTHING NEW. BUT ONCE THINGS ARE SETTLED...
I'LL COME BACK HERE TO BE WITH OTSURU, FOREVER.
HA HA! SO YOU ARE INTERESTED!
SMACK
OKAY, OKAY, SAY NO MORE.
SHAKE
SHAKE
BUT JUST PROMISE ME THIS...
COME BACK IN ONE PIECE AND MAKE OTSURU HAPPY.
I SWEAR IT!

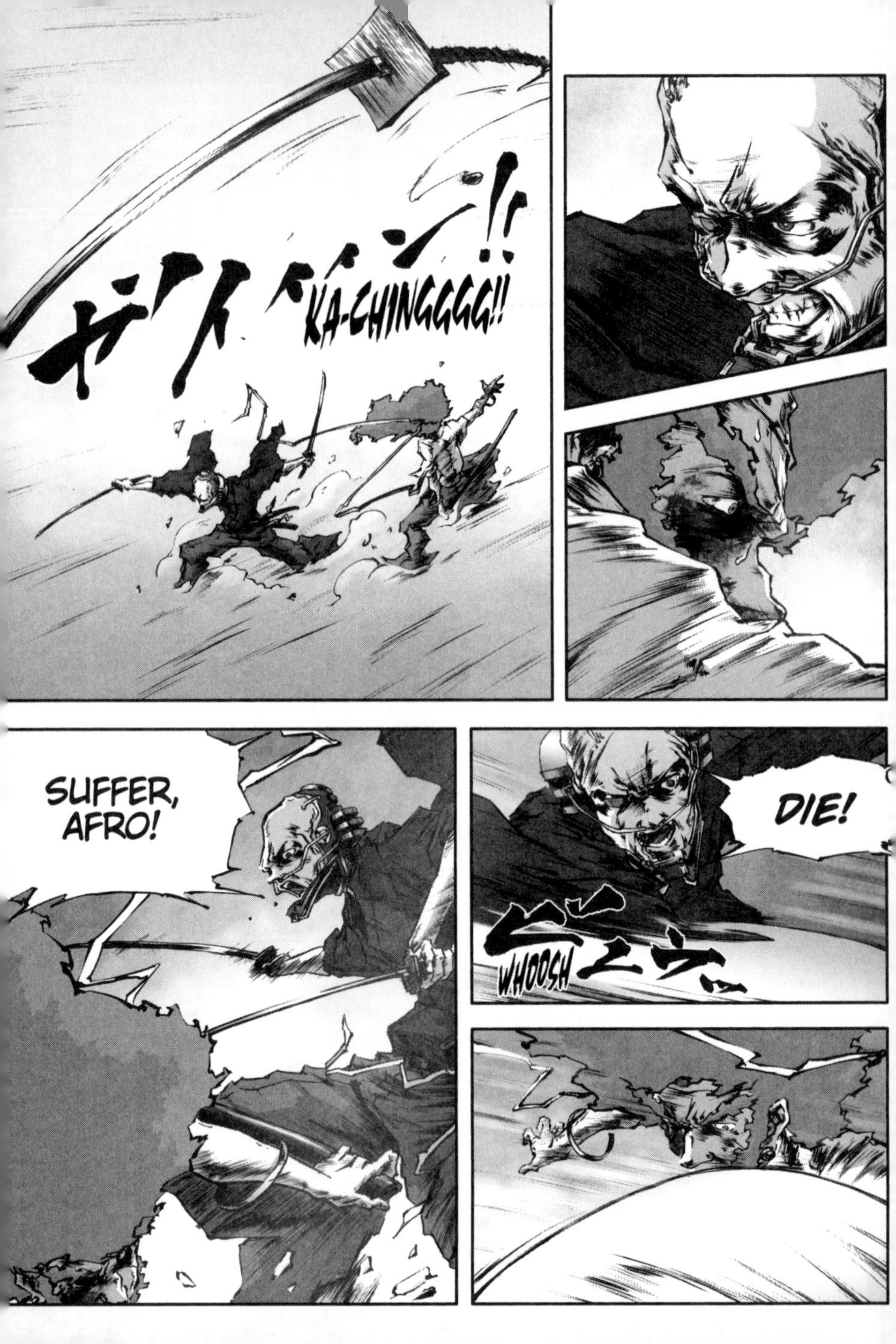
KA-CHINGGGG!!
SUFFER, AFRO!
DIE!
WHOOSH

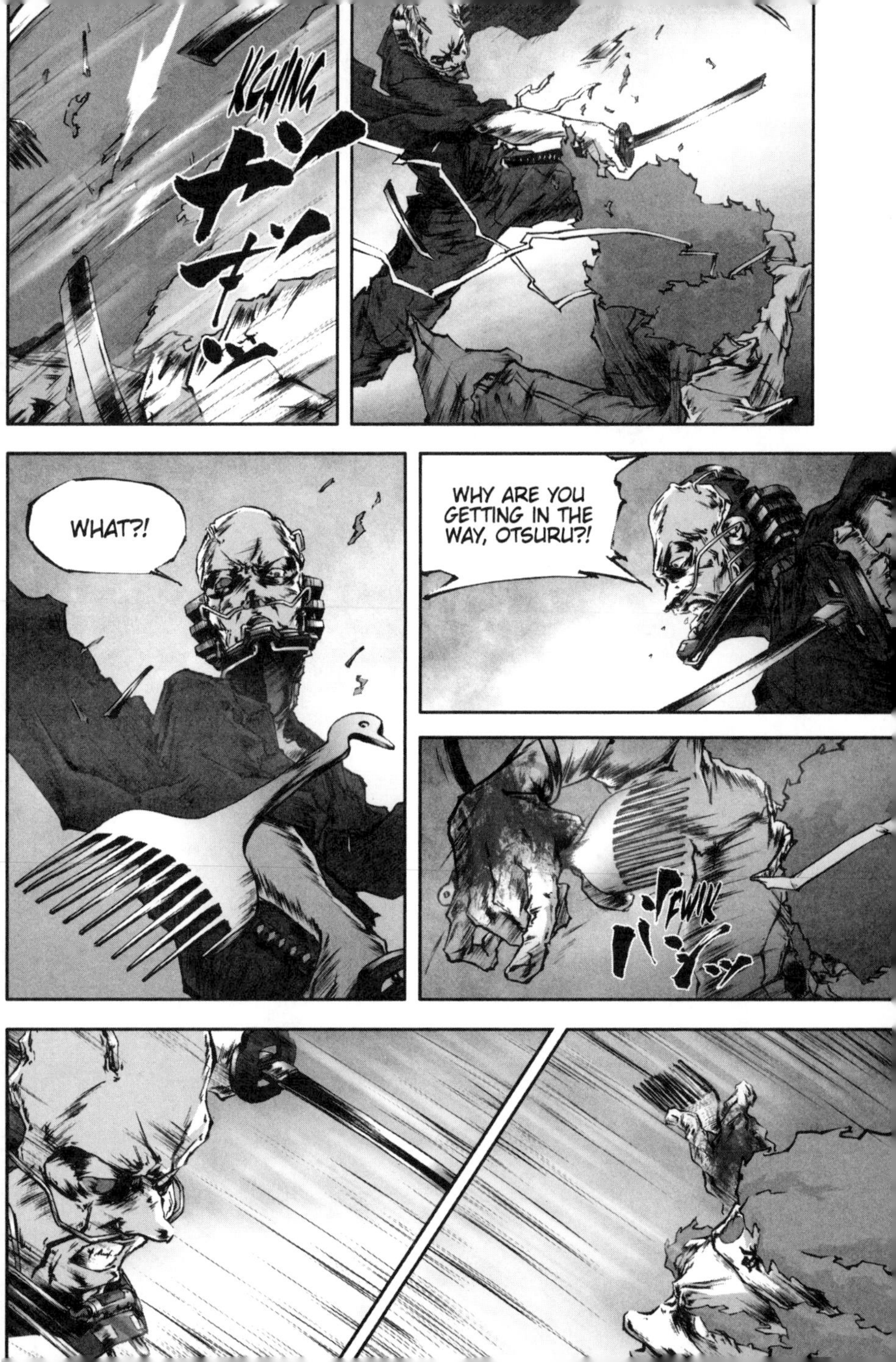
KCHING
WHAT?!
WHY ARE YOU GETTING IN THE WAY, OTSURU?!
PEWIK

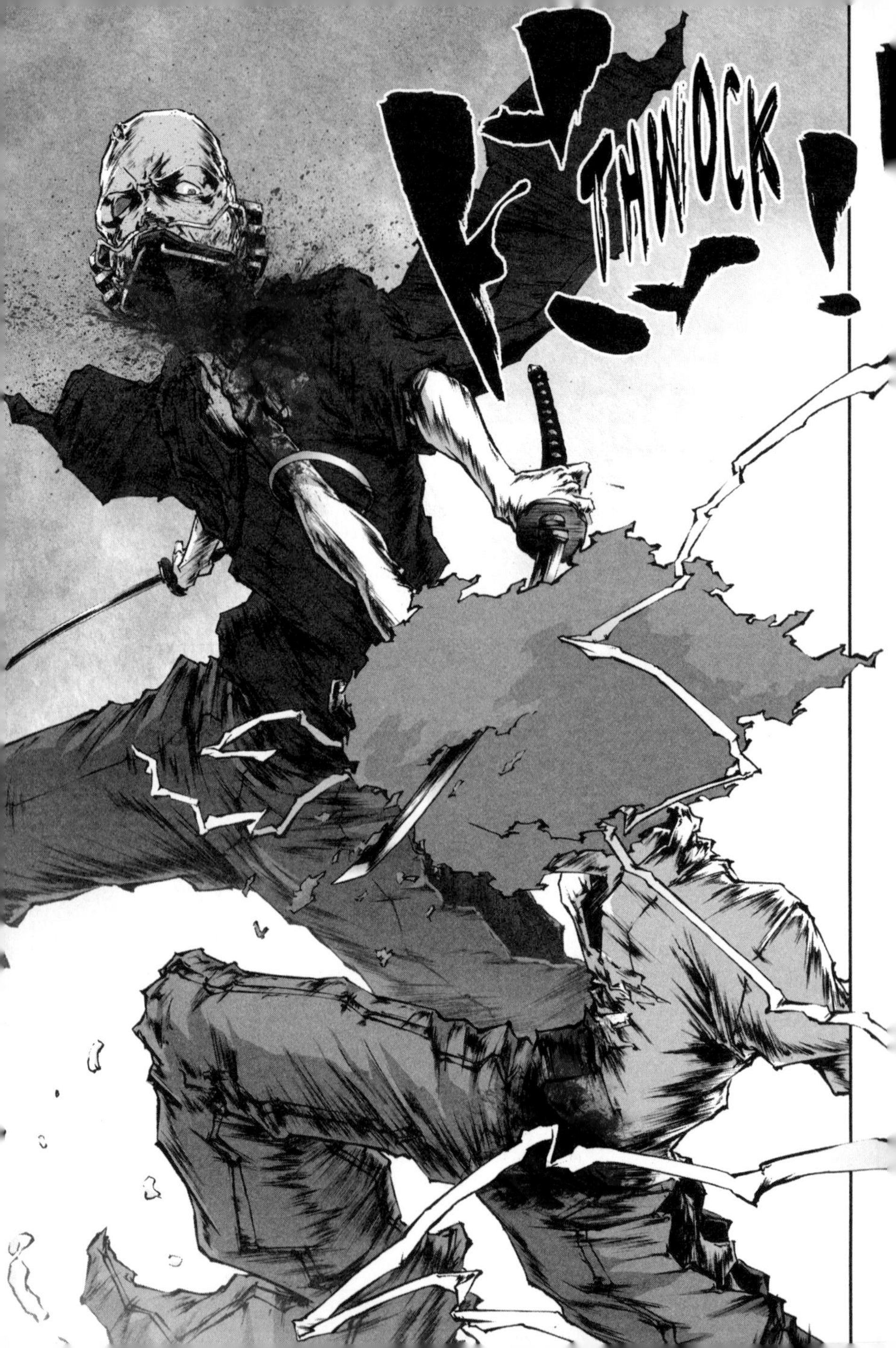
THWOCK

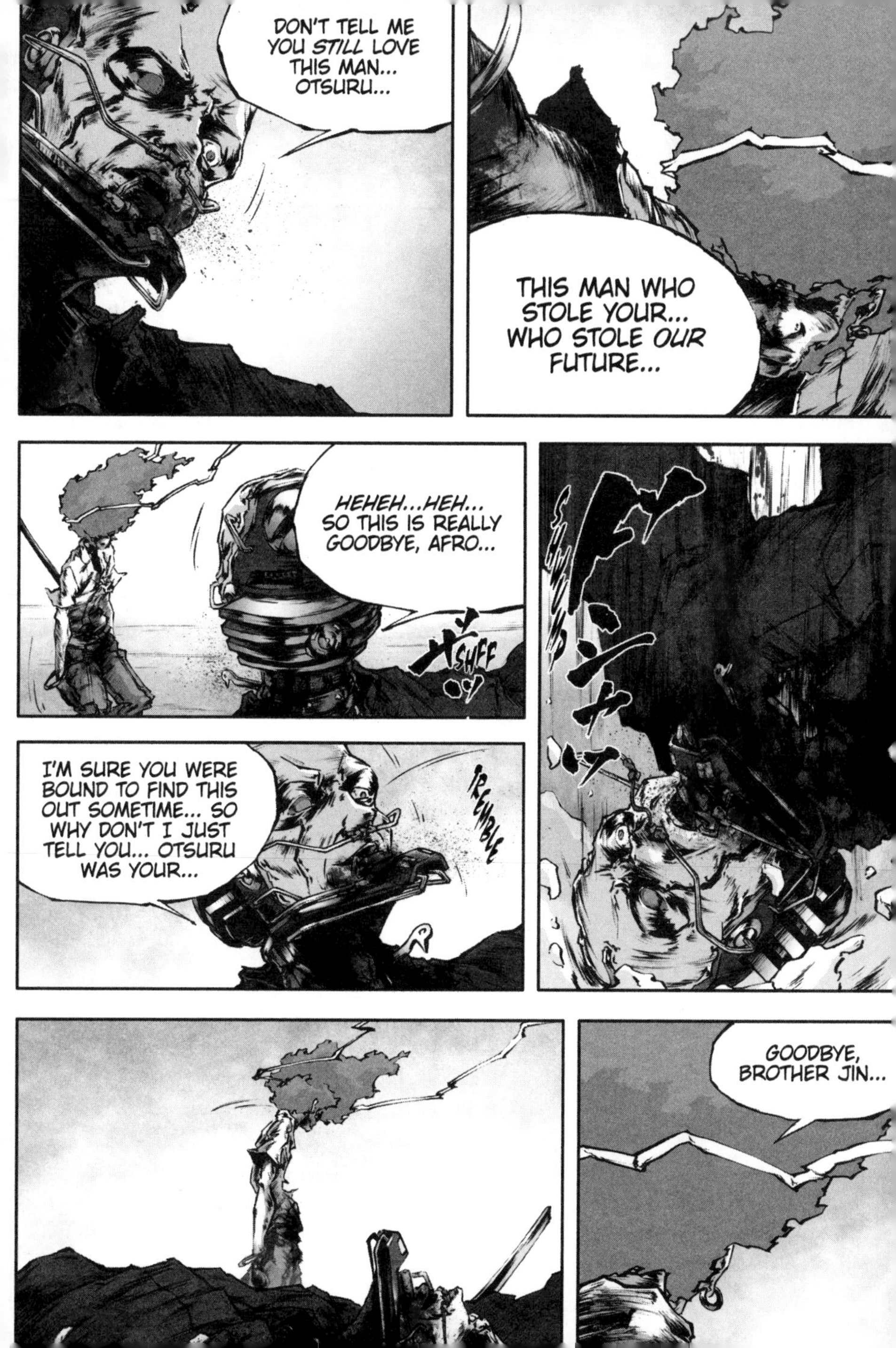
DON'T TELL ME YOU *STILL* LOVE THIS MAN... OTSURU...
THIS MAN WHO STOLE YOUR... WHO STOLE *OUR* FUTURE...
HEHEH...HEH... SO THIS IS REALLY GOODBYE, AFRO...
SHFF
I'M SURE YOU WERE BOUND TO FIND THIS OUT SOMETIME... SO WHY DON'T I JUST TELL YOU... OTSURU WAS YOUR...
TREMBLE
GOODBYE, BROTHER JIN...

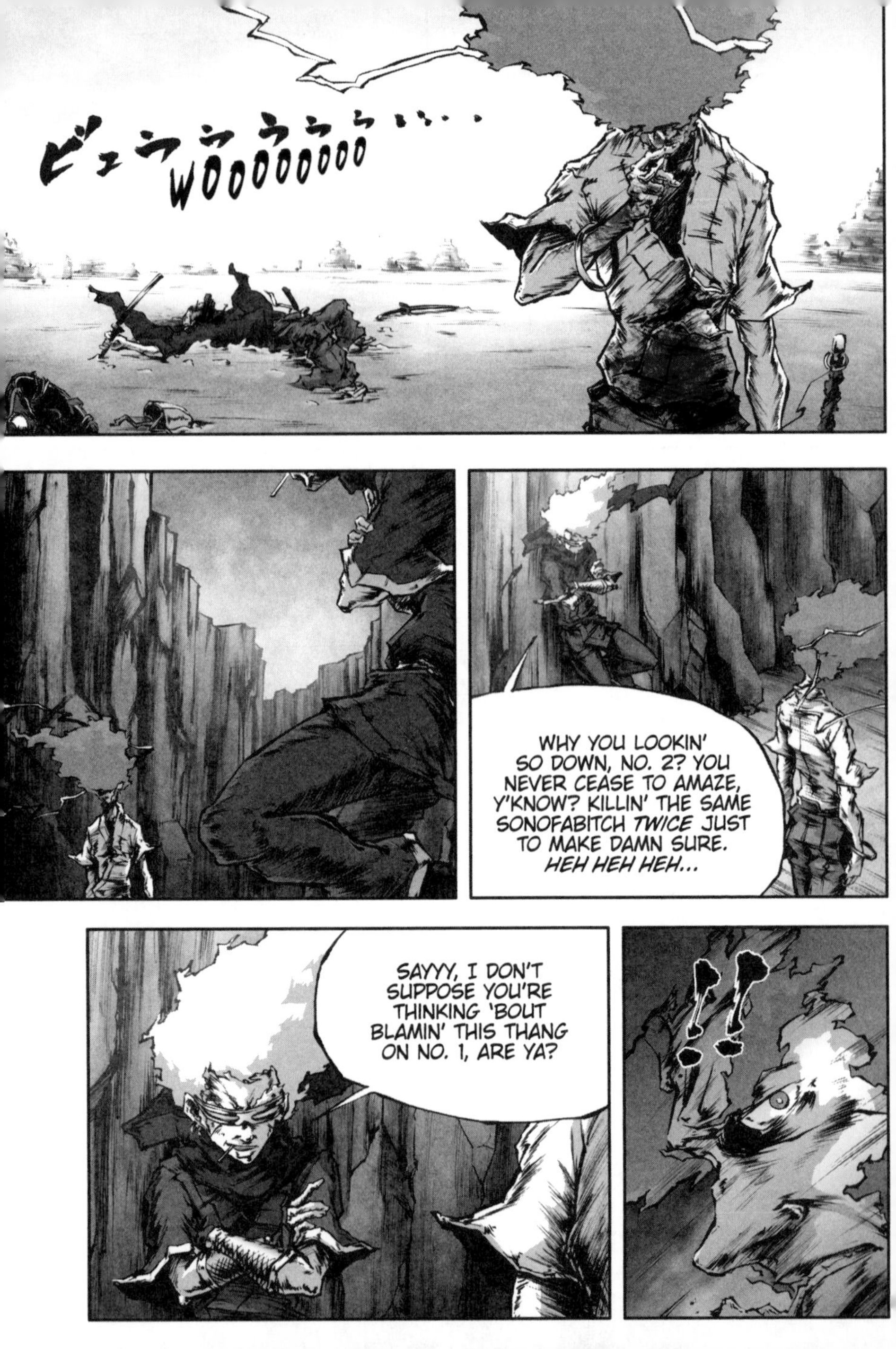

WOOOOOOOO
WHY YOU LOOKIN' SO DOWN, NO. 2? YOU NEVER CEASE TO AMAZE, Y'KNOW? KILLIN' THE SAME SONOFABITCH *TWICE* JUST TO MAKE DAMN SURE. *HEH HEH HEH...*
SAYYY, I DON'T SUPPOSE YOU'RE THINKING 'BOUT BLAMIN' THIS THANG ON NO. 1, ARE YA?
!!

HEH HEH... RIGHT ON THE MARK, HUH? YOU'RE WRONG, Y'KNOW. IF YOU ASK ME, THAT'S ALL A BIG BOWL A' *BULL.*

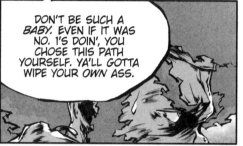

DON'T BE SUCH A *BABY.* EVEN IF IT WAS NO. 1'S DOIN', YOU CHOSE THIS PATH YOURSELF. YA'LL GOTTA WIPE YOUR *OWN* ASS.

SWOOSH

HEHEHEH, I JUST REMEMBERED WHY I HAVEN'T KILLED YOUR ASS YET. WE GOT *SHIT* TO DO, MAN. NOW PUT THAT KATANA AWAY WHERE IT BELONGS.

THE END OF ALL THIS NOISE IS RIGHT IN FRONT OF OUR EYES AND NOSES. NOW LET'S GET GOIN'. HEHEHEH.

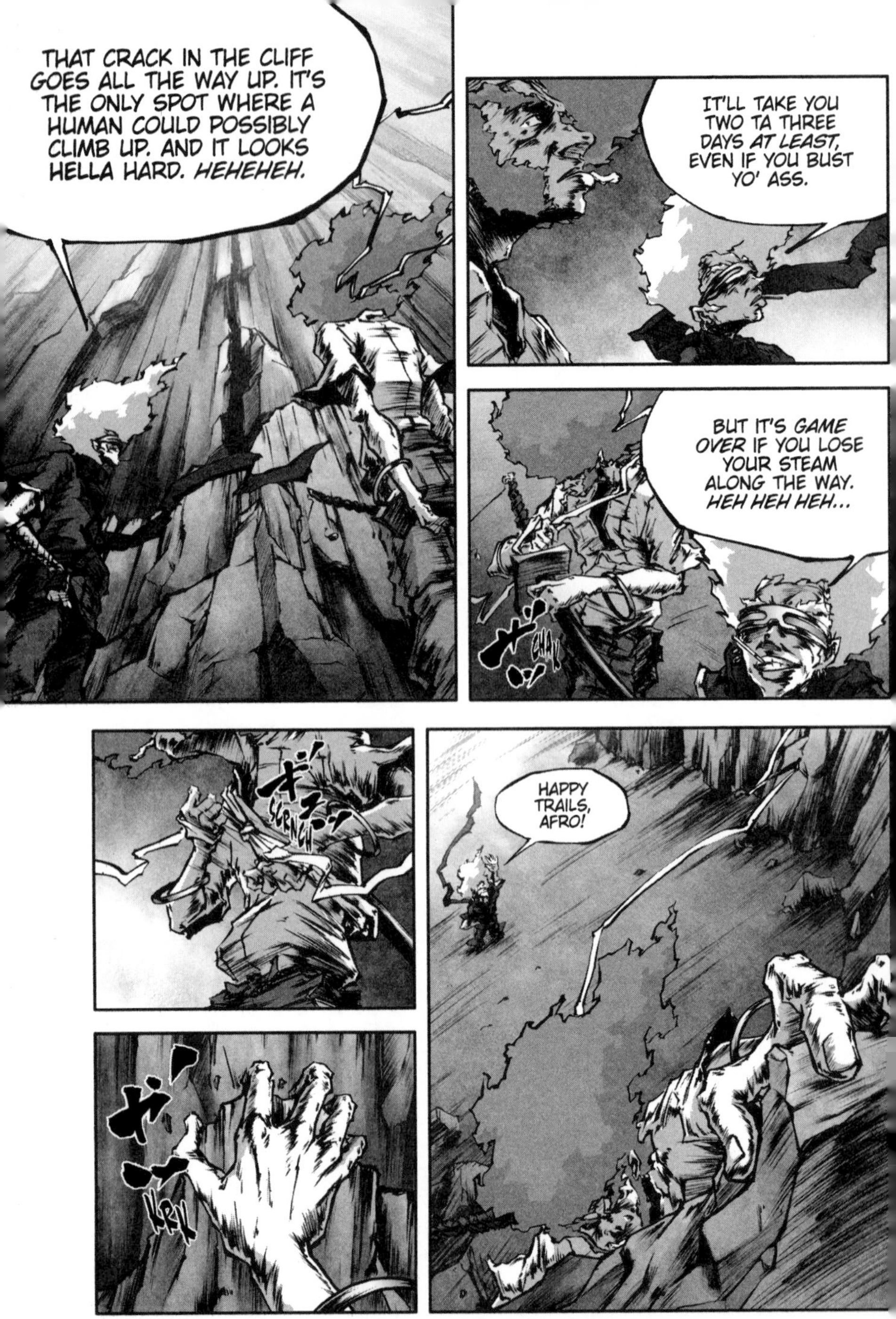
THAT CRACK IN THE CLIFF GOES ALL THE WAY UP. IT'S THE ONLY SPOT WHERE A HUMAN COULD POSSIBLY CLIMB UP. AND IT LOOKS HELLA HARD. *HEHEHEH.*
IT'LL TAKE YOU TWO TA THREE DAYS *AT LEAST,* EVEN IF YOU BUST YO' ASS.
BUT IT'S *GAME OVER* IF YOU LOSE YOUR STEAM ALONG THE WAY. *HEH HEH HEH...*
CHAK
SCRNCH
KRK
HAPPY TRAILS, AFRO!

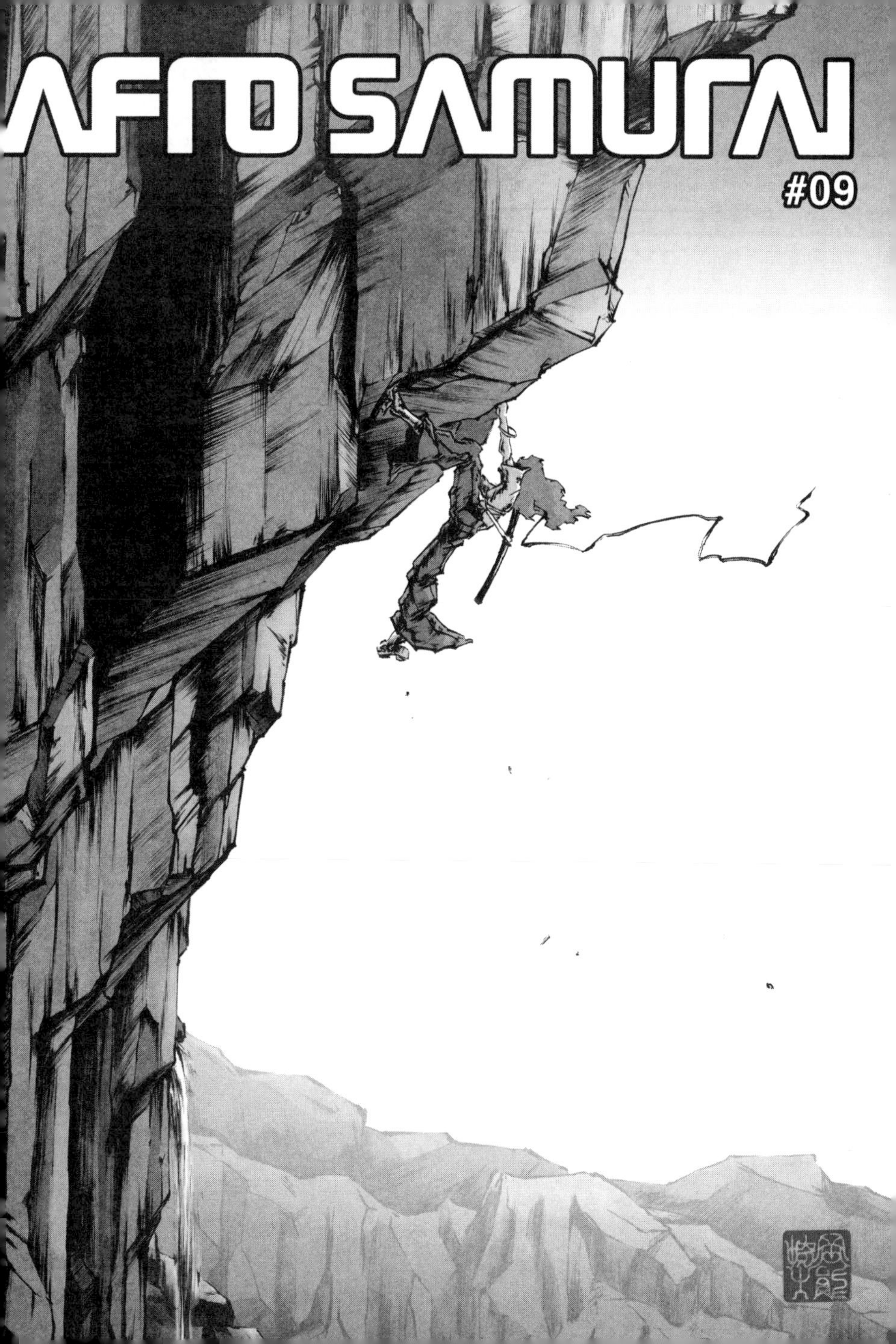
AFRO SAMURAI
#09

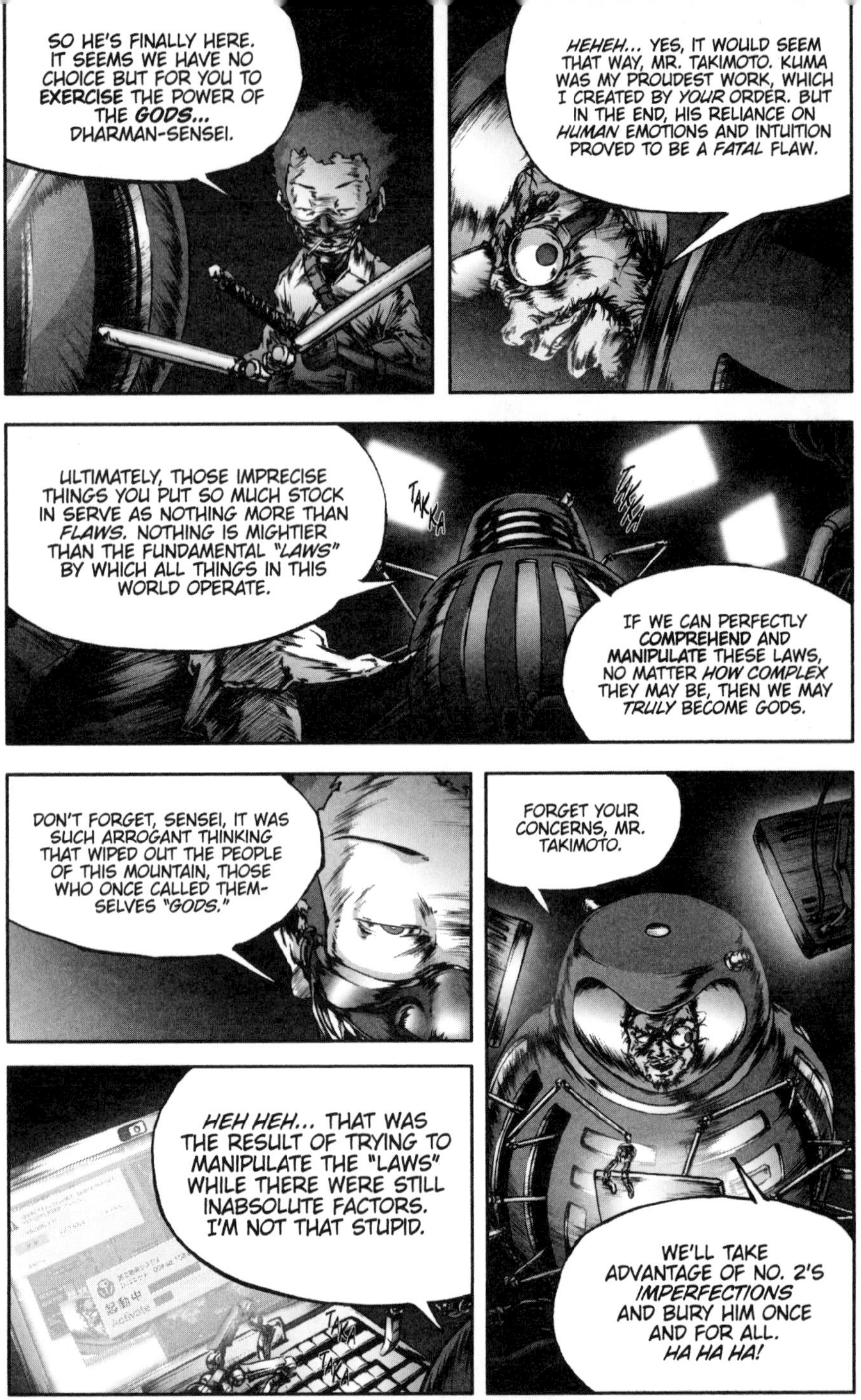
SO HE'S FINALLY HERE. IT SEEMS WE HAVE NO CHOICE BUT FOR YOU TO **EXERCISE** THE POWER OF THE ***GODS...*** DHARMAN-SENSEI.
HEHEH... YES, IT WOULD SEEM THAT WAY, MR. TAKIMOTO. KUMA WAS MY PROUDEST WORK, WHICH I CREATED BY *YOUR* ORDER. BUT IN THE END, HIS RELIANCE ON *HUMAN* EMOTIONS AND INTUITION PROVED TO BE A *FATAL* FLAW.
ULTIMATELY, THOSE IMPRECISE THINGS YOU PUT SO MUCH STOCK IN SERVE AS NOTHING MORE THAN *FLAWS.* NOTHING IS MIGHTIER THAN THE FUNDAMENTAL *"LAWS"* BY WHICH ALL THINGS IN THIS WORLD OPERATE.
TAKKA
TAKKA
IF WE CAN PERFECTLY **COMPREHEND** AND **MANIPULATE** THESE LAWS, NO MATTER *HOW COMPLEX* THEY MAY BE, THEN WE MAY *TRULY* BECOME GODS.
DON'T FORGET, SENSEI, IT WAS SUCH ARROGANT THINKING THAT WIPED OUT THE PEOPLE OF THIS MOUNTAIN, THOSE WHO ONCE CALLED THEM-SELVES *"GODS."*
HEH HEH... THAT WAS THE RESULT OF TRYING TO MANIPULATE THE "LAWS" WHILE THERE WERE STILL INABSOLUTE FACTORS. I'M NOT THAT STUPID.
起動中
Activate
TAKA
TAKA
FORGET YOUR CONCERNS, MR. TAKIMOTO.
WE'LL TAKE ADVANTAGE OF NO. 2'S *IMPERFECTIONS* AND BURY HIM ONCE AND FOR ALL. *HA HA HA!*

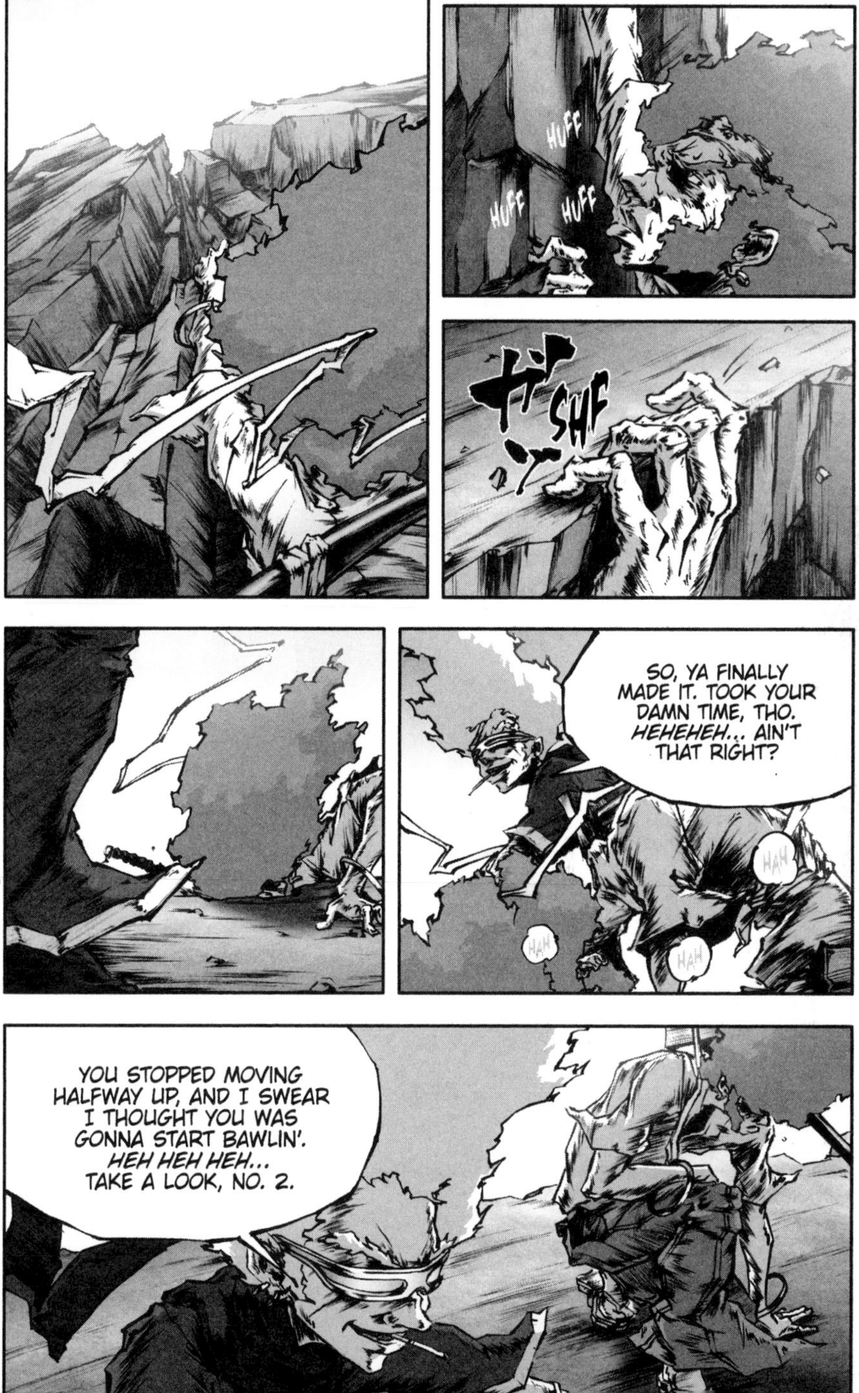
HUFF
HUFF
HUFF
SHF
SO, YA FINALLY MADE IT. TOOK YOUR DAMN TIME, THO. *HEHEHEH...* AIN'T THAT RIGHT?
HAH
HAH
HAH
YOU STOPPED MOVING HALFWAY UP, AND I SWEAR I THOUGHT YOU WAS GONNA START BAWLIN'. *HEH HEH HEH...* TAKE A LOOK, NO. 2.

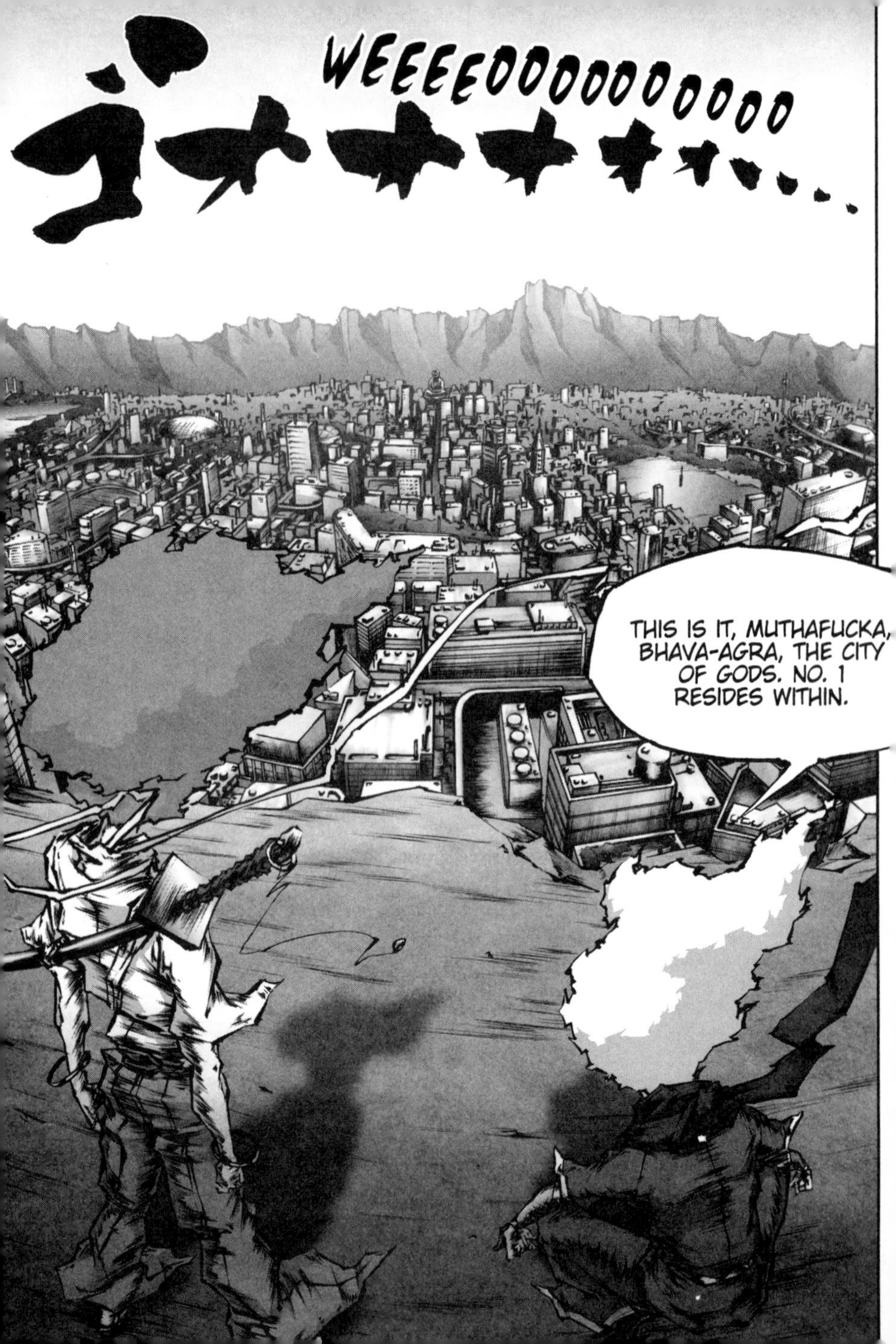
WEEEEOOOOOOOOOOO
ゴオオオオォぉ...
THIS IS IT, MUTHAFUCKA, BHAVA-AGRA, THE CITY OF GODS. NO. 1 RESIDES WITHIN.

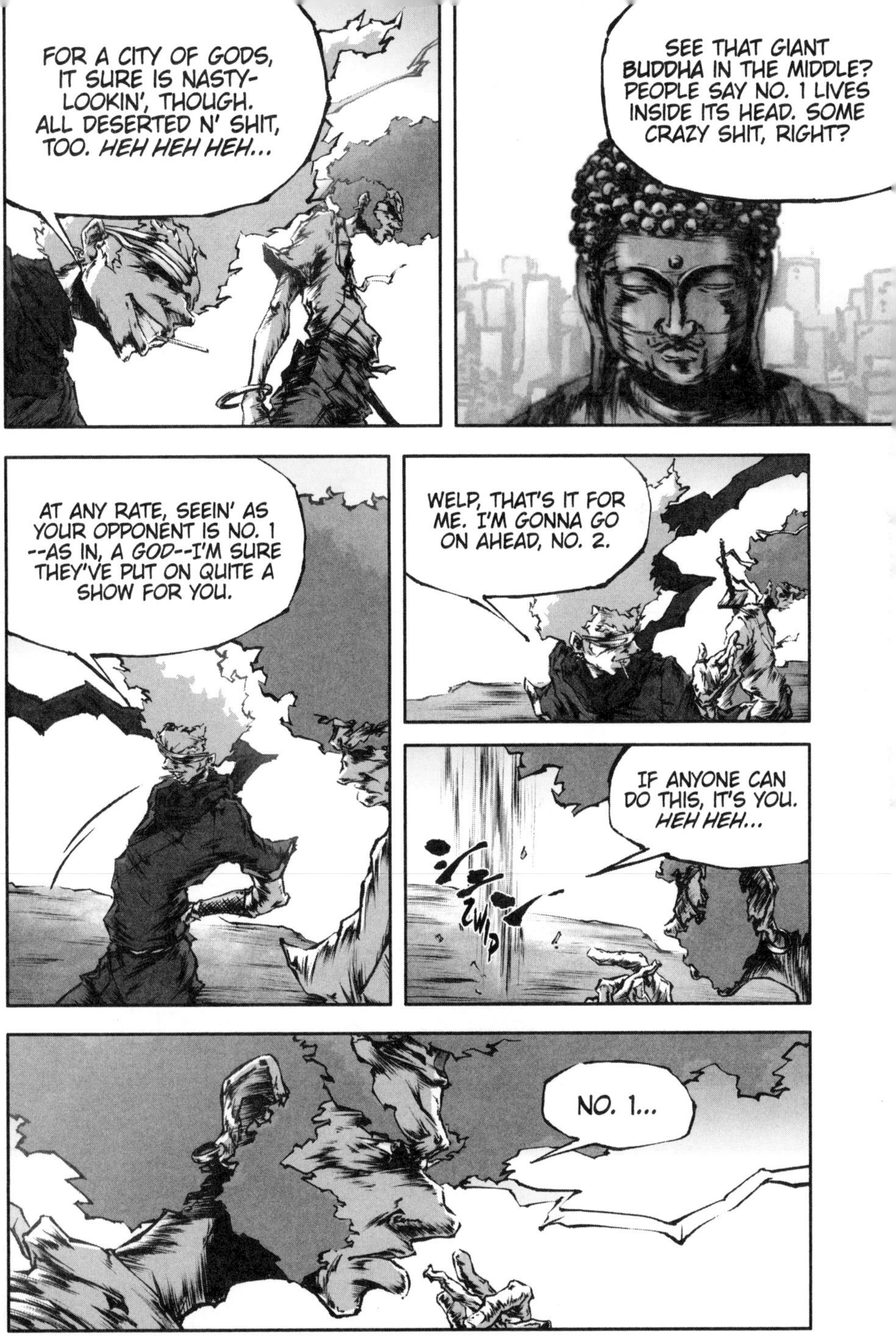
FOR A CITY OF GODS, IT SURE IS NASTY-LOOKIN', THOUGH. ALL DESERTED N' SHIT, TOO. *HEH HEH HEH...*
SEE THAT GIANT BUDDHA IN THE MIDDLE? PEOPLE SAY NO. 1 LIVES INSIDE ITS HEAD. SOME CRAZY SHIT, RIGHT?
AT ANY RATE, SEEIN' AS YOUR OPPONENT IS NO. 1 --AS IN, A *GOD*--I'M SURE THEY'VE PUT ON QUITE A SHOW FOR YOU.
WELP, THAT'S IT FOR ME. I'M GONNA GO ON AHEAD, NO. 2.
IF ANYONE CAN DO THIS, IT'S YOU. *HEH HEH...*
ZWIP
NO. 1...

VWEEEE . . . .

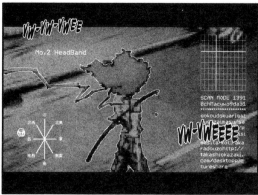

VW-VW-VWEE

No.2 HeadBand

SCAN MODE 1391
@chitacywo9da31

gokoudokuarigat
ou...zaimasu'sa
...si
...si
@asita.kotihaka
radouzhttp://
takashiokazaki.
com/desktoppic
tureshare

VW-VWEEEE

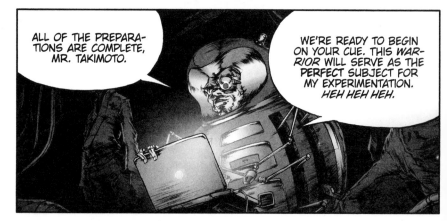

ALL OF THE PREPARA-
TIONS ARE COMPLETE,
MR. TAKIMOTO.

WE'RE READY TO BEGIN
ON YOUR CUE. THIS *WAR-
RIOR* WILL SERVE AS THE
PERFECT SUBJECT FOR
MY EXPERIMENTATION.
HEH HEH HEH.

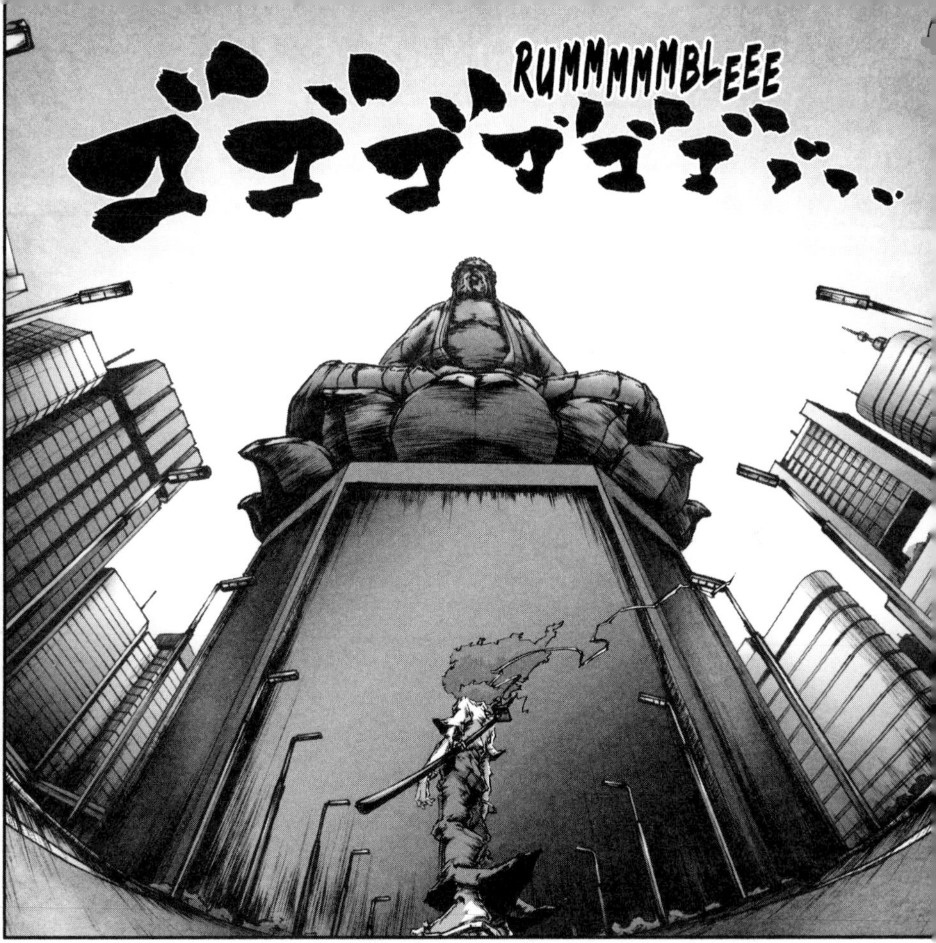
RUMMMMMBLEEE

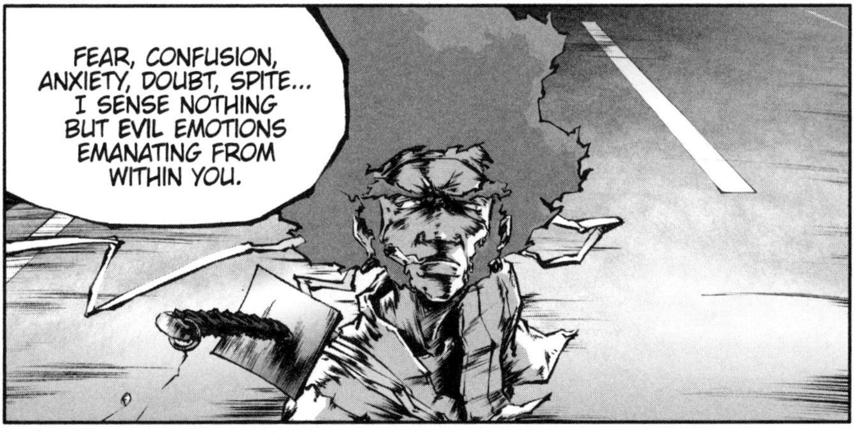
FEAR, CONFUSION, ANXIETY, DOUBT, SPITE... I SENSE NOTHING BUT EVIL EMOTIONS EMANATING FROM WITHIN YOU.

A MAN SUCH AS YOURSELF CAN'T BE ENTRUSTED WITH THE WHOLE WORLD.

I COULD KILL YOU NOW, BUT... YOU'VE MADE IT SO FAR, WHY DON'T I GIVE YOU A CHANCE? *IF* YOU'LL ACCEPT MY TERMS, THAT IS.

WHOOSH

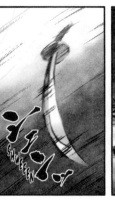

SHHINGGGNN

KEENG

TMP

HEH HEH... YOU'RE JUST LIKE A MAD DOG. I KNOW YOU'RE EXCITED, BUT YOU SHOULD AT LEAST *HEAR* PEOPLE OUT WHEN THEY HAVE SOMETHING TO SAY, NO. 2.

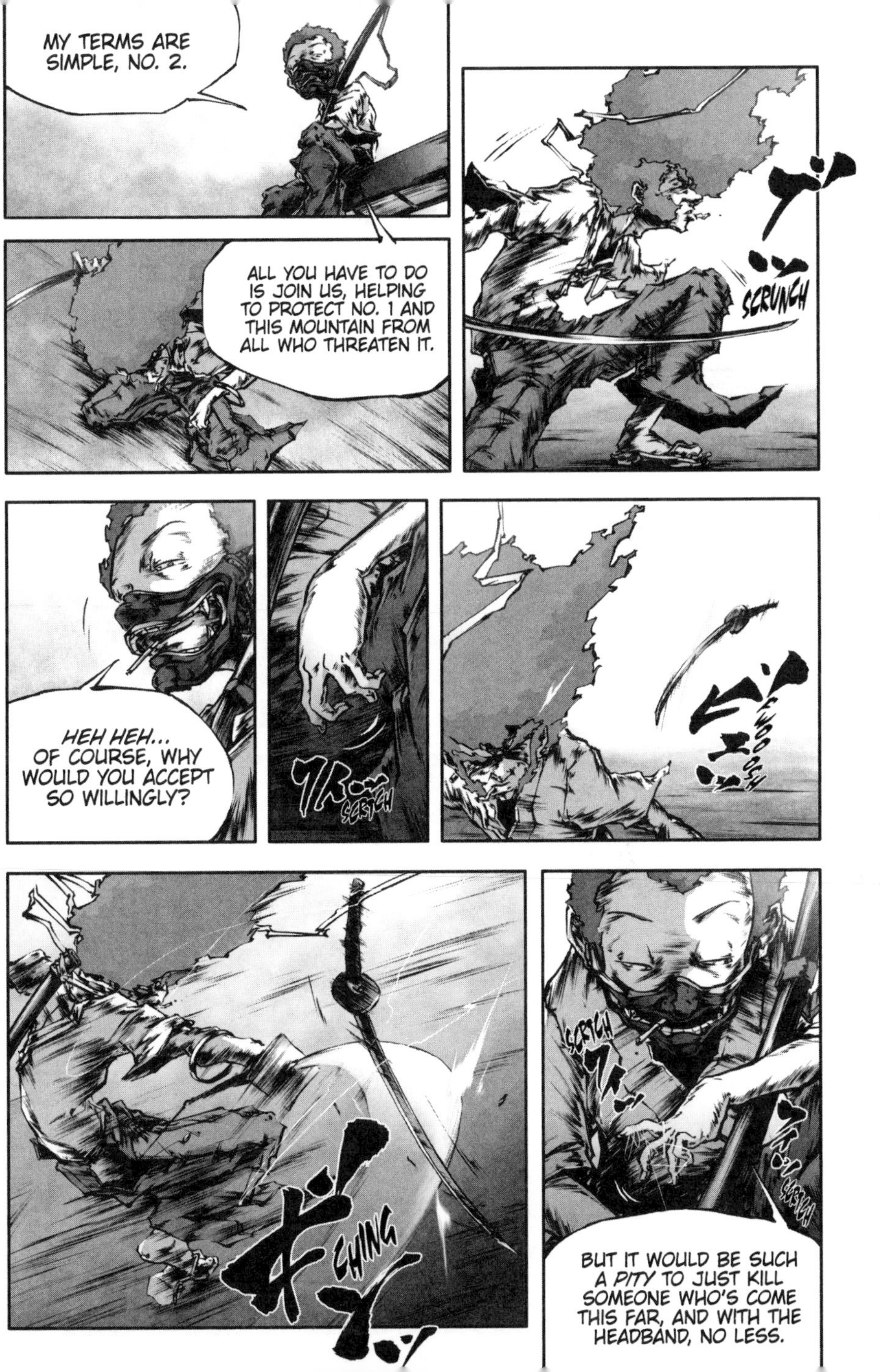
MY TERMS ARE SIMPLE, NO. 2.
ALL YOU HAVE TO DO IS JOIN US, HELPING TO PROTECT NO. 1 AND THIS MOUNTAIN FROM ALL WHO THREATEN IT.
SCRUNCH
HEH HEH... OF COURSE, WHY WOULD YOU ACCEPT SO WILLINGLY?
SCRTCH
FWOOOSH
CHING
SCRTCH
SCRTCH
BUT IT WOULD BE SUCH A *PITY* TO JUST KILL SOMEONE WHO'S COME THIS FAR, AND WITH THE HEADBAND, NO LESS.

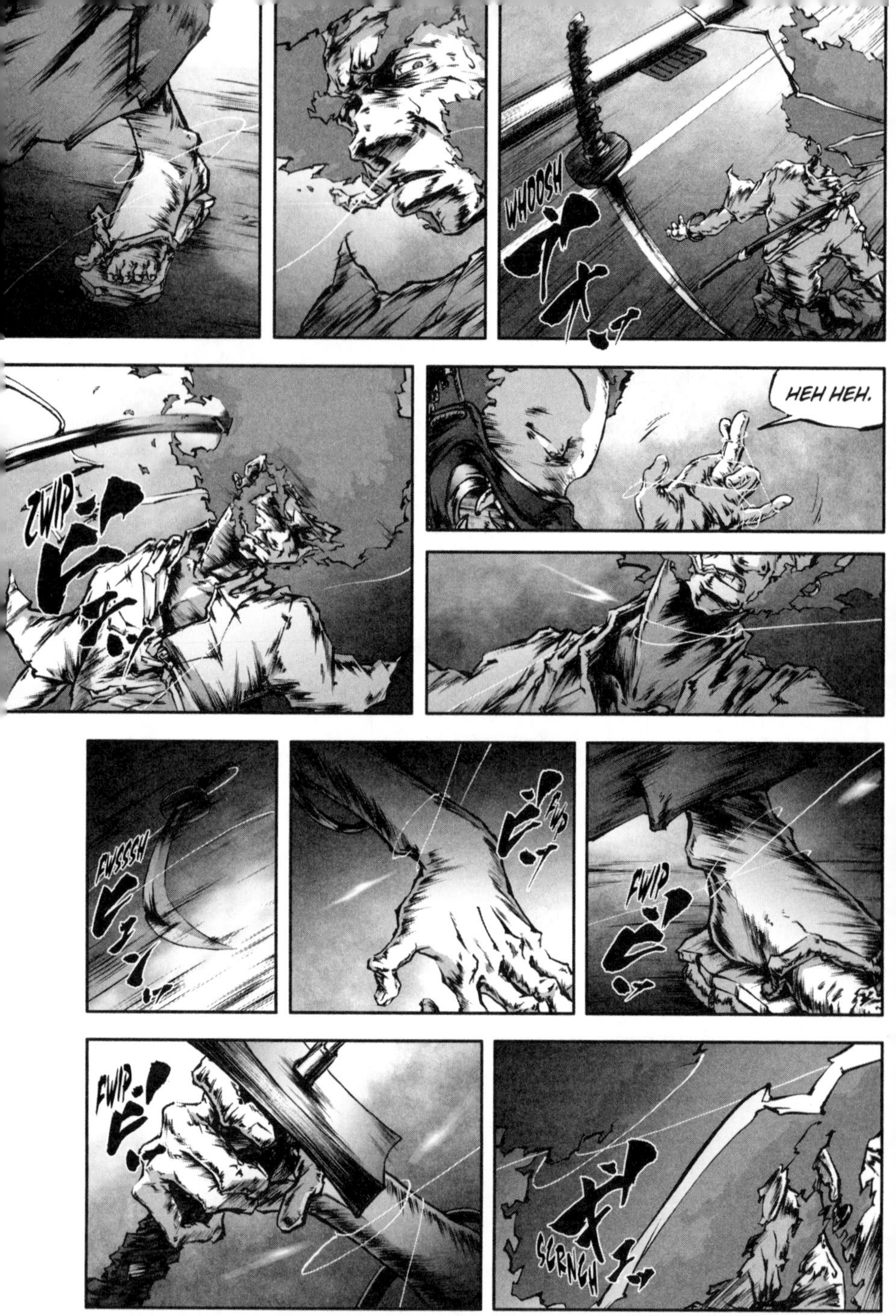
WHOOSH
ZWIP
HEH HEH.
FWSSSH
FWIP
FWIP
FWIP
SCRNCH

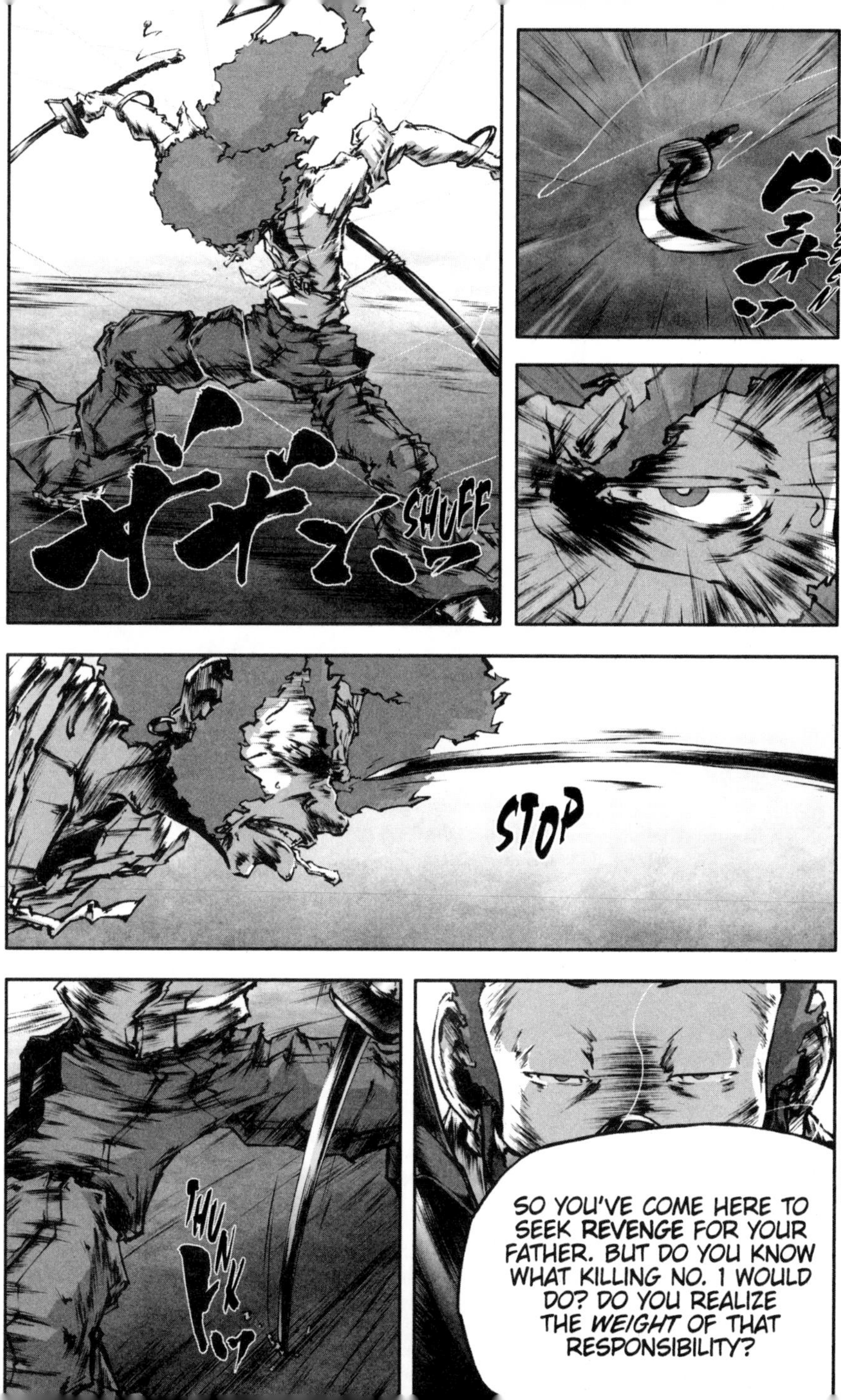
SHUFF
STOP
THUNK
SO YOU'VE COME HERE TO SEEK REVENGE FOR YOUR FATHER. BUT DO YOU KNOW WHAT KILLING NO. 1 WOULD DO? DO YOU REALIZE THE *WEIGHT* OF THAT RESPONSIBILITY?

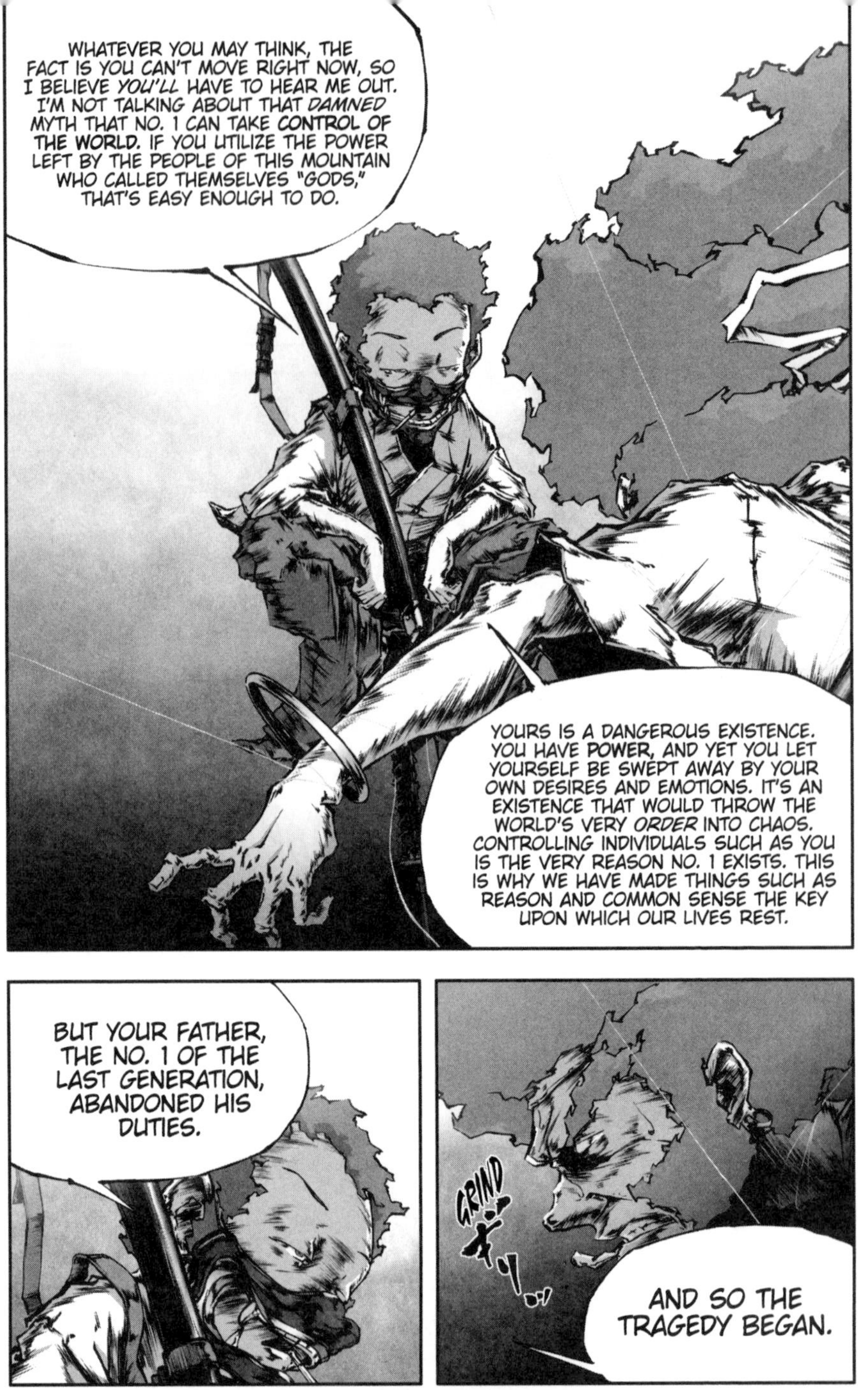

WHATEVER YOU MAY THINK, THE FACT IS YOU CAN'T MOVE RIGHT NOW, SO I BELIEVE YOU'LL HAVE TO HEAR ME OUT. I'M NOT TALKING ABOUT THAT DAMNED MYTH THAT NO. 1 CAN TAKE CONTROL OF THE WORLD. IF YOU UTILIZE THE POWER LEFT BY THE PEOPLE OF THIS MOUNTAIN WHO CALLED THEMSELVES "GODS," THAT'S EASY ENOUGH TO DO.
YOURS IS A DANGEROUS EXISTENCE. YOU HAVE POWER, AND YET YOU LET YOURSELF BE SWEPT AWAY BY YOUR OWN DESIRES AND EMOTIONS. IT'S AN EXISTENCE THAT WOULD THROW THE WORLD'S VERY ORDER INTO CHAOS. CONTROLLING INDIVIDUALS SUCH AS YOU IS THE VERY REASON NO. 1 EXISTS. THIS IS WHY WE HAVE MADE THINGS SUCH AS REASON AND COMMON SENSE THE KEY UPON WHICH OUR LIVES REST.
BUT YOUR FATHER, THE NO. 1 OF THE LAST GENERATION, ABANDONED HIS DUTIES.
GRIND
AND SO THE TRAGEDY BEGAN.

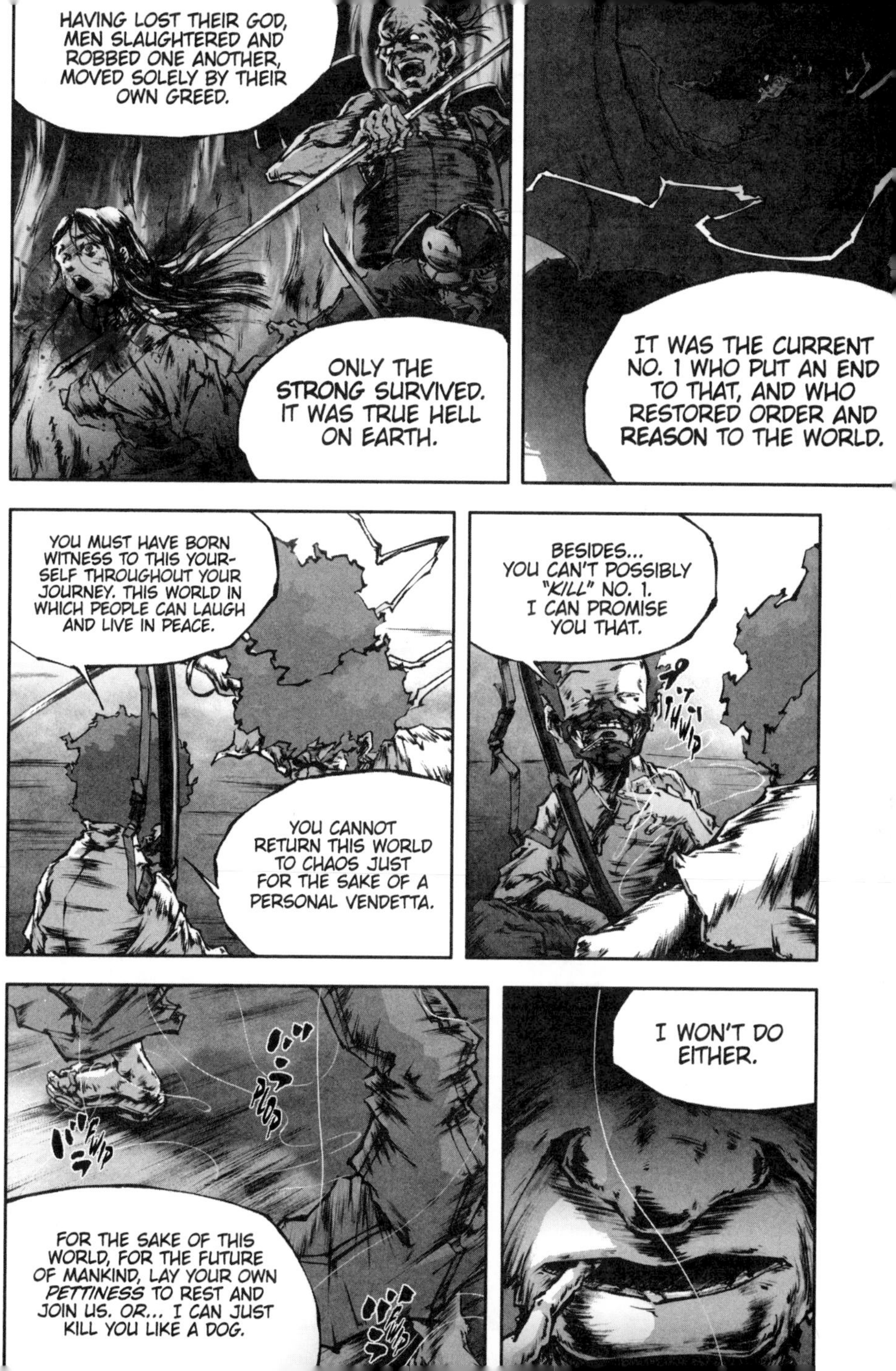
HAVING LOST THEIR GOD, MEN SLAUGHTERED AND ROBBED ONE ANOTHER, MOVED SOLELY BY THEIR OWN GREED.
ONLY THE STRONG SURVIVED. IT WAS TRUE HELL ON EARTH.
IT WAS THE CURRENT NO. 1 WHO PUT AN END TO THAT, AND WHO RESTORED ORDER AND REASON TO THE WORLD.
YOU MUST HAVE BORN WITNESS TO THIS YOUR-SELF THROUGHOUT YOUR JOURNEY. THIS WORLD IN WHICH PEOPLE CAN LAUGH AND LIVE IN PEACE.
YOU CANNOT RETURN THIS WORLD TO CHAOS JUST FOR THE SAKE OF A PERSONAL VENDETTA.
BESIDES... YOU CAN'T POSSIBLY *"KILL"* NO. 1. I CAN PROMISE YOU THAT.
THWIP
PLOP
FWIP
FOR THE SAKE OF THIS WORLD, FOR THE FUTURE OF MANKIND, LAY YOUR OWN *PETTINESS* TO REST AND JOIN US. OR... I CAN JUST KILL YOU LIKE A DOG.
FWIP
I WON'T DO EITHER.

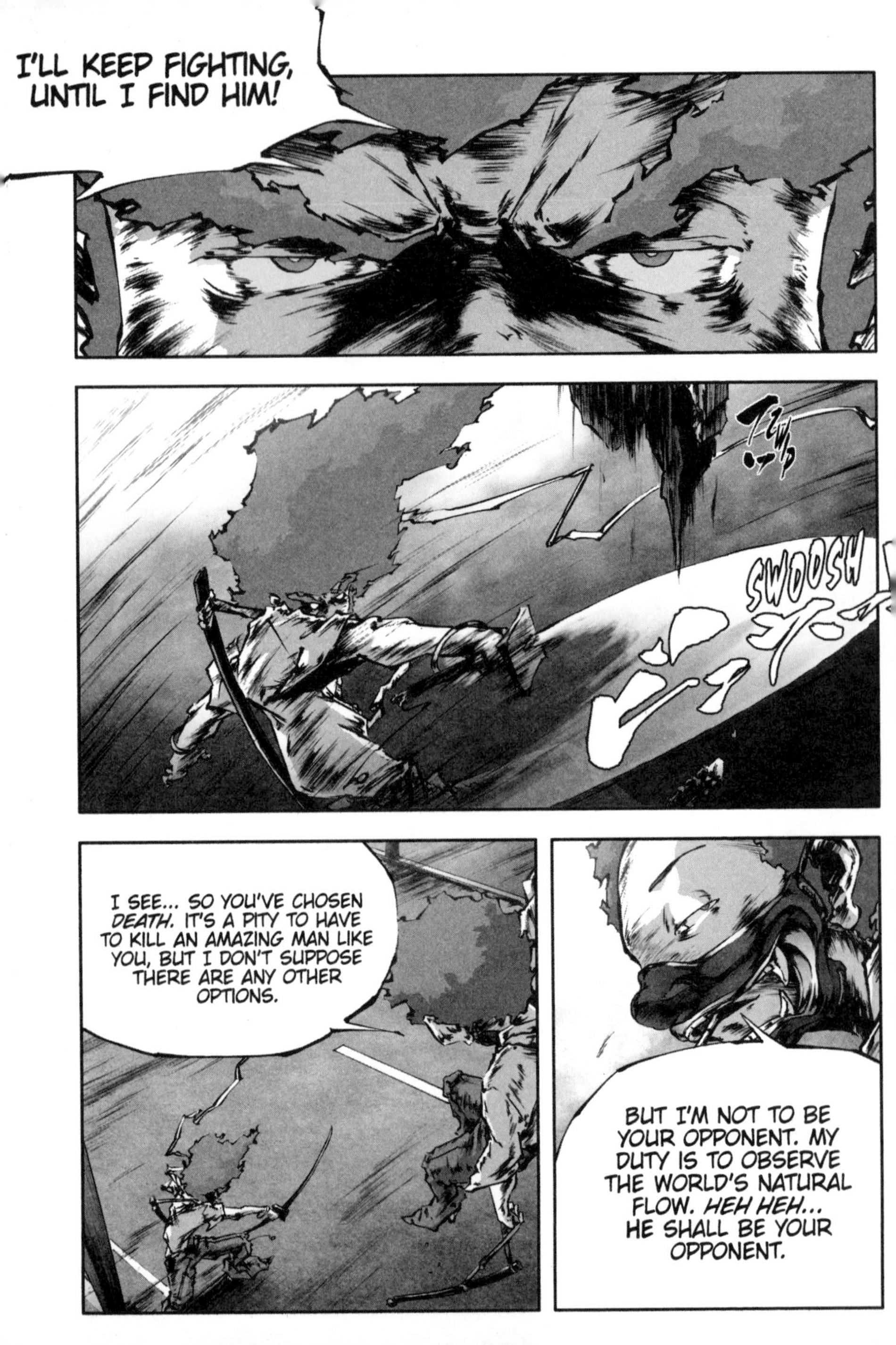
I'LL KEEP FIGHTING, UNTIL I FIND HIM!
SWOOSH
I SEE... SO YOU'VE CHOSEN *DEATH*. IT'S A PITY TO HAVE TO KILL AN AMAZING MAN LIKE YOU, BUT I DON'T SUPPOSE THERE ARE ANY OTHER OPTIONS.
BUT I'M NOT TO BE YOUR OPPONENT. MY DUTY IS TO OBSERVE THE WORLD'S NATURAL FLOW. *HEH HEH...* HE SHALL BE YOUR OPPONENT.

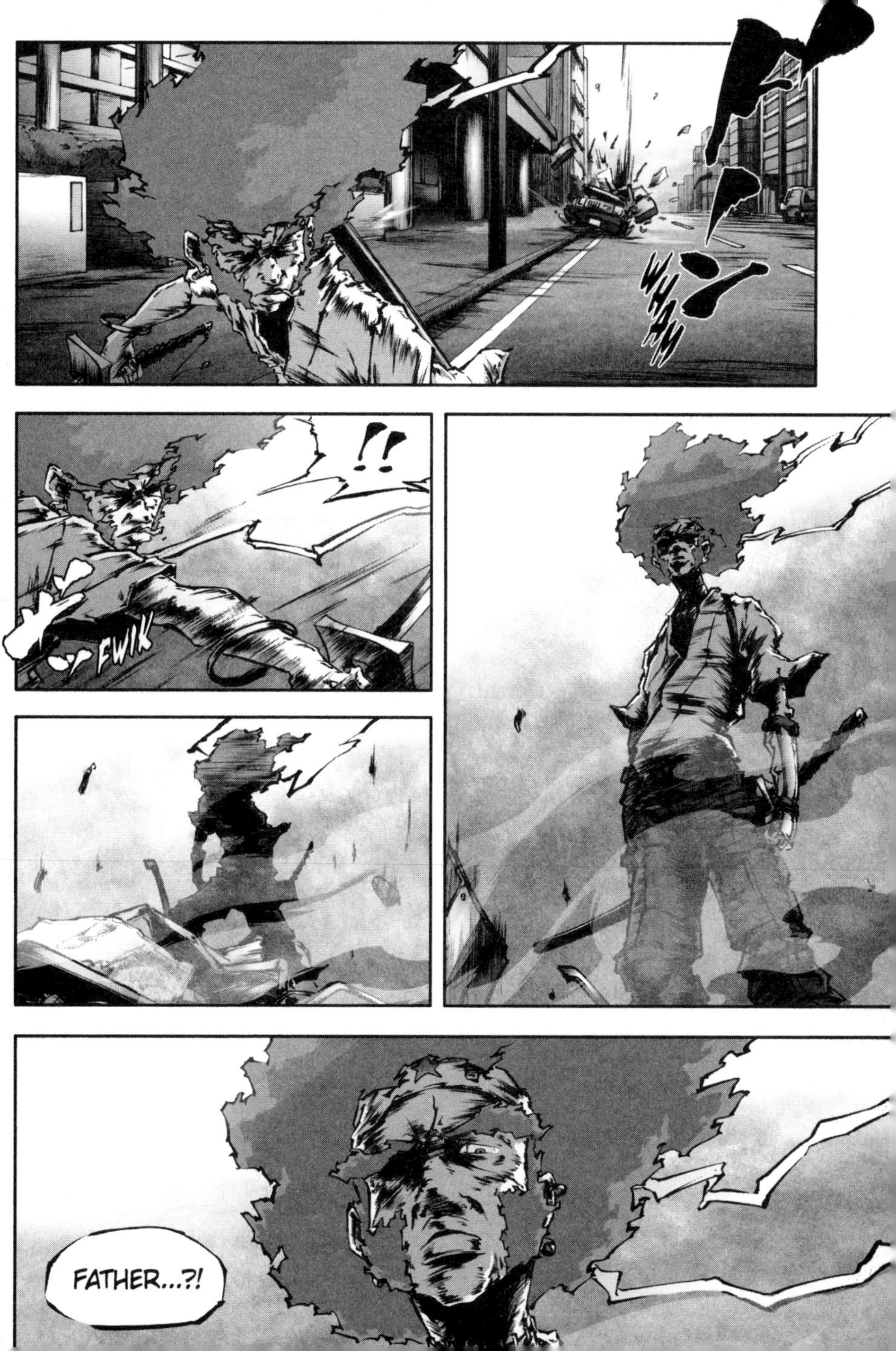
WHAM
!!
FWIK
FATHER...?!

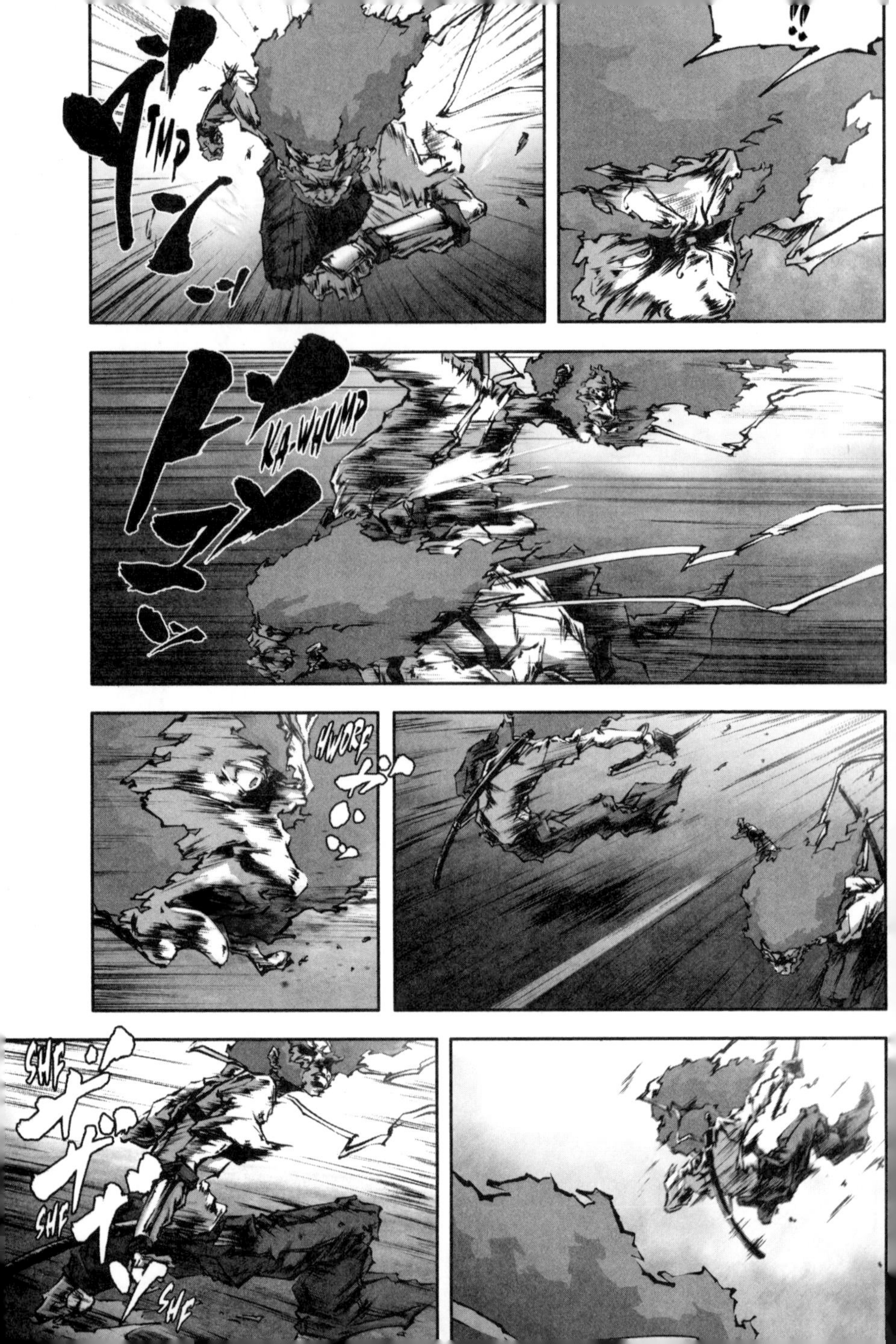
TMP
!!
KA-WHUMP
HWORF
SHF
SHF
SHF

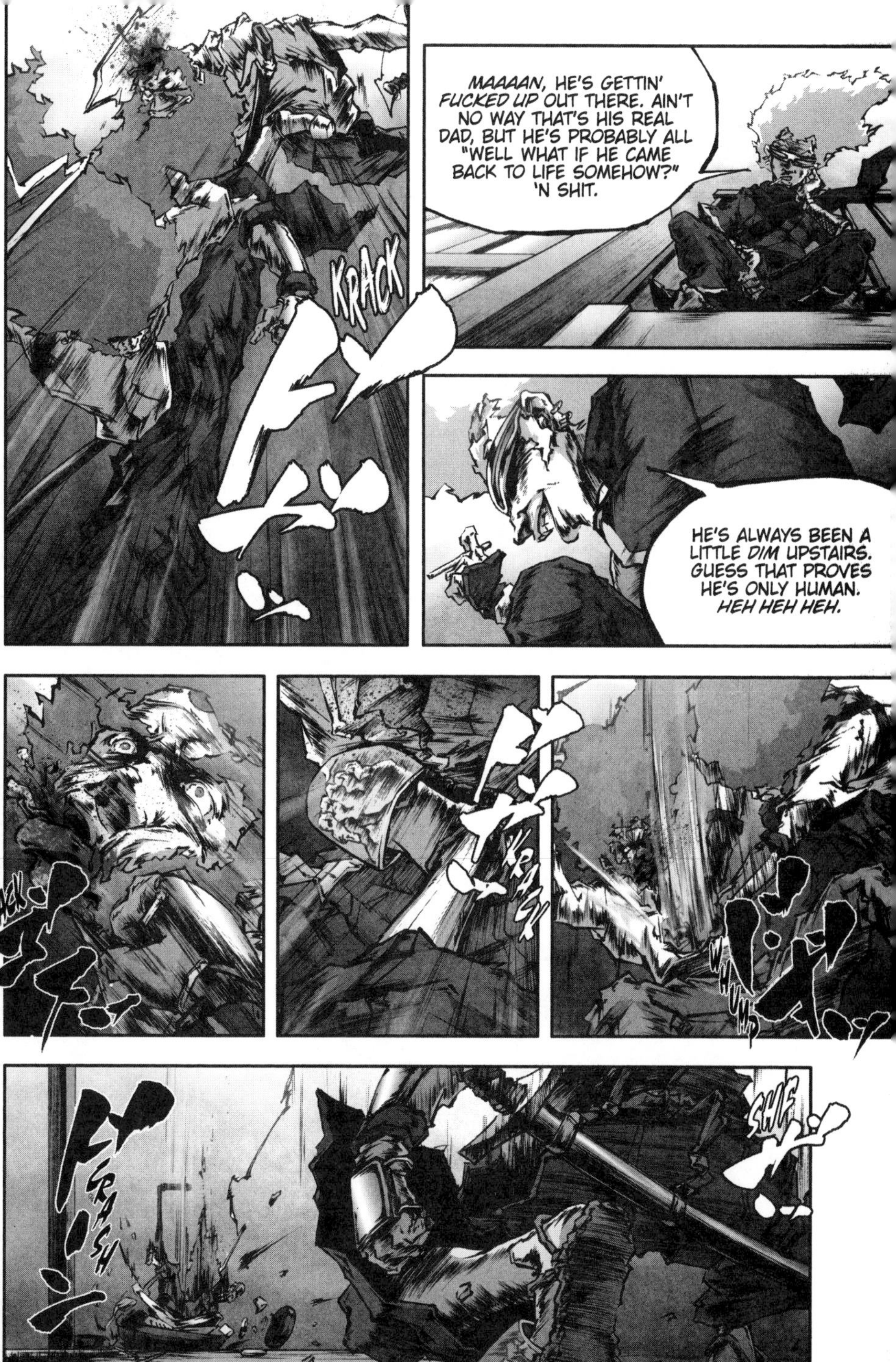
KRACK
MAAAAN, HE'S GETTIN' *FUCKED UP* OUT THERE. AIN'T NO WAY THAT'S HIS REAL DAD, BUT HE'S PROBABLY ALL "WELL WHAT IF HE CAME BACK TO LIFE SOMEHOW?" 'N SHIT.
HE'S ALWAYS BEEN A LITTLE *DIM* UPSTAIRS. GUESS THAT PROVES HE'S ONLY HUMAN. *HEH HEH HEH.*
HACK
KRASH
WHUMP
CRASH
SHIF

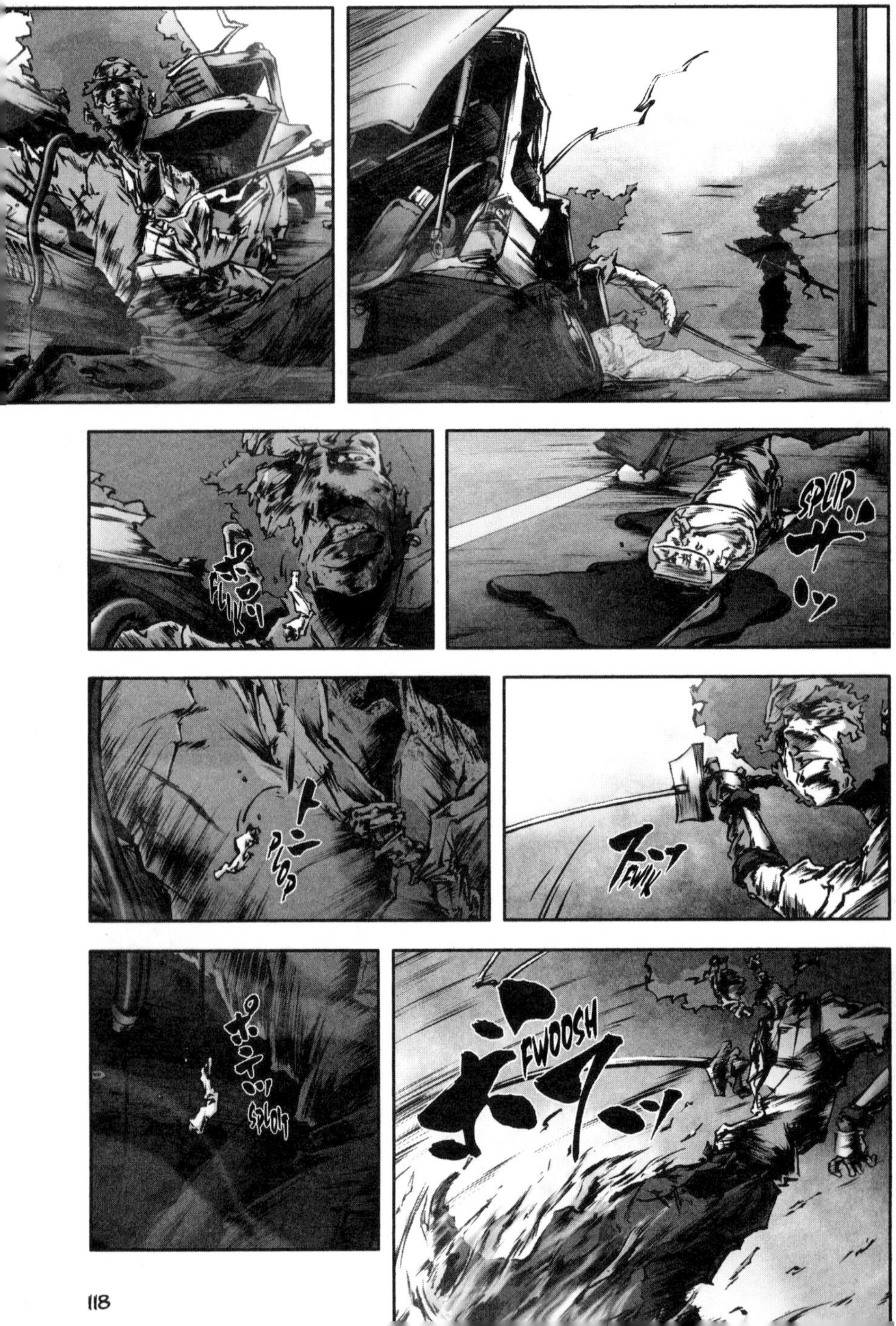
SPLIP
PLOP
FWIK
FWOOSH

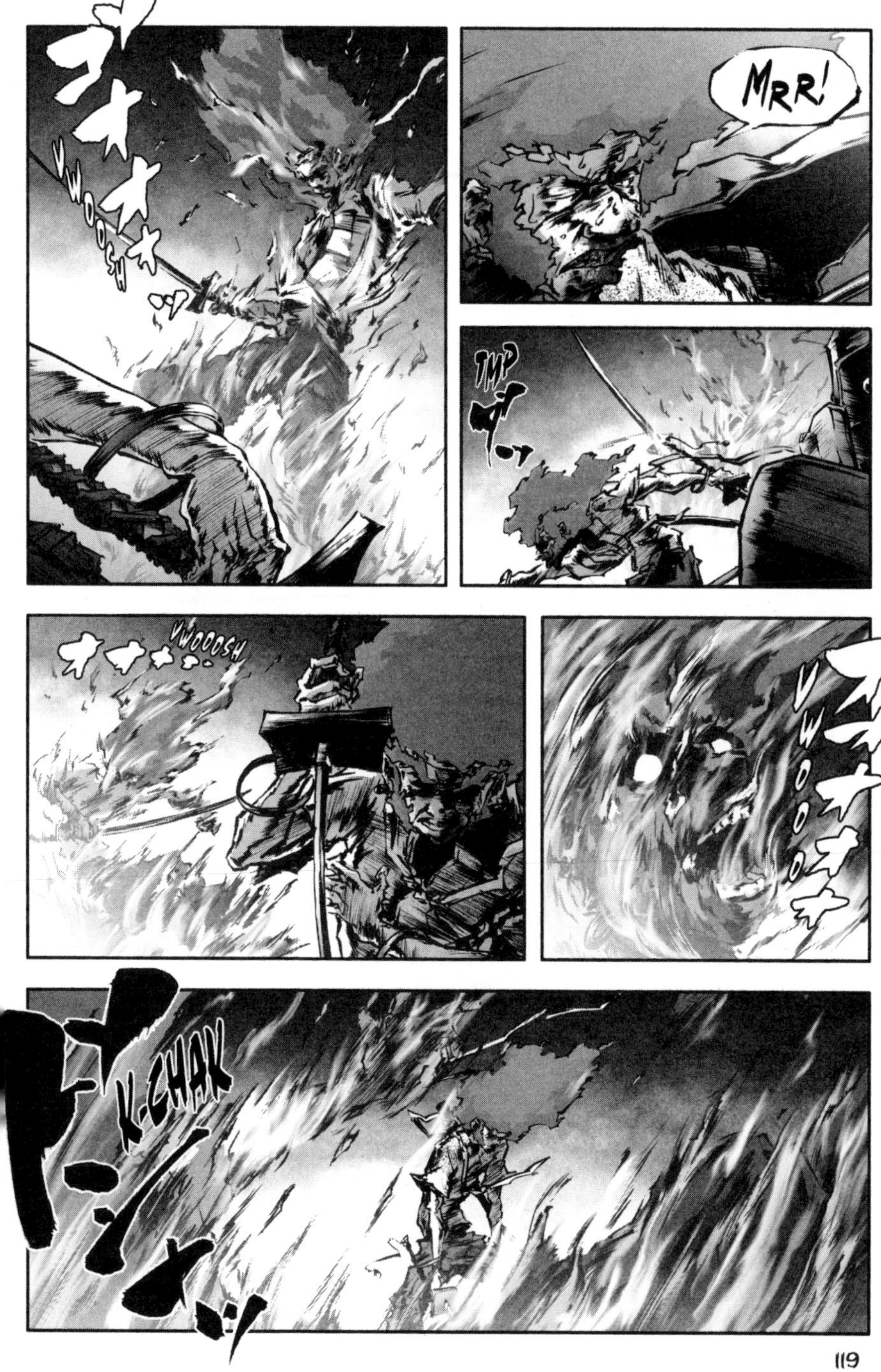
MRR!
VWOOSH
TMP
VWOOOSH
VWOOO
K-CHAK

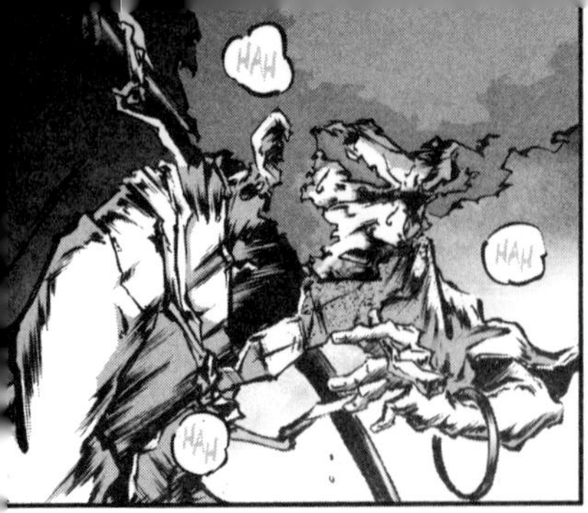
HAH
HAH
HAH
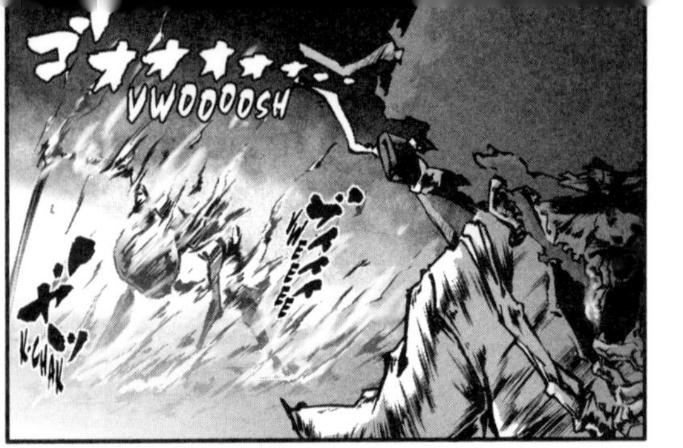
VWOOOOSH
K-CHAK
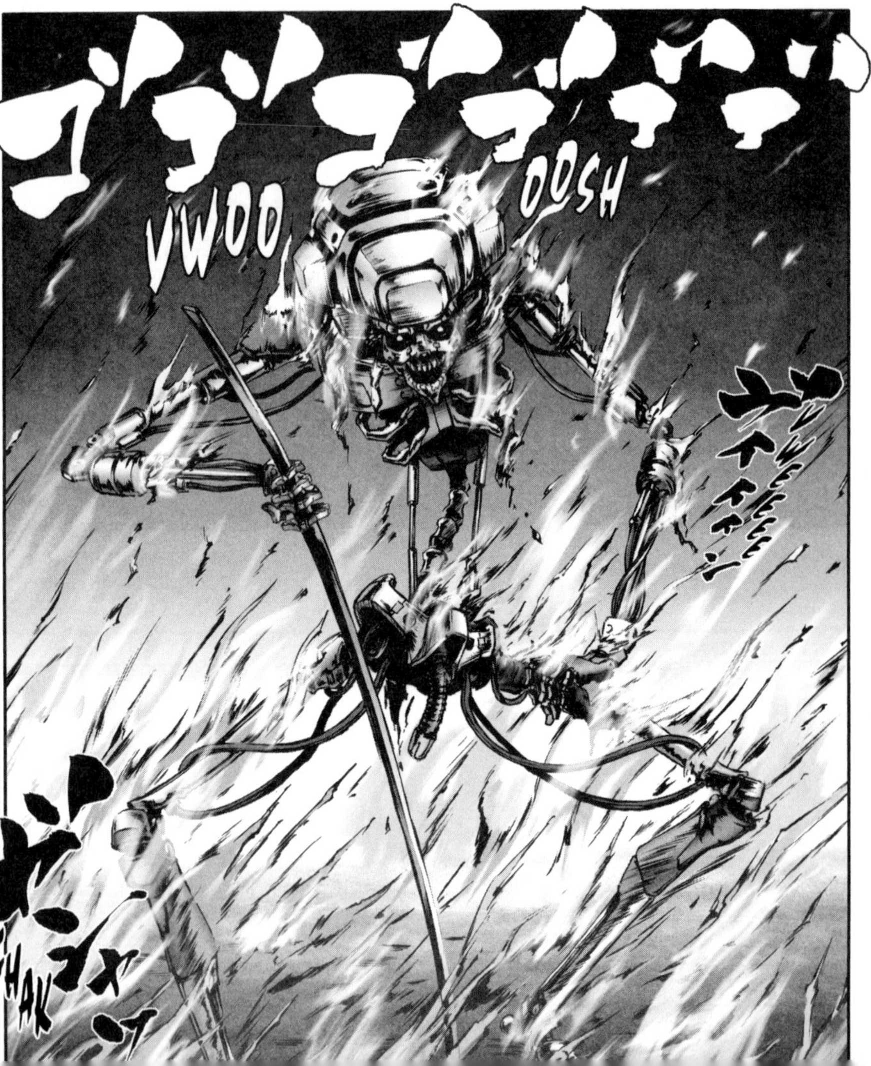
VWOOOOSH
K-CHAK

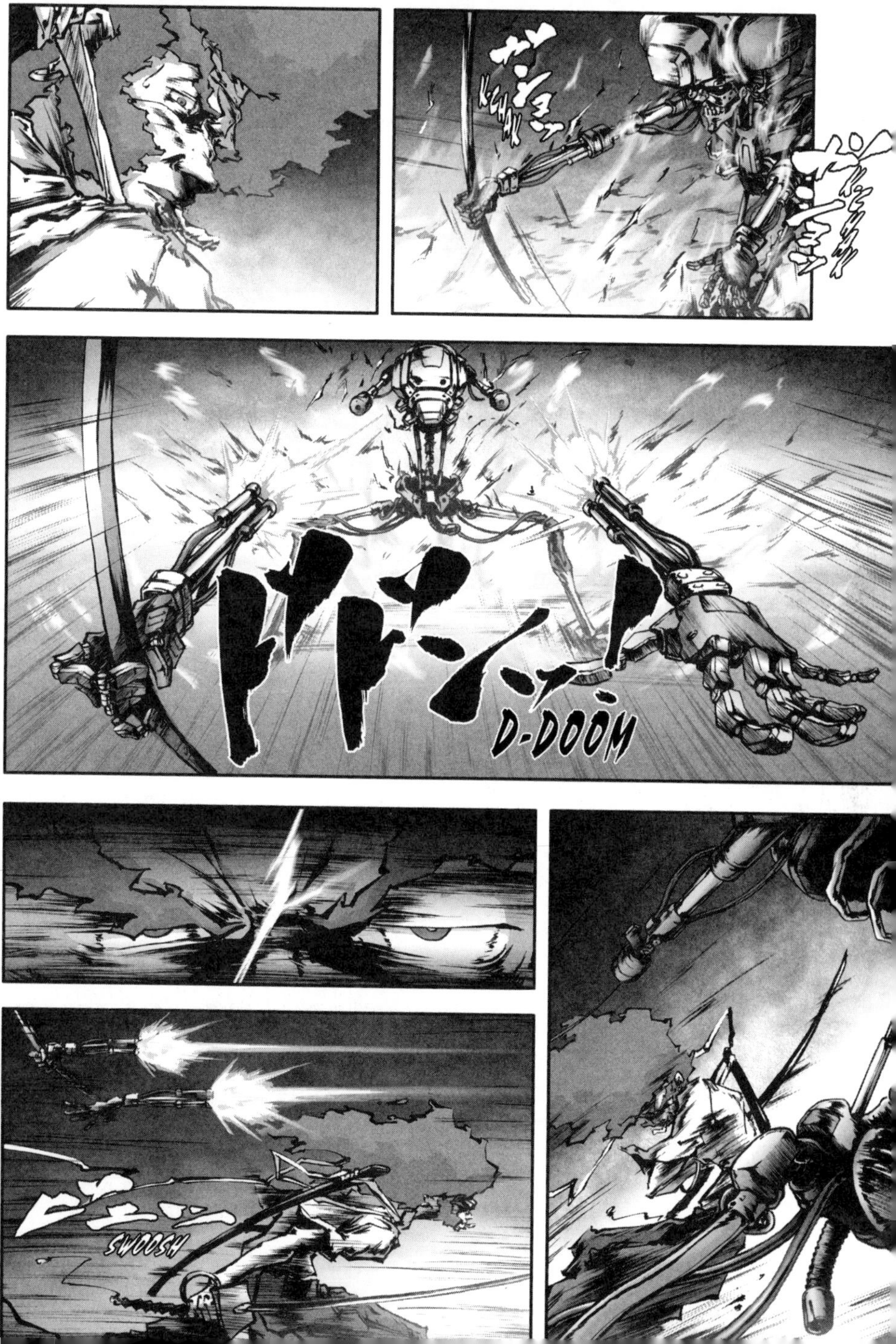
K-CHAK
D-DOOM
SWOOSH

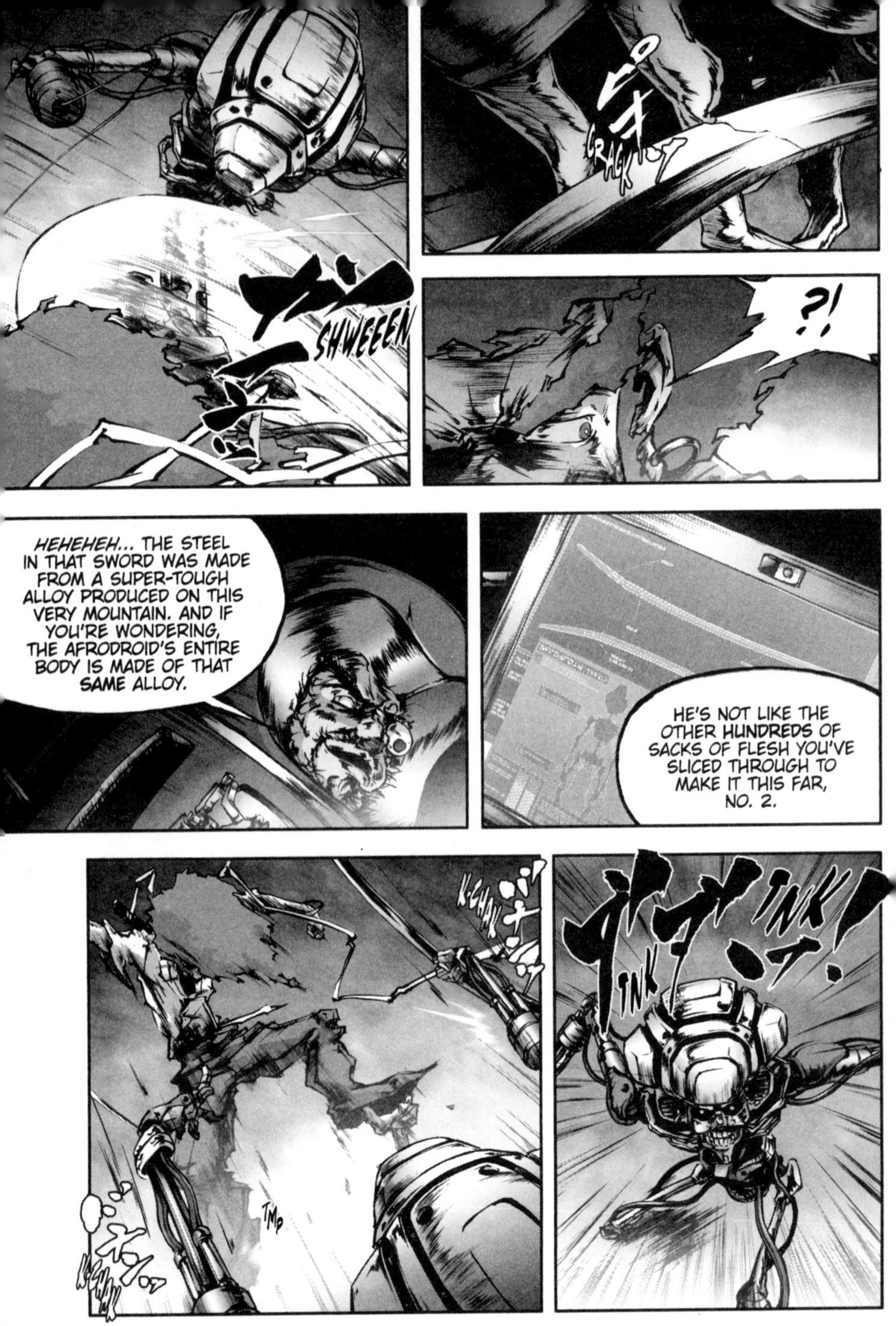
SHWEEEN
CRACK
?!
HEHEHEH... THE STEEL IN THAT SWORD WAS MADE FROM A SUPER-TOUGH ALLOY PRODUCED ON THIS VERY MOUNTAIN. AND IF YOU'RE WONDERING, THE AFRODROID'S ENTIRE BODY IS MADE OF THAT SAME ALLOY.
HE'S NOT LIKE THE OTHER HUNDREDS OF SACKS OF FLESH YOU'VE SLICED THROUGH TO MAKE IT THIS FAR, NO. 2.
K-CHAK
TMP
K-CHAK
TINK!
TINK

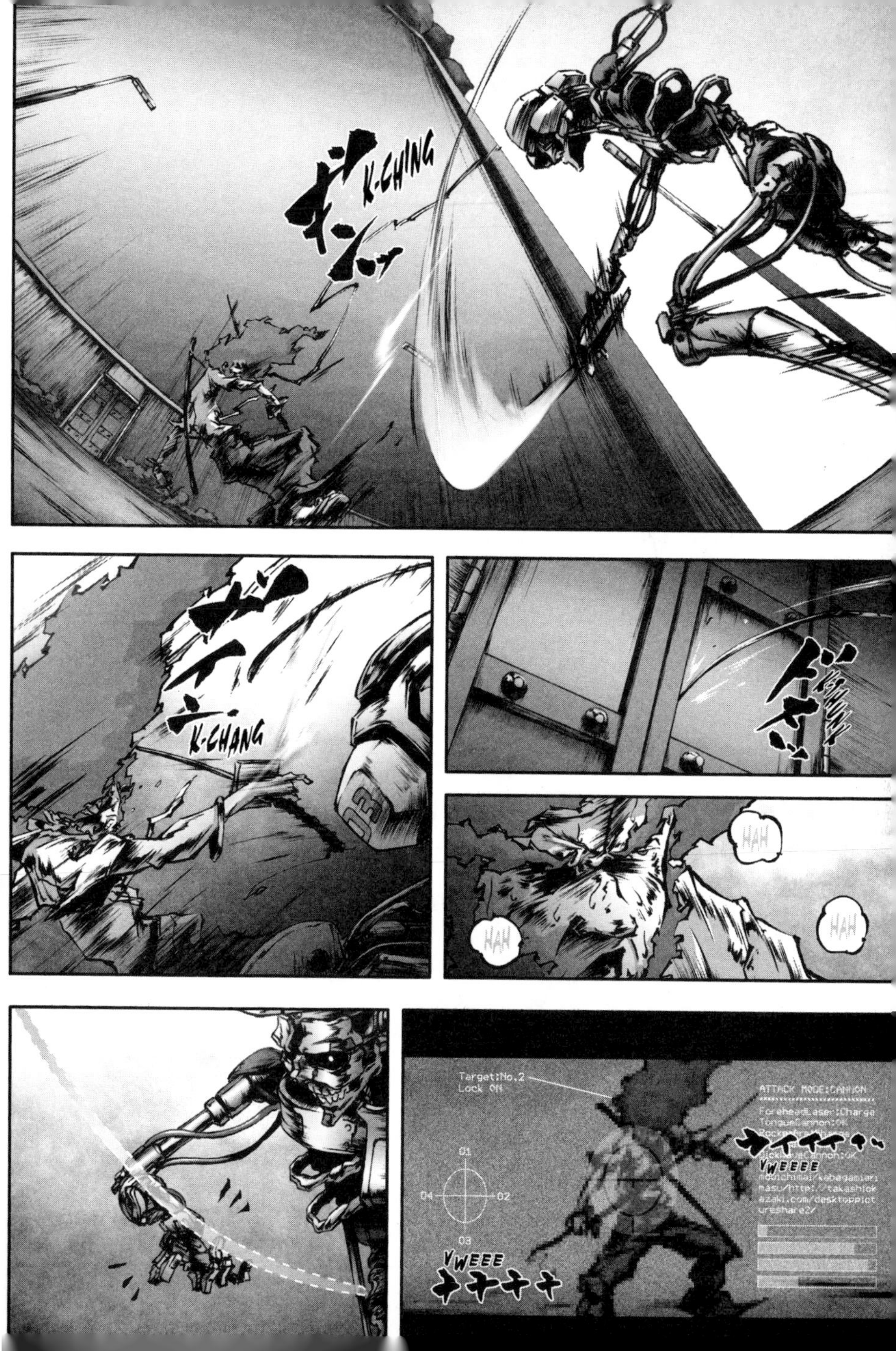
K-CHING
K-CHANG
HAH
HAH
HAH
Target:No.2
Lock ON
ATTACK MODE:CANNON
ForeheadLaser:Charge
TongueCannon:OK
VWEEEE
masu/http://takashiok
azaki.com/desktoppict
ureshare2/
01
02
03
04
VWEEE

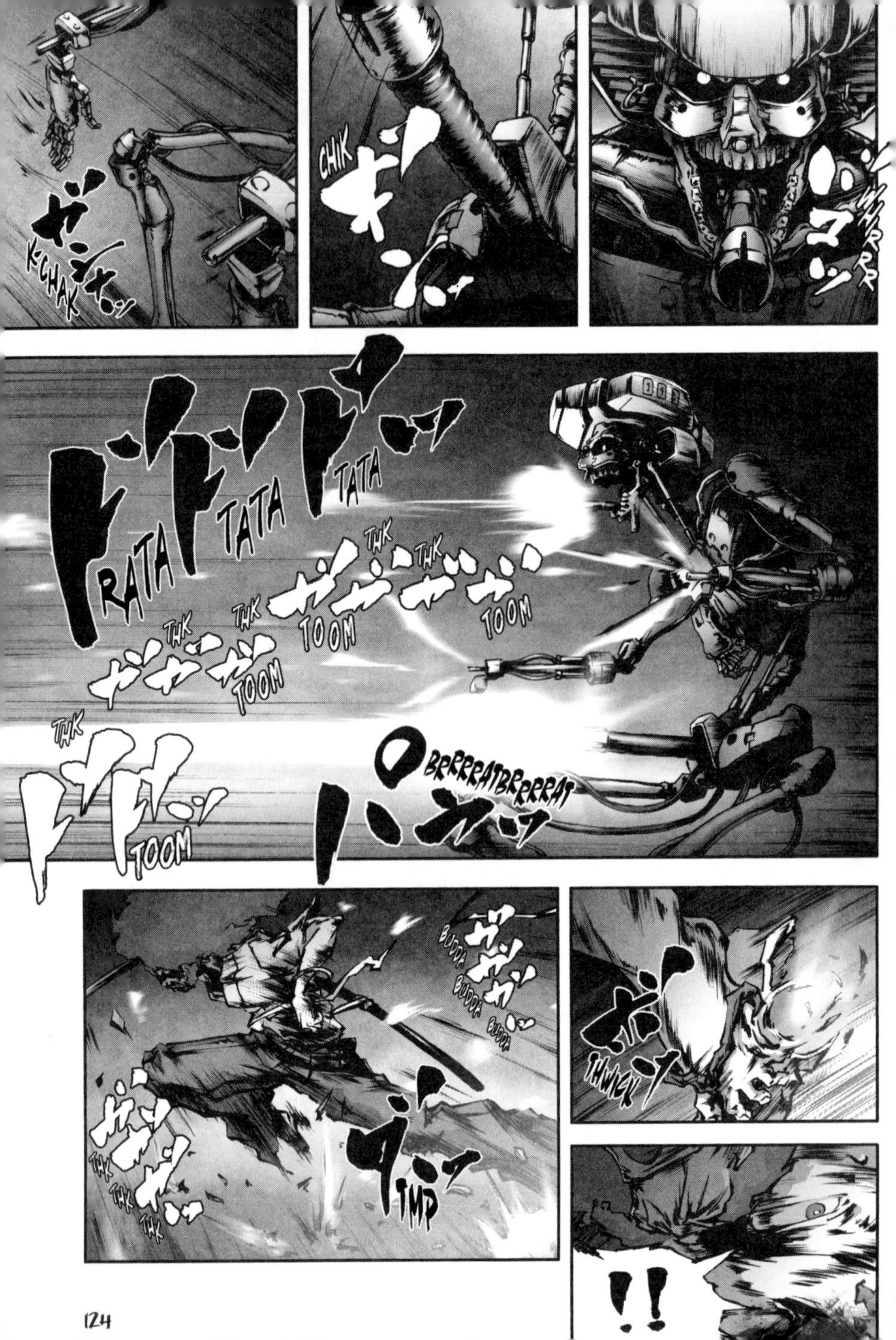
ザシャッ
K-CHAK
CHIK
ギ
VWHRRR
ゴン
ドドドドド
RATA
TATA
TATA
THK
THK
TOOM
THK
THK
TOOM
TOOM
TOOM
THK
ドドドッ
TOOM
BRRRRATBRRRRAT
パーッ
BUDDA
BUDDA
BUDDA
THK
THK
THK
TMP
THWICK
!!

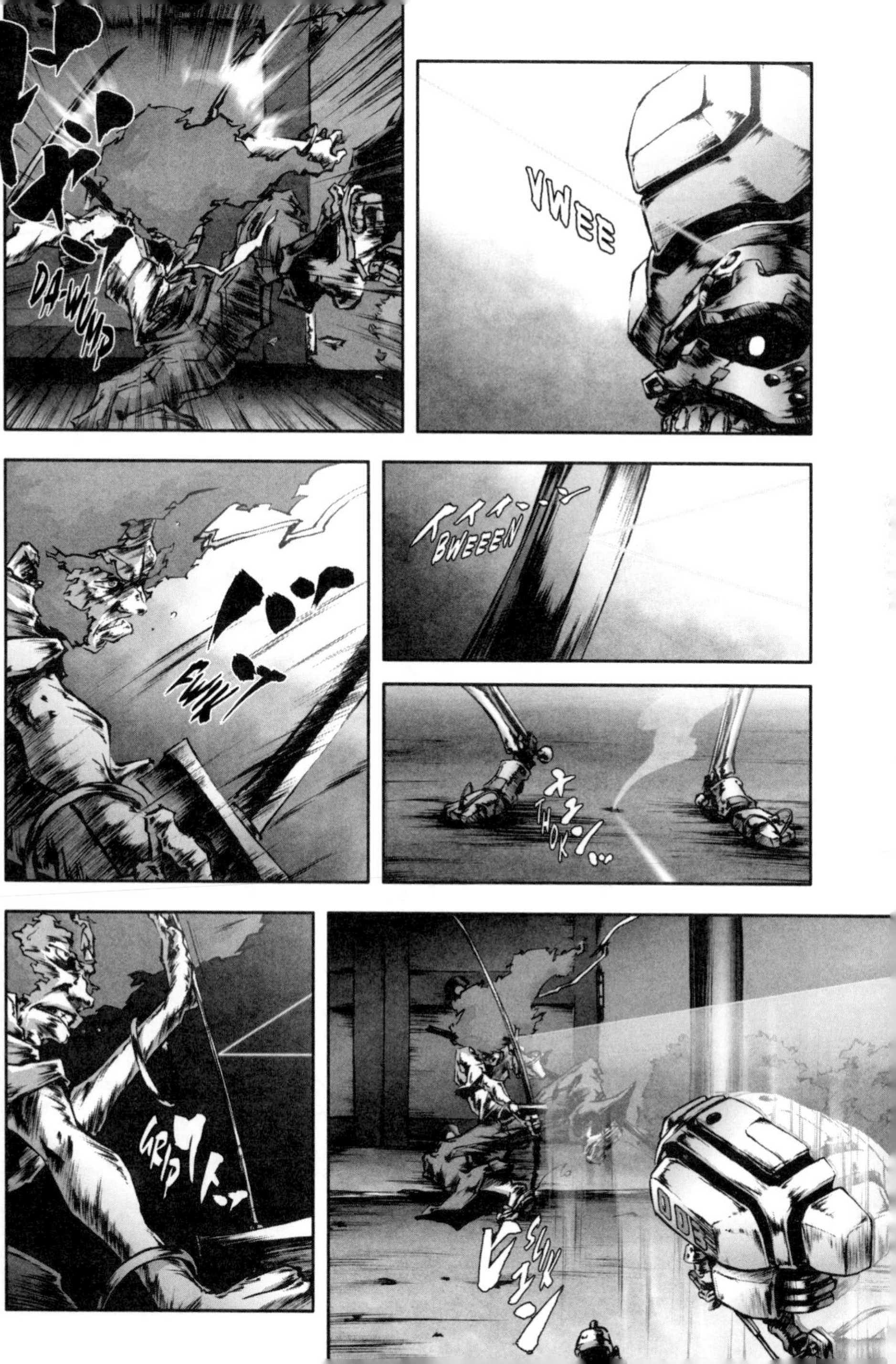
DA-WUMP
VWEE
FWIK
BWEEEN
THOK
GRIP
SLIK

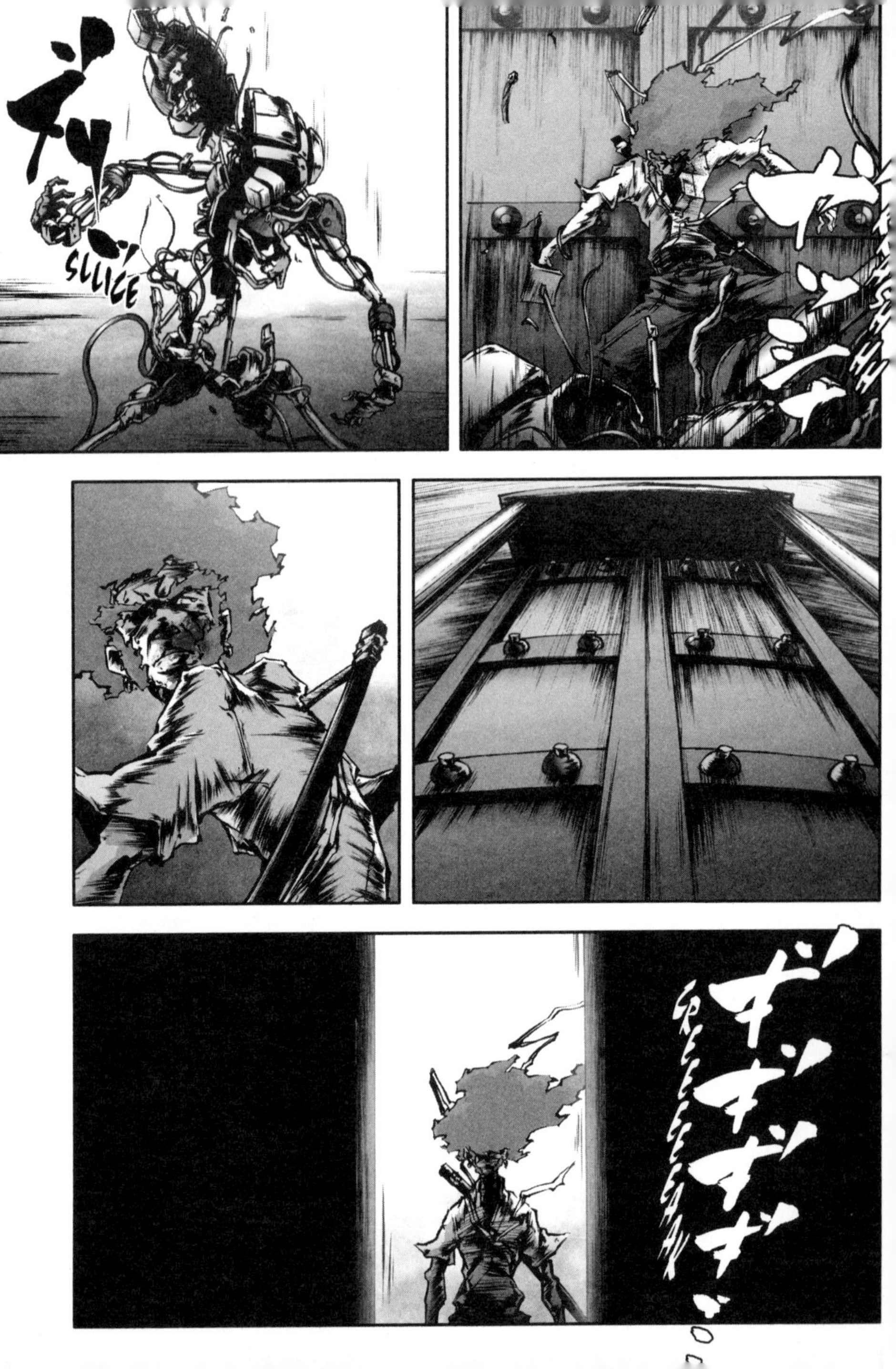
SLLICE
CREEEEEAK

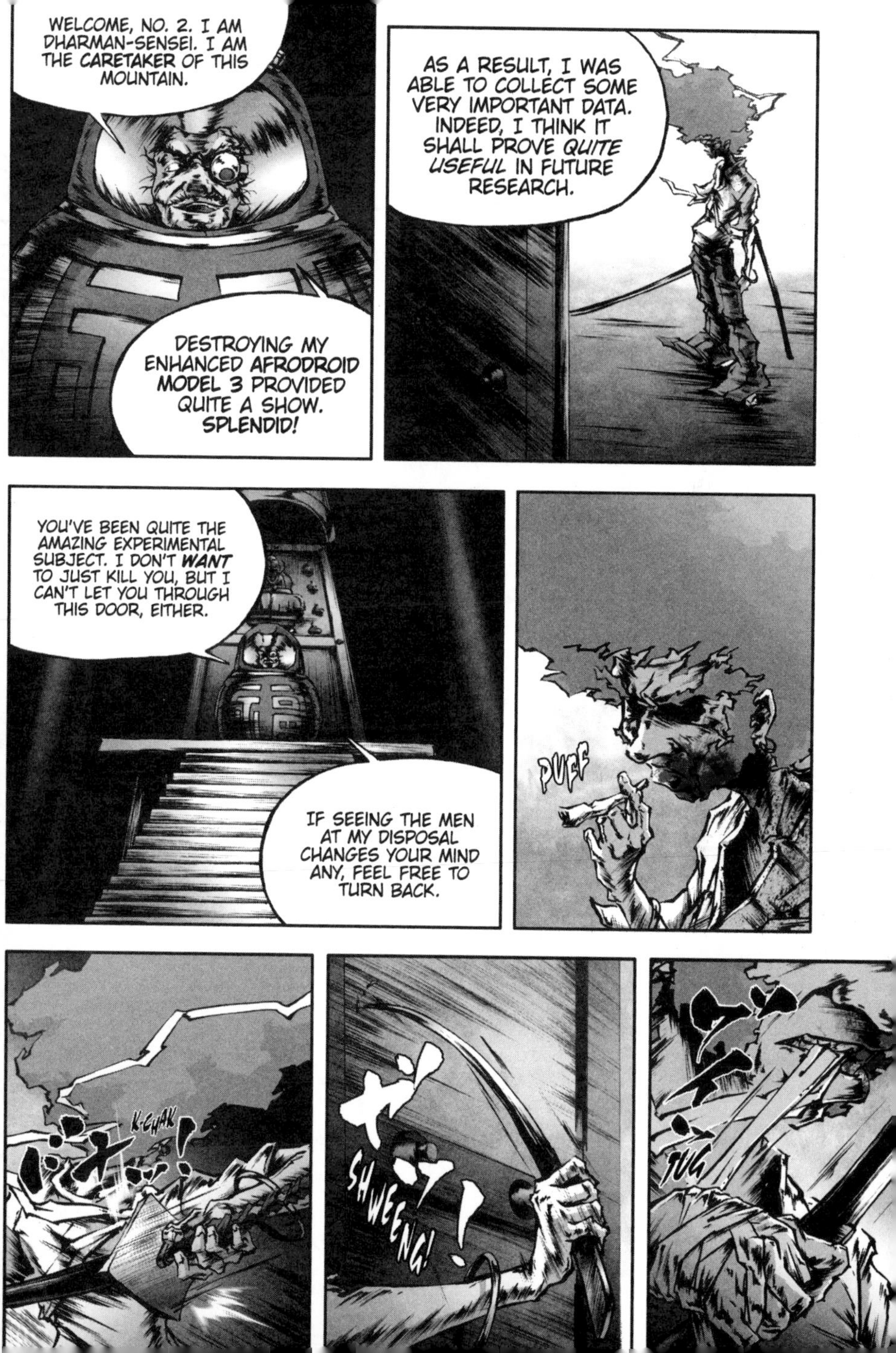
WELCOME, NO. 2. I AM DHARMAN-SENSEI. I AM THE CARETAKER OF THIS MOUNTAIN.
DESTROYING MY ENHANCED AFRODROID MODEL 3 PROVIDED QUITE A SHOW. SPLENDID!
AS A RESULT, I WAS ABLE TO COLLECT SOME VERY IMPORTANT DATA. INDEED, I THINK IT SHALL PROVE QUITE USEFUL IN FUTURE RESEARCH.
YOU'VE BEEN QUITE THE AMAZING EXPERIMENTAL SUBJECT. I DON'T WANT TO JUST KILL YOU, BUT I CAN'T LET YOU THROUGH THIS DOOR, EITHER.
IF SEEING THE MEN AT MY DISPOSAL CHANGES YOUR MIND ANY, FEEL FREE TO TURN BACK.
PUFF
K-CHAK
SHWEENG!
TUG

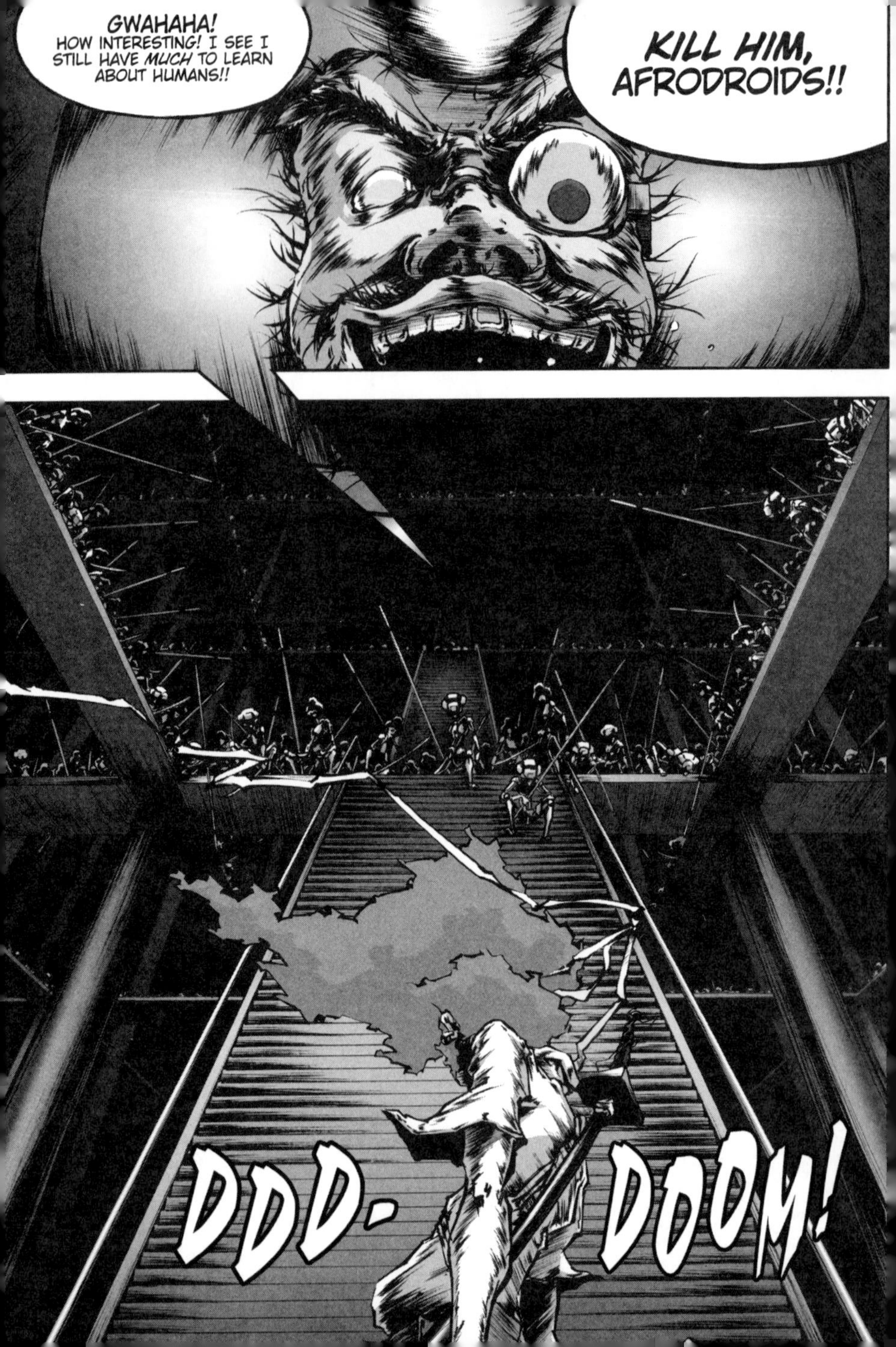
GWAHAHA! HOW INTERESTING! I SEE I STILL HAVE MUCH TO LEARN ABOUT HUMANS!!
KILL HIM, AFRODROIDS!!
DDD- DOOM!

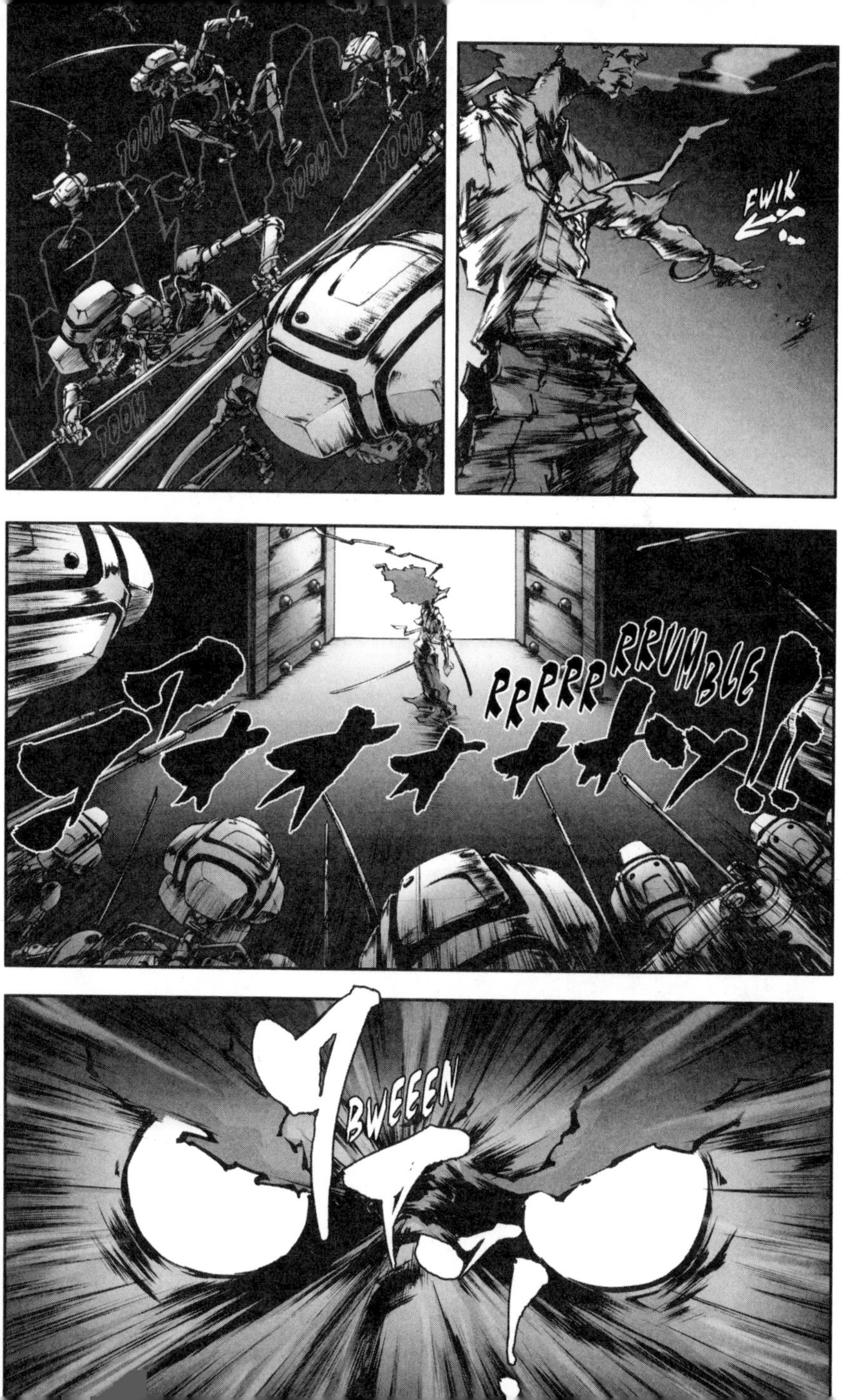
TOOM
TOOM
TOOM
TOOM
EWIK
RRRRR
RRUMBLE
BWEEEN

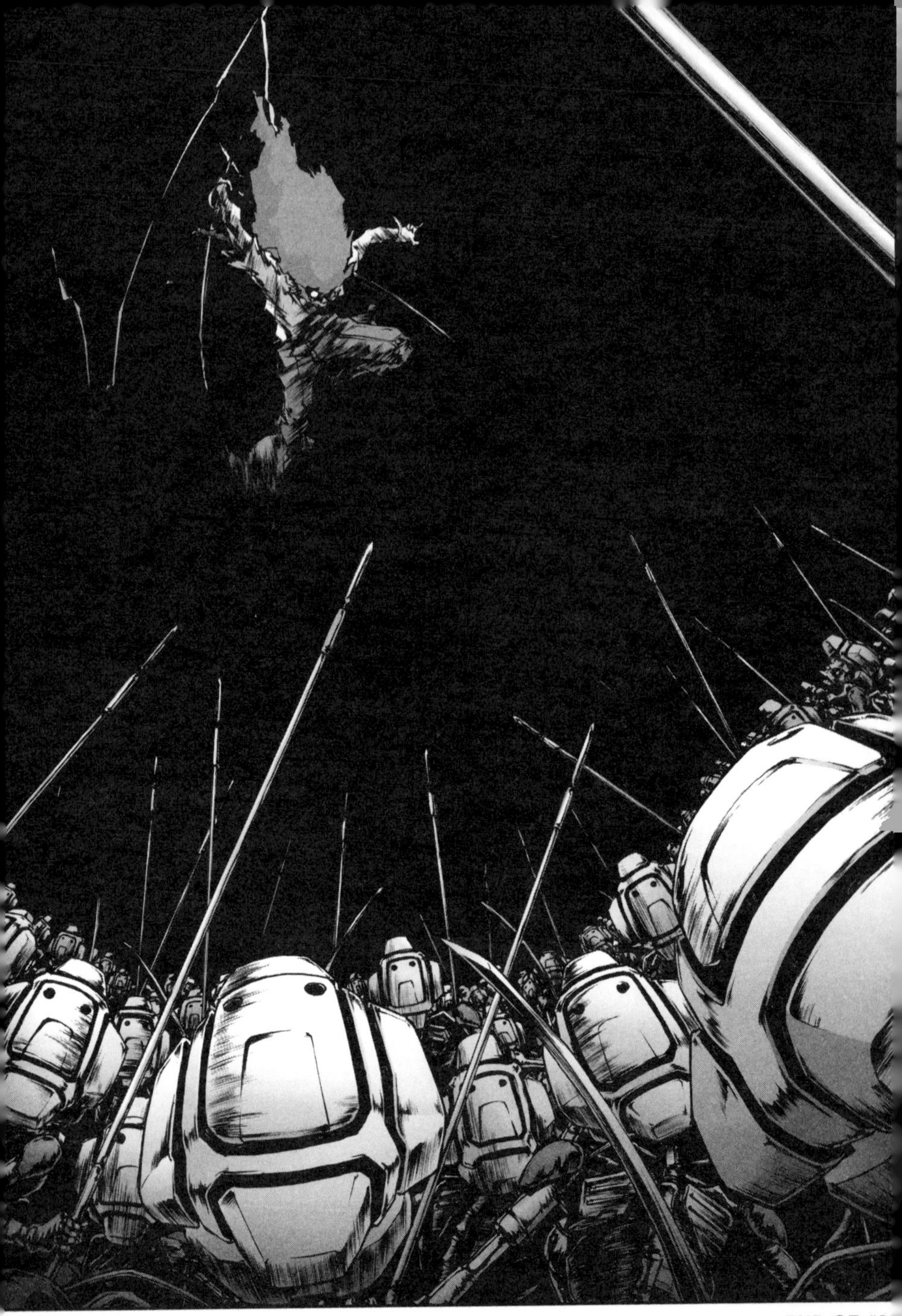

END OF #0

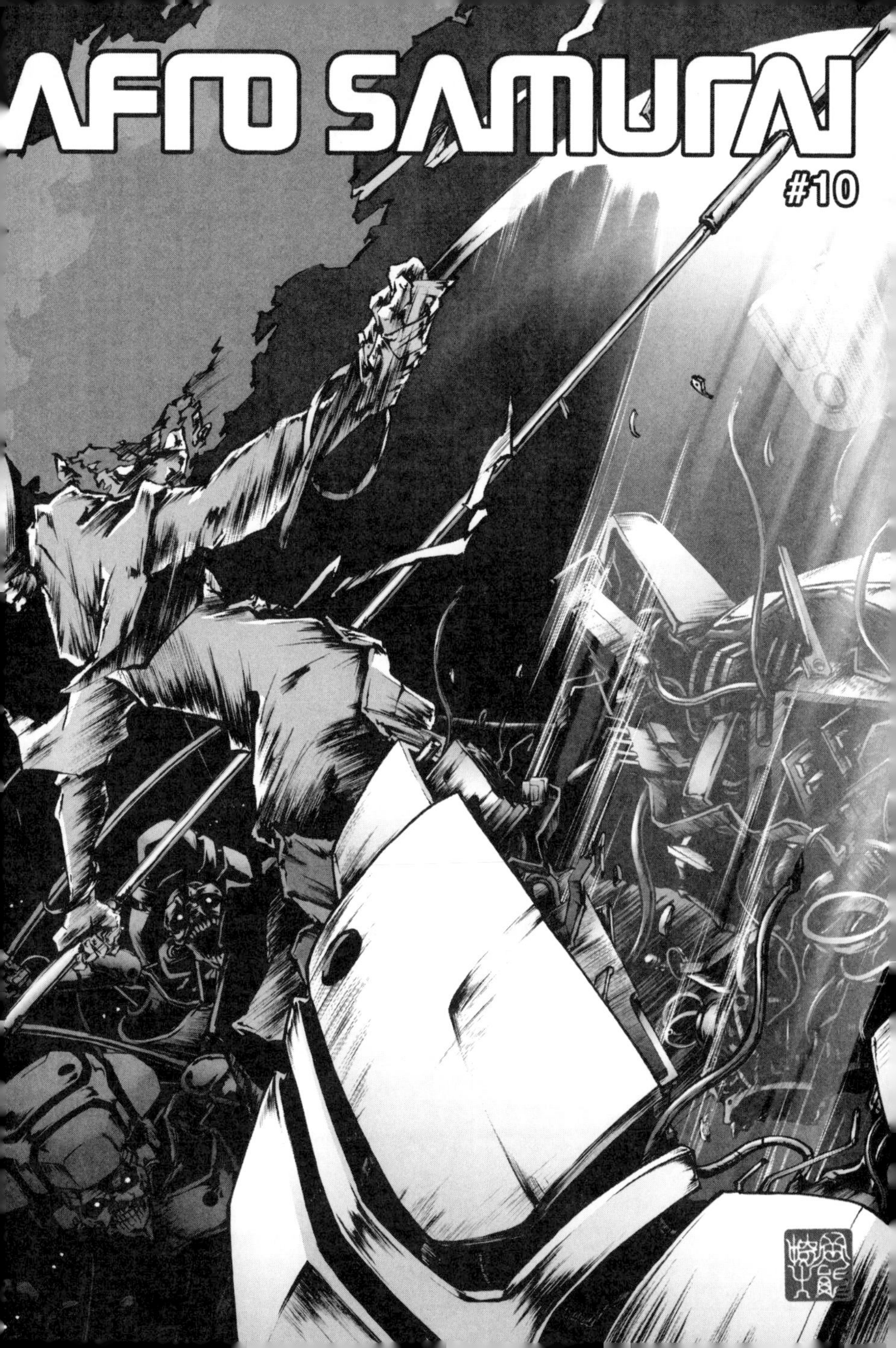
AFRO SAMURAI
#10

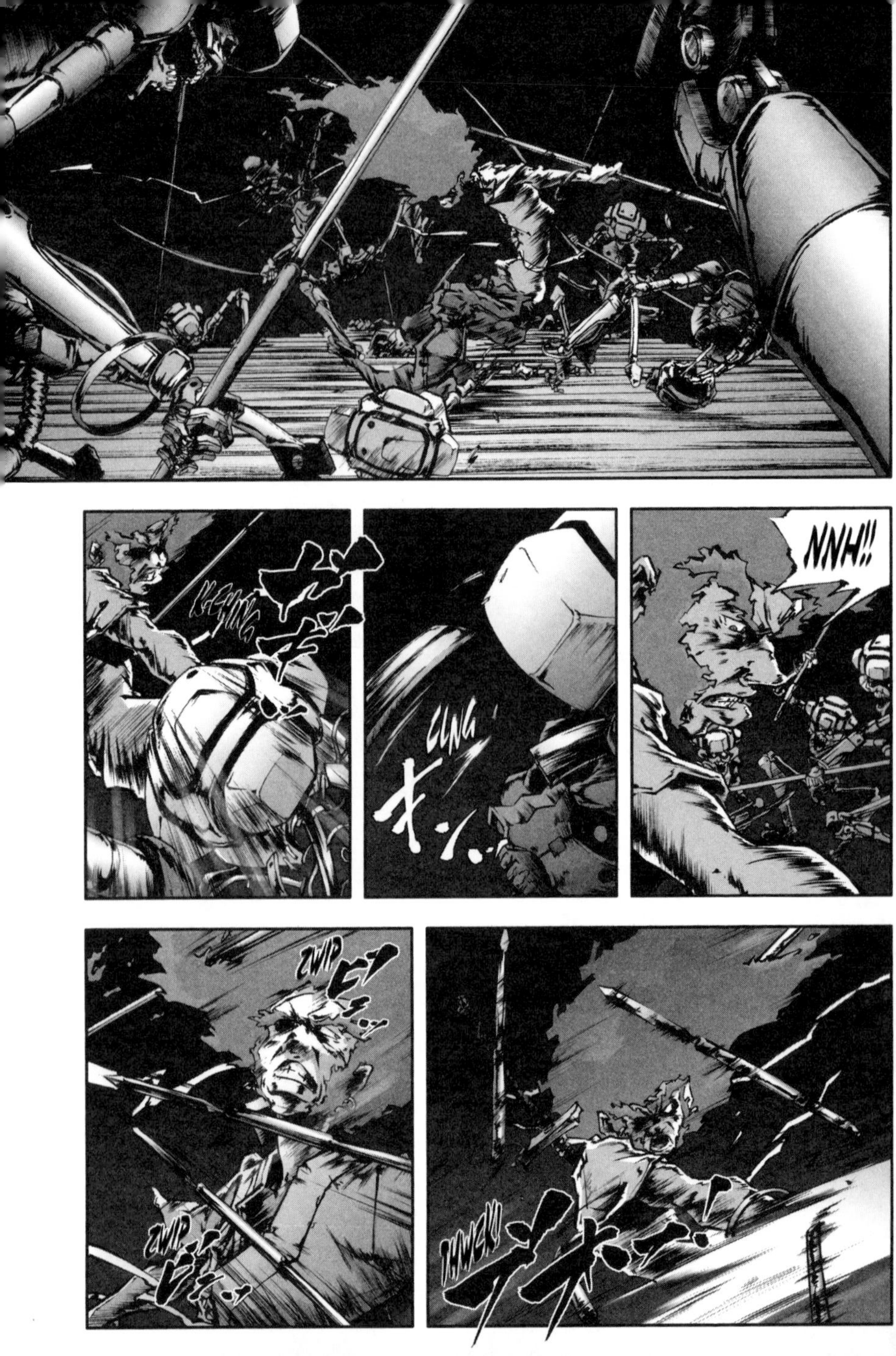
K-CHING
CLNG
NNH!!
ZWIP
ZWIP
THWACK!!

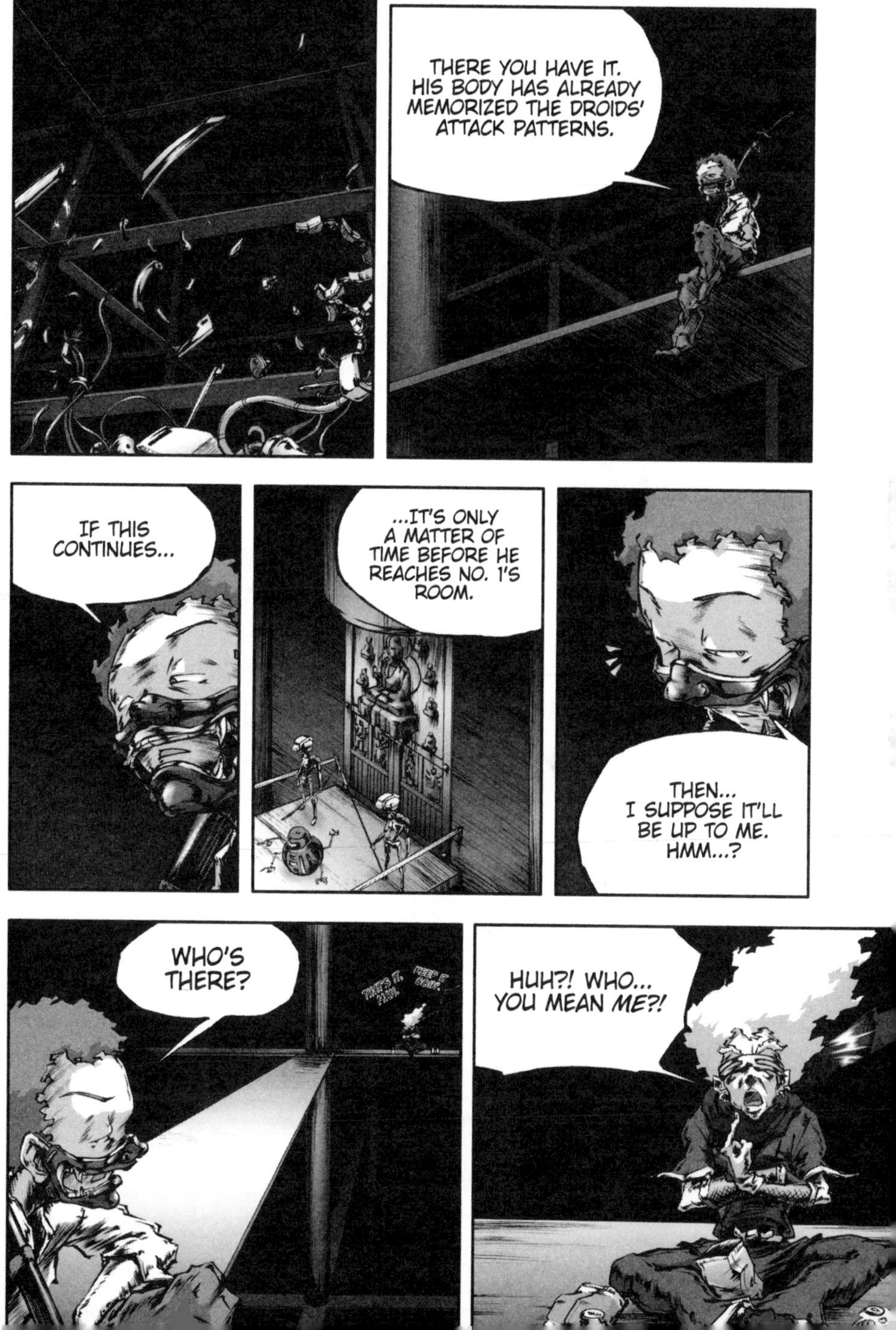
THERE YOU HAVE IT. HIS BODY HAS ALREADY MEMORIZED THE DROIDS' ATTACK PATTERNS.
IF THIS CONTINUES...
...IT'S ONLY A MATTER OF TIME BEFORE HE REACHES NO. 1'S ROOM.
THEN... I SUPPOSE IT'LL BE UP TO ME. HMM...?
WHO'S THERE?
THAT'S IT, MAN.
KEEP IT GOIN'.
HUH?! WHO... YOU MEAN ME?!

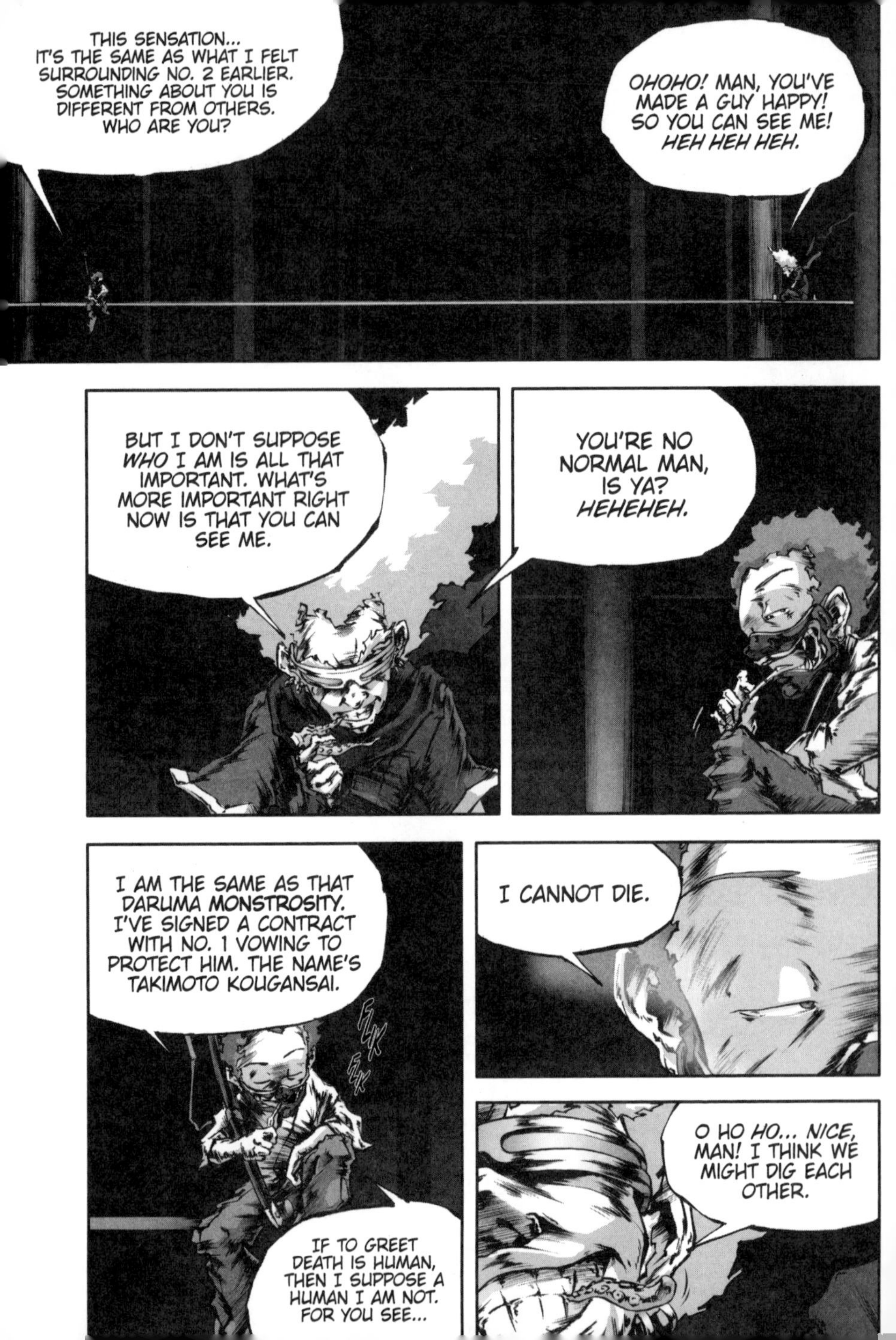
THIS SENSATION... IT'S THE SAME AS WHAT I FELT SURROUNDING NO. 2 EARLIER. SOMETHING ABOUT YOU IS DIFFERENT FROM OTHERS. WHO ARE YOU?
OHOHO! MAN, YOU'VE MADE A GUY HAPPY! SO YOU CAN SEE ME! HEH HEH HEH.
BUT I DON'T SUPPOSE WHO I AM IS ALL THAT IMPORTANT. WHAT'S MORE IMPORTANT RIGHT NOW IS THAT YOU CAN SEE ME.
YOU'RE NO NORMAL MAN, IS YA? HEHEHEH.
I AM THE SAME AS THAT DARUMA MONSTROSITY. I'VE SIGNED A CONTRACT WITH NO. 1 VOWING TO PROTECT HIM. THE NAME'S TAKIMOTO KOUGANSAI.
FLIK
FLIK
IF TO GREET DEATH IS HUMAN, THEN I SUPPOSE A HUMAN I AM NOT. FOR YOU SEE...
I CANNOT DIE.
O HO HO... NICE, MAN! I THINK WE MIGHT DIG EACH OTHER.

GRRRACK
D-DOOOOM
BWEEEN
BWEEEN
VWOOOO
K-THWAK
VWEEEEE
K-CHIK
K-CHIK

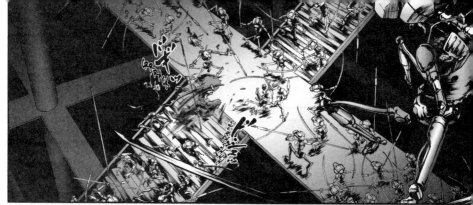

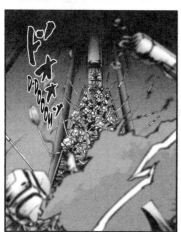

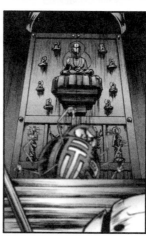

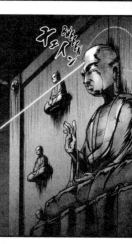

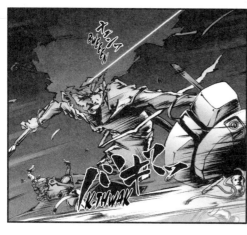

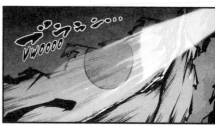

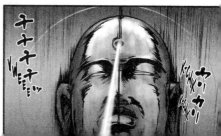

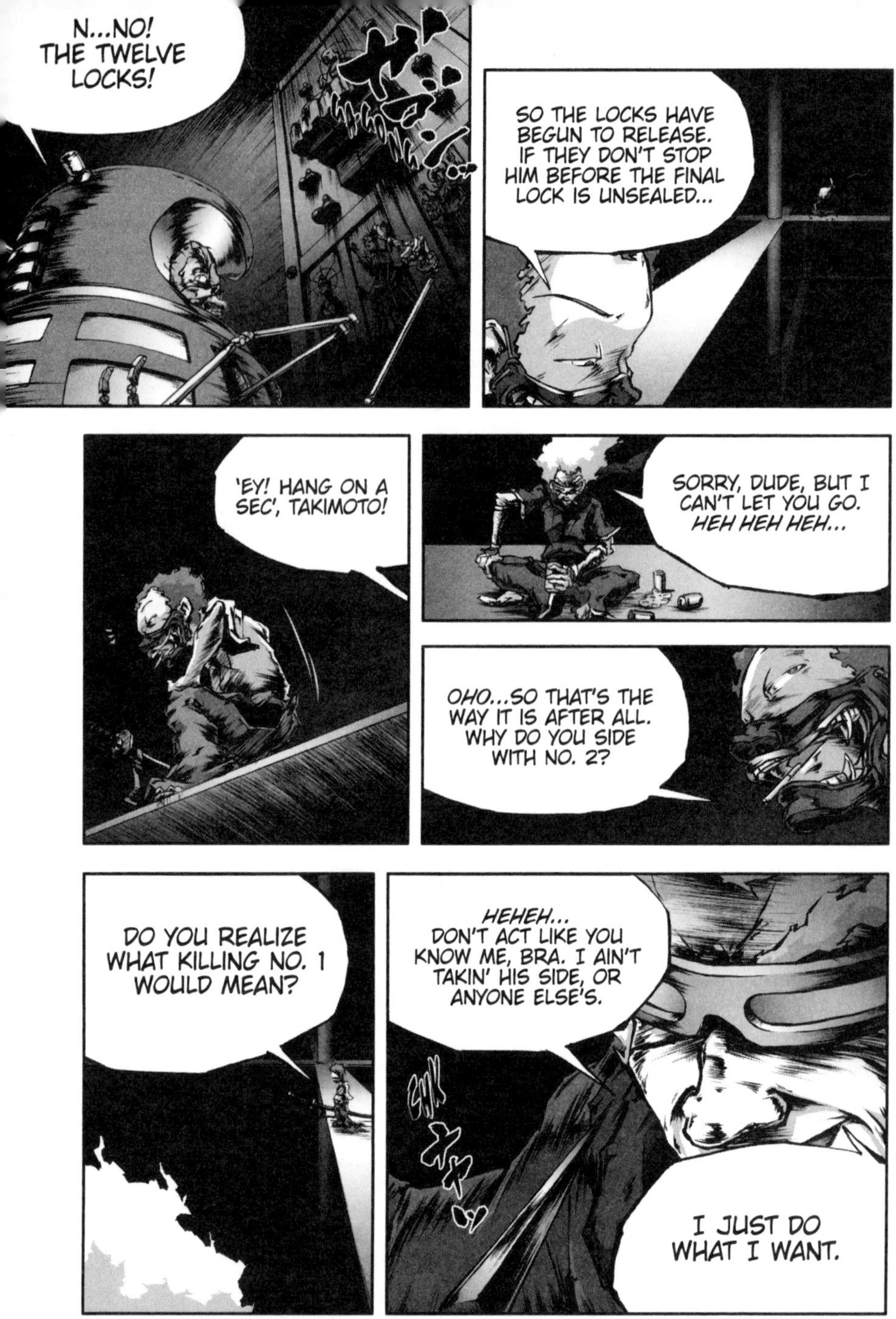
N...NO! THE TWELVE LOCKS!
SO THE LOCKS HAVE BEGUN TO RELEASE. IF THEY DON'T STOP HIM BEFORE THE FINAL LOCK IS UNSEALED...
'EY! HANG ON A SEC', TAKIMOTO!
SORRY, DUDE, BUT I CAN'T LET YOU GO. *HEH HEH HEH...*
*OHO...*SO THAT'S THE WAY IT IS AFTER ALL. WHY DO YOU SIDE WITH NO. 2?
DO YOU REALIZE WHAT KILLING NO. 1 WOULD MEAN?
HEHEH... DON'T ACT LIKE YOU KNOW ME, BRA. I AIN'T TAKIN' HIS SIDE, OR ANYONE ELSE'S.
CHK
I JUST DO WHAT I WANT.

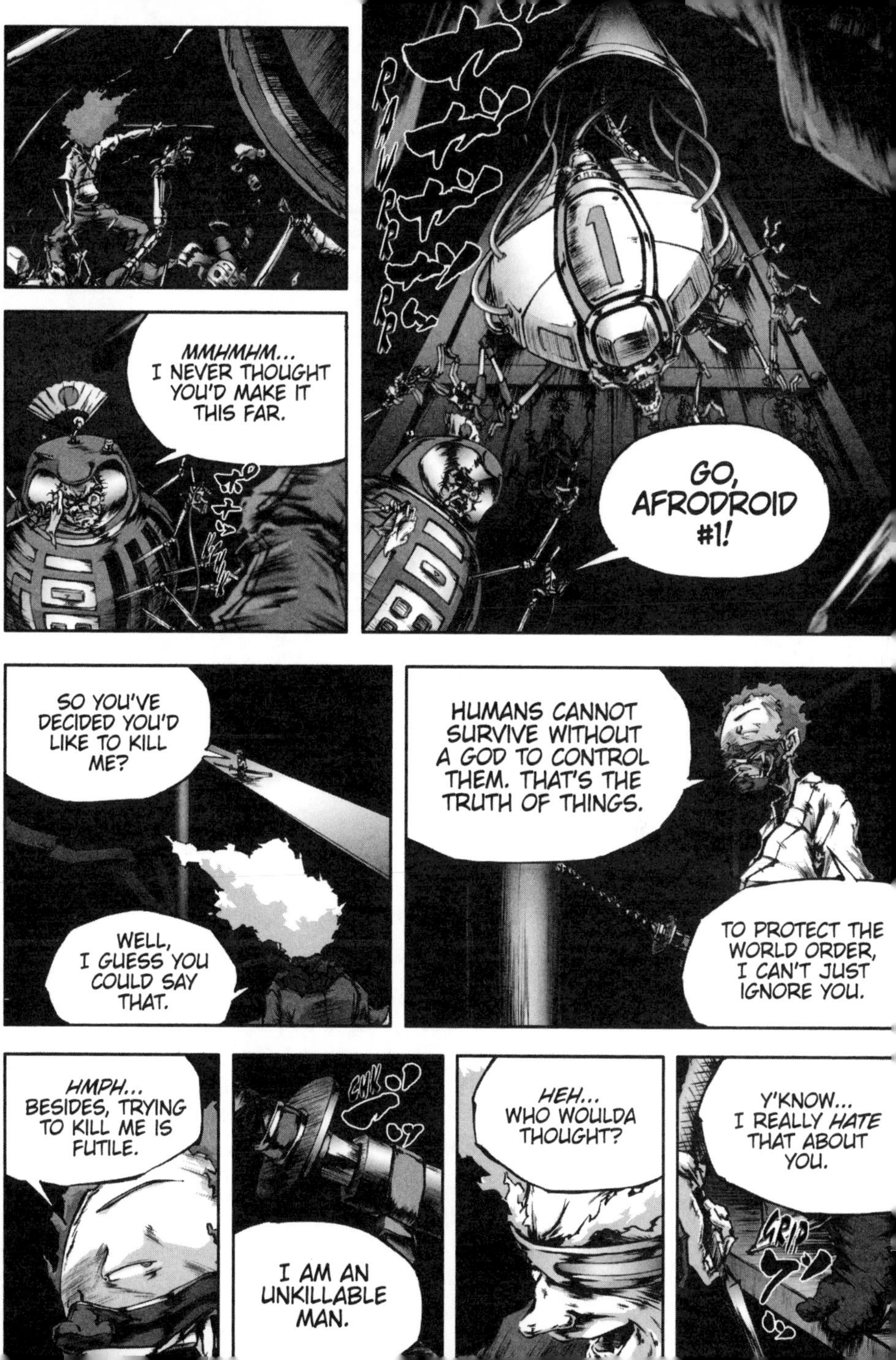
MMHMHM... I NEVER THOUGHT YOU'D MAKE IT THIS FAR.
RAWRRRR
GO, AFRODROID #1!
SO YOU'VE DECIDED YOU'D LIKE TO KILL ME?
WELL, I GUESS YOU COULD SAY THAT.
HUMANS CANNOT SURVIVE WITHOUT A GOD TO CONTROL THEM. THAT'S THE TRUTH OF THINGS.
TO PROTECT THE WORLD ORDER, I CAN'T JUST IGNORE YOU.
HMPH... BESIDES, TRYING TO KILL ME IS FUTILE.
CHK
I AM AN UNKILLABLE MAN.
HEH... WHO WOULDA THOUGHT?
Y'KNOW... I REALLY HATE THAT ABOUT YOU.
GRIP

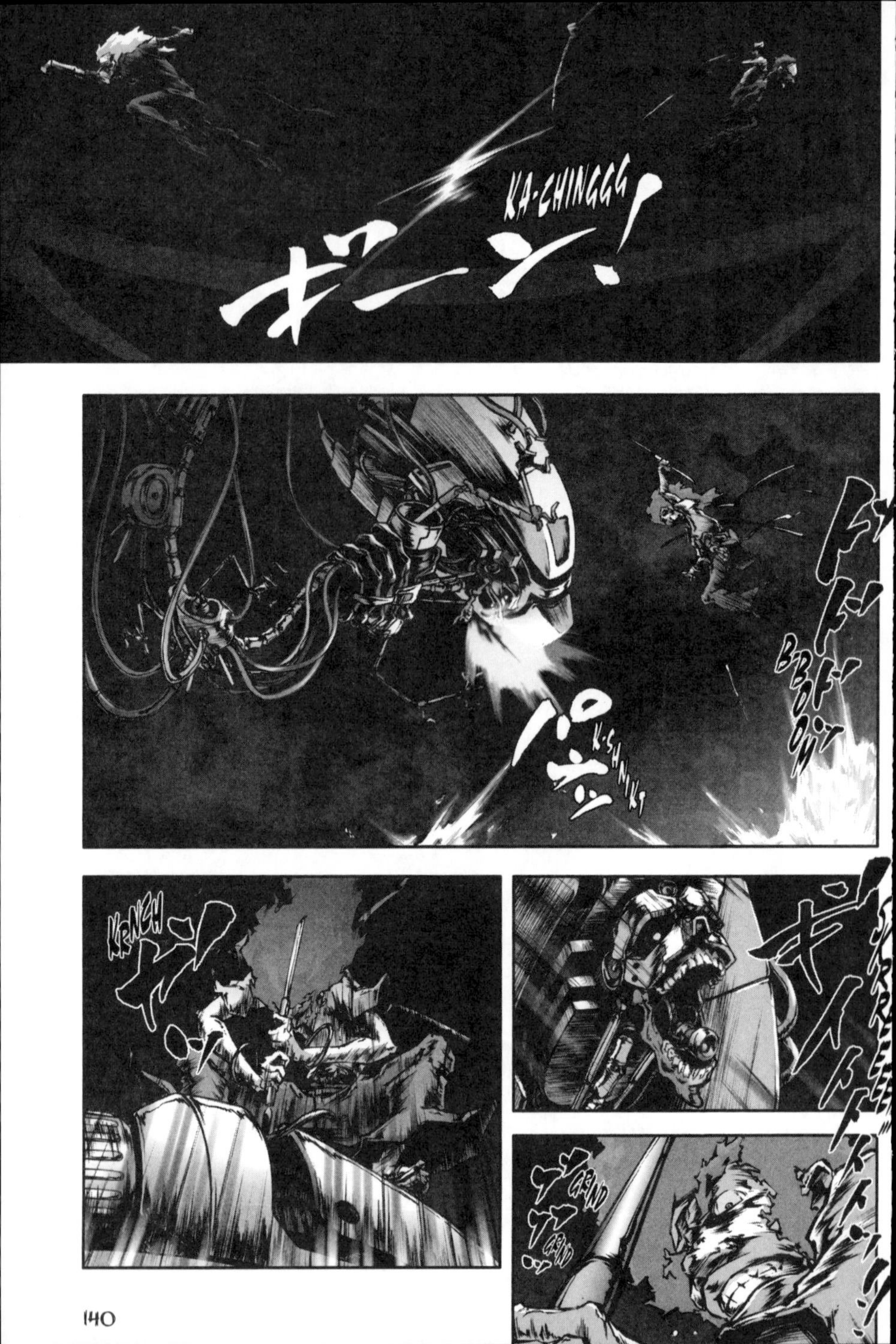
KA-CHINGGG!
ギーン!
K-SHNIKT
KRNCH
GRIND
GRIND

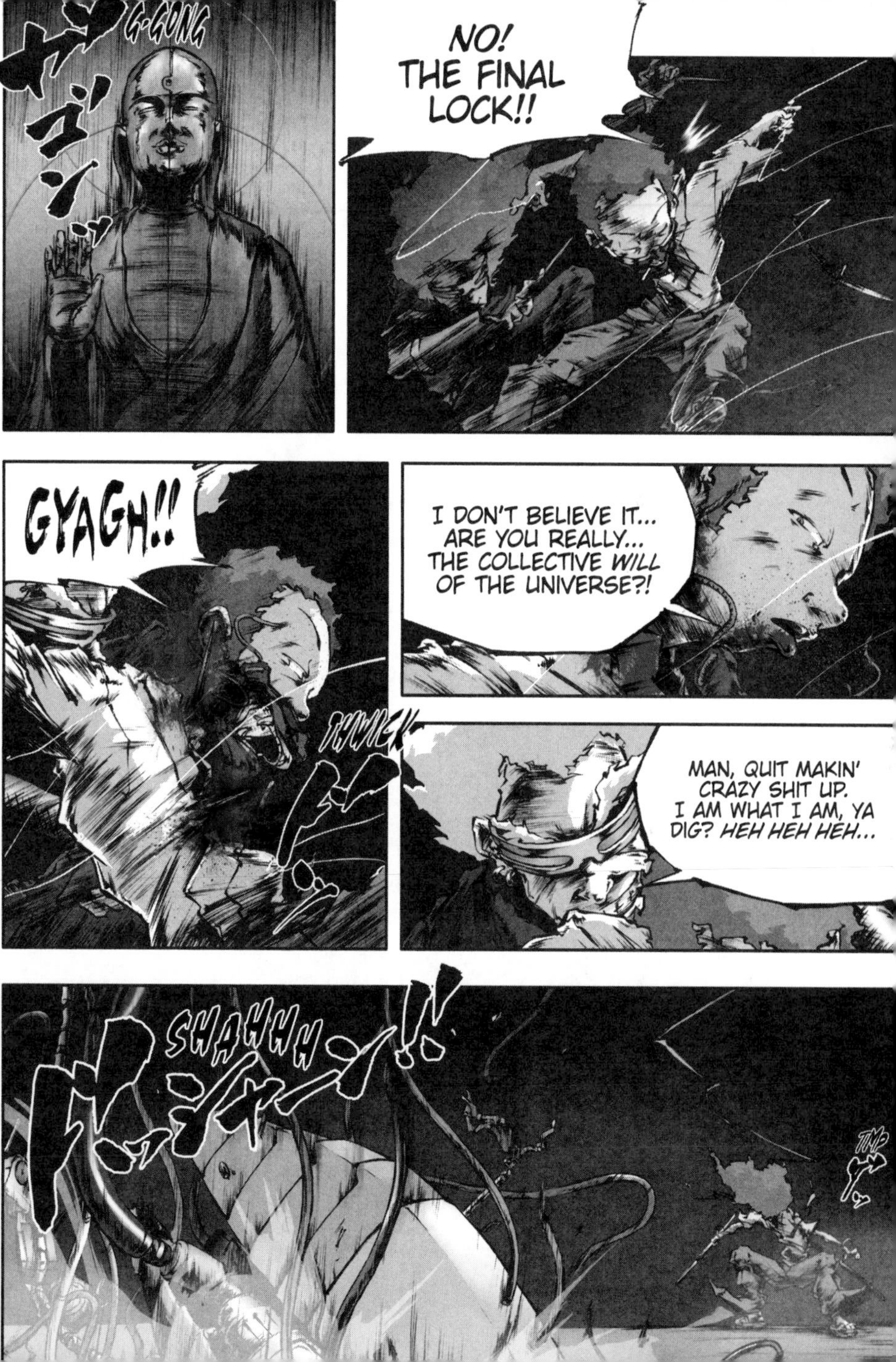
G-GONG
NO! THE FINAL LOCK!!
GYAGH!!
THWICK
I DON'T BELIEVE IT... ARE YOU REALLY... THE COLLECTIVE *WILL* OF THE UNIVERSE?!
MAN, QUIT MAKIN' CRAZY SHIT UP. I AM WHAT I AM, YA DIG? *HEH HEH HEH...*
SHAHHH
TMP

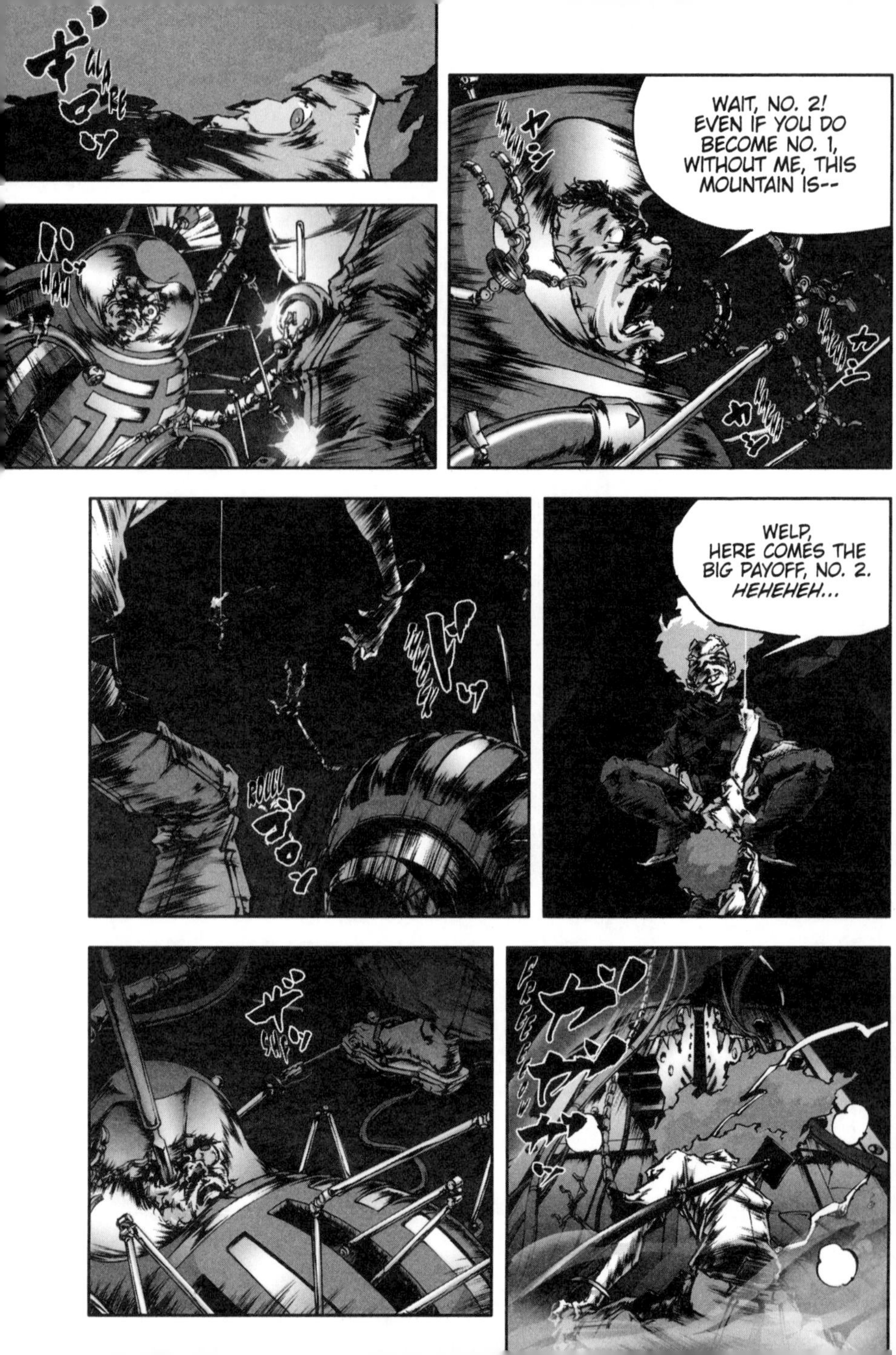
GLARE
WHAM
WAIT, NO. 2! EVEN IF YOU DO BECOME NO. 1, WITHOUT ME, THIS MOUNTAIN IS--
ROLL
WELP, HERE COMES THE BIG PAYOFF, NO. 2. *HEHEHEH...*

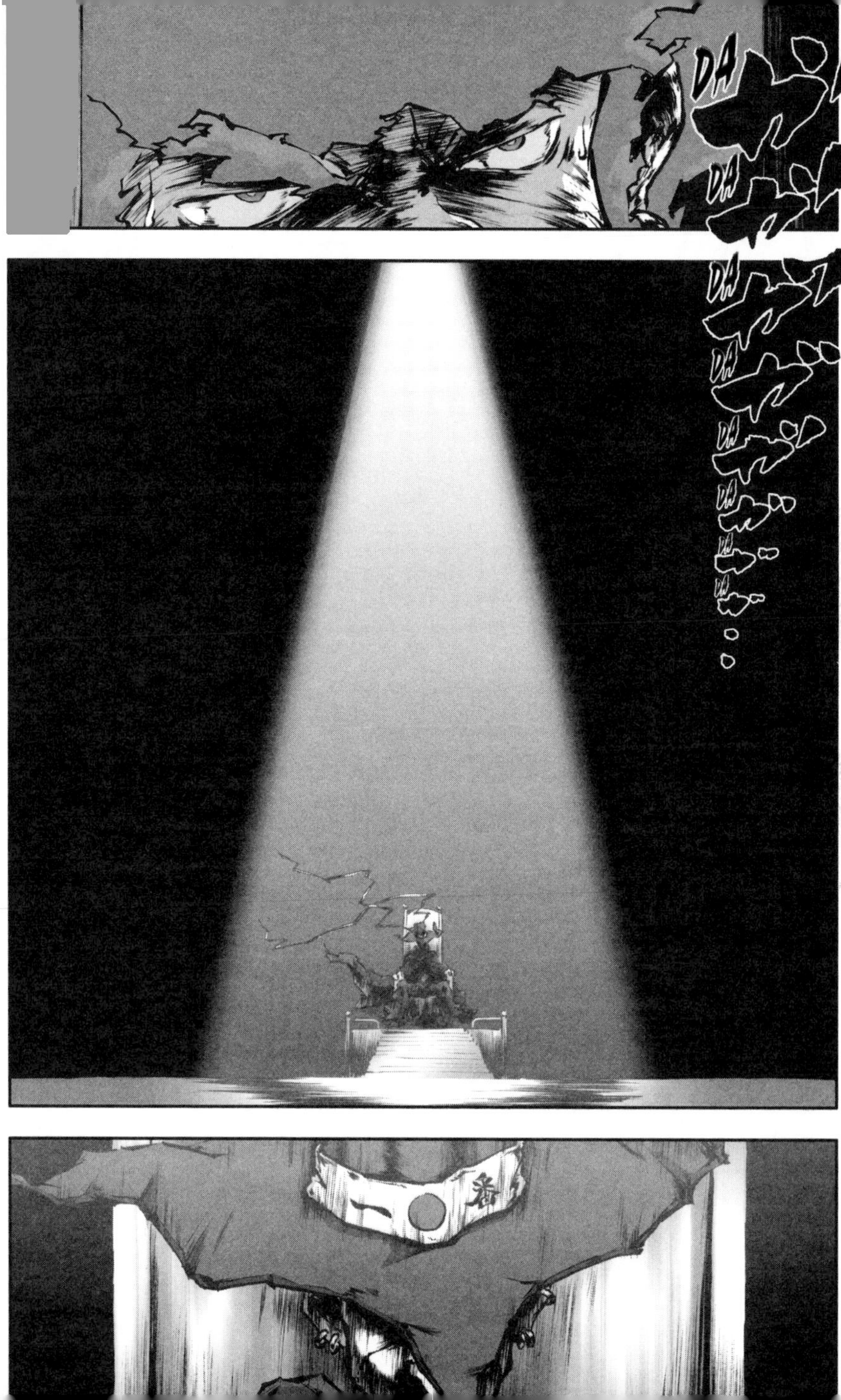
DA DA DA DA DA DA DA DA

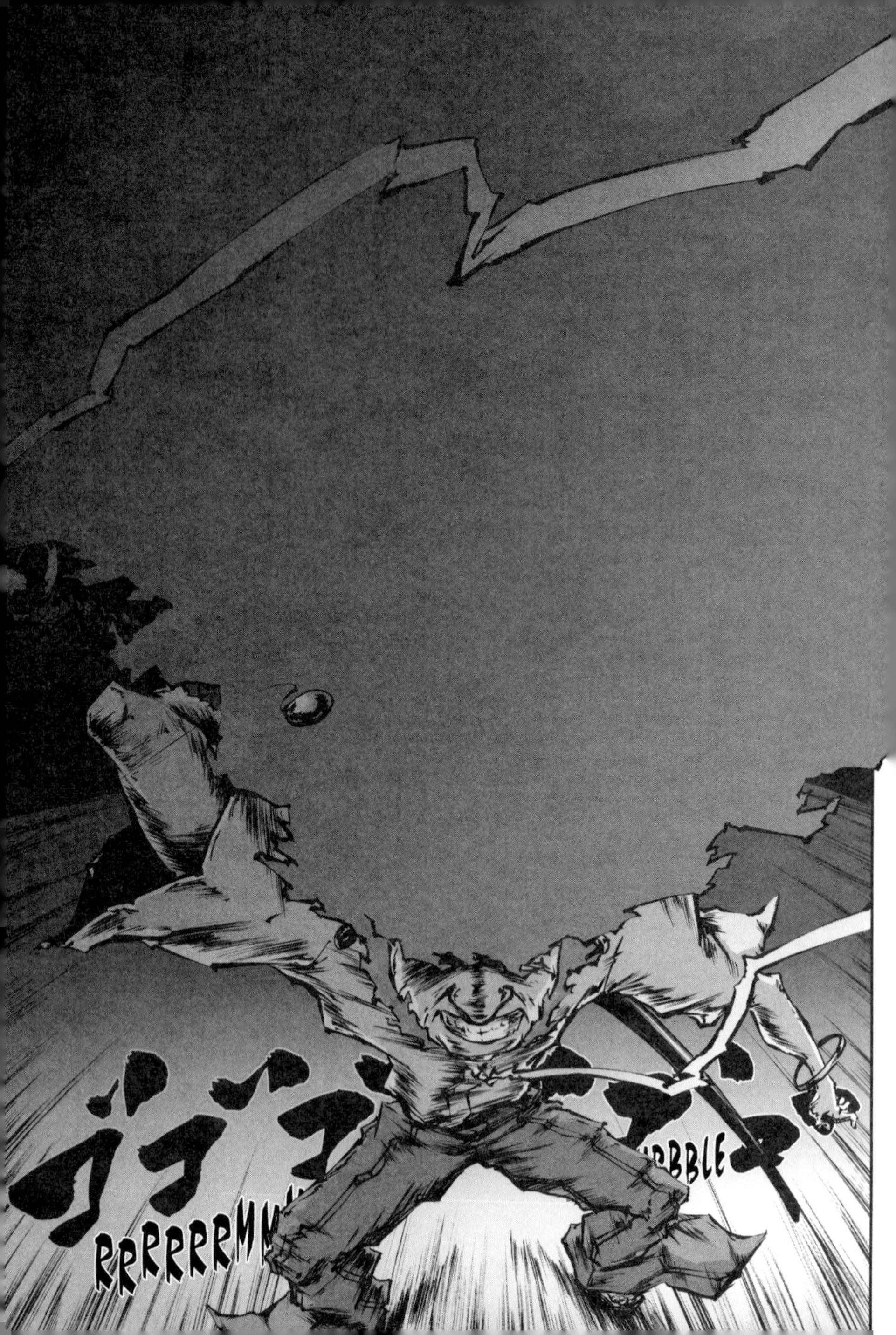
ゴゴゴ
RRRRRRMM
RBBLE

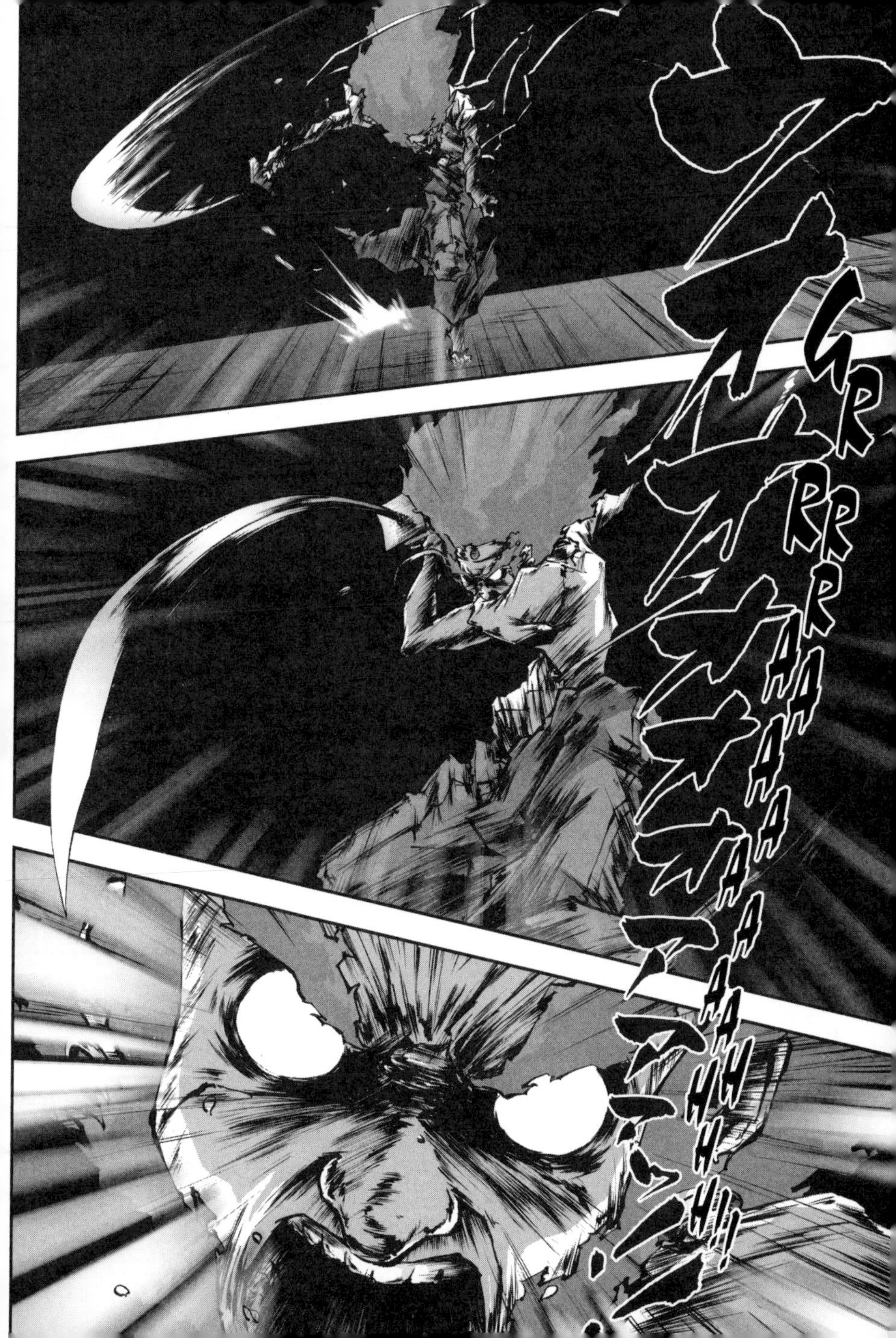
GRRRRAAAAAAAAAAHHHHHH!!

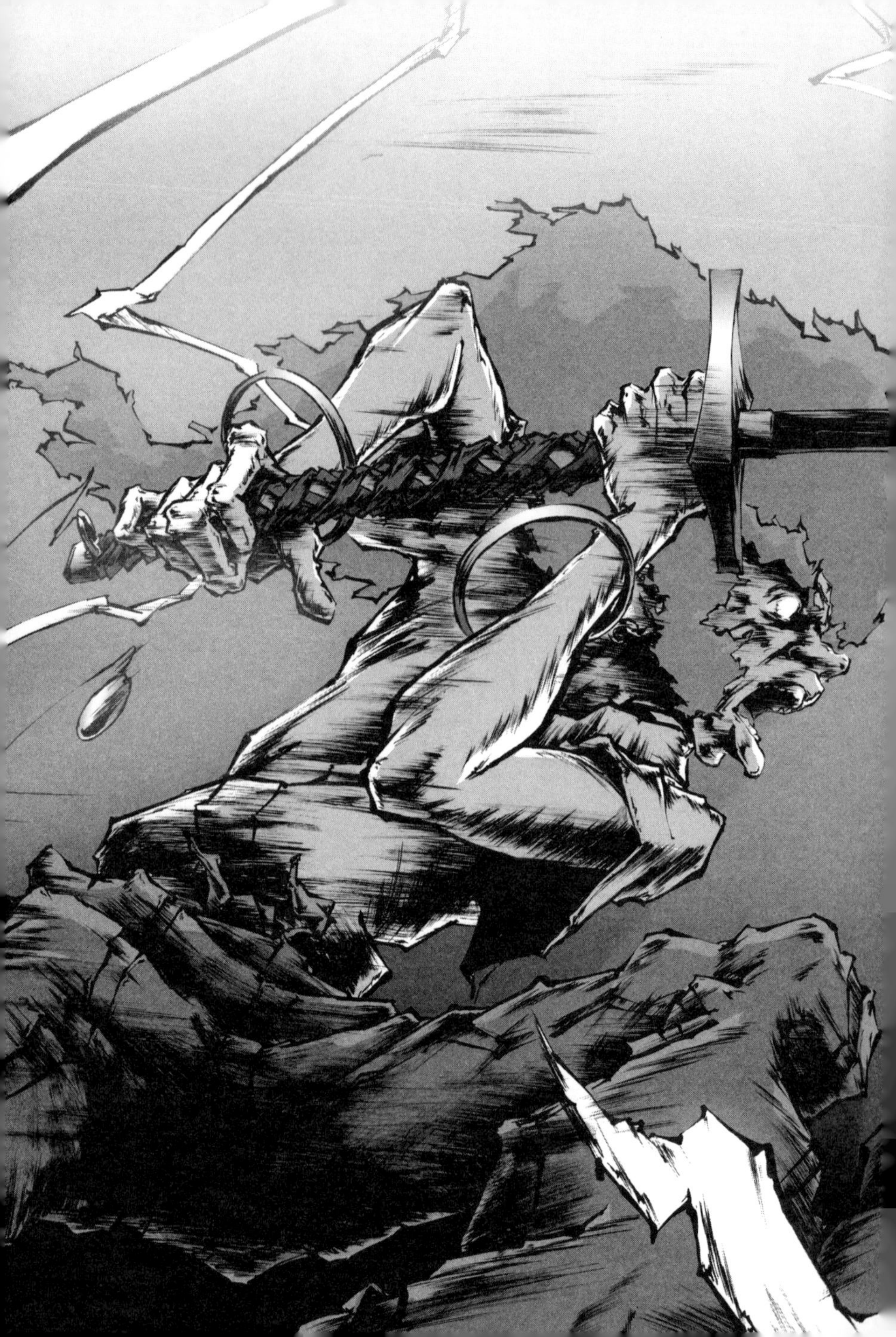

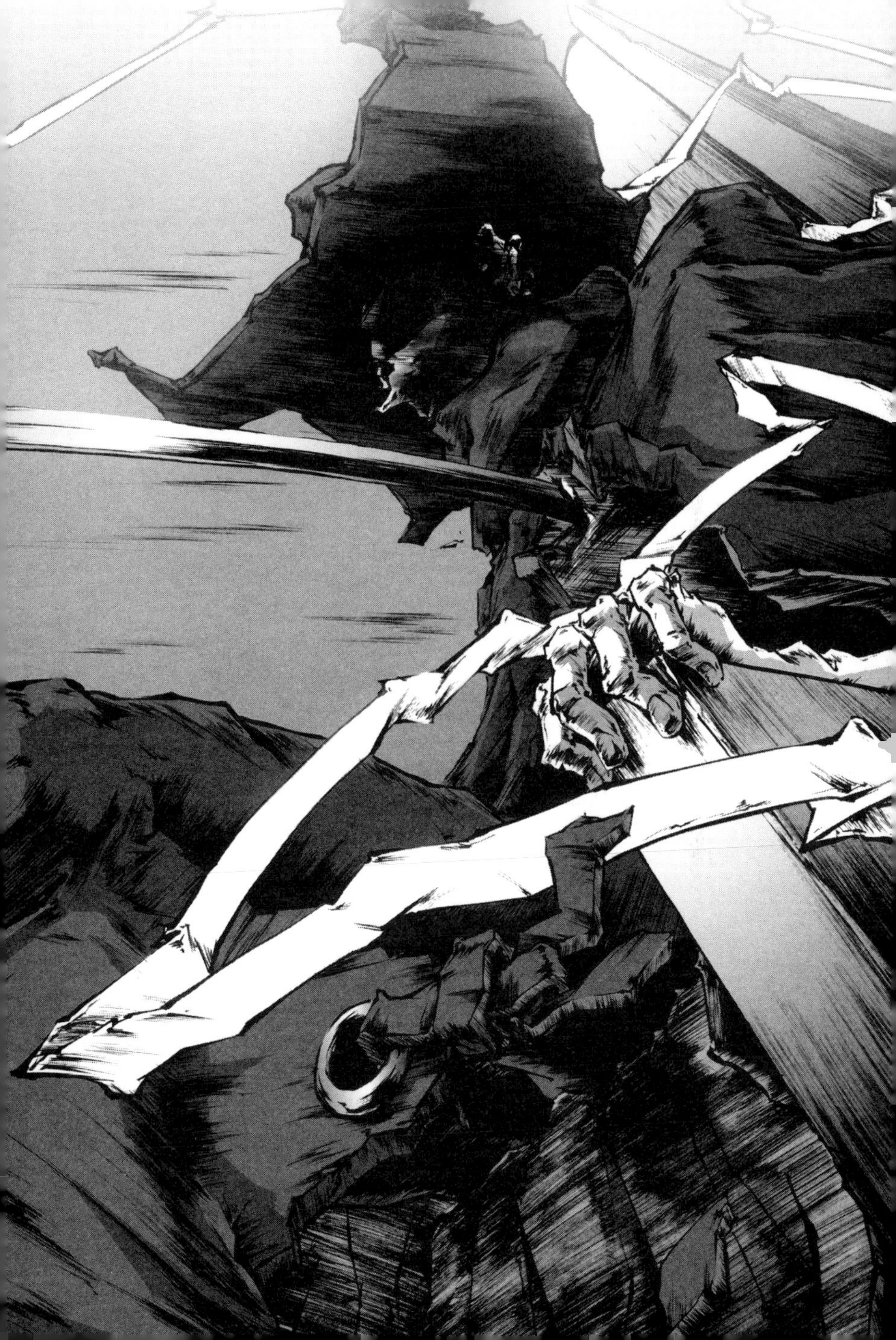

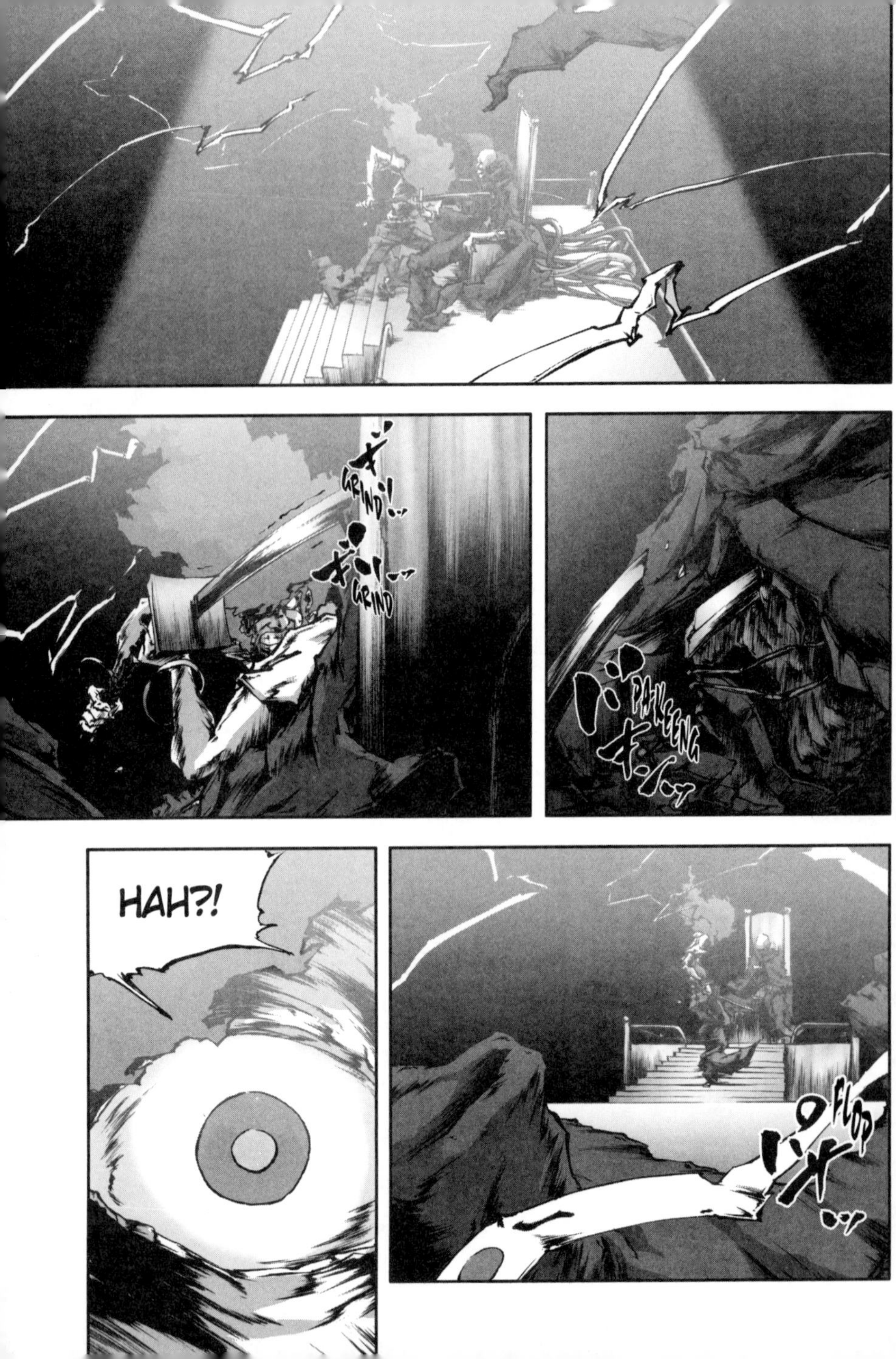
GRIND!
GRIND
PAKEENG
HAH?!
FLOP

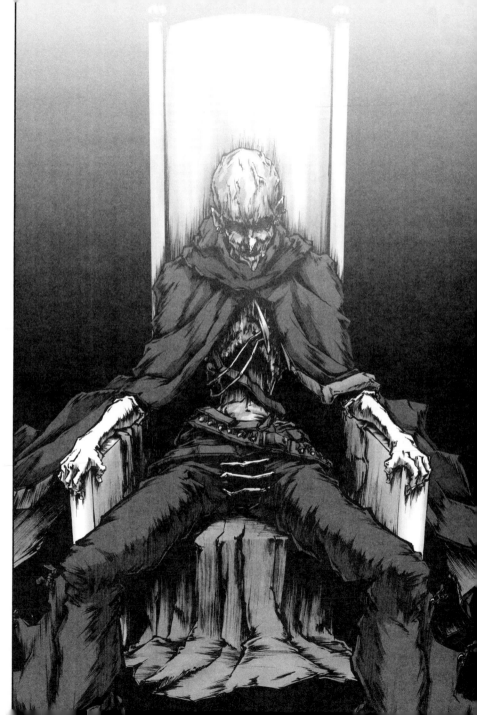

ザワンッ
CRACKLE
ボロッ
CRUMBLE
ザザー
SHHHHH...
ザー
SHHHH...
サー
SHFFFF...
ダッ
TMP
サー
SSSSS...

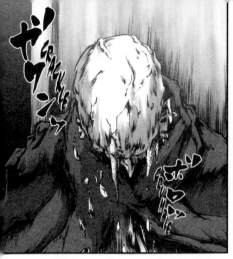

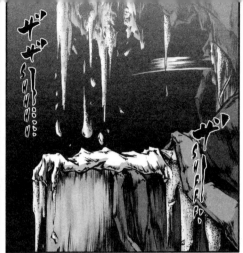

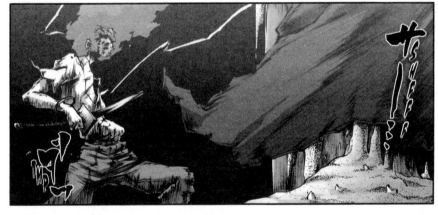

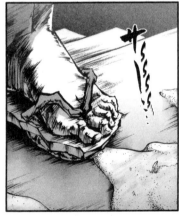

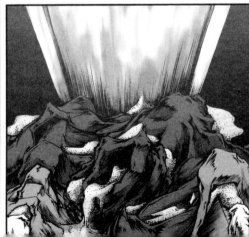

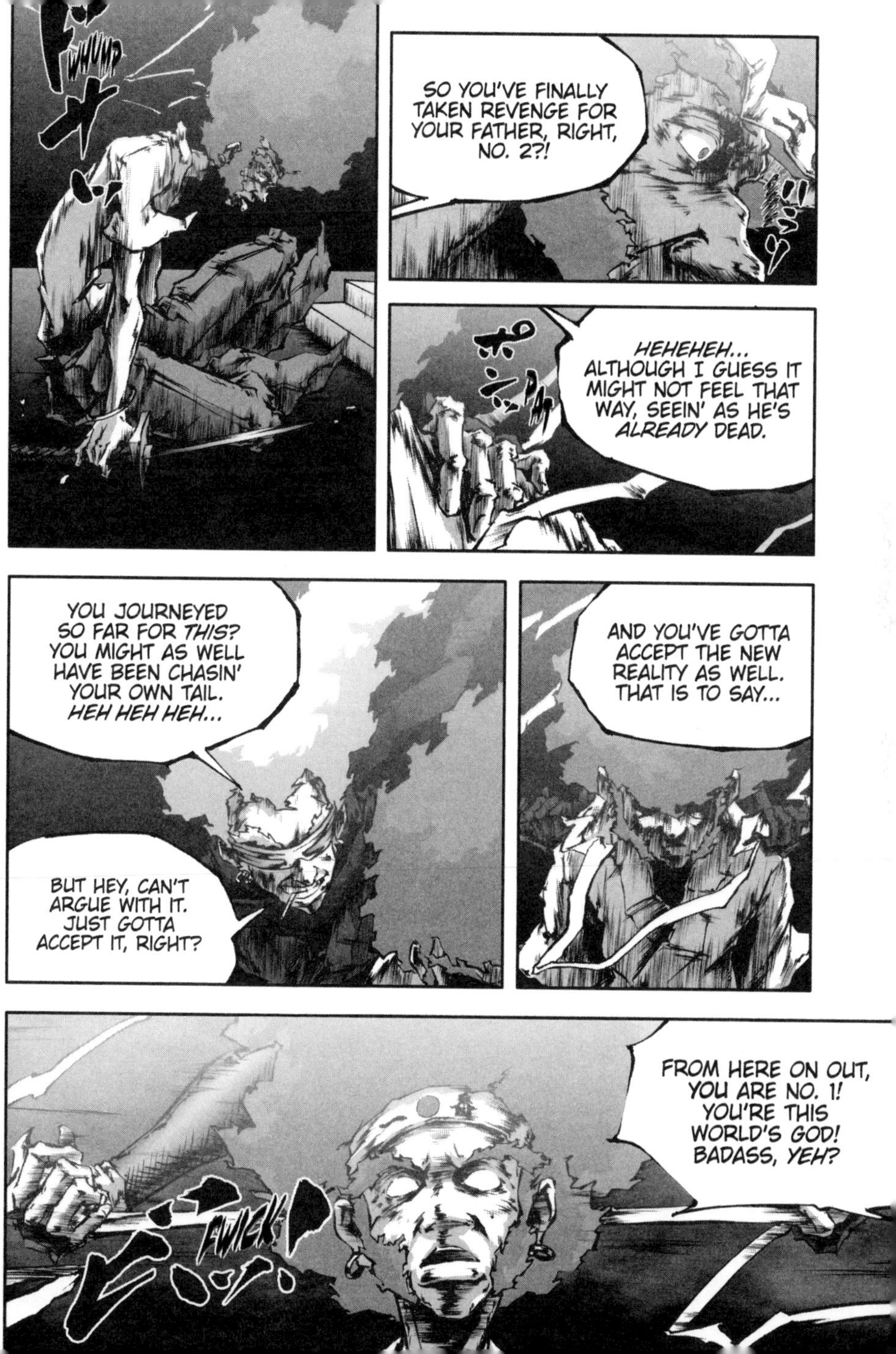
WHUMP
SO YOU'VE FINALLY TAKEN REVENGE FOR YOUR FATHER, RIGHT, NO. 2?!
PAT
HEHEHEH... ALTHOUGH I GUESS IT MIGHT NOT FEEL THAT WAY, SEEIN' AS HE'S *ALREADY* DEAD.
YOU JOURNEYED SO FAR FOR *THIS?* YOU MIGHT AS WELL HAVE BEEN CHASIN' YOUR OWN TAIL. *HEH HEH HEH...*
BUT HEY, CAN'T ARGUE WITH IT. JUST GOTTA ACCEPT IT, RIGHT?
AND YOU'VE GOTTA ACCEPT THE NEW REALITY AS WELL. THAT IS TO SAY...
FWICK
FROM HERE ON OUT, YOU ARE NO. 1! YOU'RE THIS WORLD'S GOD! BADASS, *YEH?*

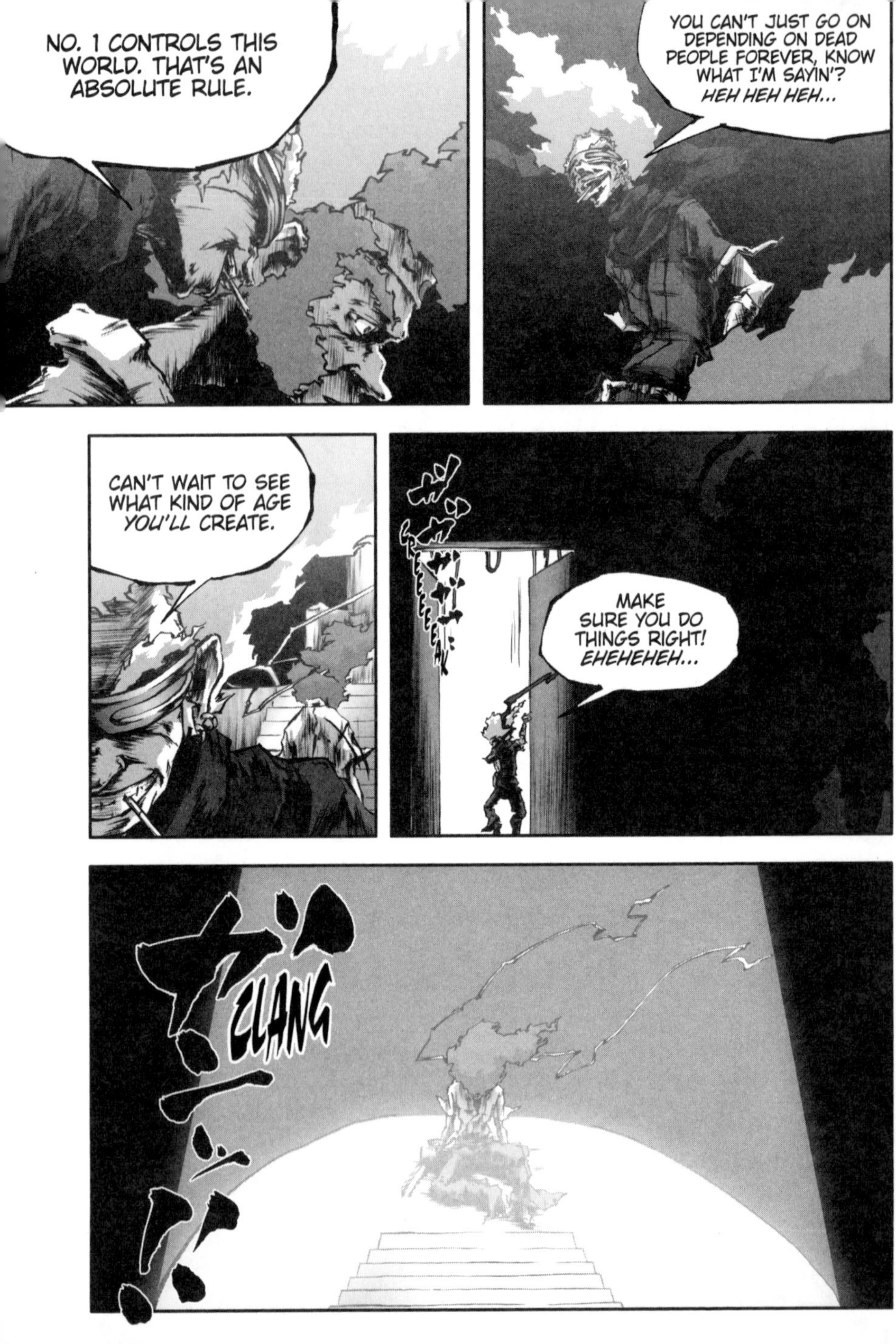
NO. 1 CONTROLS THIS WORLD. THAT'S AN ABSOLUTE RULE.
YOU CAN'T JUST GO ON DEPENDING ON DEAD PEOPLE FOREVER, KNOW WHAT I'M SAYIN'? *HEH HEH HEH...*
CAN'T WAIT TO SEE WHAT KIND OF AGE *YOU'LL* CREATE.
CREEEEEEAK
MAKE SURE YOU DO THINGS RIGHT! *EHEHEHEH...*
CLANG

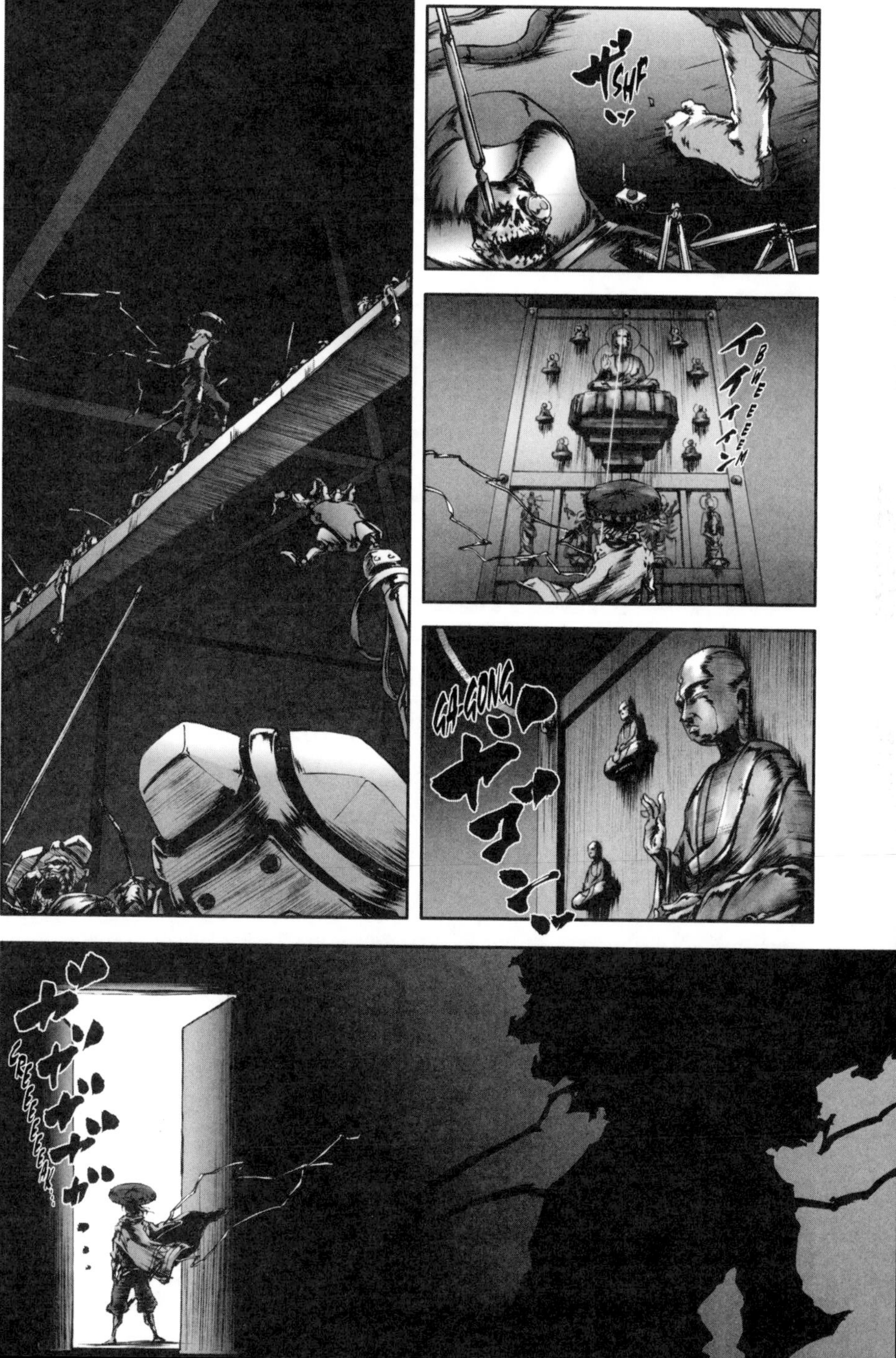

SHF
BWEEEEEM
GA-GONG
CREEEEEEEAK...

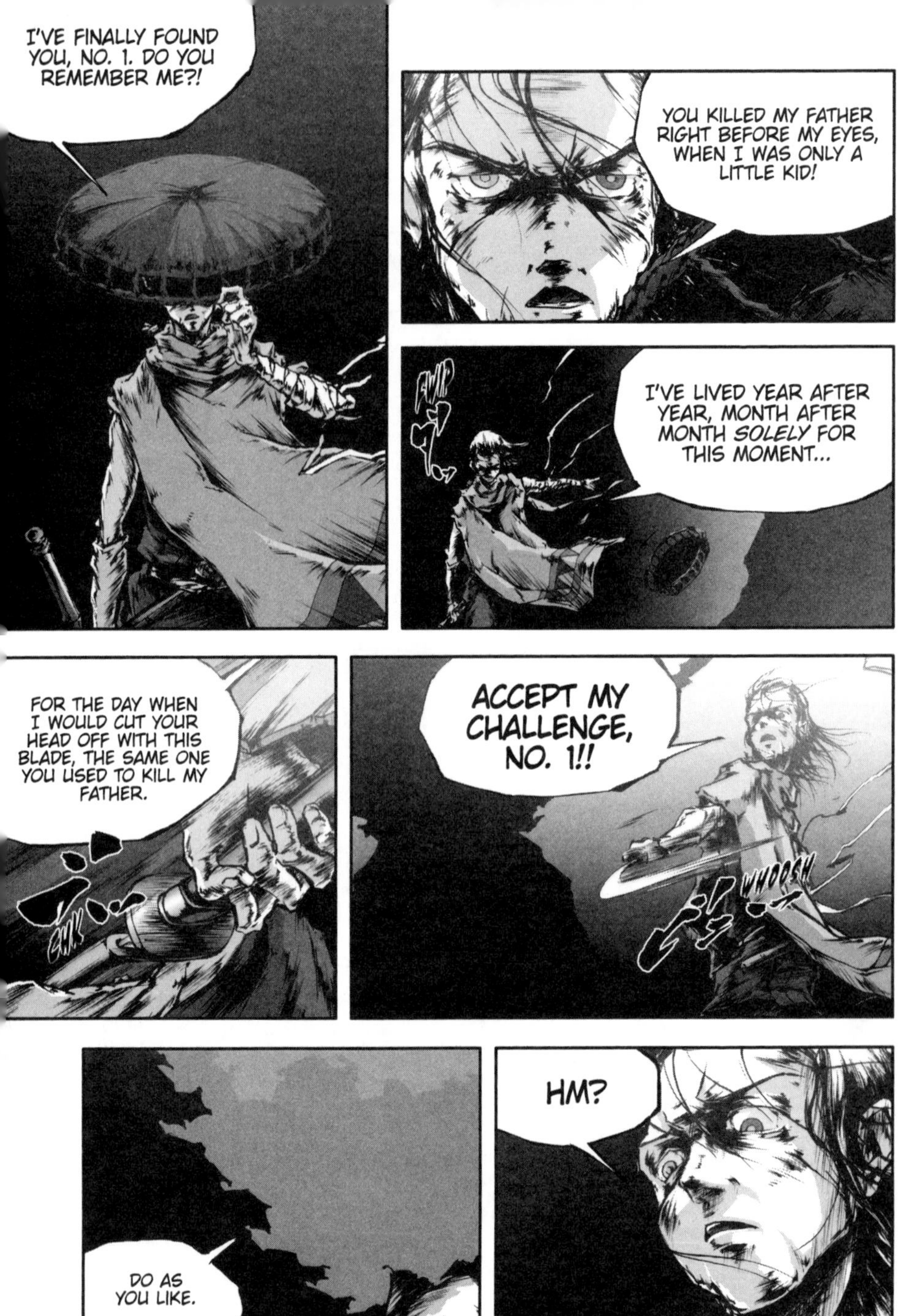
I'VE FINALLY FOUND YOU, NO. 1. DO YOU REMEMBER ME?!
YOU KILLED MY FATHER RIGHT BEFORE MY EYES, WHEN I WAS ONLY A LITTLE KID!
FWIP
I'VE LIVED YEAR AFTER YEAR, MONTH AFTER MONTH *SOLELY* FOR THIS MOMENT...
FOR THE DAY WHEN I WOULD CUT YOUR HEAD OFF WITH THIS BLADE, THE SAME ONE YOU USED TO KILL MY FATHER.
CHK
ACCEPT MY CHALLENGE, NO. 1!!
WHOOSH
DO AS YOU LIKE.
HM?

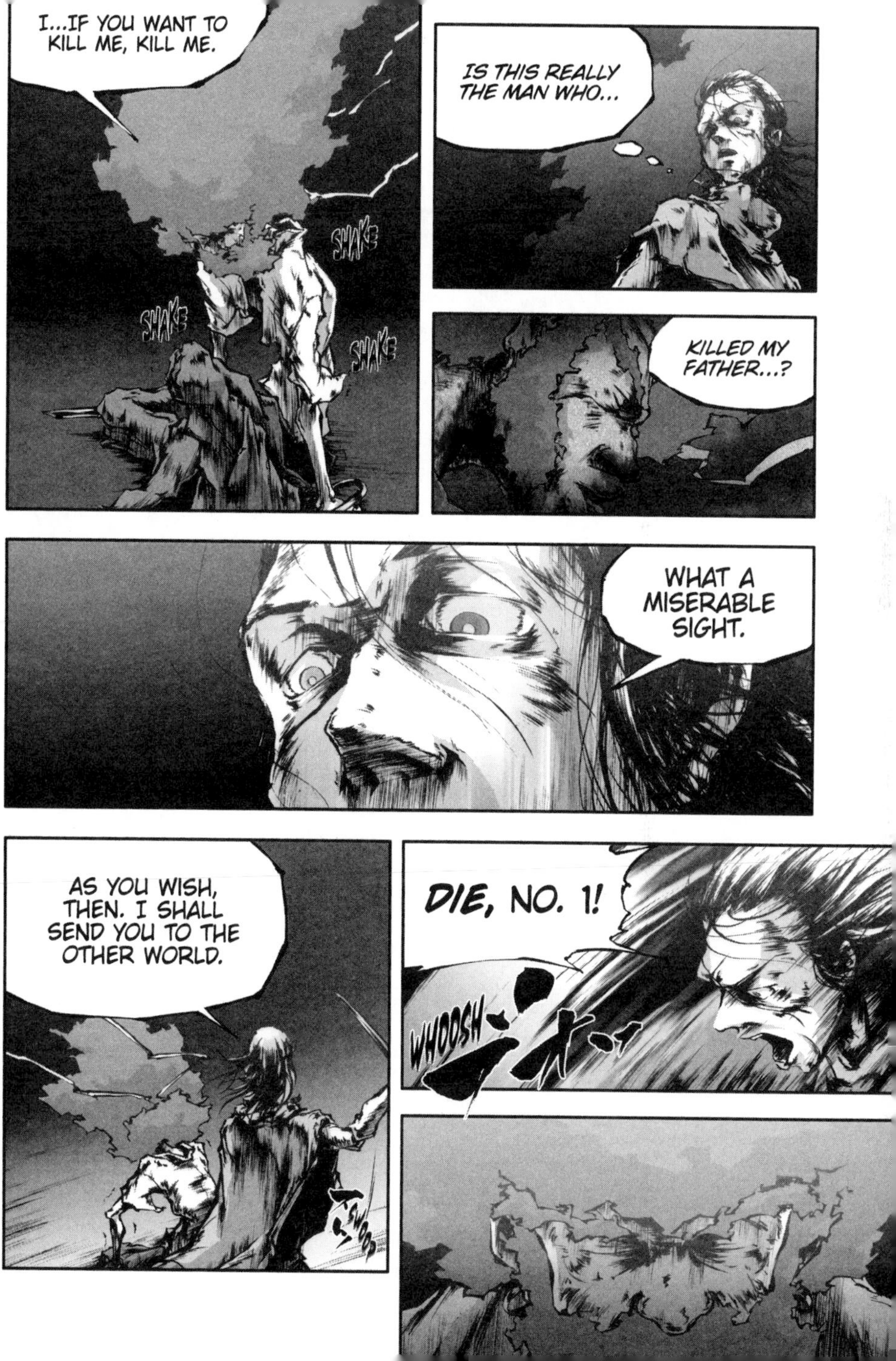
I...IF YOU WANT TO KILL ME, KILL ME.
SHAKE
SHAKE
SHAKE
IS THIS REALLY THE MAN WHO...
KILLED MY FATHER...?
WHAT A MISERABLE SIGHT.
AS YOU WISH, THEN. I SHALL SEND YOU TO THE OTHER WORLD.
SWOOP
DIE, NO. 1!
WHOOSH

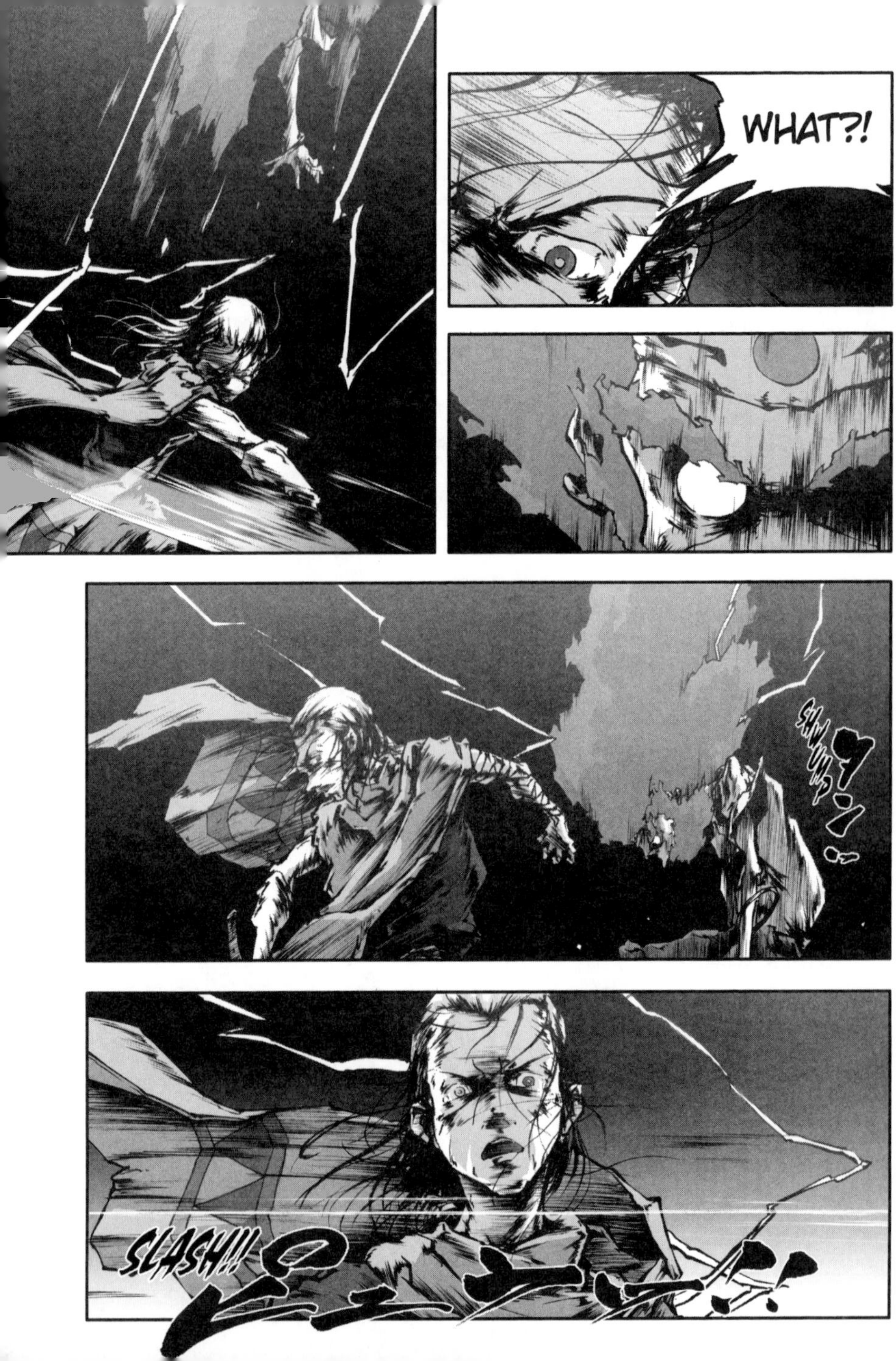
WHAT?!
SHWUMP
SLASH!!

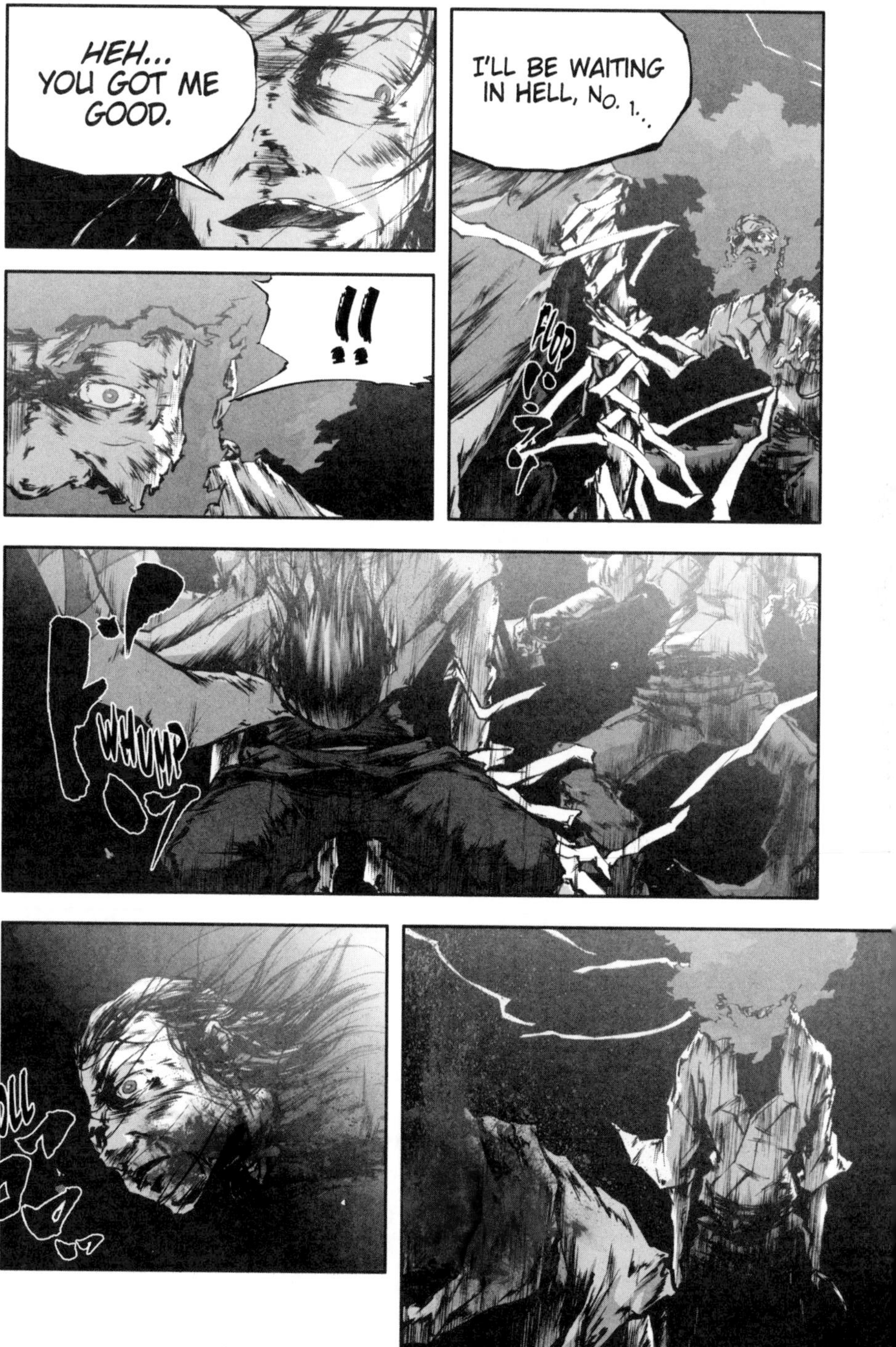
HEH... YOU GOT ME GOOD.
I'LL BE WAITING IN HELL, NO. 1...
!!
FLOP
WHUMP

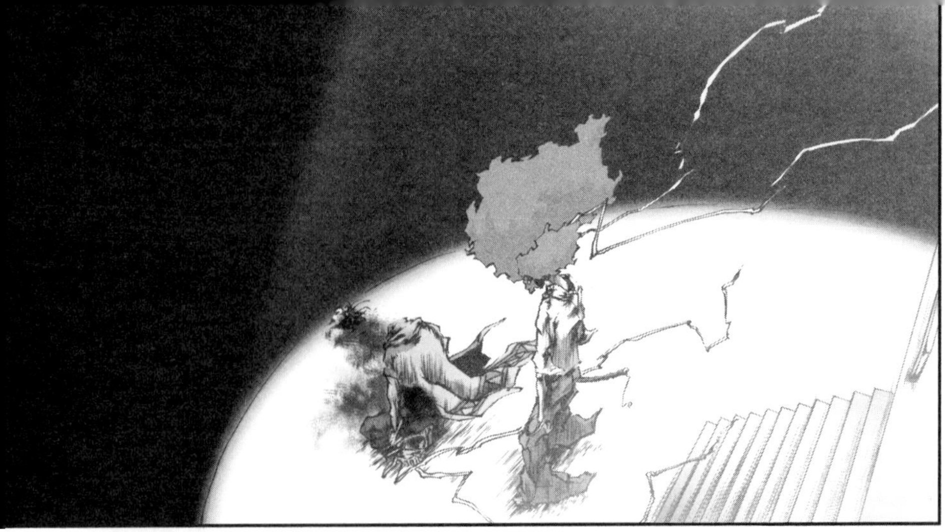

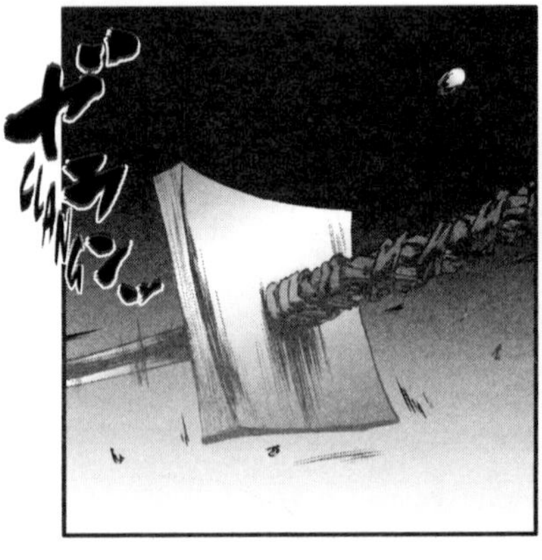
CLANG

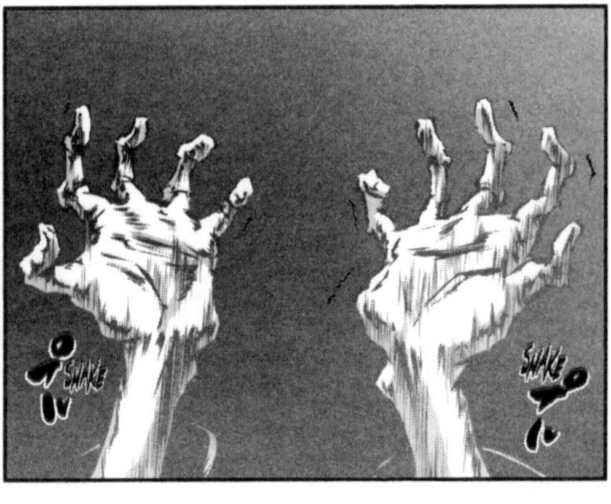
SHAKE
SHAKE

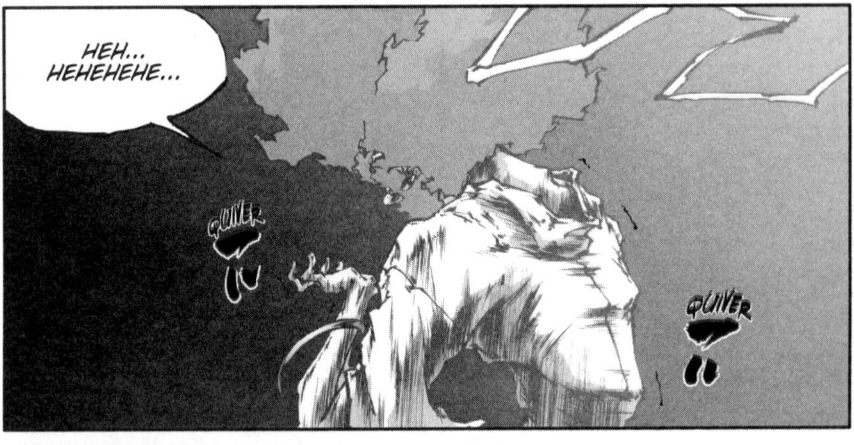
HEH... HEHEHEHE...
QUIVER
QUIVER

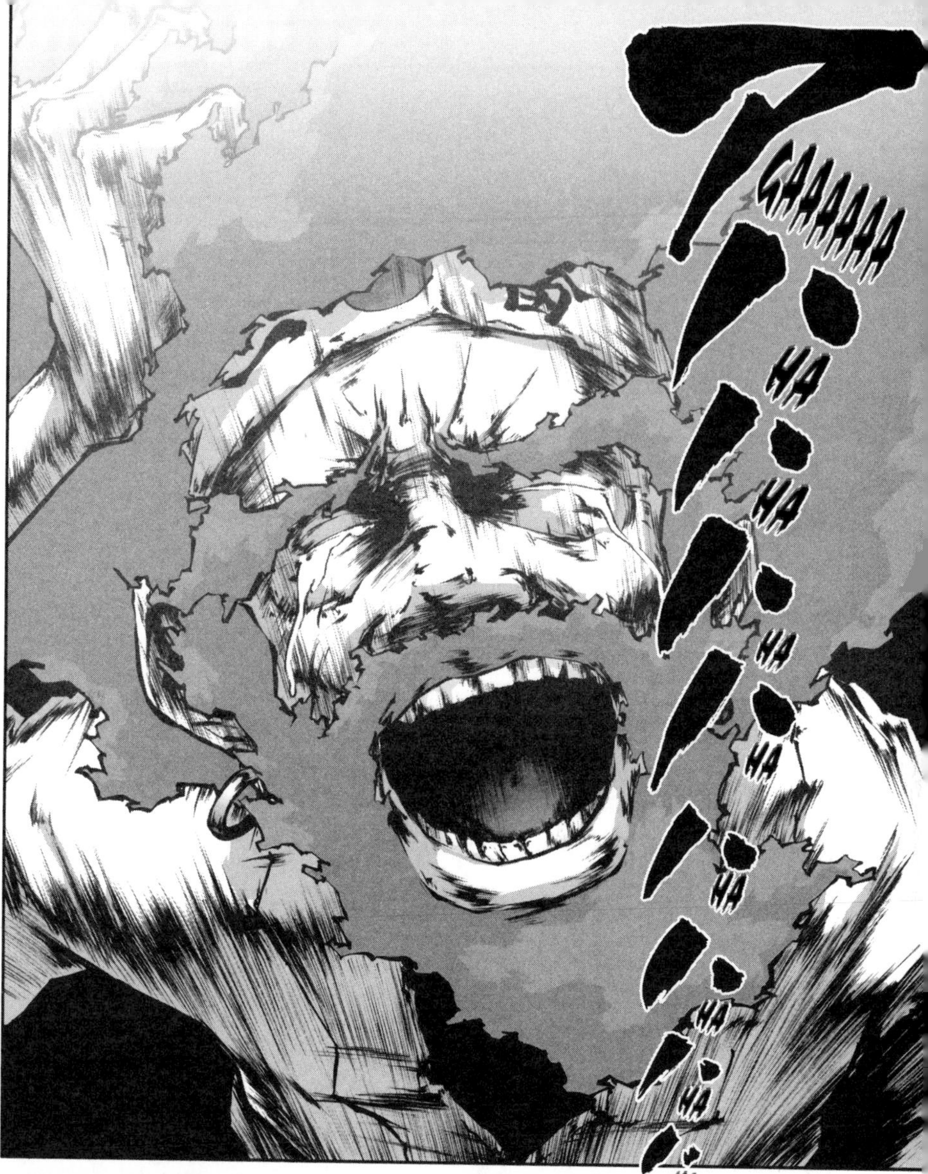
GAAAAAA HA HA HA HA HA HA HA HA

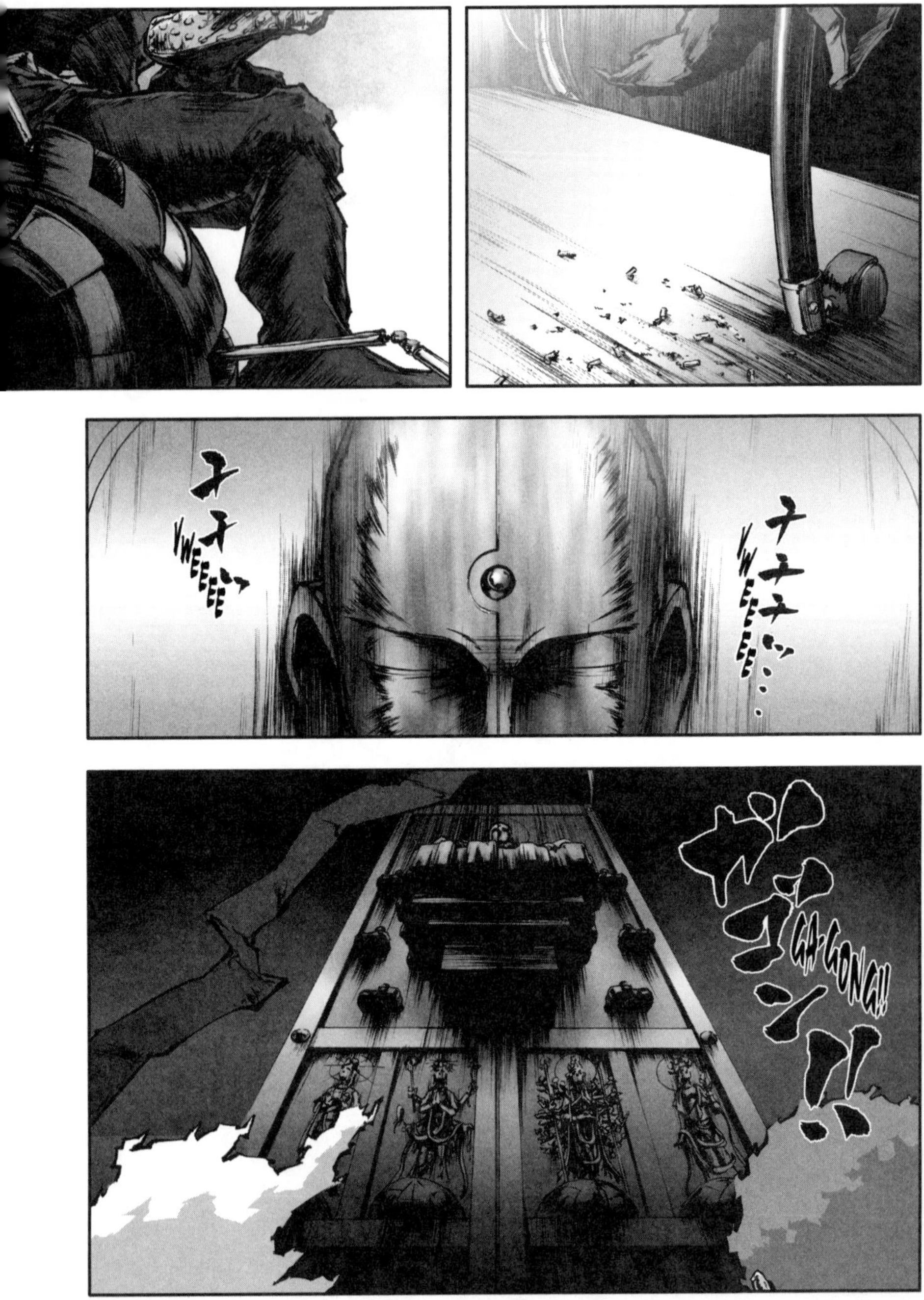
VWEEEEE
VWEEEEEE
GA-GONG!!

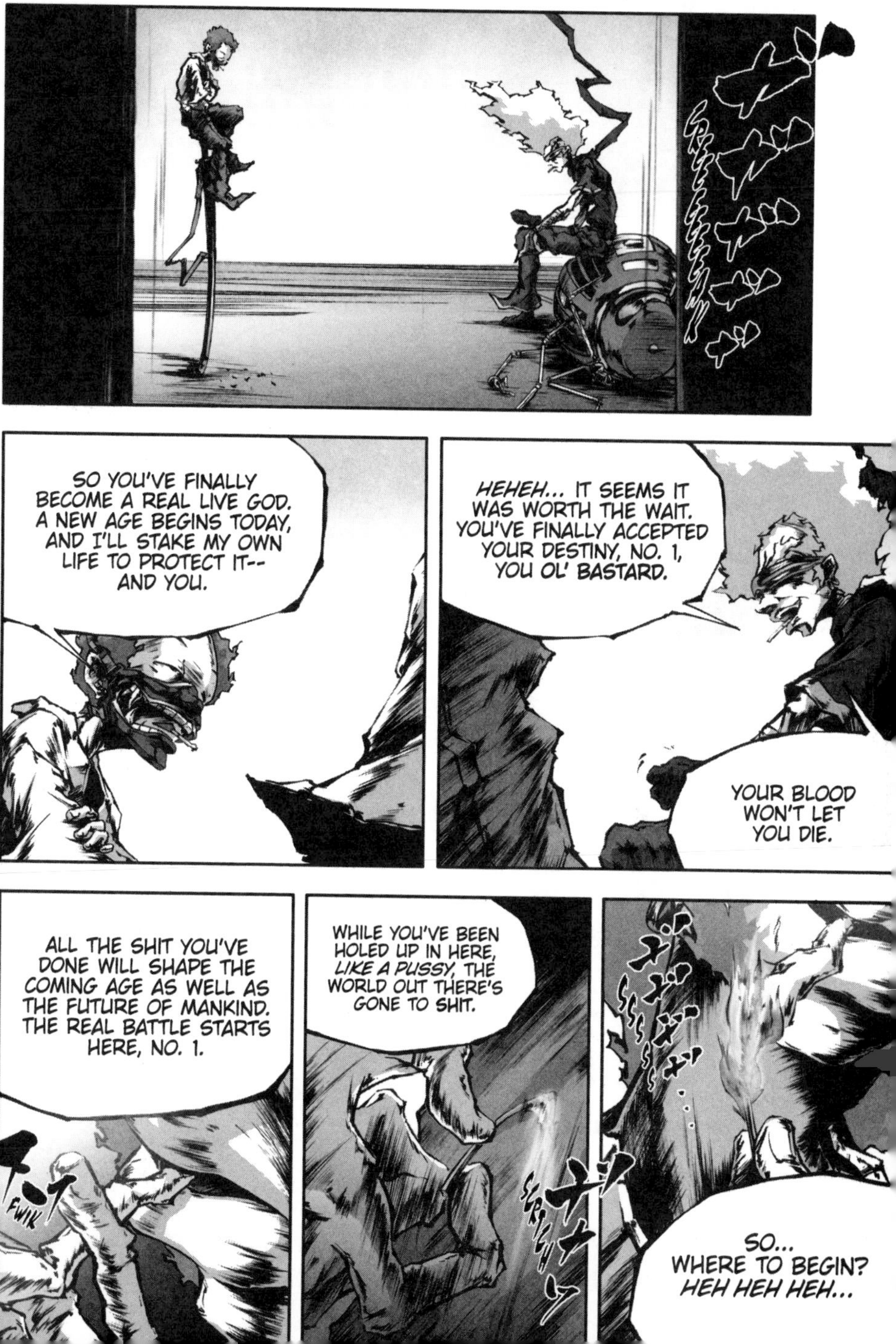

SO YOU'VE FINALLY BECOME A REAL LIVE GOD. A NEW AGE BEGINS TODAY, AND I'LL STAKE MY OWN LIFE TO PROTECT IT-- AND YOU.
HEHEH... IT SEEMS IT WAS WORTH THE WAIT. YOU'VE FINALLY ACCEPTED YOUR DESTINY, NO. 1, YOU OL' BASTARD.
YOUR BLOOD WON'T LET YOU DIE.
ALL THE SHIT YOU'VE DONE WILL SHAPE THE COMING AGE AS WELL AS THE FUTURE OF MANKIND. THE REAL BATTLE STARTS HERE, NO. 1.
FWIK
WHILE YOU'VE BEEN HOLED UP IN HERE, *LIKE A PUSSY*, THE WORLD OUT THERE'S GONE TO SHIT.
SO... WHERE TO BEGIN? *HEH HEH HEH...*

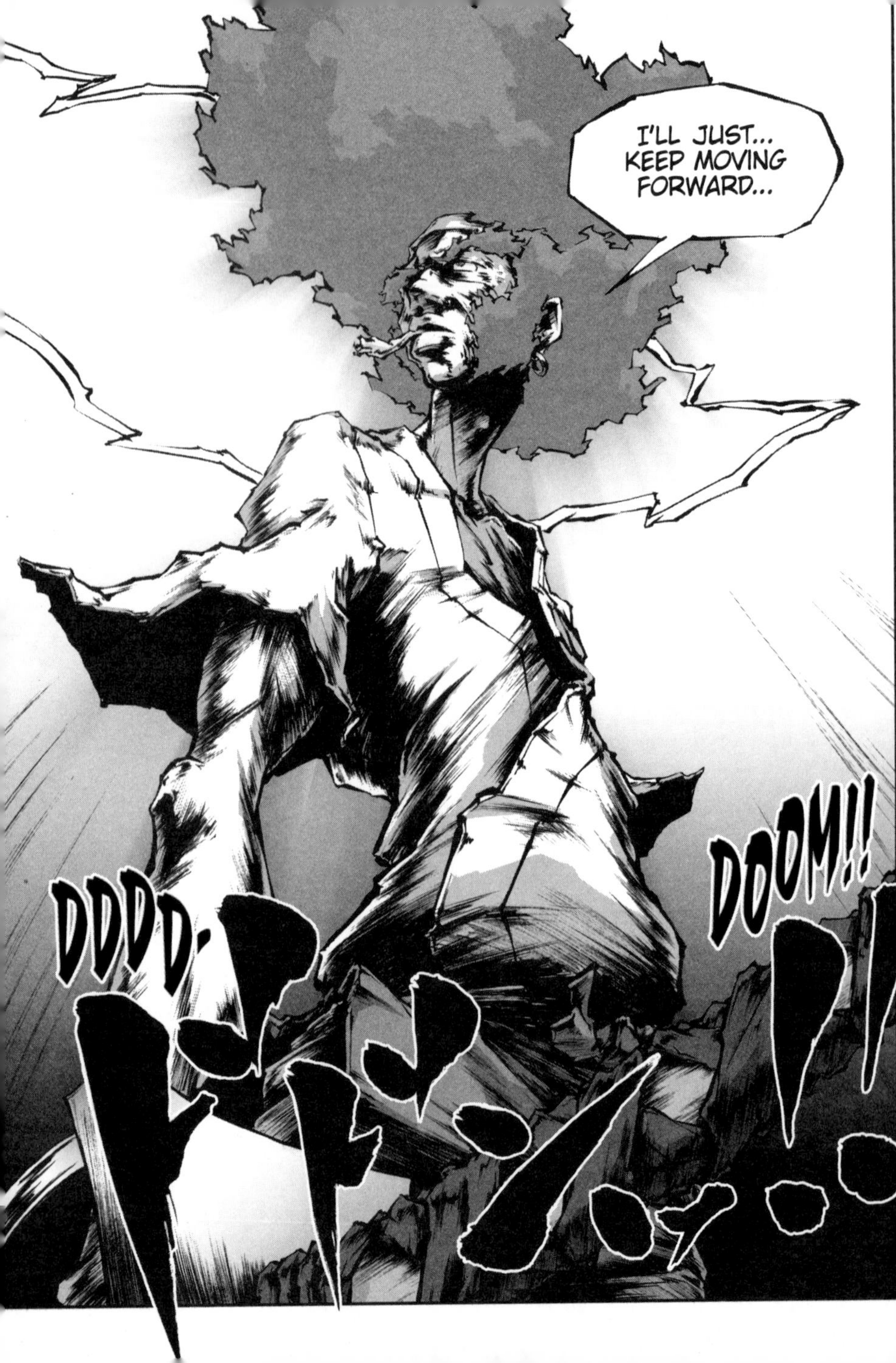
I'LL JUST... KEEP MOVING FORWARD...
DDDD-
DOOM!!

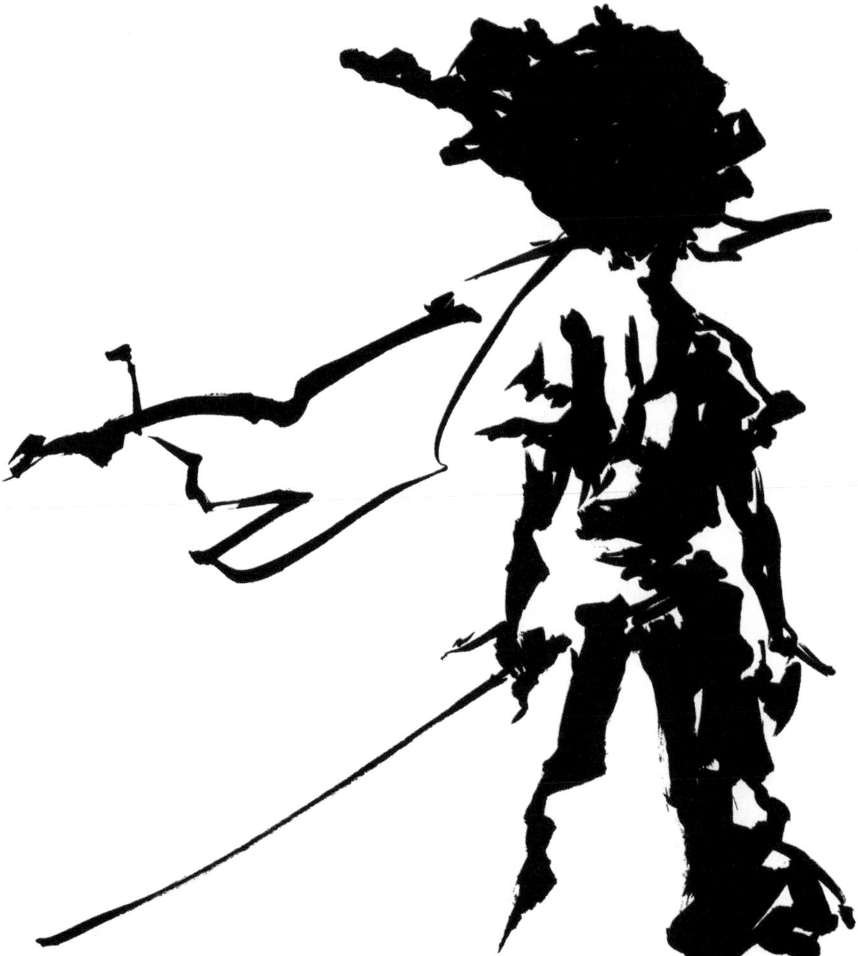

HONORIFICS GUIDE

Politeness is an integral facet of Japanese culture, and we believe that maintaining honorifics—polite speech that indicates a person's status or relationship toward another individual—in our translations helps bring out the same character nuances as seen in the original work.

In *Afro Samurai*, the common honorifics that you will come across while reading are:

-san – The most common of all honorifics, it is an all-purpose suffix that can be used in any situation where politeness is expected. Generally seen as the equivalent to Mr., Miss, Ms., Mrs., etc.

-sama – This suffix is one level higher than "-san" and is used to confer great respect upon an individual.

-chan – Another common honorific. This suffix is mainly used to express endearment toward girls, but can also be used when referring to little boys or even pets. Couples are also known to use the term to convey a sense of cuteness and intimacy.

Sensei – Literally meaning "one who has come before," this title is used for teachers, doctors, or masters of any profession or art.

TRANSLATION NOTES

Chapter 6, Page 6
In both the manga and anime of *Afro Samurai,* Afro is seen having grown up with a character who wears glasses. The manga's version of this character is a long-winded brainiac named Kazuma, while the character of Sasuke in the anime is seen to be much more of a normal kid.

Chapter 6, Page 8
Wakizashi are tradional Japanese swords that are similar to *katana,* but are much shorter (30 to 60cm, whereas a katana is anything over 60cm).
In feudal Japan, wakizashi and katana were often worn together as a pair known as *daishō.*

Chapter 6, Page 11
Afureru is a Japanese verb meaning to overflow, to run over the brim. As you can see, Afro's hair will soon overflow his head and run over the brim of his headband.

Chapter 7, Page 20
Hachimaki are Japanese headbands. These are what everyone is killing each other over in *Afro Samurai.*

Chapter 9, Page 4
In Buddhism, *Bhava-agra* is the highest level of material existence that one can reach; the fourth heaven. The Japanese word for this place would be *Uchouten* (or *Yuuchouten*).

Chapter 10, Page 4
Daruma (or *dharama*) are hollow, round wish dolls common in Japan. They are molded on the founder of Zen, Bodhidharma, and feature a mustache and beard, but the eyes are left unpainted. When making a wish, you paint in the right eye, but leave the left eye blank until your wish is fulfilled.
The character of Daruman is a pun that combines the words "Daruma" and the word "man."

Takashi Okazaki: The Man BEHIND the 'Fro

Afro Samurai originally started in the doujinshi magazine _Nou Nou Hau_. Tell us a little about that experience.

It was around 1999-2000. After I graduated from college, I started working as an illustrator. Drawing for clients was not the same as drawing what my heart wanted to express. Several of my friends in the field shared the same frustration. We blabbered drunkenly and said "what if we pay ourselves to draw what we really want to draw." That was the beginning of _Nou Nou Hau_. It started small, with a group of close friends, but I knew it'd be _Afro Samurai_ for me. We all enjoyed the balance between our main jobs and the hobby. After the second issue more friends joined, and we were up to nine artists at one point. _Nou Nou Hau_ was brought to a close when we could no longer support the printing costs, as it was not our principal to draw for sponsorship.

The version of the manga that we're publishing is actually a relaunched version of your original doujinshi. How did this relaunch come about?

It started when we began the _Afro Samurai_ project with GONZO; in the anime series we had to have mainstream entertainment elements added for the new audience. When I saw Afro animated and voiced for the first time, it felt like he left my nest. In the manga, I focused on showcasing my original _Afro Samurai_. So in essence, the manga is a relaunch of the doujinshi, but the world is bigger and the settings are stronger.

From start to finish, how long does it generally take you to complete a single page, and what's your basic process?

It took three years from the start of page one to the end of volume two. This comes out to 300 pages of art, so a simple calculation gives about three days per page!

The manga version of *Afro Samurai* diverges quite drastically from the anime version, spiraling the story into a different direction. Is this a case where your doujinshi became the basis for the anime or did you always plan for the manga to go in the direction seen in this book?

The doujinshi version of *Afro Samurai,* the current manga version, the anime version, and the game version all have slight differences from each other, but the core concept is the same. Each represents a unique world and story. Such multiple worlds coexist within the *Afro Samurai* universe, and I allowed the series to be that way from the beginning. So you can be sure that there are many more stories waiting to be told in Afro Universe.

As for the relaunch, I gained a lot more experience and knowledge during the years after finishing the doujinshi, so you can say the new manga is slightly more *otona* (adult) than the previous doujin version! (laughs)

Why did you draw *Afro Samurai* left-to-right, instead of the traditional Japanese orientation, right-to-left?

Afro Samurai was originally intended to be published as a traditional American comic book, so the pages were drawn full-size, left-to-right. It was a challenge to follow this style, though, as even the word balloons were done horizontally whereas typical Japanese manga text reads vertically and right-to-left.

In your opinion, what is the difference between Japanese manga and American comics and in which category does *Afro Samurai* fall?

As is often pointed out, Japanese manga use a style with cinematic camera angles, which was developed by the legendary manga artist Osamu Tezuka. Each frame represents a snapshot and an action. Each line and piece of dialogue is paired with a corresponding action, and it is shown visually frame-by-frame.

On the other hand, American comics are graphic novels. The story is there and inspirational visuals are there, but the dialogue and visual actions are not necessarily in sync in that way.

I think *Afro Samurai* has elements from both, and that is something not many people have done.

Is there a particular part of the manga that was your favorite to work on, and why?

My favorite is Episode #6. I also liked working on Episode #2.

These particular episodes of the manga are kind of side stories. Unlike the core story arc chapters, which I had thought through and polished up in my head a long time ago, the side story episodes had very particular themes to them and they allowed me to pursue some creative storytelling ideas and design details while also allowing me to incorporate new elements into the series itself. It was a great feeling to be able to bring *Afro Samurai* to the next level. They're essential chapters to the mythology, and I'm very happy with how episode #6 turned out. I look forward to seeing reader's response to these chapters.

In terms of your characters, what is it about the character of Afro that you like and do you see any aspects of yourself in him?

While my characters don't directly represent my experiences or personality, they are built from my subjective imagination. Of course, I couldn't draw something I'd never seen or felt or imagined, so it is possible that memories from my past influence my character expressions to some extent more than I am aware.

How do you feel now that your manga has become a sprawling franchise that spans two anime, a video game, and with a live-action movie in the works?

I want the franchise to have a variety like that seen in *Batman*.

And finally, what's your all-time favorite manga and who's your favorite artist?

I have a couple of favorite series that have given me inspiration for *Afro Samurai*. These are:
Lone Wolf and Cub
Watchmen
Batman: Year One
Kamui Gaiden
Hi no tori

STATS:

BLOOD TYPE: AB

- **FAVORITE PASTIMES:**
  Watch movies, eat good food, and play mahjong/video games

- **WHAT IS YOUR TYPICAL DAY LIKE:**
  I wake up, make a cup of coffee with a lot of milk, and work in my home office with coffee, chocolates or ice cream, and a 1.5-litter Volvic (mineral water). And I don't come out of my office for several hours.

- **WHAT WOULD I BE DOING IF I DIDN'T KNOW ART:**
  Cooking. I wanted to be a chef before I got into contemporary art.

- **WHAT I LIKE ABOUT ART:**
  I like how conceptual art leaves room for the imagination of viewers. My favorite artists are Bruce Nauman and Antony Gormley.

- **MY MOTTO / FAVORITE WORDS:**
  "上善如水" and "坐忘"
  ("Be like Water" and "Remembering to Forget")

- **MY TREASURES:**
  My family, everyone who helped Afro Samurai, the action figure signed by Sam J, the Afro T-shirt Sam J recently gave me.

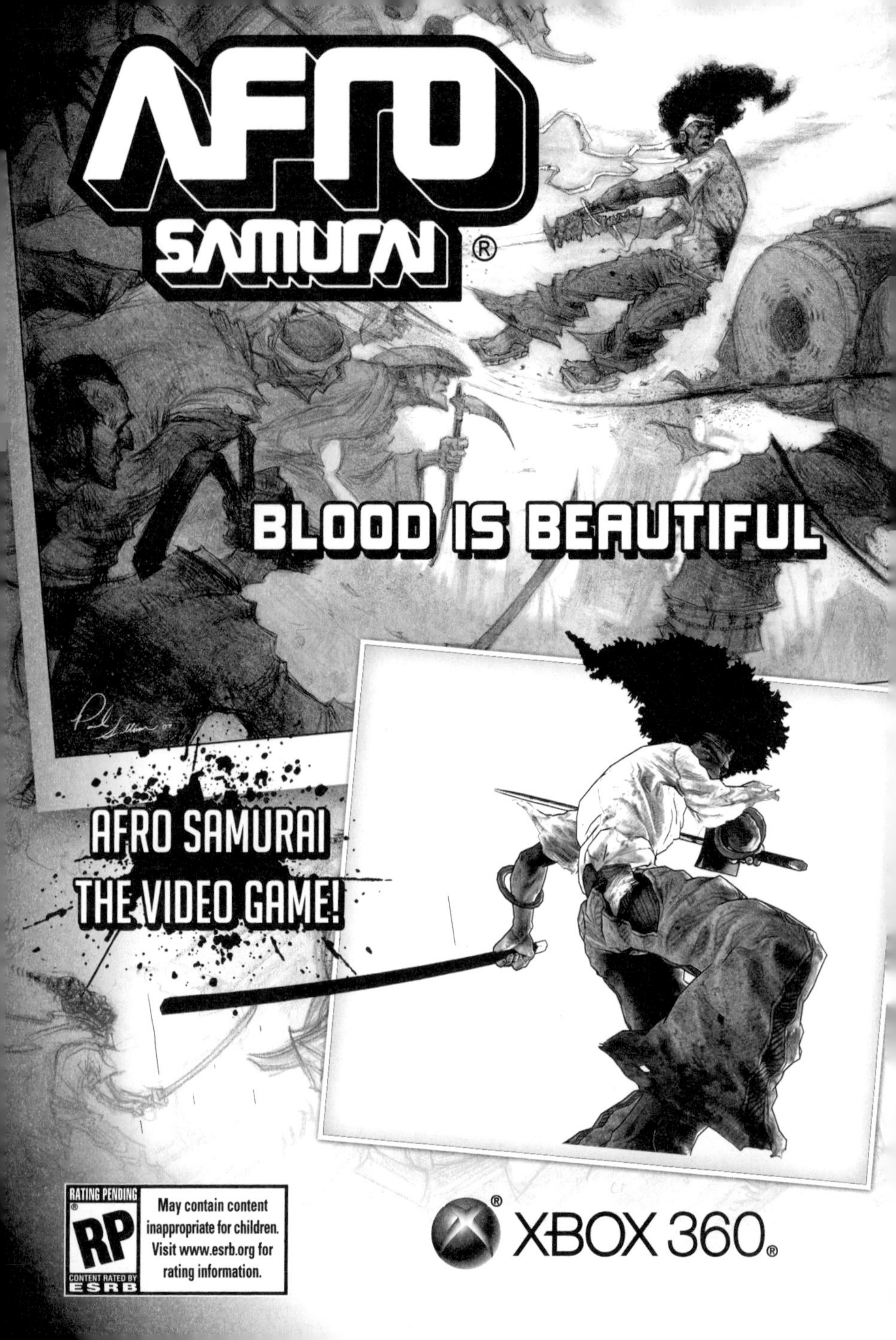
AFRO SAMURAI®
BLOOD IS BEAUTIFUL
AFRO SAMURAI THE VIDEO GAME!
RATING PENDING
RP
CONTENT RATED BY ESRB
May contain content inappropriate for children. Visit www.esrb.org for rating information.
XBOX 360®

COMING
Fall 2008

PLAYSTATION 3

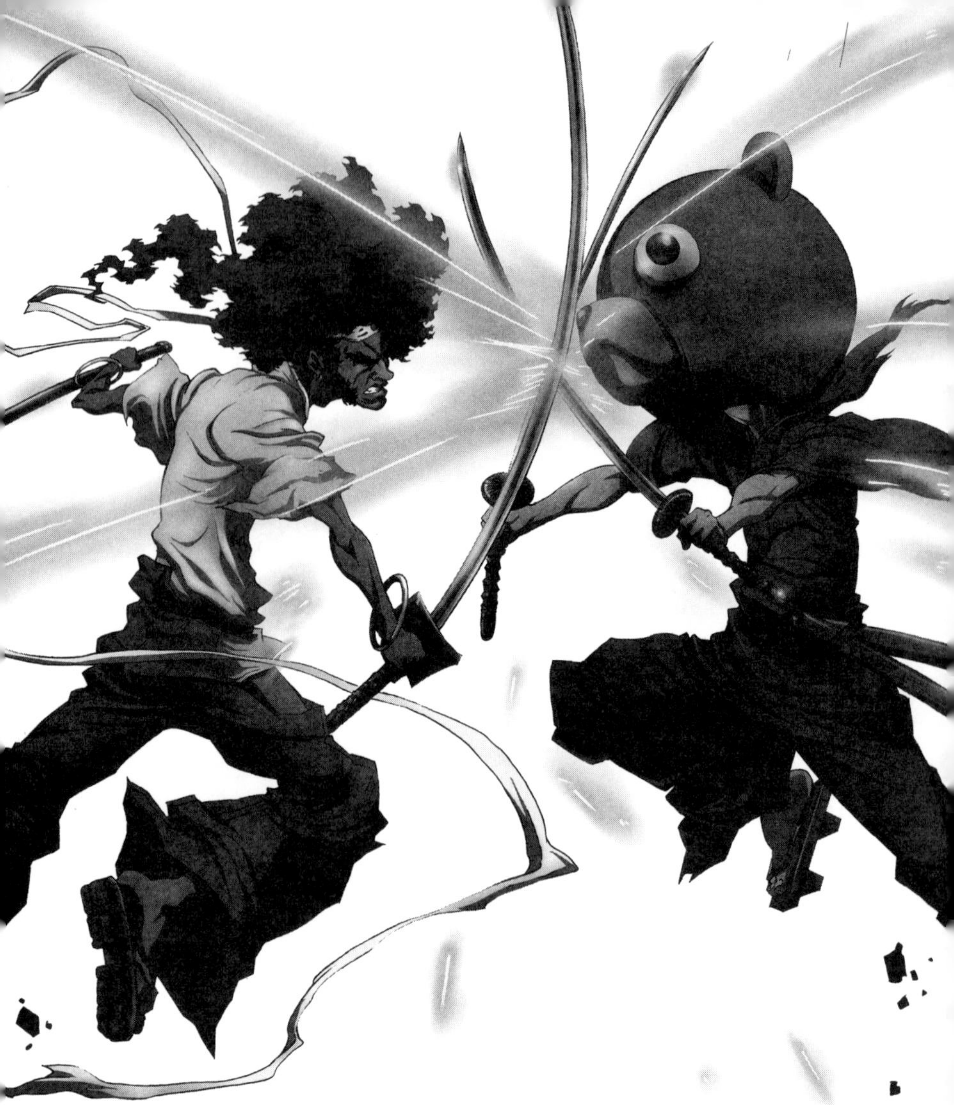

ICE COLD SOUL
AND A JONES FOR REVENGE

STARRING **SAMUEL L. JACKSON**
WITH BEATS BY THE **RZA**

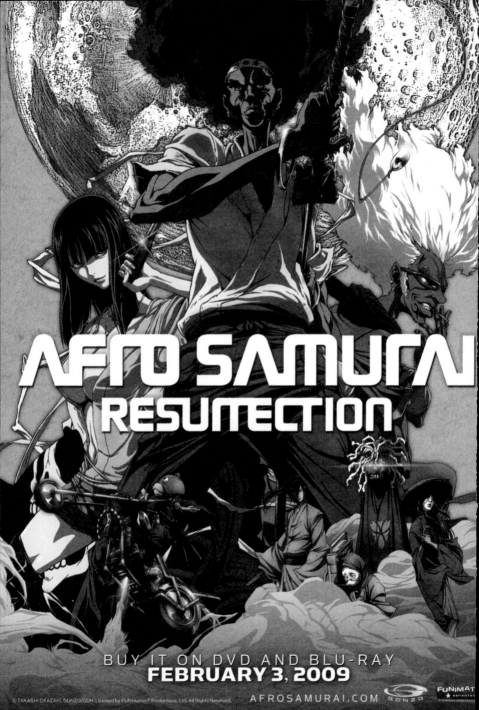

AFRO SAMURAI
RESURRECTION

BUY IT ON DVD AND BLU-RAY
FEBRUARY 3, 2009

© TAKASHI OKAZAKI, GONZO/GDH. Licensed by FUNimation® Productions, Ltd. All Rights Reserved.   AFROSAMURAI.COM

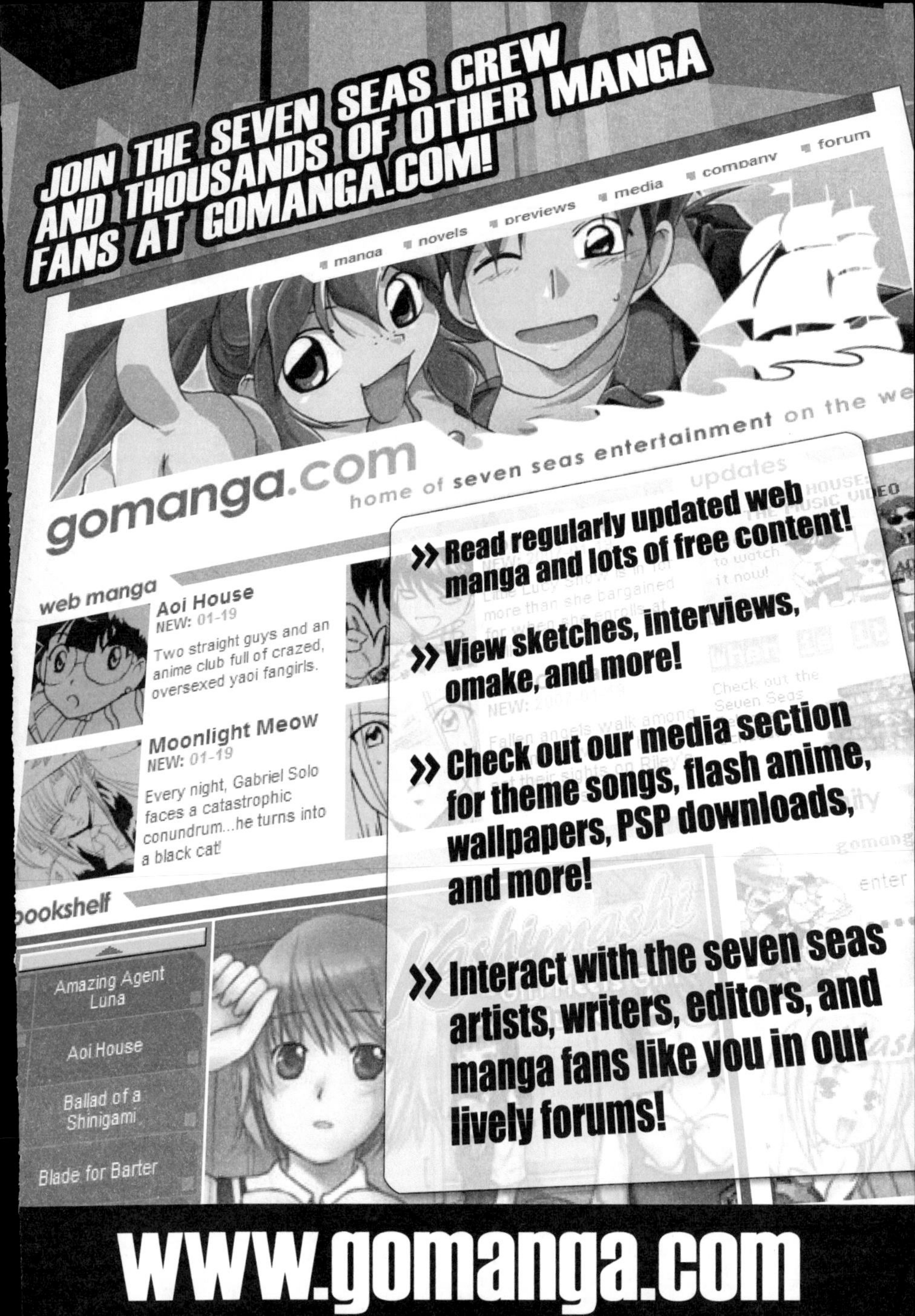
JOIN THE SEVEN SEAS CREW AND THOUSANDS OF OTHER MANGA FANS AT GOMANGA.COM!
manga
novels
previews
media
company
forum
gomanga.com
home of seven seas entertainment on the we
web manga
Aoi House
NEW: 01-19
Two straight guys and an anime club full of crazed, oversexed yaoi fangirls.
Moonlight Meow
NEW: 01-19
Every night, Gabriel Solo faces a catastrophic conundrum...he turns into a black cat!
bookshelf
Amazing Agent Luna
Aoi House
Ballad of a Shinigami
Blade for Barter
» Read regularly updated web manga and lots of free content!
» View sketches, interviews, omake, and more!
» Check out our media section for theme songs, flash anime, wallpapers, PSP downloads, and more!
» Interact with the seven seas artists, writers, editors, and manga fans like you in our lively forums!
www.gomanga.com

CREATOR BIO

TAKASHI OKAZAKI

Born in 1974 in Kanagawa, Japan.
Graduated from Tama Art University with a BA in Sculpture.

Okazaki's field of creative activity focuses on illustrations but also extends to manga, CD jacket design, sculpture, and live painting performance.

AFRO SAMURAI was originally a doujinshi manga by Okazaki that first appeared in the independent magazine *Nou Nou Hau,* and was then made into an animated TV series by GONZO. The series stars Samuel L. Jackson (who is also one of the Executive Producers), and is furnished with music composed by the hip-hop maestro RZA. After the successful US broadcast on Spike TV in 2007, the show was edited for theatrical release in Japan. DVDs are now available in six countries. Its adaptation into a Hollywood live-action film is also under way.

Representative Works:

- Designed "Metro-Taro," a fictional mascot character used in the live-action film *Negotiator Mashita Masayoshi*
- Designed "Wangan-kun," a fictional mascot character used in the live-action film *Bayside Shakedown 2*
- Provided concept design and key art for the fictional animation that appears in the live-action film *Space Travelers*
- Provided design for CD jacket and concert merchandise of Japanese rock band RIZE
- Provided artwork for the special edition of *Spider-Man 2* DVD
- Provided comic drawings for booklet of *Blade: Trinity* soundtrack CD

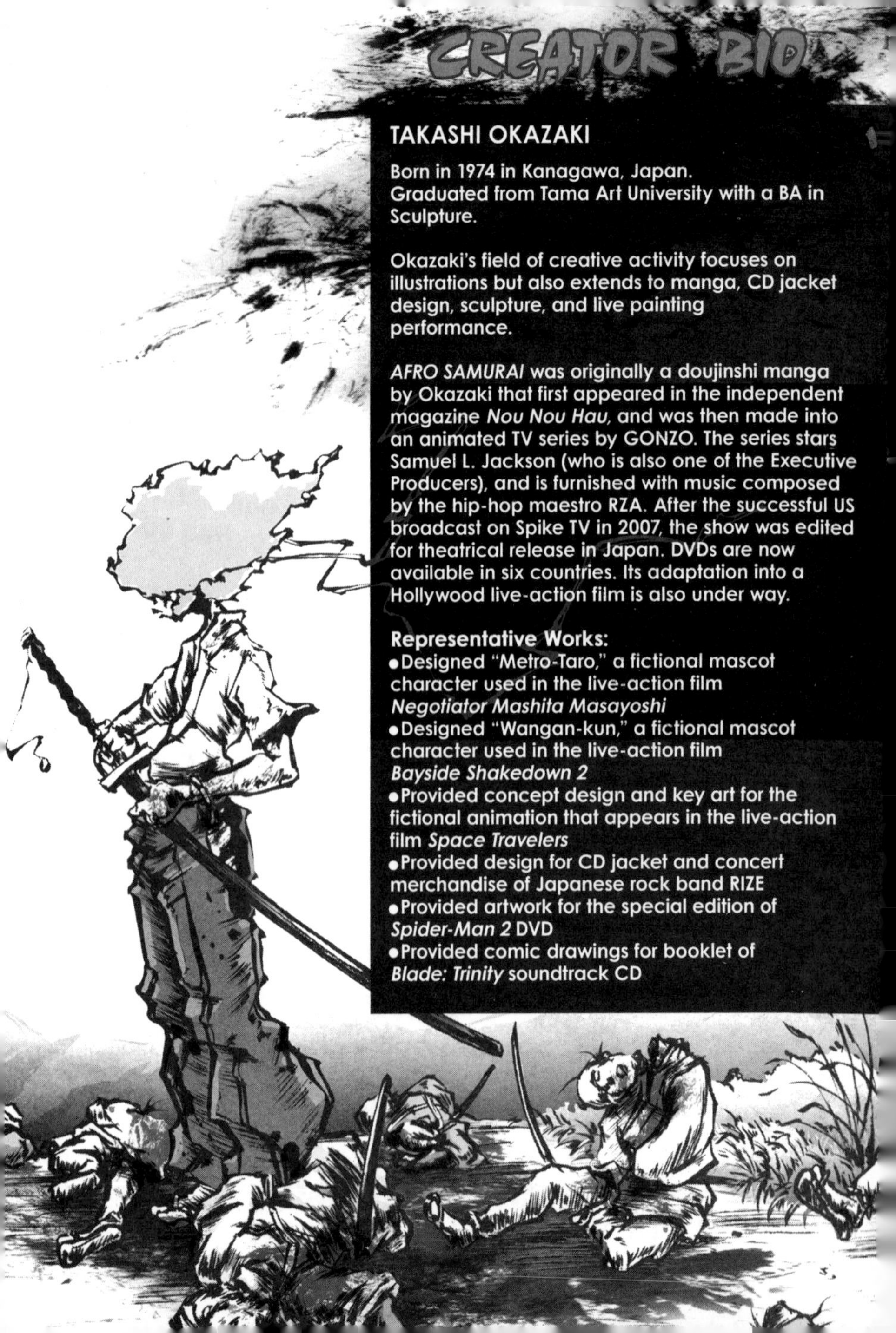